Inside the *Ring*

Inside the *Ring*

Essays on Wagner's Opera Cycle

Edited by JOHN LOUIS DIGAETANI

McFarland & Company, Inc., Publishers
Jefferson, North Carolina, and London

ALSO BY JOHN LOUIS DIGAETANI
AND FROM MCFARLAND

Wagner and Suicide (2003)

*Carlo Gozzi: A Life in
the 18th Century Venetian Theater,
an Afterlife in Opera* (2000)

LIBRARY OF CONGRESS CATALOGUING-IN-PUBLICATION DATA

Inside the Ring : essays on Wagner's opera cycle / edited by
    John Louis DiGaetani.
        p.   cm.
    Includes bibliographical references and index.

    ISBN 0-7864-2330-7 (softcover : 50# alkaline paper) ∞

    1. Wagner, Richard, 1813–1883. Ring des Nibelungen.
I. DiGaetani, John Louis, 1943–
ML410.W15I53   2006
782.1 — dc22   2005034175

British Library cataloguing data are available

On the cover: A Kirov Opera production of *Das Rheingold* in
St. Petersburg *(photograph by Natasha Razina)*

Manufactured in the United States of America

*McFarland & Company, Inc., Publishers
    Box 611, Jefferson, North Carolina 28640
    www.mcfarlandpub.com*

For Jim Holman

Acknowledgments

I would like to thank Hofstra University for granting me a sabbatical leave and travel funds to work on this book. I would also like to thank George Bernstein, Marcia Duffy, Verena Kossodo, Christine Hofmann, Elayne Horn, Mary Ann Spengler, and James Holman for their encouragement with this project.

Finally, I would like to thank Winnie Klotz of the Metropolitan Opera for the use of her wonderful photos. I would also like to thank the other photographers of various *Ring* productions illustrated in this book.

Contents

Preface

Twenty-five years ago I edited a book called *Penetrating Wagner's* Ring: *An Anthology*, and back then there were only two opera companies in the United States that ever staged the *Ring*— the Metropolitan Opera in New York and the San Francisco Opera — and not very frequently at that. How the situation has changed since then. Now every opera company in the world wants to stage the *Ring* cycle. In the United States, *Ring* cycles have appeared in many other places including Seattle, Chicago, Washington, D.C., Los Angeles, Pittsburgh, and Texas — and around the world in cities like Toronto, Tokyo, Adelaide, and London, in addition to most of the other European opera capitals.

We are clearly living during a Wagner renaissance when the *Ring* is being staged around the world — and some wealthy fans will go around the world to see various approaches to this vast tetralogy of operas. All this represents a revolutionary change in attitude, and all within twenty-five years. Back in the 1970s the problem was finding a performance of the *Ring*; now the problem is finding a ticket. Often a *Ring* is sold out a year in advance of the first performance[1] so there is clearly an increasing demand for tickets as more and more people become fascinated by the *Ring* cycle.

During the thirty years after World War II Richard Wagner had a very tainted name, especially in America, because Hitler used Wagner's tragic anti–Semitism in the cause of Nazism. Rudolf Bing in his memoirs reported that even in a city as operatically sophisticated as New York people simply did not want to hear Wagnerian opera even ten years after the war. What caused such a major change in attitude to Wagnerian opera?

Beyond the simple passage of time and the magical quality of this composer's operas, one of the major factors was the Wagner festival at Bayreuth. Winifred Wagner, the widow of the composer's son Siegfried, was a great admirer of Hitler, who was equally admiring of Wagner's music, and they both turned the summer festival into a Nazi showplace in the 1930s and until 1944, when the festival was closed. But her sons, Wieland and Wolfgang, managed to reopen the festival in 1951 and their revolutionary new approaches to staging the *Ring* and the other Wagner operas helped to revive audience interest, presenting Wagnerian opera in a new visual style and without its previous political associations.

Many people, especially the young, have been drawn to Wagner by these new approaches — not to mention the very quality of his wonderful operas. Many are too young to have the old World War II associations and thus can see and hear the operas with minds unburdened by these ugly memories. In addition, the symphonic quality of Wagner's music, coupled with its dramatic and visual powers, has excited many new audiences through recordings and videos. The use of surtitles, now in virtually every opera house in the world, has also helped Wagnerian opera. When audiences can understand what is being sung on stage, they become more engaged in opera. The age of compact discs, video cassettes, and DVDs has brought new audiences to Wagnerian opera — first in Germany and now around the world. Wagner can make music that sounds hot (the fire music of the *Ring*), sexy (the first act of *Die Walküre* and the last scene of *Siegfried*), tragic (the opening of *Götterdämmerung* and Siegfried's funeral music), and silly (Siegfried's flute playing in the second act of *Siegfried*). All these varied musical effects are cleverly woven into the drama and create symphonic sounds and theatrical sights.

The young have also been attracted to Wagner the social revolutionary. The spring of 1849 found Wagner at the barricades in Dresden, fighting the aristocratic establishment and defending the rights of the poor and the disenfranchised. The year 1848, during which he started work on *Der Ring des Nibelungen*, was also the year that Marx wrote the Communist Manifesto. The *Ring*'s own anti-materialism and anti-capitalism have been emphasized by several critics, starting with George Bernard Shaw in *The Perfect Wagnerite*, and even a casual understanding of the *Ring* forces one to ponder what happens to the gold after it is stolen from the river and transformed into the ring, with its immense wealth and power. In many ways the *Ring* is a study in greed and in the corruption that results when even noble characters like Wotan renounce love and become murderously ruthless in their determination to possess the mighty ring. Money and what it does to people are the obvious interpretation: how our ability to love can be incapacitated by our desire for money.

The dramatic and mythic qualities of the *Ring* have also attracted many new fans to its power. At a time when J.R.R. Tolkien's own *Ring* — both in its original form as novels and its newer film version — has become very popular, it is not surprising that Wagner's *Ring* (certainly the source of the Tolkien work) becomes more and more enticing. Both artists were interested in mythic patterns like love and hate, evil and revenge, water and air, earth and fire, life and death, tragedy and comedy, and death and transfiguration. It is no coincidence that the *Ring* ends where it begins, in the depths of the Rhine. Recurrent cycles are what the *Ring* is essentially about, and our lives are governed by them. A man dies of cancer, his grandson is born a month later; lovers fight and make up; water evaporates and clouds are formed; matter is destroyed but energy is created. The forces of nature occur all around us and control our lives, and they come in cycles — like Wagner's *Ring*— and these cycles both create our life and destroy it.

The scenic effects that Wagner demands, utterly impossible at the time the operas were written, provide fresh challenges to modern stage designers and inspire them to produce fascinating new *Ring* productions. So many of the visual effects Wagner wanted seem cinematic because of Wagner's impossible demands. The ending of *Götterdämmerung*, with the hall of the Gibichungs afire, Valhalla in flames, and the Rhine overflowing, seems still impossible to achieve onstage. Some great filmmaker, though, could create wonderful images with these Wagnerian demands, assuming of course that realism is worth achieving. If Wagner were alive today he would probably be turning his operas directly into films, given the impossible imagistic demands he makes of the operatic stage.

Imagination in characterization is another of Wagner's fortes. His correspondence is filled with references to people as either loving friends or dangerous enemies. In his personal life he tended to look upon other people in extremes, as heroes or villains — and indeed there is a bipolar quality to his life in general, a life lived in extremes of often suicidal depressions and paranoid manias. But one of the most wonderful and amazing things about the *Ring* is its lack of melodramatic characterization. The *Ring*'s characters remain as inexhaustible as real people because they refuse to be neatly categorized and dismissed. Who is the real villain in the *Ring*? Wotan does much more evil than Alberich ever dreams of— and often Alberich's many personal rejections and his very isolation make him a sympathetic character. In *Das Rheingold* Loge finds the gods the most culpable of beings, not the Nibelung dwarves. Wagner's characters become as confusing and fascinating and multi-dimensional as real people because they are never melodramatically two-dimensional. Even Hunding and Hagen can be portrayed onstage as suffering and sympathetic characters despite the brutality of some of their actions.

For all of these reasons and many more, a Wagner renaissance is alive and doing well today, and for the increasing number of people who become fascinated with the *Ring*, a collection of essays such as this one will be helpful. Using a variety of writing styles from the most carefully scholarly to the conversational, these essays examine many different aspects of Wagner's complex *Ring*.

Part I of the book, called the Foundation, provides a *Ring* chronology plus an introduction to the cycles in the cycle, which tries to clarify much of the plot. James Holman's essay considers the varying public perceptions of the *Ring* in this century. Vazsonyi's essay looks at Wagner the marketer, one of his many facets.

In the second part, Interpretations, Neil Friedman examines the politics of the *Ring*, Barbara Guenther's essay looks at the *Ring* as a product of the Romantic period, and the editor provides a study of the visual sources of the *Ring* in Wagner's life in Italy and Switzerland.

The next part of the collection looks at the *Ring* and Germany. Steven Cerf provides an insightful summary of Wagner's *Ring* and its influence on German culture, and Gregory Kershner shows how the *Ring* reflects the German philosophy of the period. Brigitte Heldt recounts the events around the *Ring*'s premiere in Munich — not the Bayreuth premiere, which occurred later.

The fourth part of this book examines *Ring* productions and their influence around the world. Erick Neher provides a useful overview of the production history of the *Ring*, while Joann Krieg examines the effects of the *Ring* in America, and the editor surveys the *Ring*'s literary reverberations.

The most technical of the sections of this book comes next, with a look at the language and music of the *Ring*. Stewart Spencer, a distinguished translator, examines the language of the *Ring*, from the Icelandic of the predecessor Eddas to the contemporary German. This section also includes an interview with one of the greatest current Brünnhildes, Jane Eaglen. The book concludes with a critical overview of the *Ring* on disc and on video, and a discussion of the possible trouble with Wagnerian opera.

Clearly, too many people have approached the *Ring* with fear and trembling, but the time for Wagnerian intimidation is over. More than anything else, the *Ring* was meant to be enjoyed; this book provides more information about this work for *Ring* fans, and with more knowledge of this vast work comes more enjoyment. Here a beginner can start an examination of the work but here the expert will also find new approaches and insights. This book provides an introduction to the inexhaustible *Ring*; but each new hearing, new viewing, and new production offers new insights and new discoveries. The complexities and fascinations of the *Ring* can provide entertainment and enjoyment for a lifetime — and perhaps even beyond!

John Louis DiGaetani
February 2006

A *Ring* Chronology

1813 Wagner is born in Leipzig.

1848 Wagner writes *Siegfrieds Tod*, later the basis for *Götterdämmerung*.

1851 Wagner writes *Der Junge Siegfried*, which will become the basis of *Siegfried*.

1852 The texts for *Rheingold* and *Walküre* are written. The earlier texts are changed into *Siegfried* and *Götterdämmerung*.

1853 *Der Ring des Nibelungen* is privately printed. Wagner begins composing *Rheingold*.

1854 The scoring of *Rheingold* is completed. Wagner begins composing *Die Walküre*.

1856 Wagner finishes composing *Walküre* and begins composing *Siegfried*.

1857 The first two acts of *Siegfried* composed.

1857 The first act of *Tristan und Isolde* composed.

1859 *Tristan und Isolde* finished.

1861 Paris production of *Tannhäuser*.

1865 *Tristan und Isolde* produced in Munich.

1867 *Die Meistersinger von Nürnberg* composed.

1868 *Die Meistersinger* staged in Munich; Wagner composes the third act of *Siegfried*.

1869 Wagner completes *Siegfried*, except for scoring, and begins *Götterdämmerung*. *Rheingold* is staged in Munich.

1870 Wagner continues *Götterdämmerung*. *Die Walküre* is staged in Munich.

1871 Wagner completes the scoring of *Siegfried*.

1872 Wagner finishes composing *Götterdämmerung*.

1874 Wagner finishes scoring *Götterdämmerung*.

1876 *Der Ring des Nibelungen* is performed in Bayreuth.

1882 *Parsifal* is performed in Bayreuth.

1883 Wagner dies in Venice.

Introduction: The Cycles in the Cycle

John Louis DiGaetani

The *Ring* cycle certainly remains Wagner's masterpiece, and it occupied him for almost thirty years. As was usual with him, the libretto took longer to compose than the music, the reason being that when Wagner wrote his libretto he clearly already had the music in his mind. In 1848 Wagner began with *Siegfrieds Tod,* which later became the basis for *Götterdämmerung.* Feeling that the viewer of his opera would have to know something of the youth of his hero Siegfried, Wagner wrote in 1851 *Der Junge Siegfried,* which became the basis for *Siegfried.* In 1852 the texts for *Rheingold* and *Die Walküre* were written, and the earlier texts were changed into *Siegfried* and *Götterdämmerung.*

Wagner privately printed the complete text for *Der Ring des Nibelungen* in 1853, and he then began composing *Das Rheingold.* By the next year, 1854, Wagner had completed scoring *Rheingold* and then began composing *Die Walküre.* By 1856 Wagner had finished composing *Walküre* and begun composing *Siegfried,* though (as in the previous operas) making some changes in the printed text of the *Ring* and in the final version set to music. In 1857, after having composed the first two acts of *Siegfried,* Wagner left the project temporarily and instead began composing the first act of *Tristan und Isolde.* In 1867 Wagner again interrupted the *Ring* project to begin work on *Die Meistersinger.* After that opera had its successful premiere in Munich in 1868, Wagner returned to the third act of *Siegfried.* By the next year Wagner had completed *Siegfried* and begun composing *Götterdämmerung;* also in 1869 *Das Rheingold* was first staged in Munich, over Wagner's objections. In 1870, while Wagner was working on the final opera of the tetralogy, *Die Walküre* had its premiere in Munich, also over the composer's objections. By 1874 Wagner had completed composing the final opera, and the entire tetralogy was finally staged within one week, as he intended, in his own specially-designed theater at Bayreuth, in 1876. An examination of the text of the four operas indicates that Wagner both repeated elements of his earlier literary style and developed some new techniques for this new work.

One of the major features in the text of the *Ring* operas is the repeated use of cycles — cycles of light and dark, day and night, water and land, airy mountains and watery depths, waking and sleeping, comedy and tragedy, life and death. The forces of nature are presented as controlled by cycles — forces which both give us life and take it away.

The *Ring* cycle, that vast tetralogy of operas (or music-dramas, as Wagner liked to call them), uses suicide in several important ways and it becomes a major theme in the entire work. In addition, Wagner developed a distinctive meter and style for the libretto. As many other commentators have pointed out, Wagner used a metered verse characterized by *Stabreim*—

alliteration, in English. The heavily alliterated verse that Wagner used in his *Ring* librettos was designed as a consciously antiquated form to reflect the rhetorical style of old Germanic poetry—the early medieval period of the *Ring* cycle. An equivalent in English is the heavily alliterated verse style of *Beowulf;* this form was clearly Germanic since it was also used in the poetic Eddas. Another English equivalent would be several Victorian poets who were so fond of medieval literature that they wrote in a consciously antiquated poetic style to reflect the medieval period, which became their subject matter. Even earlier, in the Romantic period, Keats used the old Spenserian stanza for his "The Eve of St. Agnes"—to reflect the period of the poem rather than the period in which the poem was written. Tennyson did this as well in his "Idylls of the King" or "The Lady of Shalott," using medieval rather than Victorian poetic forms. Clearly there was a tradition in both English and German of using antiquated poetic forms in the nineteenth century to reflect the literature of earlier periods, and Wagner used this form of medievalism as the basic style for his text in the *Ring* cycle. This nineteenth-century historicism appears also in the architecture of the period, since the taste of the period admired the use of earlier styles in contemporary buildings.

Wagner was also fond of the repetition of key words in his librettos to emphasize key ideas. He created a verbal equivalent of his musical *leitmotiv* system by the repetition of words and images to reflect some of the major ideas in each of his four *Ring* librettos. "Schmach" (shame) and "Liebe" (love), for example, are repeated often in *Die Walküre*, in addition to repetitions of key images. Light and darkness, which Wagner used very often in his libretto for *Tristan und Isolde*, also appear in the *Ring* cycle, often with symbolic meanings. The use of these cycles again connects the *Ring* with Vico's concept of the cycles of nature which control our lives. Wagner uses irregular line lengths in these four librettos, but usually the lines are short, with six syllables, generally iambic trimeter but often varied. Wagner was clearly imitating the Old High German poetic forms like those in the *Nibelungenlied*.

One of the central concerns of the tetralogy is suicide. Suicide does not appear in *Das Rheingold* or *Siegfried*, but it appears significantly in *Die Walküre* and especially *Die Götter-dämmerung*. In these two of the *Ring* operas suicide appears as a major subject, so clearly its treatment deserves close attention. The subject of suicide first appears in the second act of *Die Walküre*, during Wotan's famous dialogue with his daughter Brünnhilde. As he confesses to his favorite Valkyrie daughter:

Ich berührte Alberich's *Ring*	I once held Alberich's ring,
gierig heilt ich das Gold!	greedily grasped the gold!
Der Fluch, den ich floh,	The curse that I fled
nicht flieht er nun mich:—	won't flee from me now:—
was ich liebe, muss ich verlassen,	what I love I must leave,
morden, wen je ich minne,	murder him whom I cherish
trugend verrathen	and falsely betray
wer mir traut!	him who trusts me!—
Fahre denn him,	Farewell, then,
herrische Pracht,	godly power,
göttlichen Prunkes	divine show's
prahlende Schmach!	resplendent shame!
Zusammen breche	Let all I built
was ich gebaut!	now fall in ruins!
auf geb' ich mein Werk!	I give up my work!
nur Eines will ich noch:	one thing only do I crave:
das Ende—	the end—
das Ende!—	the end—
Und für das Ende	And Alberich will accomplish
sorgt Alberich!	that end!

Wotan yearns for the end of his suffering, the end of his struggles with Alberich over the gold; and yet what he seems to want most is his own death. In calling for the end, Wotan seems to be yearning for his own annihilation even if that means leaving Alberich in control of the ring.

This same suicidal quality appears in his son Siegmund during the same act of *Die Walküre,* specifically during the "Todesverkündigungmusik" or Death Announcement music. As Brünnhilde tells Siegmund when she appears to him:

Nur Todegeweihten	Only the death-doomed
taugt mein Anblick:	are allowed to look on me—
wer mich erschaut,	he who sees me
der scheidet vom Lebens-Licht,	leaves from the light of life.
Auf der Walstatt allein	In battle only
erschein'ich Edlen:	I appear to heroes:
wer mich gewahrt,	he who perceives me
zur Wal kor ich ihn mir.	I've picked as one dead.

This passage indicates the deadly nature of Brünnhilde's task: she is announcing to Siegmund that he must now leave life and his wife and sister Sieglinde to join the Valkyries and the other heroes in Valhalla. When he refuses to leave Sieglinde, Brünnhilde insists that (because he has seen her) he must now go to Valhalla. Siegmund then threatens to commit suicide.

Diess Schwert—	This sword—
das dem Treuen ein Trugvoller schuf:	which a traitor gave to an honest man:
diess Schwert	this sword
das feig vor dem Feind mich ver-	which betrays me, alas, to my enemy,
rath:—	then let it strike against a friend!
frommt es nicht gegen den Feind,	two lives
so fromm'es denn wider den Freund!	laugh at you here:—
Zwei Leben	take them, Nothung,
lachen dir hier:—	useful steel!
nimm sie, Nothung,	Take them at a stroke!
neidischer Stahlt!	
Nimm sie mit einem Strech!	

What Siegmund threatens to do here is first to kill Sieglinde, and then to kill himself. (Some critics have suggested that Siegmund is threatening to kill Sieglinde and her unborn child, but he is not sure she is pregnant—in fact, she herself will not find this out until the next act.) And the threat works very well, since Brünnhilde promises to help him in his upcoming battle with Hunding instead of following her orders from Wotan to let Siegmund die.

His sister Sieglinde also becomes suicidal during the next act, when she stands with Brünnhilde and her sister Valkyries as Wotan is approaching. As she says to Brünnhilde:

Nicht sehre dich Sorge um mich:	Don't worry because of me:
enzig taugt mir der Tod!	death alone can help me!
Wer heib dich Maid	Who told you, o maid,
dem Harst mich entführen?	to carry me away from this battle?
Im sturm dort hätt' ich	In the battle there
den Streich empfah'n	I've been struck
von derselben Waffe,	by the same spear
der Siegmund fiel:	which killed Siegmund:

das Ende fand ich	I've met my end
vereint mit ihm!	united with him!
Fern vom Siegmund —	Far from Siegmund —
Siegmund, vor dir!	Siegmund from you!
O deckte mich Tod,	Let death come to me
dass ich's denke!	lest I think of it!
Soll um die Flucht	Before I curse you, maid,
dir Maid ich nicht fluchen,	for saving me,
so höre heilig mein Flehen	hear my holy plea and
stosse dein Schert mir in's Herz!	drive your sword into my heart!

Sieglinde, as suicidal as her Walsung twin Siegmund, wants Brünnhilde to kill her rather than face the future without him. Of course Brünnhilde gives her the will to live (at least temporarily) by telling her that she is pregnant and will soon bear the glorious hero Siegfried.

When Wotan arrives soon afterwards, he vents his fury on his favorite daughter Brünnhilde for disobeying his orders and defending Siegmund instead of Hunding. Wotan threatens to put her into a sleep, saying that whatever man finds her thus unprotected can then have her. By the end of the scene, Brünnhilde acts just as Siegmund had behaved in the previous act, becoming suicidal to get what she wants. She asks that she be surrounded by fire to protect her from cowards, so that only a hero will possess her.

Diess eine	This one thing
musst du erhören!	you must grant me!
Zerknicke dein Kind,	Kill your child
das dein Knie umfasst;	who holds your knee,
zertritt die Traute,	trample your favorite
zertrumm're die Maid:	and dash her to pieces:
ihres Leibes Spur	let your spear destroy
zerstore dein Speer:	all trace of her body:
doch gieb, Grausamer, nicht	but, merciless god, don't allow her
der grässlichsten Schmacht sie pries!	the most foul of fates!
Auf dein Gebot	At your order
entbrenne ein Feuer:	let a fire spring up;
den Felsen umgluhe	let its hot flames
lodernde Fluth:	encircle her:
es fresse ihr Zahn	its tongue shall lick,
den Zagen, der frech sich wagte,	its tooth attack
dem Freislichen Felsen zu nah'n!	any coward who dares to approach
	the fearsome rock in his rashness.

Here we find a powerful plea for self-destruction — suicidal behavior indeed — since Brünnhilde is asking Wotan to destroy her rather than leave her unprotected. She is threatening suicide if Wotan does not allow her request, and her threat works. Wotan immediately agrees to surround her with fire and so protect her: only the hero who does not know fear will dare to approach his sleeping daughter.

The single *Ring* opera which makes the greatest use of suicide is the grand finale of the tetralogy, *Die Götterdämmerung,* where suicide and suicidal behavior dominate, and in fact the tetralogy ends with an act of suicide. Waltraute appears to her sister Brünnhilde toward the end of the first act, describing the condition of their father Wotan:

So — sitzt er,	So he sits,
sagt kein Wort.	saying not a word
auf hehrem Sitze	silent and solemn

stumm und ernst	on his sacred seat,
des Speerest Splitter	with the broken spear
fest in der Faust:	held tight in his hand:
Holda's Apfels	Holda's apples
ruhrt er nicht:	he does not eat:
Staunen und Bangen	shame and fear
binden starr die Götter.	possess the Gods!

What Waltraute is describing here is clearly suicidal behavior since, if Wotan does not eat the apples of Friea, he will soon grow old and die.

In fact, the suicide of both Brünnhilde and Wotan — as well as of the rest of the gods — is clearly envisioned in the immolation scene that ends the tetralogy. As Brünnhilde sings:

Das Feuer, das mich verbrennt,	Let the fire that destroys me
rein'ge vom Fluche den *Ring*:	clean the ring of its curse:
ihr in der Flut	in the waters
löset ihn auf,	let it dissolve
und lauter bewarht	and safely protect
das Lichte Gold	the shining, pure gold
das euch zum Unheil geraubt. —	that was stolen to your grief. —
Fliegt heim, ihr Raben!	Fly home, ravens!
Raunt es eurem Herren,	Whisper to your lord
was hier am Rhein ihr gehort!	what you overheard here by the
an Brünnhilde's Felsen	Rhine!
fahrt verbeit:	Fly past Brünnhilde's rock:
der dort noch lodert	tell Loge, who burns there,
weiser Loge nacht Walhall!	to go to Valhalla!
Denn der Götter Ende	For the end of the gods
dämmert nun auf:	has now come:
so — werf'ich den Brand	so do I throw this torch
in Walhall's prangende Burg.	into Valhalla's proud castle.
Grane, mein Ross,	Grane, my horse,
sei mir gegrüsst!	hear my message!
Weibt du auch, mein Freund,	Do you know, my friend,
wohin ich dich führe?	where I'm directing you now?
im Feuer leuchtend	Lit by fires,
lieg dort dein Herr,	your lord lies there,
Siegfried, mein seliger Held.	Siegfried, my blessed hero.
Dem Freunde zu folgen,	You whinny with joy
wieherst du freudig?	to approach your friend?
Lockt dich zu ihm	Does the laughing fire
die lachende Lohen?	take you to him?
Fühl' meine Brust auch,	Feel how the flames
wie sie entbrennt,	burn in my breast,
helles Feuer	bright fires
das Herz mir erfasst:	seize my heart:
ihm zu umschlingen,	to clasp him to me
umschlossen von ihm,	while held in his arms
in mächtigster Minne	and in greatest love
vermählt ihm zu sein	to be wedded to him!
Heiajaho! Grane!	Heiyaho! Grane!
Grüss deinen Herren!	Greet your lord!
Siegfried! Siegfried! Sieh!	Siegfried! Siegfried, See!
Selig grüsst dich dien Weib!	In bliss your wife greets you!

What we have here is a double suicide, for Brünnhilde kills not only herself by throwing herself into Siegfried's funeral pyre. She is also killing Wotan, who obviously wishes this death as well. Brünnhilde's final vision, like Isolde's final vision at the end of *Tristan und Isolde,* is a fantasy, a daydream of her lover alive and her joining him. So the *Ring* ends in sacrificial and exalted suicide. Does Wagner suggest here that the greatest happiness can occur, in some situations, only in suicide — especially in a death pact with a person one loves? Both Brünnhilde and Wotan commit suicide, and for Brünnhilde this ends with her vision of being reunited with Siegfried. But here, unlike in the end of *Der Fliegende Holländer,* there is no promise of an afterlife — only the exaltation of that final vision of being united with the beloved. And exaltation remains clearly the final vision, the final sounds, and the final emotion of the *Ring* cycle.

But is this great tetralogy really a tragedy if its ending is so happily triumphant? In these four librettos, Wagner uses comic relief—something which we connect with Shakespearean tragedy and which Wagner has only rarely attempted before. In his theoretical writing, Wagner always exalted Greek tragedy, which certainly does not use comic relief but instead emphasizes the value of the elegiac tragic tone. Wagner, however, abandons his theory to add comic relief to his *Ring* cycle, and Cosima repeatedly emphasizes her husband's love of Shakespeare in her memoirs. For example, Cosima wrote in her diary for July 28, 1881:

> Our morning conversation revolves around *A Midsummer Night's Dream,* and we find ourselves still laughing heartily at Bottom's "Not a word of me," which shows him to be a complete original, a being such as only Nature and Shakespeare can bring forth. And how individual all his comedies are, whereas in Calderon the characters are always the same! We surrender entirely to the magic of Oberon and Titania in our memories. R. works [Cosima Wagner, *Diaries,* 434].

It is interesting that a few days later when Cosima is playing the piano for her husband, he comments negatively on the overly literal labeling of the leitmotivs in editions of his works. Her entry of August 1, 1881, reads: "I play excerpts from *Götterdämmerung,* arranged for piano duet, with Loldi. R. says he is pleased with the work. Unfortunately in this edition there are a lot of markings such as 'wanderlust motive,' 'disaster motive,' etc. R. says 'And perhaps people will think all this nonsense is done at my request!'" (Cosima Wagner, *Diaries,* 435). Clearly Wagner wanted his use of leitmotivs to be seen as subtle and complex and not easily labeled.

Wagner himself wrote of his indebtedness to Shakespeare, in his autobiography. Very early in *Mein Leben* the composer wrote, "One of the main ingredients of my poetic fancy I owed to Shakespeare's mighty diction, emotional and humorous" (Wagner, *My Life,* 27).

Perhaps because of the extended time Wagner had to work on his tetralogy, both aspects of his personality — the manic and the depressive — inevitably entered this largest of his operatic works. The French writer Edouard Schure caught this aspect of Wagner when he met him after the premiere of *Tristan und Isolde* in Munich.

> Oh, what a strange whirl of emotions one felt on peering into this brain. It was, as the poet [Dante] says, *la bufera infernal che mai non resta.* And dominating all these characters, there were two that revealed themselves almost always simultaneously, like the two poles of his nature: Wotan and Siegfried! Yes, on the deepest level of his thinking, Wagner resembled Wotan, this German Jupiter, this Scandinavian Odin whom he created in his own image, a strange god, a philosopher and pessimist, for ever troubled by the end of the world, for ever wandering and brooding on the enigma of all things. But in his impulsiveness he resembled Siegfried more than anyone else, the strong and ingenuous hero, who knows neither fear nor scruples, forging a sword for himself and setting out to conquer the world. The result was the constant union between profound reflection and ebullient spontaneity [Spencer 180–181].

Here Schure has captured Wagner's bipolar nature, which includes both the suicidal god

Wotan and the young hero Siegfried, who does not know fear. Both the tragic and the comic are united in the *Ring* cycle, with comic relief in all four operas. As Wylie Sypher has pointed out, "Perhaps the most important discovery in modern criticism is the perception that comedy and tragedy are somehow akin, or that comedy can tell us many things about our situation even tragedy cannot" (Sypher 93). There could be no better illustration than the totality of the *Ring*.

Nature, the green world, is victorious by the end of the *Ring*, with its representatives, the Rhinemaidens, on stage and in possession of their ring at last, followed by human beings observing Valhalla burning and the dawn of a new day. The green world triumphs over the greedy feuding of a corrupted divinity and a corrupted humanity. To see comedy as more than a vehicle for a belly laugh, to see it in larger social and anthropological terms, is to understand the comedic aspects of the *Ring*. Overtly comic, even laughable, elements of the plot, staging specifications, and especially the various uses of lighting, as well as the music itself, must be seen as part of a whole — a whole that is ultimately a mythic representation of loss, change, and redemption.

Comedy, and especially its relationship to light and darkness, will help us to comprehend the *Ring*. *Das Rheingold*, which preserves the Aristotelian unity of time by occurring within the space of one day, opens in the murky darkness before dawn with the Rhinemaidens happily swimming about their treasure. The Rhinemaidens seem the very essence of comedy as they swim about their gold singing, blissfully naïve in the presence of its power and beauty. This light, happy mood is disturbed by the heavier, darker sounds from the orchestra as Alberich, the creature of darkness and night, appears. As he says in his opening lines:

Hehe! Ihr nicker!	Haha! You nixies!
Wie seid ihr neidlich,	How graceful you are,
neidliches Volk!	desirable creatures!
Aus Nibelheims Nacht	From Nibelheim's night
naht' ich mich gern,	I would gladly approach,
neigtet ihr euch zu mir.	if you would come down to me.

One of the Rhinedaughters, Flosshilde, says, "Es dammert und ruft" (It grows darker and someone is calling"). What attracts this dwarf Alberich from the darkness of Nibelheim is the gold and its glimmer of light.

As Alberich says of the Rhinemaidens, "Wie scheint im Schimmer/ ihr hell und schoen!" ("How you shine in the glimmery light so bright and beautiful!") Just as naturally as man seeks the light and avoids darkness, Alberich tries to capture these bright creatures, and they feign interest in his amorous advances, then laugh and swim away when he approaches. This teasing, cruel nature remains with the Rhinemaidens throughout the *Ring* until they finally taunt Siegfried in the last act of *Götterdämmerung*. Here, however, the Rhinemaidens confront only the ugly dwarf Alberich, yet they enjoy making fun of him for as long as he endures it. For example, the water makes Alberich sneeze, which inspires Woglinde to say, "Prustend naht; meines Freiers Pracht!" ("Sneezing my wonderful suitor approaches!") Wellgrunde is even nastier, and when she has finally encouraged Alberich to chase her, she says:

Bist du verliebt	Are you a lover
und lüstern nacht Minne?	and do you crave love's rapture?
lass' sehn, du Schöner,	Let us see what you
wie bist du zu schau'n?	are like, handsome fellow —
Pfui! du haariger,	Ugh! You hairy,
Hoeckriger Geck!	hunchback beau!

Das Rheingold, Metropolitan Opera: Diane Kesling, Meredith Parsons, and Karen Erickson as the Rhinemaidens. (Photograph: Winnie Klotz)

Scharzes, schweiliges	Black, horny,
Schwefelgezwerg!	sulfurous dwarf!
Such' dir ein Friedel,	Find yourself a sweetheart
dem du gefällst!	whom you can please!

Clearly the maidens enjoy provoking the ugly dwarf, and they swim about laughing as he tries to capture them. Their very cruelty makes the dwarf a sympathetic figure who finally seeks power since he will never get love.

The stage brightens as the rising sun strikes the gold and fills the whole scene with its golden light. The Rhinemaidens sing, "Rheingold! Rheingold! Leuchtende Lust,/ wie lachst du so hell und hehr!/ Bluehnder Glanz,/ entgeleisset dir weihlich in Wag!" ("Rheingold! Rheingold! Gleaming joy, how bright and gloriously you laugh! Glowing brightness, you brighten the waves!") The gold itself, protected by the Rhinemaidens, here symbolizes the beauty of nature, so that its seizure suggests the rape of nature by forces of greed and corruption. But at this point the gold seems safe, for only he who will renounce love can tap its power, and the Rhinedaughters are sure that Alberich is much too lusty a dwarf ever to make such a sacrifice to gain their beautiful hoard. Yet he fools them and makes just such a sacrifice by the end of the scene. As Alberich says when he steals the gold:

So buhlt nun im Finstern,	Then make love in darkness,
feuchtes Gezücht!	watery brood!
Das Licht lösch' ich euch aus....	I extinguish your light.

By the end of this first scene of the opera, Alberich has become the creature of darkness who destroys light, and the laughing Rhinemaidens laugh no longer, for he has destroyed the

Das Rheingold, Scene 1, Saxon State Opera, Dresden: Franz-Josef Kapellmann as Alberich. (Photograph: Matthias Creutziger)

Das Rheingold, **Metropolitan Opera: Horst Hiestermann as Alberich. (Photograph: Winnie Klotz)**

comedy of their existence — but only temporarily. By the end of the tetralogy's last scene we are shown that the theft caused only an interruption in normal life.

The rising sun provides the transition to the second scene, for here the day dawns on the mountainside before Valhalla, which the gods will finally possess. The repeated use of day and night in the lighting directions clearly exemplifies Wagner's use of Giambattista Vico's natural cycles. This new day will be the most crucial day in Wotan's life, but it begins comically. Dreaming about his beautiful new castle, the chief of all the gods is awakened by his nagging wife. Fricka, utterly incapable of keeping the philandering Wotan by her side, has become in her bitterness the typical shrew of comedy, whose very nagging drives her husband further away. As she tells Wotan, "Auf, aus der Träume/ wonnigem Trug!/ Erwache, Mann, und erwage!") ("Arise from the pleasant deception of dreams! Wake, man, and reflect!") With those irritating words Wotan is awakened. This is a light, bright scene with the new castle glowing in the background, for the giants Fasolt and Fafner have finally completed it and are arriving to collect their wage, the goddess Freia. Fasolt tells Wotan, "Sanft schloss/ Schlaf dein Aug': wir beide bauten/ Schlummers bar die Burg.") ("While your eyes were gently closed in sleep, we, sleepless, both built the castle.") Toil and darkness and sleeplessness are thus linked to the new home of the gods. So far, Alberich, the giants Fasolt and Fafner, and the new castle have been connected with the darkness; however, the gods are usually associated with bright, gleaming light. We first see them with the fresh light of a dawn. Fasolt calls Wotan "Lichtsohn du!" (You son of light!) But the chief of the glittery race wants to renege on his agreement with the giants, so he summons the crafty Loge to find him a way of getting out of this pact.

As the god of fire, Loge is lightness and brightness, personified here in the flickering figurations of his motif. Because of his insightful wit and cleverness he functions comically, but his is an evil, self-serving wit that isolates him from the other characters in the *Ring*. He comments in the final scene of the opera that he finds the actions of the gods immoral, but this does not stop him from helping Wotan to trick the giants and to steal the ring from Alberich.

Darkness dominates the third scene of *Das Rheingold*, which is set in Nibelheim. In those murky depths Alberich taunts Mime, flaunting his powers over his own race. Since earlier in the day when Alberich stole the ring, he has immediately enslaved the people around him. The Nibelungs had been happy and carefree, but now they are miserable slaves who have to mine gold for their master, Alberich. He indicates the darkness of his motives when he tries on his new helmet, the magic Tarnhelm, and says, "Nacht und Nebel — neimand gleich" ("Night and mist — resembling no one"). The orchestral colors darken for this scene, with a more pronounced use of the lower woodwinds and strings. "Nibelheims nacht'gem Land" ("Nibelheim's night-born land"), Wotan calls the place, and it certainly is dark in many different ways. In this scene we also find out that Loge is a cousin of Alberich's, a highly significant relationship because of the similarities it suggests between the two characters. "Den Lichtalben/ lacht jetz Loge; der listige Schelm," ("Loge is hobnobbing with the light-gods now, crafty knave)," says Alberich to his cousin. The word "Nacht" is used repeatedly in this dark scene, which captures the sad enslavement of the dwarves and the haughty and taunting power of Alberich. He has been rejected by the lovely Rhinedaughters, but he can get his revenge on his fellow dwarves in dark Nibelheim.

David Levin and some other commentators on the *Ring* have argued that the Nibelung dwarves (and other dwarves in European literature) are actually meant to be Jews, but there is no evidence in Wagner's text or the music to prove this. The same logic would have to apply as well to all the dwarves in European mythology, from the stories of Hans Christian Andersen to the brothers Grimm and even earlier. Do the dwarves in Walt Disney's film *Snow White and the Seven Dwarves* prove that dear old Walt was anti–Semitic? Hardly. Wagner presents Wotan and Alberich as polar opposites, though similar in some ways, basing this polarity on the composer's own personality.

The fourth and last scene of *Rheingold* is characterized by the general gloom and darkness of a murky twilight. When Donner and Froh clear the clouds away at the end of the scene, we see a sunset in the distance, which tells us that we have come to the end of this fateful day. As Wotan sings at the end of the opera:

Abendlich strahlt	In the evening light
der Sonne Auge;	the sun's eye gleams;
in prächtiger Glut	in its beautiful glow
prangt glanzend die Burg.	the castle shines bright.
In des Morgens Scheine	In the light of morning
mutig erschimmernd,	bravely glittering
lag sie herrenlos,	it stood without a master,
hehr verlockend vor mir.	lofty and inviting before me.
Von Morgan bis Abend,	Between dawn and sunset
in Müh und Angst,	in toil and suffering
nicht wonnig ward sie gewonnen!	it was not happily won!
es naht die Nacht!	Night draws on!

With these lines Wagner reminds us of the movement of the sun during this day, which gives a form to this opera. Cycles and cyclical movement clearly provide a structure for Wagner's tetralogy. This sunset also becomes symbolic, for with its waning light the gods grandly parade into Valhalla, which has already been linked for us with darkness and suffering. The intellectual, witty Loge closes the opera with a clever rejoinder to the wailing Rhinemaidens, telling them to bask in the glorious light of the gods. The gods think that their day has ended successfully, for they can now occupy their new home, Valhalla, accompanied by the strains of suitably triumphal music. But the sunset in the distance reminds us that this is the beginning of the end for these proud but tainted creatures.

Die Walküre is the most somber of the *Ring* operas, containing only one scene with any light, witty touches. A misguided production can, of course, add hours of merriment to the work, but this was not Wagner's intention. The lighting effects of this opera are very different from any used in the other three, with repeated moments of fragmented and weak lighting; and this is the cloudiest of the four *Ring* operas as well. The first act opens in Hunding's house as a storm rages outside. The room is dark, for according to Wagner's stage directions only an occasional glimmer from the fire at the hearth lights the scene. Even this flicker finally dies out as the act progresses, but eventually the storm clears and moonlight from outside floods the room. Siegmund, by the middle of the first act, notices the flicker of flame from the hearth.

Was gliesst dort hell	What is it glints brightly there
im glimmerschein?	in the gloom?
Welch ein Strahl bricht	What ray of light
aus der Esche Stamm?	shines from the ash tree's trunk?
Des blinden Auge,	A flash of lightning
leuchtete ein Blitz;	strikes the blind man's eyes;
lustig lacht da der Blick.	the light sparkles there happily.

The flickering light from the dying fire reveals the sword in the ash tree. After he pulls it out, Siegmund and Sieglinde declare their incestuous love in the beauty of the spring moonlight, which comes flooding even into Hunding's dark hut. As Siegmund tells Sieglinde:

Im Lenzesmond	In the spring moonlight
leuchtest du hell;	your face shines radiantly;
hehr umwebt dich	framed by your lovely
das Wellenhaar;	waving hair;
was micht berückt	what bewitched me

Das Rheingold, Metropolitan Opera: Siegfried Jerusalem as Loge. (Photograph: Winnie Klotz)

Das Rheingold, Metropolitan Opera: Jan-Hendrik Rootering as Fafner and Matti Salminen as
Fasolt. (Photograph: Winnie Klotz)

Das Rheingold, Scene 3, Saxon State Opera. (Photograph: Matthias Creutziger)

| errat' ich nun leicht — | now I can see clearly — |
| denn wonnig weidet mein Blick. | as I rapturously feast my eyes. |

This beautiful but fragile lighting will repeatedly be connected with the doomed figures and their tragic love. Later, sunlight will be associated with the more forceful Siegfried and Brünnhilde, but for Siegmund and Sieglinde moonlight and firelight are more fitting. This contrasting lighting for contrasting lovers creates yet another polarity in the *Ring*, but (as Vico would undoubtedly point out) both sunlight and moonlight are created by the cycles of nature.

Act II of the opera takes place in a rocky gorge, where Brünnhilde compares Fricka's entrance to a storm, and the storm punctuates this act. More and more clouds darken the stage as Wotan is forced to yield to Fricka's demands that he abandon the Walsungs and uphold her rights as goddess of the vow of marriage. Even more darkness gathers as Wotan explains to his daughter Brünnhilde the trap that he is in, and then he orders her to announce Siegmund's death to him. When Wotan talks about Alberich, he mentions the fact that the dwarf has begotten a son, and that when this happened, Erda had predicted that the downfall of the gods would soon follow. In the next scene, with the incestuous lovers returning, the only light they can see is the light in each other's eyes, along with occasional flashes of lightning that frighten Sieglinde. By the end of this act, when Siegmund is finally killed by Hunding, who is in turn killed by Wotan, the stage is engulfed in darkness. We see the action through a series of lightning flashes, our only source of light in the stormy gloom. Thunder and lightning end this act as Wotan rages at his disobedient daughter.

The last act of *Die Walküre* also uses storms, storm clouds, and occasional flashes of lightning to accompany the general murkiness and moral cloudiness of the action on stage. For the ride of the Valkyries there are again sudden flashes of lightning, many threatening

Das Rheingold, **Metropolitan Opera: James Morris as Wotan. (Photograph: Winnie Klotz)**

passing clouds, and general gloom. But the girls themselves provide the opera with its one bit of comedy, for they often laugh at their horses' nipping each other and engaging in sexual play. Later, the darkness and storm are directly connected with Wotan and his anger when Waltraute sings, "Nachtige zieht es/ von Norden heran" ("Darkness is coming from the north"). Then Ortlinde answers: "Wüthend steuert/ hier der Storm" ("The raging storm is coming this

***Die Walküre*, Metropolitan Opera: Placido Domingo as Siegmund. (Photograph: Winnie Klotz)**

way"). The storm gets more intense until Wotan himself finally appears on the scene, raging at Brünnhilde, and at the other Valkyries for defending her disobedience.

The stage is darkest when Wotan is angriest, but as he softens in his confrontation with Brünnhilde, gradually the clouds clear and the fragmented lightning gives way to a lovely,

Die Walküre, Metropolitan Opera: Jessye Norman as Siegline. (Photograph: Winnie Klotz)

clear twilight. In this twilight — the only clear, steady light we have seen so far in this opera — Wotan agrees to protect his sleeping daughter with a wall of fire. The act and the opera end with the flickering light accompanied through Loge's flickering fire-music.

This, the least humorous of the four *Ring* operas, ends with a lovely firelight. Weak light, darkness, clouds, and flashes of lightning have suggested the fragmented, morally weak world

Die Walküre, Metropolitan Opera: Christa Ludwig as Fricka. (Photograph: Winnie Klotz)

of *Die Walküre*. A word that recurs frequently is "Schmacht," or shame: the shame of Sieglinde, who must submit to Hunding though she does not love him; the shame of Wotan, who must submit to Fricka, though he no longer loves her, and who cannot control his own daughter; and the shame of Siegmund, who must leave his lover and sister in such terrible need. Such pervasive shame requires obscurity and cover, which is precisely what the opera's lighting

Die Walküre, Saxon State Opera: Jukka Rasilainen as Wotan, Birgit Remmest as Fricka. (Photograph: Matthias Creutziger)

effects provide. But in the general darkness another repeated word is "Liebe" (Love): Siegmund's love of Sieglinde and Wotan's love for Brünnhilde.

In direct contrast, *Siegfried* is the most comic of the *Ring* operas, but it remains a Wagnerian comedy, and that means that there are smiles and ideological conflicts rather than belly laughs and slapstick. People have often maintained that Wagner lacked a sense of humor; they are wrong. He had one, but it was, well, Wagnerian, as this masterpiece reveals. The opera includes comic situations, comic lines, comic music, and a happy ending. Too often, however, conductors and directors have approached *Siegfried* with all the grim determination that should be reserved for *Walküre*. In fact, the comic situations and characters in the opera are often dismissed as embarrassing or eliminated, and the result is bad theater for this opera and lack of tonal variety in the whole cycle. Now that most opera companies use some form of surtitles, one can hear more audience laughter during many performances of *Siegfried*.

Act I of *Siegfried* takes place in a dark interior, a cave, and the only source of light is a low fire burning near an anvil. From the opening of the first act the orchestra sounds very gloomy, with somber and dangerous-sounding bassoons, tubas, violas, cellos, and basses for Fafner and Mime. The first prolonged use of violins occurs when Siegfried makes his entrance; he and his music brighten up the general gloom and he even enters with a bear and chases Mime around the cave with it, laughing at his practical joke. He then complains of not having a decent sword, which establishes the major problem of the first act. Yet the darkness of the cave also suggests Siegfried's lack of knowledge about himself and his ancestry. He sees the animals in the forest with their young and asks Mime about his parents, for he does not believe that Mime is his real father; but the dwarf avoids most of his questions and just keeps reminding the boy of all that has been done for him.

Mime uses gratitude on Siegfried in the way that most people use a hammer. He is the

***Siegfried*, Act I, Seattle Opera: Siegfried and Mime. (Photograph: Chris Bennion)**

stereotypical over-possessive parent when he nags at the boy, cooks food for him, then reminds him of all he has done for him. Mime tells him that his mother died giving birth to him, and then sings a little refrain over and over about "the helpless orphan born in the woods" to remind him of his debt of gratitude. Mime knows how to make guilt work to benefit himself. He is also sardonically comic in his silly and inept attempts to teach the boy fear by conjuring up the dark, dense forest and the big teeth of Fafner the dragon. But with Mime's plan to chop the naïve boy's head off after he gets the ring, we can see the real evil in the old dwarf.

To kill a dragon Siegfried needs a sword, and his desire to find it in Act I is connected with his patrimony, for the broken fragments of Nothung, which Mime finally gives him, originally composed the sword of his father Siegmund. Freudian and phallic implications aside, Nothung provides a tangible connection between Siegfried and the parents he has never known. The solemn-sounding brasses that announce the arrival of the Wanderer, Wotan, on the scene also connect to Siegfried's ancestry, since the audience (unlike Siegfried) knows that Wotan is his grandfather. Here, the Wanderer's confrontation with the suspicious and nasty old Mime is organized around three questions that they ask each other, and then bet their heads on, but even here there is comedy. When the Wanderer first enters the cave, Mime tells him to live up to his reputation and keep on wandering. Wotan himself ironically addresses Mime as "wise smith," "wily dwarf," and "honest dwarf," all to comic effect. But the dialogue between the two characters has serious functions as well, for Wotan's three answers to Mime's questions about the races that inhabit the world are used to structure the entire opera.

Wotan describes the world of the *Ring* as having three major segments. The first, Nibel-heim, is the land of the elves and darkness, ruled by "Schwarz-Alberich" (dark-Alberich). The

Siegfried, Act I, Seattle Opera: Siegfried and Mime. (Photograph: Chris Bennion)

setting for Act I of *Siegfried* strongly suggests Nibelheim. Wotan says that the second part of creation is Riesenheim, ruled by Fafner, and it exists on the surface of the earth. Act II of *Siegfried* takes place on this plane, with a dense forest for the setting and with the shady and splotchy lighting typical of a forest. In the bright heights, on the other hand, live the gods, ruled by "Licht-Alberich" (Light-Alberich, or Wotan). Most of the last act takes place on the top of Brünnhilde's rock and in the full blaze of sunlight, at least according to Wagner's stage directions if not in some productions. The opera, then, as outlined by Wotan himself in his responses to Mime's questions, moves from darkness to light. While the variations become more subtle within each act, this is the overall pattern, and the contrast between Licht-Alberich and Schwarz-Alberich described by Wotan creates yet another Wagnerian polarity.

This pattern of contrasting lighting is sustained in the middle of the first act when Mime curses the light ("Verfluchtes Licht!"). Being a creature of caves and caverns, he is naturally more comfortable in the darkness, which is symbolic as well of his character and his evil designs on Siegfried's life. The general darkness of this Mime-dominated act is eliminated only during the Forging Music at the end. Siegfried is angry at Mime's inept attempts at forging and decides to act for himself. His effort to repair his father's shattered sword, Nothung (literally, "Found in Need"), creates the only bright passage in this dark act. The music here employs the motif associated with Loge, god of fire, for Siegfried must build a large fire to have enough heat to reforge the sword, and it is also significant that he uses wood from an ash tree. Wotan's spear is ash. Siegfried's new sword is forged symbolically with the remains of the old order of the gods. With Nothung Siegfried has established a tie with his mysterious past, acquired some new knowledge about his parents, and created a weapon for asserting and defending himself.

Siegfried, **Act II, Metropolitan Opera: Siegfried Jerusalem as Siegfried. (Photograph Winnie Klotz)**

The second act of *Siegfried* takes place in Riesenheim, in the depths of a dense forest, according to Wagner's stage directions. The act opens in "dark night" and the music helps create this ominous darkness with sounds suggesting the presence of the dangerous dragon Fafner. The ensuing confrontation between Alberich and Wotan occurs in almost total darkness, a lighting scheme that tends to equate these two characters for the audience. Both are after the ring and both want to use Siegfried for their own purposes. Wotan's motives center on the survival of the gods and the defense of his moral and legal system, while Alberich's motives are more selfishly evil and greedy; but both want to use Siegfried, and the blackness of the scene suggests Wagner's dark opinion of their motives.

With the dawn, Siegfried and Mime enter. The light in the middle of a dense forest is alternately shady and sunny and this is reflected in the often undulating Forest Murmurs music. As Siegfried wonders about his past, his parents, and his future, the gently shimmering music suggests the delicate forest light and various bird sounds. Now that Siegfried is alone, the tone in the act brightens. His natural curiosity about the birds and the bees becomes naïvely charming and typically adolescent. He becomes especially comic when he cuts a reed, whittles a rough flute, and tries to imitate the sound of the birds in the forest. The sour, flat notes he produces are musically comic. The audience laughs at the silly music written for the English horn, and regards the heroic "Dummer," Siegfried, with amusement. Significantly, all the other characters in the opera address him as "Kind" (child) or "Knabe" (boy). He is charmingly adolescent here, though some of the less pleasant aspects of adolescence — impatience and impetuosity for example, — appear in other parts of the score.

The music sounds fatally dangerous after the Forest Murmurs scene and during the major confrontation of this act, the fight between Siegfried and Fafner. Yet who can take it seriously? The fairy-tale quality of the scene makes most members of the audience smile, and as the dragon's roars become more ferocious, the fun grows. By the end of the fight Fafner has been mortally wounded, but he can still be comically perceptive about Siegfried. "Who gave you this idea, for it couldn't have come from your head?" the dragon asks. Mime is also unintentionally comic when he becomes so excited by the immediate presence of the ring and the power of the Tarnhelm that he can not help chattering too loudly about his eagerness to kill the stupid boy. Once Siegfried has killed the two immediate threats to his life, Fafner and Mime, the orchestral tone brightens again. The Forest Bird promises the boy the companion he has been seeking throughout the opera who will relieve his loneliness. The bird describes Brünnhilde as perched atop a fiery rock and declares that only he who does not know fear can win her. Significantly, she is immediately associated with light.

Like Act II, Act III begins with a stormy night just before the dawn, and with Wotan on stage. Once again we see him in a darkness that must soon give way to dawn, an optimistic light that is often connected with Siegfried in this opera. The old generation must give way to the impetuous and often careless new generation just as surely as day conquers night, or so Wagner is telling us in the opera's lighting. But here at the beginning of this last act the initial confrontation is between Wotan and Erda and, except for her bluish glow, it is a murky scene. Wotan is at his most pathetic here in his noble but anxiety-ridden attempts to avoid his certain fate. The all-wise Erda is sleepy and as unconcerned as any other impersonal force of nature, and thus she provides a dramatically effective foil for Wotan's anxiety. Erda wants to go back to sleep and keeps putting Wotan off, but she is finally angered enough by his persistence to tell him that he is a liar. In fact, the cycle of waking and sleeping occurs here and elsewhere in Wagner's *Ring* cycle, for the cycle of sleeping and waking governs much of our lives. Wotan counterattacks by telling Erda that she is not all-wise since she can not help him to avoid his doom. In the monologue that follows, Wotan comes to realize the hopelessness of his situation and to accept it with resignation. He now knows that his reign and that of the gods has ended. Siegfried represents the new order, and not even Erda can help Wotan avoid his destruction. With the approaching dawn the boy himself enters, following the Forest Bird, which flies off at the sight of Wotan's fierce ravens.

The dialogue between Wotan and Siegfried becomes a musical and dramatic conflict of the generations. Siegfried is tired of listening to old men and wants to get to the sleeping Brünnhilde, but Wotan wants the respect due his age and position and he is reluctant to lose control of his daughter, even though he knows that his loss is inevitable. Though Wotan calls Siegfried and the Walsungs "deine lichte Art" ("Your radiant kind"), he is angered by the boy's impatience and lack of understanding. Hence he tries to block the boy's way to the sleeping girl. In the ensuing fight Siegfried's sword Nothung breaks Wotan's ash spear, and the old generation of the world's rulers is defeated by the new. Wotan never again appears onstage in the *Ring*, though his daughters Brünnhilde and Waltraute do refer to him in his absence.

After this final conflict of the opera, all becomes bright and radiant. Fire music, appropriately, describes Siegfried's journey through the flames to reach Brünnhilde. The act, like the entire opera, has moved from darkness to light — another one of Vico's patterns. As Siegfried steps onto the top of the mountain, the scene is bathed in brightness and the audience gets its first view of total sunlight — in Wagner's stage directions, at least. Siegfried and Brünnhilde, and their relationship, glow with sunlight, while, as we have seen, various shades of murky grays represent the other characters in the opera.

Siegfried's description of what he sees as he comes onto the top of the mountain reinforces the message expressed by the many violin crescendi and the stage picture in any good production: radiant sunlight and the sleeping maiden. As a goddess, albeit an ex-goddess, she dwells in the domain of light and air that Wotan had described in the first act. Here there are

Siegfried, **Metropolitan Opera: Hildegard Behrens as Brünnhilde. (Photograph: Winnie Klotz)**

Freudian overtones as well, for when Siegfried first sees Brünnhilde's body he is afraid. It is she and her sexuality, then, that have finally taught him the fear that neither Mime, Fafner, nor Wotan could teach him. The boy calls out to his mother to calm his rising fears; Wagner, well before Freud, combines newly experienced sexuality with the figure of the mother. Yet Siegfried's boyish fear of a woman's body is so typical that it is comic. Wagner cleverly indicates this with the marvelous naïveté of Siegfried's response when he first removes Brünnhilde's shield — "That is no man!" he says.

As anyone could have predicted, curiosity and physical attraction overcome fear, for

Siegfried kisses the sleeping maiden. As she awakens, the first thing she says is "Heil dir, Sonne! Heil dir, Licht! Heil dir, leutender tag!" ("Hail to you, sun! Hail to you, light! Hail to you, shining day!") In the first scene of this act Erda is awakened by Wotan, and now her daughter Brünnhilde is awakened by Siegfried — sleeping and waking being one of the many natural cycles in this tetralogy. The union of Siegfried and light is established here too, for he has become a sun god for her and, just as surely, he gets a first glimpse of total sunlight in the opera with her. What, then, do Brünnhilde and the light symbolize? For him the woman and the light are basically love and knowledge. She immediately loves him, as a result of knowing his parents and of Wotan's spell in the last scene of *Die Walküre*; and the love is of course mutual. The boy has been lonely and seeking a companion for most of the opera, and here, at last, he has found her; but she also represents knowledge. As a child of Wotan and Erda, Brünnhilde has the wisdom that Siegfried knows he lacks in himself. She tells him about his past and his dead parents, which he has been curious about since the beginning of the opera. Potentially, then, presented here is the ideal matching of active energy and wisdom.

At first Brünnhilde, like a typical nineteenth-century virgin, fears the loss of her virginity; she is also consciously aware of her new position as a defenseless woman rather than a goddess. She asks Siegfried to love her but not to touch her, but he is too aroused to be satisfied with something so platonic. "Wake up! Wake up and see the sunlight," he pleads. The woman in her, luckily for him, overcomes the chaste goddess and she becomes inflamed with love's sexual passion, as he already is. The music at this point, with all its mounting crescendi and fast rhythms, is reminiscent of the *Liebesnacht* in *Tristan und Isolde*, and the opera ends with a glorious duet for the lovers that affirms all that the light on stage at this time symbolizes. The final two lines of the opera summarize the lovers' emotions: "Leuchtende Liebe, Lachtender Tod!" ("Shining love, laughing death!") Their radiant new love will defy even death, they sing, as the primordial life force of the green world is reaffirmed in this dazzling final scene. But the mention of death and its laughing defiance seems vaguely ominous for the future, despite the triumphant, happy present. Siegfried has at last found all that he has sought in this opera, and he shows that he can even laugh at death, but his actions contain the seeds of a sad future and the suggestion of a bipolar cycle of life and death. Here at *Siegfried*'s finale, we have come to the core of Wagner's theory of comedy. To make a joke or get a laugh was never enough for Wagner. He did want his audience to smile and occasionally to laugh but only within the scope of larger ideological conflicts between good and evil, youth and old age, hate and love, naïveté and wisdom, life and death, and — between darkness and light. What we have here is bipolar comic relief.

Götterdämmerung provides the culmination of the *Ring* in more than one way, including as it does the various comic elements and lighting effects already noticed in the other *Ring* operas. The prologue to the first act of this opera begins with the darkness before dawn, a lighting effect that Wagner is especially fond of because it enables him to suggest both darkness and imminent new light. The darkness is, of course, entirely suitable for the Norns scene, for they predict the destruction of the gods; but with the first glimmers of the new day we see the happy lovers Siegfried and Brünnhilde. The light of day returns the Norns to Mother Earth, for they remain most content in her slumbering darkness; but Siegfried and Brünnhilde, while singing their love music together, refer often to light. Dawn and light are here repeatedly connected with the couple's love, for, unlike Hagen and Alberich, they are the forebears of a radiant new race.

Each of the three acts of this monumental opera preserves a unity of time, for each of them occurs during a single day — Wagner being careful to indicate the progression of the sun during every act. By the end of the prologue to *Götterdämmerung*, the sun has risen and, as

Götterdämmerung, **Saxon State Opera: Katharina Peetz, Ursula Hesse von den Steinen, the Three Norns. (Photograph: Matthias Creutziger)**

the action of the first act proceeds, the sun continues to climb in the sky. The lightning and thunder often associated with the gods' stormy existence dominate the stage briefly during the second scene of this act when Brünnhilde is visited by her Valkyrie sister Waltraute. In contrast to the dark unhappiness of the gods, Brünnhilde sings of the brightness of her love for Siegfried and tells her sister that she will never give up the token of that love, the ring. But by the end of this scene twilight has fallen and in the gathering darkness Siegfried comes to the rock and, transformed by the Tarnhelm into the shape of Gunther, captures Brünnhilde. We know by her speech that she does not recognize him. "Wer bist du, Schrecklicher? Stammst du von Menschen? Kommst du von Hella's nächthchem Heer?" ("Who are you, terrible creature? Are you a man? Do you spring from Hell's night-born race?") Thus Brünnhilde associates trickery, deceit, and evil with the dark powers of the night, while for her Siegfried remains a sun god. Yet across their happiness a fatal shadow has fallen and by the end of this first act of *Götterdämmerung* total darkness has enveloped the stage.

Act II of this opera, like the prologue of Act I, begins with the pre-dawn darkness. In this murk Alberich appears before his son Hagen, reminding him of the rightness of his cause, of the power of the ring, and, most of all, of his determination to possess the ring once again. The lack of bright lighting on stage is reflected in Alberich's language.

die wir bekämpfen	Those whom we fight
mit nachtigem Krieg	with the forces of darkness
schon gibt ihnene Not unser Neid.	already our envy gives them grief.

As the dawn approaches, Alberich must leave, warning his son to remain true to him. It is interesting how frequently Alberich repeats the phrase "Mein Sohn" ("My son"), implying that Hagen has a duty to his father. Alberich intends to use this duty, of course, to ensure his own ultimate possession of the ring; he feels no paternal affection. But with the dawn Siegfried returns, and the dawn motif takes on a significance that is similar to that of the nature motif, for light and nature are permanent elements that can survive the total destruction at the end of the opera.

The second act of this opera uses the very dramatic situation of a ruined wedding party, just as the second act of *Lohengrin* did. Brünnhilde cannot believe her eyes when she sees her

Götterdämmerung, Metropolitan Opera: Matti Salminen as Hagen. (Photograph: Winnie Klotz)

husband Siegfried eagerly awaiting a marriage to Gutrune. As she expresses it, "Mir schwendet das Licht" ("I am losing the light"), for indeed the light has gone from her life. Siegfried's response to her charges is: "Gunther, dein Weibe is übel! Erwache, Frau! Hier steht dein

Gatte." ("Gunther, your wife has become sick! Awake, lady! Here is your husband."). That Siegfried should awaken her to this sham marriage is an ironic reversal of his earlier action in awakening her during the last act of *Siegfried*. As the sun sets at the end of this act, the gathering darkness conceals Brünnhilde, Gunther, and Hagen, all plotting Siegfried's death. The trombones accompany Hagen's fatal blast as he calls for Siegfried's death, and henceforth the harsher qualities of the brass will be used more and more frequently as the opera moves ahead.

The final act of what has been called the greatest of Wagner's tragedies begins comically. The Rhinemaidens, foolish teases that they are, bewail the loss of their gold, but they do a lot of laughing as well. They begin the act by singing about the brightness of the sunlight and the sad lack of it in the murky depths of the Rhine since their gold was stolen.

Frau Sonne	Lady Sun
sendet lichte Strahlen:	spread beams of light;
Nacht liegt in der Tiefe:	in the depths it is night:
einst war sie hell,	once it was bright there,
da heil und hehr	when, safe and beautiful,
des Vaters Gold noch in ihr Glanzte.	our father's gold glittered there still.
Rheingold!	Rheingold!
klares Gold!	Pure gold!
wie hell du einstens strahltest,	How brightly once you did shine,
hehrer Stern der Tiefe!	resplendent star of the deep!

When Siegfried arrives, the girls immediately tease him cruelly with questions like

Was schiltst du so in den Grund?	What are you grumbling about?
...	...
Welchen Alben bist du gram?	What elf has annoyed you?
...	...
Hat dich ein Nicker geneckt?	Has a Nixie been fooling you?

The girls laugh at his inadequate attempts to answer all their absurd questions seriously, but then they ask for the return of their ring. Siegfried answers:

Verzeht' ich an euch mein Gut,	If I wasted my goods on you,
das Zurnte mir wohl mein Weib.	my wife would be angry with me.

The Rhinemaidens quickly respond:

Sie ist wohl schlimm?	Is she bad-tempered?
Sie schlagt dich wohl?	Does she beat you?
Ihre Hand fühlt schon der Held!	The hero can feel her hand already!

Thus these teasing Rhinedaughters make fun of the great hero who is fearful of his wife, and they then go on to taunt him for being a miser.

Just when Siegfried seems most inclined to give them the ring, they explain the curse on it, linking the ring with darkness and death. They tell him that if he does not give them the ring he will die that night, but here Siegfried's pride and naïveté become painfully apparent. He insists that he is not afraid of their threats, just as he would not give in to their teasing. So they swim off humming their motif, sure that they will get their ring back by the end of the day. Their final comments become teasing once again as they call him a fool, laugh at him, and then swim away.

While Siegfried's refusal to be intimidated by these comic, silly girls is understandable, they remain nevertheless right about what is going to happen to him by the end of the day, and the comic relief early in the act is soon replaced by tragedy. Hagen arrives, and Siegfried shows himself to be generally witty and humorous. When he mixes a drink for himself in his horn, he spills some by accident and then says that it will bring refreshment to Mother Earth. When Hagen asks him if he can still understand the songs of birds, he responds, "Seit Frauen ich singe horte, vergass ich der Voglein ganz." ("Since I heard women singing, I have quite forgotten the birds.") Suddenly, though, as the sun slowly sets in the background, Hagen plunges his spear into Siegfried's back. Significantly, Siegfried's dying words are not of revenge or betrayal; instead, he sings of the beautiful light that comes from Brünnhilde's loving eyes. As he dies, he affirms the beauty of love and light instead of the horrors of death, betrayal, and darkness.

In the second scene of the third act, set in the hall of the Gibichungs, Wagner dramatically portrays Gutrune's fears of her bad dreams and of the general darkness. Here she becomes an interesting contrast to Brünnhilde; while Gutrune has always been the passive female who is the puppet of the men around her (her brother Gunther and her half-brother Hagen), Brünnhilde initiates action. Wagner portrays the women as polar opposites. During this murky night, Hagen arrives and kills his half-brother, Gunther, but very quickly Brünnhilde assumes a dominant role, singing the famous immolation scene to bring the tetralogy to its glorious finale. As Carolyn Abbate has pointed out, "Brünnhilde is, then, at once a commanding prophetic voice and a unique listening ear. In her operatic form, both elements are greatly multiplied.... The commanding prophecy and the sibylline ear are finally brought together at the end of *Götterdämmerung*" (Abbate 215).

In the gloom, the flickering firelight brightens as Brünnhilde ignites Siegfried's funeral pyre. From the beginning of her oration, what she remembers most about Siegfried is his radiance. This is a funeral oration, but it remains a joyful one, which ends happily for her. As she sings before she leaps into the flames:

Ihr zu umschlingen,	To clasp him to me,
umschlossen von ihm,	to be held in his arms,
in machtigster Minne	to be united with him
vermahlt ihm zu sein!	through the power of love!
Hei-a-ja-jo! Grane!	Hei-a-ya-ho! Grane!
Grüss deinen Herrn!	Greet your lord!
Siegfried! Siegfried! Sieh!	Siegfried! Siegfried! See!
selig grüsst dich dein Weib!	Your wife greets you joyfully.

Brünnhilde imagines herself joined again with her light-bearing hero, happy and safe in his arms. This is not tragedy, but comedy, for great evil has been purged from the world through her triumphant suicide. By the end of the opera, however, we are again engulfed in that fertile pre-dawn darkness with which the whole tetralogy opened. A new and better day will dawn, for the evil in this world has been purged and the green promise of new life has been preserved. Wagner has shown us the powers of evil and corruption, but his final scene in the *Ring* restores nature's purity and innocence through eroticized suicide—here of Brünnhilde and Wotan—but also a stark reminder of what we saw at the ends of *The Flying Dutchman* and *Tristan und Isolde*. This familiar operatic statement fulfills Wagner's sense of an appropriate end.

Hagen's final grab for the ring is unsuccessful, for the Rhinemaidens are on stage again to pull him down into the depths and to laugh, as they generally do, at his death from greed. They are happy because they have their ring back and the world has been saved — the green, sunny, and essentially innocent world that had been threatened for so long by evil and darkness. The redemption motif ends the opera with tones of fulfillment, restoration, and peace.

The enduring ring in this vast tetralogy becomes the ultimately victorious ring that the earth makes around the sun. The sun god is dead, but the radiant sun endures, implying that finally the *Ring of the Nibelungs* is a bipolar totality that includes cycles of both tragedy and comedy, both light and darkness, both mania and depression. This larger theme reflects Giambattista Vico's famous theories about the eternal cycles of nature and the possibility of the merged polarities which can govern our lives. The cycles in the *Ring* cycle — a ring itself is an image of cyclical rather than progressive movement — are, I feel, related to the mood swings in Wagner's own life. Bipolar — or manic-depressive — illness has often been connected with artists and writers. Wagner probably suffered from bipolar illness, and that is why cycles of both comedy and suicide, of life and death, are evident in his *Ring* cycle. An examination of Wagner's letters indicates suicidal thoughts as well as manic visions of what his art could do for both Germany and the world. He realized his greatest achievement in his *Ring*, which continues to fascinate the world primarily because of its fascinating cycles.

Bibliography

Abbate, Carolyn. *Unsung Voices: Opera and Musical Narrative in the Nineteenth Century.* N.J.: Princeton University Press, 1991.

Barondes, Samuel H. *Mood Genes: Hunting for Origins of Mania and Depression.* New York: W. H. Freeman, 1998.

DiGaetani, John Louis, ed. *Penetrating Wagner's* Ring: *An Anthology.* New York: Da Capo, 1991.

_____. *Wagner and Suicide.* Jefferson, N.C. and London: McFarland, 2003.

Frye, Northrop. *Anatomy of Criticism.* New York: Atheneum, 1957.

Jamison, Kay Redfield. *Touched with Fire: Manic-Depressive Illness and the Artistic Temperament.* New York: Free Press, 1993.

_____. *An Unquiet Mind: A Memoir of Moods and Madness.* New York: Vintage Books, 1996.

Levin, David J. *Richard Wagner, Fritz Lang, and the Nibelungen: The Dramaturgy of Disavowal.* N.J.: Princeton University Press, 1998.

Spencer, Stewart. *Wagner Remembered.* New York: Faber and Faber, 2000.

Sypher, Wylie. *Comedy.* New York: Doubleday, 1956.

Wagner, Cosima. *Cosima Wagner's Diaries: An Abridgment.* Translated by Geoffrey Skelton. New Haven, Conn.: Yale University Press, 1997.

Wagner, Richard. *My Life.* Translated by Andrew Gray. New York: Da Capo, 1992.

_____. *Wagner's* Ring *of the Nibelung.* Translated by Stewart Spencer with commentaries by Barry Millington. London: Thames and Hudson, 1993.

Wright, William. *Born That Way: Genes, Behavior, Personality.* New York: Alfred A. Knopf, 1998.

"O, most excellent gold! Who has gold has a treasure with which he gets what he wants, imposes his will on the world, and even helps souls to paradise."

—*Christopher Columbus*, in a letter
to King Ferdinand and Queen Isabella, 1503

I. THE FOUNDATION

1. The Golden *Ring* in a Golden Age
James K. Holman

On a warm summer evening in July 1951, patrons of the Bayreuth Festival strolled up the Green Hill and into the Festspielhaus for the first time since 1944. Wilhelm Furtwängler, cleared of charges of Nazi collaboration, and unseen in the "mystic abyss" of the orchestra pit, opened the festival, not with the music of Wagner, but with Beethoven's Ninth Symphony.

Under the circumstances — painful memories and uncertainties about the future — it was apparent to those assembled, and to the music world at large, that an attempt was being made at a new beginning: here, in the Franconian village chosen by Wagner as home both for his family and his musical works, the world was being asked to embrace, again, the artwork of a future now long past, and degraded in that very hall. Few of those patrons, I suspect, would have predicted the magnitude of that renaissance.

The Bayreuth performances in 1951 inaugurated what has grown to become a golden age for Wagner, in some ways *the* golden age. And it is a half-century in which *Der Ring des Nibelungen* has been revived as one the most compelling touchstones, and most glamorous vehicles, of our high culture.

The broad sweep of Wagner, in the hundred years before 1951, was marked by ascendant triumph followed by bitter catastrophe. Both of these epochs, and the reception of Wagner's operas during them, were shaped to a considerable, perhaps unique, extent by forces ultimately exterior to the quality of the operas themselves, by what I will refer to as twin shadows: Wagner as man and Wagner as philosopher. His life and personality, and his "theories" and other writings, have served to, to obscure the operas as much as they have revealed them. No other artist has cast shadows as long as these, for we know too much about him and what he thought, and we remain amazed, repulsed and endlessly fascinated.

It is safe, now, to reach the conclusion that in our half-century the twin shadows have been slowly but surely receding. The passage of time, and the thirst for great music, can do that. This withdrawal, a kind of normalization, is permitting the operas to speak for themselves as they could not in the shadows, but as they should.

The Triumph of Wagnerism

Imagine the Green Hill at the moment of the inaugural festival, August 1876, and the first performance of the full *Ring* cycle.[1] Young Tchaikovsky, "watching Wagner pass in his sumptuous carriage rolling directly behind the Kaiser's, wrote, 'What pride, what overflowing emotions must have welled up at this moment in the heart of that little man who, by his powerful determination and great talent, has defied all obstacles to the final realization of his artistic ideals and audacious beliefs!'"[2]

There were others present, serious men, who soberly considered the inauguration of the festival theater and the *Ring* as "not just the cultural event of the century, (but) one of the greatest moments in cultural history."[3] No moment, no event can have represented more effectively Wagner's ultimate victory, and the triumph of Wagnerism itself.

"Wagnerism"—what is it? There are as many attempts at definition as there are users of the term. In view of such diversity, I purposefully attempt no definition here. Yet "Wagnerism" must mean something; the word survives in common usage, and one cannot find an "ism" so commonly applied to any other composer. Whatever it may signify with regard to the historical significance of Wagner's personality, or theories, or music dramas, it was certainly made vital by Wagner's insatiable (and successful) need to dominate, and to make people see the world, and himself, in the way he did.

Success—respect, fame, wealth and great influence—did not come easily or by accident. The incessant labors of Wagner's life, and the relentless self-promotion of that life—a conscious effort to turn biography into legend, and to turn theory into art—succeeded beyond any reasonable expectation, but would return to cast disturbing shadows over his legacy and accomplishments.

Not an Ordinary Life

It is futile to suggest that Wagner's life can be ignored. It is a life so rife with controversy and spectacle that it has launched a thousand books, and continues to induce unceasing analysis and speculation. By any standard, even an outline of the objective facts is astonishing.

He was born in Saxony in 1813, in between and not far from Napoleon's last great battles before Elba: victory at Dresden, defeat at Leipzig. His mother's risky visit across the battlefields to Ludwig Geyer during the campaign has given rise to the question of paternity, still unanswered, a question that has commonly tortured and stimulated creative men. Whatever the truth, it is likely that Wagner could not have been sure who his father was.[4]

Boyhood and adolescence were undistinguished, but not unhappy. There was teen-age drinking and gambling, and not much interest in school, except for stage drama and, he later claimed, the language and dramas of classical Greece. But there were artists in the family, and a kindly uncle, Adolph Wagner, who stabilized the boy and directed him toward music.

Wagner must have made the startling discoveries, sometime in his early twenties, that his God-given talent was in musical composition, and that music must be the outlet for the expression of his dramatic ideas. It may or may not be true that he quickly surpassed the capabilities of Christian Weinlig, his (only) teacher of composition, or that he learned orchestration by writing a piano transcription of the Ninth Symphony. But it does ring true that Beethoven's conversion of symphonic music into "a self-sufficient means of expressing the most highly personal, and in that sense, dramatic, emotional conflicts,"[5] and his need, at the end of his final symphony, to revert to the human voice provided Wagner with the revelation that opera—music and stage drama—would of necessity be his life's labor.

There is a search, for want of a better word, for a style. Unafraid to experiment, or to borrow, and having no real voice of his own, he writes three operas. *Die Feen* is a child of German romantic opera, and Weber; *Das Liebesverbot*, of Italy and Bellini; *Rienzi*, of (not yet despised) France and successful Meyerbeer, who would become his self-inflicted nemesis (and muse).

The 1830s also bring instruction, love and adventure. He is chorus master and conductor in Würzburg, Königsberg, Magdeburg, and Riga. There is successful pursuit of the actress, Minna Planer, who brings along a girl named Ernestine. At some later time Wagner discovers that the girl is not Minna's sister, as he was led to believe, but her illegitimate daughter, the offspring of her seduction at fifteen. There are debts everywhere, and escape from Cossacks in Riga — a storm-tossed voyage that inspires *Die Fliegende Holländer*.

That voyage brings the Wagners to Paris, glittering center of grand opera and grand ambition, and it is Paris that will be, ever after, Wagner's antipode, more influential, both creatively and destructively, than Bach's Leipzig or splendid, imperial Dresden.

There is not much, anymore, of the youthful and charming melodramas of earlier episodes. There is poverty and, Wagner's ability to borrow (temporarily) exhausted, pawn shops and, briefly, debtors' prison. There are no orchestras to conduct, but odd and menial jobs. There are friendships, many of which will survive, but with strugglers who are in no position to help. There is one friendship, that will not survive, with one who helps beyond measure and propels him toward genuine achievement, for it is Meyerbeer who arranges, among other things, the 1842 premiere of *Rienzi* in Dresden.

Paris is a crucible. Exposure to Berlioz, both music and man, is a revelation of future possibilities. He comes to terms with his real talent, writing both the libretto and the music of *Holländer*. Later, returning to Paris in 1850, he will attend a performance of *Le Prophète*; experiencing Meyerbeer's stupendous success will be a shattering experience. It is in Paris, in defiance of both Paris and Meyerbeer, that Wagner determines to seek artistic achievement and professional glory that would strike a reasonable man as utter fantasy.

Other things stir in Paris: envy, frustration and resentment — and a need to settle scores with those who have not yet yielded to his superiority, even if that has been hardly manifest. Perhaps he recalls the Napoleonic subjugation of Saxony. Still inchoate hatred of France, and of Meyerbeer and his art, pushes Wagner toward the embrace of home and Germanism. In 1871 he will gloat appallingly at Paris's humiliation. He leaves for Dresden in 1842, but Wagner and Paris are not done with each other.

The Dresden years, 1842 to 1849, are filled with accomplishments. There is professional recognition and real fame. Within a period of two months, both *Rienzi* and *Holländer* are premiered. He is made Royal Kapellmeister to King Friedrich.

He also completes *Tannhäuser* and *Lohengrin*. The former is premiered in 1845, Wagner conducting. *Lohengrin* must wait until 1850, when friend Liszt stages the work in Weimar, Wagner in exile.[6] These hybrid operas, Janus-like, represent both the endgame of German romantic opera and a preview into the music of the future.

In Dresden, Wagner is propelled into political adventure. The state bureaucracy does not support the staging of *Lohengrin*, much less his proposals to reorganize, under himself, the Royal Theater. As always, there are mounting (capitalist!) debts. Still a royal servant, he addresses the radical *Vaterlandsverien*. The collapse of Louis Philippe and the rise of the Second Republic ignite turmoil across the Continent, and Wagner falls into the arms of the great anarchist, Bakunin.[7]

In 1849 King Friedrich dissolves the Saxon Diet, and Saxons rise in protest. Wagner takes to the streets, longing for the immolation of his own theater, which has rejected *Lohengrin*. Prussian troops are dispatched, compatriots are arrested, and Wagner flees. Compromising documents are found, and a death sentence put on his head. Friends help him into exile in Zurich. Is it not true, then, that Wagner's life was not ordinary?

We cannot leave Dresden without noting a quality that creates space between Wagner and most other composers: relentless intellectual curiosity and voracious reading. In Dresden, with money in his pocket, he assembles an enormous personal library.[8] By 1849 he has set forth in extraordinary detail and precision the remainder of his creative life. He is committed to the subjects of *Tristan, Meistersinger,* and *Parsifal,* and, having plumbed the Teutonic and Scandinavian sources, has written *The Wibelungs,* "The Nibelungen Myth as Scheme for a Drama," and the poem for *Siegfried's Death.*

The Interlude — 1849–1853

In exile, there is a period of intellectual speculation and synthesis. There is (almost) no musical composition. The philosopher pours out essays that every Wagnerian knows, and almost none has read. The subjects are the state of European art: music and drama, Greek achievement, contemporary decline, and formulae for the redemption of all. He does not stop there, but moves on to matters of national character and, for the first time, race.

The essays are a mélange of brilliant insights, and the working out of personal aesthetics, wrapped around nonsensical confidences, born of ambition and frustration, that will unwittingly tarnish his reputation. All this is written in a convolution of high and low German that has stymied German-speakers, not to say translators, since they were first published.

Thus the twin shadows — how Wagner lived, and what he thought and wrote — grow longer. But Wagner's virtual *absorption* of Schopenhauer at this time was more than just philosophical; for him it was a fundamental personal and ultimately *artistic* act, "enabling him to find himself, and to get at one with himself on every level."[9] What is often misunderstood is that the influences of the philosophies of Feuerbach and Schopenhauer did not make Wagner a philosopher; rather, they helped him "to crystallize ... an outlook on life ... [and] an approach to art and a whole aesthetic that gave freest rein to the gifts with which he was most lavishly endowed."[10]

The mature poet emerges now, too. In Zurich, drawing on the German and Icelandic sagas and eddas, and on Feuerbach and Schopenhauer, he completes the texts of all four *Ring* operas. (That is, nearly completes; the ending, Brünnhilde's peroration, will elude him until 1876, and perhaps forever.) He has the poems published, and reads them to patient friends.

He dreams outrageous dreams, and dares to publish those, too. In exile, out of work, with few prospects and no money, and before a note is composed, he proposes that this monster work, this *Ring* cycle, can actually be staged, and as a sort of national anthem. Twenty-five years before the fact, he suggests that the world will come to hear this work in a theater to be built as a monument to this artwork of the future, and to him. Impossible!

The Artist in Full

In 1853, gestation explodes into creation. The waters at La Spezia murmur, and *Das Rheingold* is composed in eight months. Here, indeed, is the music of the future, and it would never stop coming, growing and evolving, for thirty years. Seven masterpieces, each a "sound world" unto itself, both confirming and contradicting Wagner's own attempts at explanation and theory.

Love and Romance

During those thirty years, there is an endless series of ups and downs. With each episode of love, sex and marriage, the shadow of Wagner's biography deepens. But these constant entanglements need to be considered, because the issues of the eternal feminine and the redemptive power of women are themes throughout the music dramas. But they also were viewed then, and they are now, as the stuff of gossip and scandal, and condemnation.

Three women play major roles. First, and saddest, is Minna. Her hopes — for a respectable life as Frau Royal Kapellmeister — are dashed with the uprising in Dresden, and clearly her husband's talents and aspirations far outstrip her ability to accept or understand them. Her loyalty, and his abuse, are well known, but his early passion is often forgotten, as are his ongoing bouts of tenderness, even during the long process of abandonment.

Mathilde Wesendonck has had the good fortune of being immortalized by her affair with Wagner. She is the ideal, both the object of desire and the inaccessibility of it. Under the influence of Schopenhauer and *Tristan*, she represents, consciously or not, unrelieved longing, ecstasy and suffering. The matter of consummation no longer seems relevant, nor does the question of whether Mathilde inspired *Tristan*, or as seems more likely, the compulsion to compose *Tristan* inspired the affair.

The biography is further enlivened by Wagner's willingness to take for himself the wife of his best friend and most ardent champion. Cosima (she and von Bülow had visited at the Wesendoncks on their honeymoon) was the illegitimate daughter of Marie, the Countess d'Agoult, who left her husband to become mistress to Liszt. After giving Liszt three children — Cosima was the second — she returned to the Count.

Cosima has children with Wagner, but there is a sense of worship on her part, detachment on his. For "in a homely, masculine girl, almost a quarter of a century his junior, Wagner came to find the mother-sister of his dreams," who fulfilled her "higher duty by allying herself to one of the giants of the age."[11]

Intermixed in this romantic tapestry are many other threads, denoting bold advances and dramatic retreats: among them Jessie Laussot, Friedericke Meyer, Mathilde Maier, and Judith Gautier.

Miracle

By 1864, Wagner faces artistic and financial ruin. Composition of the *Ring*, abandoned in 1857 to make way for *Tristan*, is not resumed. *Tristan* itself proves unplayable, unsingable and unperformed. Paris has struck back; the revised *Tannhäuser* performances are a fiasco. The *Meistersinger* libretto has been finished, but the music will not come to him.

None of this prevents self-indulgence in Vienna — a mansion, silks and satins, champagne and flirtations — but creditors close in as if they mean it, and so he flees once again, to Stuttgart. He writes that only a miracle can save him.

And so it comes to pass. Pfistermeister, Secretary to the king of Bavaria, enters his room bearing "a photograph and ring of the Bavarian king and [hands] these relics to the dumbfounded composer.... It was the king's desire that Wagner proceed to Munich, where, under royal protection, he was to live free from material care and bring his artistic mission to completion."[12]

Art and the Artist

The events of Wagner's life, only briefly summarized here, are so extraordinary as to explain their endless fascination. Other forces during the course of the century, including the force that was Wagner himself, were changing the way society would regard both art and the artist.

In the year of Wagner's birth, only a generation removed from the events of 1789, high culture remained the playground of the highly privileged: royalty, and the very (generally landed) rich. Works were commonly the result of patronage, and performance depended on the generosity, or social ambition, of the patron. One recalls, in Strauss's *Ariadne*, that the *nouveau riche* Viennese required both *opera seria* and *opera buffa* to be performed simultaneously, so that guests could enjoy the fireworks by nine.

Political upheaval, economic industrialization, and the ultimately triumphant expansion of the middle class brought about enormous changes. Performance came to rely on public attendance and the box office, and success on something new: critics! The upwardly mobile began to embrace art as a prerequisite of upward mobility, and a means of feminine liberation.

The patron, Otto Wesendonck, was a successful purveyor of that staple of the Industrial Revolution, machine-made textiles, and Mathilde was given over, like others of her class, to the seduction of poetry, both moralizing and sexually dangerous.

Both the content and overt purpose of art were redirected, as surely as frivolous Fragonard gave way to heroic David, and royal Louis to Napoleon. Much of eighteenth-century music was written as entertainment and ornament, or for the achievement of the merely beautiful, or as a demonstration of brilliant technique. Mozart, best known during his life as prodigy and pianist, had to be careful with *Figaro*, Beaumarchais's play having been banned by the Emperor as politically dangerous for Vienna.[13] But by Wagner's heyday, the very word "Verdi," like Verdi's operas themselves, had become a powerful political force for Italian unification.[14]

It was natural, in these circumstances, that the successful artist, no longer a faceless technician and employee (Kapellmeister!) of the patron, headed toward the center of attention. He began to enjoy high levels of public recognition, of fame and respect. There were economic consequences, too, for it became feasible for the commercially successful writer or composer or painter to make good money on his own, and thus independently direct the course of his own handiwork.

These changes were everywhere caught up in the career of Wagner. He was instinctively attracted to social and political change, the quest for financial independence, and liberation from the frustrations of patronage. Wagner, it is true, was the beneficiary of one of history's most storied patronages, but it is impossible to imagine Wagner (or anyone else) turning down what Ludwig had to offer, and Ludwig was for Wagner a means to an end. He ruthlessly exploited the besotted youth, until resistance at court propelled him and his art to Bayreuth.

It was Wagner, above all, who articulated the new purposes of art. He was disgusted less by the quality of music in opera than by opera's absence of moral purpose. Everything Wagner wrote, be it essay or opera, is infused with intention, with the object of instruction and improvement.

Wagner's goal would be no less than to redeem the German people through the reformation of German musical theater. His model, though, would not be German at all, and certainly not Scandinavian, but Greek. Especially from Aeschylus, he would project the engagement with universal human problems, even the performance structure, of the classics into the artwork of the future.[15]

At least to Wagner, it would follow as night follows day that the credit for redeeming society belongs not to the patron, nor the politicians, but to the creative artist. These radical notions, the sanctity of high art and the sainthood of the artist, inconceivable in Haydn's day, would be commonplace a century later, as they remain today.

The Wagner Industry — I

Among the many sides of Wagner's complex persona, we dwell here on only one, but for our purposes the most decisive: the need to dominate. In Ernest Newman's words: "Wagner had the need that many men of immense vitality have felt ... of dominance for dominance's sake; there is something aquiline in them that makes it impossible for them to breathe anywhere but on the heights."[16] Or in Bryan Magee's: "If ever there was a human being who could be described as the embodiment of will, in the ordinary sense of the word, it was Wagner.... He had an overwhelming personality, a seemingly uncontrollable drive to dominate everybody and everything around him."[17]

Nicholas Vaszonyi has described the way this need to dominate, this drive for fame and fortune, and professional supremacy, resulted in nothing less than the creation of what he calls a "Wagner industry."[18] Employing unprecedented techniques of self-promotion, Wagner established himself as "artist superstar," probably the first of the modern type.

Wagner understood the socio-economic changes we have observed. He understood the emerging power of the new commercial class to patronize the artist, and to attend his operas — novel possibilities open to men of genius and great energy.

Wagner's self-promotion was facilitated by his insatiable need to communicate, to make sure there was a public record of his opinions on every subject, but in addition to tell us everything about himself. Wagner's writings fill twelve volumes — more words, surely, than musical notes! The essays are brilliant, insightful, learned, inscrutable, and repulsive. And swirling around these are thousands of letters. Even though it was an age of letter-writing, one is impressed at the persistent determination to explain himself and to persuade.

It came naturally to Wagner, too, to forge a coterie, a phalanx of highly gifted men, to expand the acceptance of the master's genius. The inner circle, to name only a few, is impressive: Röckl, Uhlig, Nietzsche, Ludwig II, Wolzogen, Levi, Richter, Bülow, Bruckner. The list of female advocates is longer still. On a more democratic level, he succeeded in forming Wagner clubs throughout Germany. Ostensibly, these celebrated the greatness of the music dramas, but were effectively used as sources of funding for the Bayreuth theater.

The Wagnerians even initiated, in 1878, their own propaganda organ, the *Bayreuther Blätter*. This publication solicited funds for Bayreuth, but also gave Wagner the regular opportunity to "bring his salon harangues to a wider public."[19] The dedicated young Prussian, Wolzogen, was brought to Bayreuth as editor, under the watchful eye of Cosima.

So we come back once more to Bayreuth: a festival, a theater, a whole city! dedicated to the artworks of a single artist. Wagner invented the very idea of the modern summer festival, and Bayreuth — if waiting lists are the measure — remains to our day the most successful of all.

Has there been a more apt — or self-absorbed and self-erected — monument? The idea for his own theater came in 1848, along with the concept of a Nibelung trilogy, at a time of professional self-destruction, personal danger and the absence of prospects. Its realization could not have been imagined, much less achieved, by a man of lesser vitality, will, or the compulsion to dominate. Victory would come, but it would also sow the seeds of backlash and contempt.

The Wagner Industry — II

The tide of Wagnerism continued to rise, beyond Wagner's death in 1883 and on into the new century. For other artists, Wagner "provided the spectacle of an artist who had conquered stupid resistance from stuffy bourgeois and academics and had died wealthy and revered in his own country. Accounts of him pictured a lord receiving tribute in his castle and a demigod worshipped at Bayreuth. He was the emblem of vindication for every artist."[20]

The composers, other artists and men of letters who came to Bayreuth until 1914 are too numerous to mention here. Many came away under the Wagnerian spell, ready to become Wagnerians, and to preach the dogma, whatever they thought it was, of Wagnerism. So it spread, to England and Italy, and to France — especially to France.[21]

Meanwhile, the coterie kept the Wagner Industry in high gear. It was perhaps easier to revere a dead Wagner than a live one. But Wagner, like Napoleon, was ill-served by those he elevated to perpetuate his achievements. Cosima — a highly intelligent and in many ways sympathetic woman — served so effectively as archivist that festival performances would become, and struggle to remain, a museum of recalled gesture. The inept Wolzogen would commit serious damage by trivializing Wagner's motivic "method," and stamping it with the imprimatur of Bayreuth.

There is the protracted attempt to protect the picture of the man. As Ernest Newman wrote: "It has been Wagner's peculiar misfortune to have been taken, willy-nilly, under the protection of a number of worthy people who ... have painted for us a Wagner so impeccable in all his dealings ... so invariably wise of speech, a Wagner brutally sinned against and so pathetically incapable of sinning, that one needs not to have read a line of his at first hand to know that the portrait is an absurdity."[22]

Posthumously, Wagner contributed mightily to this portrait. He dictated his autobiography, *Mein Leben*, to Cosima in 1865 (it was not updated beyond that year). Gutman suggests that, having achieved a (precarious) position at the court of Ludwig II, Wagner needed to re-position, that is to say obscure, anti-royalist adventures of the past.

It was pro-Wagner Newman himself who first demonstrated the extent to which Wagner's accounts were frequently one-sided, unfair, or false. For Newman, separating truth from fiction was of great value in analyzing and understanding the man, for there has "never been a more complex artist.... A soul and character so multiform are an unending joy to the student of human nature."[23] Others would not be so generous.

Decline

It is tempting to see signs of decline at moments of great triumph. The inaugural *Ring*, overwhelming centerpiece of the first festival, was a financial disaster, inadequately sung and poorly staged, and patrons complained, then as now, about poor housing and wretched food. The second festival would be postponed until 1882, offering *Parsifal* only. The *Ring* would not appear again at Bayreuth until 1896.

Wagner's fragile health and psyche were battered by the experience, and he condemned the German people for inadequate appreciation. Nor could he escape at this point from financial responsibilities. So off he went again, on the road, to raise money to cover the losses.

The underside of triumph is impermanence, and the weakening of Wagnerism, as a direct force and current taste, was both inevitable and self-induced. Some of Wagner's specific music-dramatic innovations — chromaticism, post-romanticism, *Gesamtkunstwerk*, and music as moral drama, for example — stimulated more aberrant tonalities, neo-classicism, opera *verismo*, and "art for art's sake." It is one of the Wagnerian puzzlements, in fact, that one so influential had so few direct imitators.[24]

As Victorians became Edwardians, the cutting edge moved to others. While *Salome* and

Elektra were astonishing audiences in Dresden, "Bolero" incited riot in Paris. Cezanne gave way to deconstruction, Fauvists to cubists.

The twin shadows of Wagner's personality and "philosophy" were ripe to spur an historic reversal. "Anti-Wagnerism" was, of course, not new. Wagner's paranoia was well-founded in that he had always had his detractors — many of them personal victims of his ascent. And Wagner's provocative theories, and the operas themselves, created as much outrage as submission.

So the publication of *Mein Leben*, postponed until 1911, ironically stimulated a process that led to the regular vilification of the Wagner persona. Misuse of the essays would lead to much worse.

Catastrophe

Young Kaiser Wilhelm may not have been the only royal cousin, or bourgeois politician, to feel, in 1914, aggrieved, alarmed and imperial, but he did personify the most brutish (until then) side of Germanism, and without Bismarck to restrain him, pursued an oversize notion of Germany's place in the sun. By 1919, Europe's most prosperous and art-loving country would be deemed and held accountable, by its conquerors, as sole cause of the debacle. There would be no more "Wagner Nights" in New York.

The wise men at Versailles determined to make Germany writhe, and writhe she did, until inevitably, riding a crest of disorder and victimization, Germanism rose again, this time with a vengeance, and in the name of Wagner, too. The most ardent Wagnerian cannot deny that Hitler embraced Wagner's music and a conception of Wagner's philosophy. Now, and only now, were Wagner's old-age anti-Semitic ravings seen to be not quite so harmless.

The brightest and most human of all the operas was employed in the obscene interests of National Socialism, and *Meistersinger* still suffers the effects. Never mind that *Parsifal*, a story about a weak ruler's decadence and failure, was banned by the Nazis throughout the War, or that Tristan's nihilistic writhings in Act Three were considered unsuitable for German war-wounded.[25]

The remains of Wagnerism were buried in that Berlin bunker, swept aside as surely as the Third Reich itself. Under the rubble, too, lay a diminished public will to accept and enjoy the beauty and innovation and majesty of the music, the music dramas' exploration of the possibilities of redemption, and indispensable reflections on the human condition. Wagnerism had risen to the heights, not just on the qualities of the artwork, but on the personality and written word of the artist. The shadows cast by both were now long and dark indeed.

The Case of Jacques Barzun

Jacques Barzun was an important historian of high culture, and man of "good letters," for seventy years. In music, his contribution is to have helped re- establish, in his 1949 *Berlioz and His Century*, that composer's rightful and substantial place.

Our attention here is directed at an earlier book, *Darwin Marx Wagner*, first published in 1941. Barzun cites these three contemporaries (seminal works of all three were published in 1859) as the towering figures in a culture moving past the Romantic age, and their "power over the modern mind" ever since.[26] It is a stature that Barzun regrets, representing a turning away from human sensibility toward faith in scientific materialism, or "mechanical change and moral fatalism"[27] through which "Darwin and Marx as scientists and Wagner as artist had seemingly made final the separation between man and his soul."[28]

We are grateful to have *Berlioz and His Century*, which unwittingly draws an unmistakable parallel between the things in music and opera that both Berlioz and Wagner tried to change and to accomplish. It is as absurd for Wagnerians to regard the Frenchman as merely a "proto-Wagner" as it is for Barzun to regard Wagner as a mere populizer of Berlioz's innovations.

Barzun makes the error of judging Wagner on the basis of our twin shadows, the personality and essays. He should be given leeway here, for he writes about culture, beyond music, and Wagner's persona and ideas, however misunderstood, have had, as we have seen, enormous influences. Also, Barzun wrote the Wagner book at a time of Germanism run amok, when one had reason to wonder about the survival of western values, not to mention Jews.

Barzun spends pages vilifying Wagner's character: Wagner, he says, "could have no critical or personal ethics. He must damn, cheat, and lie about the very ideals which he presumably revered but rarely used."[29] Barzun is particularly hurt by Wagner's personal mistreatment of Berlioz, whom he failed to acknowledge as master or to convert to Wagnerism.

Barzun is somewhat perceptive about Wagner's intentions: "it was not his art that Wagner strove to impose, but himself. It was as the master magician of Bayreuth that he wanted to succeed."[30] We have already agreed that Wagner's need to dominate was a central feature of his persona, but Barzun misses the more telling point: that Wagner's battles did indeed ensure the recognition of his artwork. More importantly, there is no evidence — none! — that Wagner's personal foibles ever compromised his artistic integrity; it is far more likely that Wagner's failures as a man enriched his art. In all the long hours of the music dramas there is not a measure that can be said to pander, to self- promote, or in Barzun's words, to cheat and lie.

Barzun's vision is also obscured by Wagner's other shadow — that is, in believing that there is some rational or literal connection between the content of the essays and the quality of the music dramas. To say that Wagner fails because of "an array of provocative theories"[31] is like saying Babe Ruth failed at baseball because his speech was ungrammatical.

Everybody agrees with Barzun that many of the things Wagner wrote are dense, self-serving, occasionally repulsive, inconsistent, and rarely read. Digested and explained, as they have most recently been by Bryan Magee,[32] they reveal historical and analytical heft, and a titanic intellectual struggle and "working out" that resulted not in great ideas, but in great art.

It is in his summation of Wagner's alleged *musical* shortcomings that Barzun's argument deteriorates into mere prejudice, more hurtful to Barzun's reputation than to Wagner's. He claims that Wagner's music is a synthetic borrowing from others, mainly Berlioz; that his harmony, or "enharmony," is merely "Chopin reduced to a system"; that his orchestration is no more than "borrowings from the more truly orchestral masters."[33]

The concept of the music drama is stolen from Meyerbeer, and Barzun cites "conclusive" proof that Wagner's librettos do not, as intended, move the drama forward.[34] Worst of all, Wagner's empty mechanism is bound up in the "system" of leitmotif. It is the old Debussy argument about "calling cards," that Wagner (or Wolzogen and other disciples) could teach audiences the music of the future by means of a scorecard.

We take Barzun here as an example of the depth of anti-Wagnerism. The generosity we are inclined to extend to Barzun's views, written in the awful days of 1941, is muted by his never having revised them in the 1957 and 1981 editions of *Darwin Marx Wagner*, nor in the 2000 *From Dawn to Decadence*.

Liberation

Four years after Barzun's book was published, both Germany and the position of Wagner in world music lay in ruins. Out of the rubble, parallel efforts were undertaken to reform and rehabilitate. Germany would become a model of democracy and hard-earned prosperity. In the case of Wagner, a series of milestones would begin a reversal of fortune; and the twin shadows of persona and theory would begin to give way, properly seen as clues into the accomplishments of the music dramas, rather than the other way round.

The end of Nazism at Bayreuth came the way it did to many German cities. The Wehrmacht chose to withdraw rather than fight for the town. The SS told Winifred Wagner, English-born wife of Wagner's son Siegfried, and now in charge, that to remove the master's personal effects into storage was defeatism. A bomb damaged part of the Wagner home, Wahnfried, and destroyed Wagner's desk, but not his piano. The Festspielhaus was not targeted.

A couple of weeks later, an opera-loving G.I. (later a distinguished writer on opera) named Joseph Wechsberg went over to have a look. He found Hans Sachs's workshop on the stage, sat in the cobbler's chair, and sang the "Wahn!" monologue. He would be the first but not the last Jew to redeem Wagner over the next sixty years.[35]

Bavaria was in the U. S. occupation zone, and American occupation forces took de-Nazification seriously. Winifred, more devoted to Hitler than any of the German Wagners, would be banned from Festival administration until her death in 1980. That responsibility would pass, when the festival was permitted to re-open in 1951, to her two sons, Wieland and Wolfgang.

Rehabilitation and "New Bayreuth"

So we return to the Green Hill, where we started, to the most influential and admired stage productions in the history of the music dramas. Frederic Spotts's summary of the opening *Parsifal* could be applied equally to the *Ring* that followed: "From the moment the performance began that afternoon it was apparent that a sacred rite had been rigorously secularized. By the time it ended, no doubt remained that the old orthodoxy in interpreting and staging Wagnerian opera had been irreparably shattered."[36]

The key stylistic elements were "light and shadow rather than solid sets, a disc defining the acting area, plain costumes, indeterminate time and place."[37] The staging implied not so much a Nordic or German saga as a Greek one. Audiences were compelled toward the inner meaning of the dramas, and the psychological implications were made patent as never before.

"New Bayreuth" was so successful as to become instantly traditional, dominating Wagner productions worldwide until 1976. Ardent Wagnerians considered them so true to the inner intention of the master that they did not admit to the radical nature of the stagings, so different than Wagner's specific instructions. It was an auspicious beginning to the half century.

Solti

Between 1958 and 1965, London/Decca records accomplished the first modern studio recording of the *Ring*. It is still regarded as the greatest achievement in recorded music, and its historical importance to Wagner can hardly be over- stated: it was a giant leap forward in making the tetralogy accessible to a hugely expanded audience in a manageable format.

The project brilliantly exploited two new technologies: long-playing records and stereo-phonic sound, providing the twin advantages of extended listening and the impression of live, stage-quality sound — without the coughing. In a way, a whole new art form was established, elevating the recording producer, at least in this case, to the level of creative artist.[38]

The project was undertaken with an unprecedented level of artistic talent and techno-logical sensibility. The singers were drawn from a hall of fame of postwar Wagner singers, and the Hungarian Georg Solti, conducting the Vienna Philharmonic, accomplished a read-ing that was intense, if not manic, but also delicate and subtle. Each opera won the Grand Prix du Disque Mondial as the best recording for that year, and the *Götterdämmerung* has been called "the best recording ever made of anything."[39] Most of all, Solti demonstrated the artistic and commercial potential of the *Ring*, extending the position of the cycle into the main-stream of high culture consumption.

Chéreau

By the mid-1970s, Bayreuth still stood as the arbiter of Wagner productions, but there were grumblings. New Bayreuth had dominated for a quarter century, and a Stuttgart *Ring*, in an unmistakable if feeble challenge to the festival, offended everybody but the German avant-gardists.

Wolfgang Wagner decisively answered his critics by announcing that the centennial *Ring* would be staged (the film director Ingmar Bergman having become unavailable) by the French stage director, Patrice Chéreau. This was an Industrial Revolution *Ring*, wonderful to look at, but above all, remembered for its integrated and compelling dramatic acting. The con-ductor, Pierre Boulez, famously resisted by the Bayreuth orchestra, stirred the pot by demand-ing, and getting, chamber music-like playing of great subtlety and clarity.

Encountering unprecedented hostility at the first performance, the Chéreau *Ring* accu-mulated a wide and telling critical approval, and by its close, in 1980, the final ovation lasted ninety minutes. Chéreau demolished any remnants of the tradition that the *Ring* was a some-how sacrosanct Victorian classic. The door was wide open to personal or revisionist *Ring*s, now with the imprimatur of Bayreuth itself.

Chéreau had a second, perhaps more telling impact in propelling Wagner and the *Ring* toward a golden age: television. It is statistically certain that more people watched the Chéreau broadcasts — whose success surprised everyone — than had attended *Ring*s over the past hun-dred years. The broadcasts would be followed by videotapes (and later DVDs), so that the *Ring* could be enjoyed at home at the discretion of the viewer.

Sadler's Wells and Seattle

In the English-speaking world, two other approaches to the *Ring* had a material role in extending the popularity of the cycle. In 1969, Sadler's Wells (now the English National Opera) launched a *Ring*, like all its productions, in English. Graced by wonderful singing from Rita Hunter and Norman Bailey, and even more by unanticipated orchestral majesty under Reginald Goodall, the production was a surprising and smashing success. An added benefit was a new translation by the eminent critic Andrew Porter, whose achievement was to craft a text that both made good sense and was particularly singable.

In the mid-1970s, the general director of the Seattle Opera, Glynn Ross, staged a com-plete cycle, complete with bears and bearskins. Ross cannily chose the monumental work as a way of differentiating his company and putting it on the map, which it did, but it also demonstrated that the *Ring* was not beyond the capabilities of regional companies.

The *Ring* at Seattle has been continued and enhanced by the company's next director, Speight Jenkins, who staged not only two new *Ring*s, both artistic successes, but all ten major Wagner operas over the past twenty years. None of Seattle's other considerable achievements over that time are as pronounced as its worldwide reputation for Wagner.

The Met Strikes Back

Since Chéreau, unrestricted interpretive license has become a norm. The stage director and designer have as a rule replaced the conductor as the centerpiece of artistic control in opera. Personal-vision *Ring*s in Germany were influenced by the East German stage director Walter Felsenstein — for example, in the work of Götz Friedrich and Harry Kupfer. Friedrich's so-called "Washington Subway" *Ring* for the Deutsche Oper offered a tunneled world without escape, or the slightest sign of natural beauty. The Kupfer *Ring* at Bayreuth, 1988–1992, presented an even bleaker, environmentally ruined world.

The Metropolitan Opera, perhaps rekindling its own glorious heritage of Wagner performance,[40] threw down the gauntlet in the late 1980s by staging a new *Ring*. It was called an expression of the New Romanticism by its designer, Gunther Schneider-Siemssen. The production was informed by a deliberate effort to let audiences see what Wagner wanted them to see, by this time a radical approach.

Critics were skeptical, uncomfortable perhaps with the conservative notion of fidelity to the vision of the composer. The public, on the other hand, was enthusiastic, grateful to be welcomed into the *Ring* experience rather than being left out, if not taunted, by the obscure deconstruction of the German elites; and audiences flocked to New York.

The Met production did not sweep the field, but it did provide a sturdy alternative, and sent a powerful message to opera administrators more interested in selling tickets than offending ticket buyers.

Barenboim and Levine

The final, and most agreeable, milestone in our chronology, and a subject that should not be avoided in any case, concerns the weakening, if persistent, allegation of anti-Semitism in Wagner. This remains the longest, and darkest, shadow still cast by Wagner's persona and theories.

Bayreuth's rehabilitation since 1951 has included a deliberate and patently sincere effort to expunge any trace of anti-Jewishness, or other forms of bias, from the festival. Two vibrant cases in point are the invitations to Daniel Barenboim and James Levine to take major conducting roles, and their enthusiastic acceptance of those engagements.

Levine first conducted in Bayreuth in 1982, with *Parsifal,* and he conducted the *Ring* cycle from 1994 to 1998. At the Met, Levine has been a fervent and highly admired conductor of Wagner, and has missed no opportunity to stage all the music dramas in New York. Levine's soaring musical credentials and enthusiasm for Wagner have constituted an advocacy of the quality in Wagner's music that speaks for itself.

Barenboim first conducted at Bayreuth in 1981, with *Tristan,* and he conducted the Kupfer *Ring* from 1988 to 1992. He led performances of all ten Wagner operas in Berlin in April 2002. And of course Barenboim dented, if he did not knock down, the unofficial ban on performing Wagner in Israel by leading the Berlin State Orchestra in a short excerpt from *Tristan* on July 7, 2001.[41]

There are, of course, those who still wish to make us believe that Wagner's defects, in persona and in theory, are manifest in his artwork. Not all of these are as patently unhinged as Gottfried Wagner, whose hatred of his father Wolfgang is clear (if nothing else is) as motivation for his anti-Wagner campaign. For better or worse, the Wagner Industry, after all, grinds on, and the charge of anti-Semitism in the music remains a tempting sideshow for some.

It is best here to give the final word to Barenboim himself:

> In the operas themselves, there is not one Jewish character. There is not one anti-Semitic remark. There is not anything in one of the ten great operas of Wagner even approaching a character like Shylock. That you can interpret Mime or Beckmesser in a certain anti-Semitic way (in the same way, you can also interpret *The Flying Dutchman* as the errant Jew), this is a question that speaks not about Wagner, but about our imagination and how our imagination is developed, coming into contact with these works.[42]

Wagner's Golden Age

So we have moved, step by step, into a millennial era for Wagner. What does that mean? It is a time in which the twin shadows of Wagner's persona and theory are fading, and the music dramas are increasingly able to stand clear of them, on their own. The passage of time has been critical in this, especially as the interval has grown from World War II to the present, but also because Wagner himself has now been dead for more than 120 years. New audiences are coming forward to experience the music dramas directly, less conditioned by history, bias and cliché.

This writer has indulged, to be sure, in a cascade of over-simplification — deliberately — to draw a brief but broad picture of Wagner and Wagnerism over the past two centuries. We have conceded that Wagner's life and his influence on our culture were so extraordinary as to be irresistible to all kinds of people. Further, that life was so self-revealed as inescapably to demand scrutiny, conjecture, awe and revulsion, not to mention the determined search — a fair subject — for autobiography in the artworks themselves.

It is not my intent to suggest that Wagner's operas have ever been absent from the mainstream repertory, the way the works of many worthy composers have been. But something different is happening, a trend that I will attempt to demonstrate by quantifying it, if not explaining it. Opera houses are now offering more and more Wagner, and it has become a commonplace that Wagner performances sell faster and more reliably than the rest of the repertory — a stunning reversal.

The case of the *Ring* is especially dramatic. In the 1950s the *Ring* was viewed as well beyond the resources of most houses. There would be an occasional cycle in New York, San Francisco or London, but the costs of staging, singing, and orchestral playing were daunting, and general directors were always concerned that audiences would not (pay to) sit through the long and intimidating piece.

Now it is all upside down. The Met *Ring* has been revived twice since its inception in the late 1980s. Three complete cycles were offered in the spring of 2004 and, in an otherwise dismal year for ticket sales, were sold out well in advance. Seattle launched its third *Ring*, directed by Stephen Wadsworth, in 2001, a critical and box office success. Three cycles were staged again in August 2005, with tickets sold a year in advance.

The Canadian Opera Company has chosen to open its new house in 2006 with a new *Ring*, and the novel notion of engaging four different directors. In London, the Royal Opera staged a new cycle in the late 1990s, and a new *Ring* for 2006. A mile away, the English National Opera has launched its first *Ring* since Goodall, staging, as is now common, one new opera per year, with Phyllida Lloyd (*Mamma Mia!*) directing. Londoners may thus have a choice of simultaneous *Ring*s, and might also have taken the train up to Edinburgh for Scottish National Opera's *Ring* in 2003.

The Lyric Opera offered a new *Ring* by August Everding in the early 1990s. Chicagoans were able to reprise these productions in three complete cycles in spring 2005. The Washington National Opera staged a Francesca Zambello *Die Walküre* for 2005 and *Das Rheingold* for 2006. That company's first complete cycle cannot be far behind.

Other major houses are turning back to the tetralogy. The Vienna *Staatsoper* presented the cycle in 1993, did so again, both in 2004 and 2005, and has announced a new *Ring* for 2009. The Easter Festival in Salzburg will present each of the four operas, respectively, in the years 2006 to 2009. The Opera National du Rhin (Strasbourg) will do the same thing.

In Germany itself, *Ring*s were economically, and politically, impossible in the early postwar years. That has all changed; *Ring* cycles are ubiquitous, often probing, in an almost proprietary way, that country's own tragic lust for power. Bühnen (Cologne), Karlsruhe, Munich, Chemnitz, Stuttgart, Wiesbaden, Deutsche Oper (Berlin), and Mannheim have announced *Ring* cycles. As noted above, in 2002 audiences flew to Berlin from all over for a cycle of *all ten* major operas, directed and conducted by Kupfer and Barenboim, respectively.

Even more surprising is that the *Ring* is now turning up at houses which, a generation ago, had no business thinking about a *Ring*. Warsaw staged the *Ring* at the very twilight of communism. Helsinki staged the cycle in the summer of 2004. The Netherlands Opera presented three cycles in 2005. In 2003, at the St. Petersburg tri-centennial, the Mariinsky Theater presented the first *Ring* by a Russian company in over 100 years. The State Theater in Budapest staged two cycles in 2005.

The State Opera of South Australia produced the first-ever Australian *Ring* several years ago, an engagement so successful that it staged the *Ring* again in late 2004. Two cycles were staged in 2005 at the Teatro Amazonas in Manaus, far up the Amazon. The *Ring* operas have even been performed at the Tyrol Festival in Erl, Austria, and the Longborough Opera Festival in the Cotswolds.

Der Ring des Nibelungen has become, in our time, the superstar of the performing arts.

Conclusion

This author has often wished that we knew as little about Wagner as we do about Bach. What do we know about Bach — what do we need to know? — except that he got up in the morning, walked over to St. Thomas's after breakfast, wrote music of immortal quality, and went home for lunch?

It is not to be. But we can remember that Wagner's biography and writings survive only because Wagner was among the greatest of musicians, and that they are of value in helping us understand the events and thinking that influenced the creation of wonderful operas.

In matters such as these, it is always wise to give the last words to those who have understood these things best. One of them is Owen Lee, whose 1998 lectures directly explored how it is "that a man some regard as morally corrupt could produce works of art that are, to many people of good conscience, indispensable."[43] And another, finally, is Ernest Newman, whose writings on Wagner are still needed, and who wrote, in 1924: "There is no need, no reason to discuss the 'philosophy' of such a mind. [Wagner] is no philosopher: he is simply a perplexed and tortured human soul and a magnificent musical instrument. All that concerns us today is the quality of the music which was wrung from the instrument under the torture."[44]

Notes

1. The first festival could claim the premieres of *Siegfried* and *Gotterdämmerung* only. *Das Rheingold* and *Die Walküre* debuted in Munich in September 1869, and June 1870, respectively. Ludwig II, who owned the rights, ordered them performed over the objections of Wagner, who stayed away. The Beethoven Ninth opened the festival on three other occasion, in 1933, 1953, and 1954.

2. Gutman, *Wagner: The Man, His Mind and His Music*, p. 383.

3. Spotts, Frederic, *Bayreuth*, p. 71.

4. For an account of the question of Wagner's paternity, see Gutman, pp. 1–10.

5. Magee, *Wagner and Philosophy*, p. 212.

6. Wagner himself would not hear his opera until 1861, in Vienna. The opera "was made the occasion of a demonstration of respect and affection such as Wagner had never experienced before." Ernest Newman, *The Life of Richard Wagner*, Vol. III; see pp. 138–140.

7. Mikhail Bakunin remained the great hero of anarchists into the 1930s, when the movement itself was snuffed out by its supposed communist allies during the Spanish Civil War.

8. Intellectual curiosity was an often overlooked quality of Wotan, and for that matter, of Siegfred. For a good description of Wagner's library at Dresden, with particular emphasis on the *Ring* sources, see Elizabeth Magee, *Richard Wagner and the Nibelungs*, pp. 25–37.

9. Bryan Magee, *Wagner and Philosophy*, p. 185. This 2001 book (called *The Tristan Chord* in America) is a near-miracle of clarity and good sense, and easily the best work on this subject.

10. Magee, p. 185.

11. See Gutman, pp. 230–233. The conditions under which Cosima grew up were disturbing, if not cruel, and her fears about her own ancestry might have fueled her own virulent anti-Semitism.

12. Gutman, p. 248.

13. Gerhart von Westerman, *Opera Guide*, p. 88.

14. *Risorgimento* rallies in Italy were enlivened by chanting or posting the composer's name, an acronym of Vittorio Emanuele, Re d'Italia.

15. For an especially trenchant discussion of Wagner and his love of the classics, see Owen Lee, *Athena Sings*. This critical subject has never been treated so admirably.

16. Ernest Newman, *Wagner as Man and Artist*, p. 14.

17. Magee, p. 183.

18. Vaszonyi is Professor of German at the University of South Carolina. He spoke about the "Wagner Industry" at a lecture before the Wagner Society of Washington, D. C. in 2003, and is writing a book on this subject. *Ed. note*: A portion of that book forms the next essay in this one.

19. Gutman, p. 432.

20. Jacques Barzun, *From Dawn to Decadence*, p. 638.

21. For a summary of the almost pervasive impact of Wagnerism on the leading artists and intellectuals in France during the last quarter of the nineteenth century, see Robert Hartford, *Bayreuth: The Early Years*, pp. 181–186.

For a superb overview of Wagner's broader influence, see Father Owen Lee's intermission talk at the Met's Saturday broadcast of April 17, 2004. Lee's survey includes a short list of artists shaped in part by Wagner's art, including Verlaine, Mallarmé, Mann, Virginia Woolf, Van Gogh, Kandinsky, Richard Strauss, Bruckner, Elgar, Puccini, Debussy, D. H. Lawrence, Schoenberg, Conrad, Forster, Cather, Diaghilev, Shaw, Berg, Sibelius, Nietzsche, Mahler, and above all, Eliot and Proust.

22. Newman, p. 3.

23. Newman, p. 3.

24. Westerman's view is that "it is understandable that such a towering, exceptional personality as Wagner never established a school, that no further development was possible along his exact lines, and that not even a new style of singing grew up, for his highly complex work depended too much on its creator." See Westerman, p. 234.

25. Spotts, p. 192.

26. Jacques Barzun, *Darwin Marx Wagner*, p. 7.

27. Barzun, p. 5.

28. Barzun, p. 3.

29. Barzun, p. 273.

30. Barzun, p. 273.

31. Barzun, *From Dawn to Decadence*, p. 637.

32. Barzun, *Darwin Marx Wagner*, p. 247.

33. Barzun, p. 247.

34. Barzun, p. 248.

35. See Joseph Wechsberg, "My Grandfather Would Be All For It," in John DiGaetani, *Penetrating Wagner's Ring*, pp. 417–432.

36. Spotts, p. 212.

37. Spotts, p. 213.

38. See John Culshaw, *Ring Resounding*, an account of the making the Solti recordings. It is a charming and informative account of the most celebrated collaboration in recorded music, but more, a blueprint for excellence on any project.

39. Magee, *Aspects of Wagner*, p. 38.

40. From its first season in 1883, the Metropolitan took on, largely from its German-American patrons, a decidedly German character. For years, all operas were sung in German. It is amazing to think that *all four Ring* operas were staged in thirty-four of the fifty-two seasons from 1898–1899 through 1950–1951, including the war years, 1939–1940 through 1944–1945. (*Madama Butterfly* was banned immediately after Pearl Harbor). From its Met premiere in 1884–1885, *Die Walküre* was omitted in only nine seasons through 1950–1951, which include the anti-German years 1917–1918 through 1920–1921, and the 1892–1893 season, when the house burned down and the season was cancelled. See "Met Archives CD," 2000.

41. For Edward Said's account of this episode, see Daniel Barenboim and Edward W. Said, *Parallels and Paradoxes*, pp. 175–184.

42. Barenboim and Said, p. 98.

43. M. Owen Lee, *Wagner: The Terrible Man and His Truthful Art*. Toronto: University of Toronto Press, 1999.

44. Newman, p. 324.

Bibliography

Barenboim, Daniel and Said, Edward W. *Parallels and Paradoxes*. London: Bloomsbury, 2003.

Barzun, Jacques. *Darwin Marx Wagner*. Chicago: University of Chicago Press, 1981.

_____. *From Dawn to Decadence*. New York: HarperCollins, 2000.

Culshaw, John. *Ring Resounding*. New York: Viking, 1967.

DiGaetani, John. *Penetrating Wagner's Ring*. New York: Da Capo, 1978.

Gutman, Robert W. *Richard Wagner: The Man, His Mind, and His Music*. New York: Time-Life Records Special Edition, 1968.

Hartford, Robert, ed. *Bayreuth: The Early Years*. Cambridge: Cambridge University Press, 1980.

Holman, J. K. *Wagner's Ring: A Listener's Companion and Concordance*. Portland: Amadeus, 1996.

Lee, M. Owen. *Athena Sings*. Toronto: University of Toronto Press, 2003.

_____. *Wagner: The Terrible Man and His Truthful Art*. Toronto: University of Toronto Press, 1999.

Magee, Bryan. *Aspects of Wagner*. Oxford: Oxford University Press, 1968.

Magee, Elizabeth. *Richard Wagner and the Nibelungs*. *Wagner and Philosophy*. London: Penguin, 2001. New York: Oxford University Press, 1990.

Newman, Ernest. *The Life of Richard Wagner*. Cambridge: Cambridge University Press, 1941.

_____. *Wagner as Man and Artist*. New York: Vintage, 1960.

Spotts, Frederic. *Bayreuth*. New Haven: Yale University Press, 1994.

Westerman, Gerhart von. *Opera Guide*. London: Thames and Hudson, 1964.

2. Selling the *Ring*: Richard Wagner's "Enterprise"[1]

Nicholas Vazsonyi

In an 1873 letter to Emil Heckel — founder of the original Wagner Society in Mannheim — Richard Wagner asks his most "energetic" friend to put together promotional materials informing the general public about the planned world premiere of the complete *Ring* cycle at the first Bayreuth festival. Once Wagner had approved the text, Heckel was then to "bring the matter to the public, and indeed with awesome publicity, so that no one can say 'I haven't heard anything about it.'"[2]

By the early 1870s, Wagner was fully committed to "selling the *Ring*" together with the Bayreuth festival as parts of a conceptual package Lore Lucas has dubbed "the trinity": Gesamtkunstwerk — *Nibelungenring* — Festspiel.[3] For Wagner, "enjoying the *Ring*" meant nothing less than grasping and savoring the concept in its entirety. He writes disdainfully of those who are satisfied to see the *Ring* "cozily at home" sitting "comfortably" in their local opera houses after a day at work. By doing so, they "transform the extraordinary into the ordinary."[4] Wagner would surely also object to today's idea of enjoying the *Ring* in one's living room, seated comfortably in a favorite armchair, listening to the best recording that digital technology can muster. Ideally, Wagner wanted the *Ring* to be performed and experienced only in his specially-designed festival theater. He was serious about restricting access to his artwork; enjoying the *Ring* was to require the effort of "for once undertaking the somewhat arduous trip to Bayreuth, in order to experience carefully prepared festival plays," a journey which in Wagner's own words takes on the characteristics of "a pilgrimage."[5] The "extraordinariness" and exclusivity entailed in such an experience would seem to eliminate the need for the massive publicity Wagner sought in the 1873 letter to Heckel. But there is no contradiction between the esoteric and the mass-market Wagner. Theodor W. Adorno already suggested as much in reference to the "magic" of Wagner's music dramas, which "simultaneously function as commodities that satisfy the needs of the culture market."[6]

But what Adorno sensed in the music is even more evident in Wagner's extra-musical activities and declarations. Richard Wagner was, among other things, an entrepreneur, albeit an idealistic one.[7] He consistently referred to his *Ring*/Bayreuth project as an "enterprise" (Unternehmung) and, although it goes against convention to think of creative artists as salesmen, in the following I will discuss Wagner's varied, deceptively complex, occasionally contradictory, and remarkably innovative efforts to "sell the *Ring*."

Wagner's "Enterprise"

The French sociologist Pierre Bourdieu continued the Frankfurt School discussion of modernist movements and the "avant-garde" by analyzing them not so much in terms of aesthetics, but rather as a set of practices which began to emerge in Paris around 1840, culminating early in the 20th century.[8] Using Charles Baudelaire and Gustav Flaubert as his examples, Bourdieu argued that their break with commercial publishers and insistence on writing "difficult" (meaning: unprofitable) literature — literature for which there was no ready market — was, paradoxically perhaps, also a marketing pose. Their non-commercial stance came to be known as art for art's sake (*l'art pour l'art*). Turning conventional economics on its head by assuming a "loser wins all" strategy, they contended that only inferior art for mass consumption made money.[9] Their audience would be the select few who would appreciate innovative aesthetic risk-taking. However, notwithstanding their opposition to the commercialism, consumerism, and resultant commodification of art characteristic of modernity, the avant-garde nevertheless had an "obsession with publicity" and hence the marketplace.[10]

Somewhat curiously, Wagner is often not mentioned in discussions of the avant-garde, even though the conceptually esoteric dimension of his enterprise, not to mention his call for an "Art-work of the Future" and his participation in the so-called "New German School," is best understood within its framework. The French avant-garde — notably Baudelaire — were among the most enthusiastic early Wagnerites. But even beyond Wagner's progressive aesthetics, some of the ways in which he went about selling his works also anticipate tendencies which became characteristic of the avant-garde.

But if for no other reason than its sheer scope and dimension, Wagner's enterprise was also different from anything undertaken by both his contemporaries and successors in the avant-garde; and, as Adorno suggests, it brought him into even closer proximity with the commercial establishment from which — rhetorically at least — he sought to distance himself.[11]

A case in point is the innovative scheme to raise capital for the construction and start-up costs of the festival theater. Shortly before his untimely death in 1871, Carl Tausig, the German-Jewish pianist and Wagner devotee, came up with the idea to create a *Patronatverein* (Patron's Association) whose members would purchase a total of 1,000 *Patronatscheine* (Patron Certificates) for 300 thalers each, to raise the estimated 30,000 thalers needed. The owner of each *Patronatschein* was guaranteed a seat for all three of the *Ring* cycles planned for the first Bayreuth festival. Should three patrons share the cost of a single *Patronatschein*, each of them could attend one complete cycle. Emil Heckel's concern was that even a three-way split would prevent those with modest financial resources from going to Bayreuth, and so the idea of the Wagner Society was born, allowing exponentially more people to participate in the purchase of a certificate. Attendance at the festival was then to be decided by lot. Both Tausig's idea and Heckel's amendment met with Wagner's enthusiastic approval.

Even today, the *Patronatschein* is reminiscent of stock shares though, as Michael Karbaum points out, with the important difference that it offered artistic rather than economic dividends.[12] In 1871, when the idea was conceived and implemented, public and press reaction was mixed, affected in part by significant contemporary events in Germany. The lightning victory over France which abruptly ended the Franco-Prussian war early in 1871 was immediately followed by the long-awaited creation of a unified German nation-state, and an unprecedented industrial and commercial boom known as the "Gründerjahre" (founding years).[13] Wagner and his friends capitalized on the national (ist) frenzy by referring to the festival theater repeatedly as "this national undertaking" which was "in the service of German art," etc.[14]

Wagner also allowed for comparisons with the world of commerce. For instance, he hoped the *Patronatscheine* would sell quickly "just like with public offerings of shares and state securities" and he talks plainly about raising "outstanding capital."[15] While the national implications of the venture were harder to resist, the public was more negative about the fundraising scheme, reflecting a general mistrust of stocks as well as the rejection of what appeared to be Wagner's questionable mixture of commerce and a high-art project made more distasteful by his seemingly aggressive efforts at promotion.[16] In retrospect, the marketing campaign was innovative. It entailed fund- and awareness-raising concerts, numerous pamphlets and notices, and copious correspondence. At the same time, Wagner marketed himself as a distinct personality and leading cultural figure, for which the publication of his nine-volume *Collected Works* (*Gesammelte Schriften und Dichtungen*, 1st ed. 1871–1873), culled from over three decades of writings, serves as only one, though significant, example.[17]

Ideologically, Wagner had only contempt for any form of "profit-making" which would "funnel dividends to shareholders" who had provided the necessary capital.[18] Stung by the comparisons to commercial ventures, he would repeatedly refer to "my enterprise which eschews all profit."[19] Wagner was also dismayed that Wagner Societies outside of Germany were being formed to raise funds for travel and tickets. This made getting to Bayreuth seem too easy, again transforming the extraordinary into the ordinary or, to quote Wagner, as if "we were talking about theatrical productions ... which could be viewed simply by paying 100 thalers (perhaps even at the box office)."[20] Wagner insists that his name not be used for such societies, because "they conform so little to the intention with which the originally German societies were formed."[21] He continues:

> My intention was to offer the public free performances, solely supported by individual contributions. But in Germany I did not find those thousand generous patriots. Worse still, the entire press turned its back on my idea and stood against me. No segment of society, neither the nobility, nor the financiers, nor the academics wanted to support me.[22]

Wagner seemed to want it both ways. He rejected both pre-modern notions of patronage and the modern reliance on commercial viability. But he needed money. Instead of selling tickets — like ordinary theaters — Wagner hoped to chart a middle course between the older and newer forms of funding by having a conglomerate of small-scale patrons (dubbed "friends of his art") rather than the single benefactor. This would avoid the medieval custom whereby art served to enhance the greater glory of the individual autocrat, while it would also evade the mercantilism of selling tickets. Instead, Wagner "wanted ... to collect contributions for the realization of a national idea."[23]

Wagner's plan failed. He had wanted to found the quintessential anti-industry — a noncommercial venture where art was enjoyed for art's sake, and where only the truly devoted would participate and attend. The realization of this idea would have sealed Wagner's public break with conventional theater and theatrical practice. In the end, he found himself engaged in a relentless effort to attract attention and raise operating capital which made his venture appear not that different from the kinds of "industry" he condemned. Adorno puts it succinctly:

> In the midst of liberal culture the aim was to set up a cultural monopoly; the taint of this sullies the purity of Wagner's criticism of the commercialization of the arts.... [T]he whole conception of Bayreuth is inseparable from the wire-pullings designed to eliminate the competition from the repertory theatre.[24]

Worse still, Wagner succumbed to both the pre-modern and modern forms of fundraising. But even the large contribution from Bavaria's King Ludwig II, and the sale of tickets, did not save the first Bayreuth festival from posting a significant loss.[25]

In the longer view, however, the result of Wagner's entrepreneurial efforts looks quite different from the apparent failure of 1876. In the meantime, he had constructed a complex "institutional network"[26] consisting of the festival theater as the main physical plant, his residence the Villa Wahnfried as a research and development center, along with an expanding web of funding organizations and fan clubs like the *Patronatverein* and the Wagner Societies. In 1878, he launched the house journal *Bayreuther Blätter*, an official public relations arm which ran until 1938. According to Karbaum, this "institutional network" is nothing but a thinly disguised marketing and distribution machine with little beyond its aesthetic value to separate it from the thoroughly commercialized world.[27] Karbaum's study, whose publication Wolfgang Wagner apparently tried to sabotage, suggests Wagnerian hypocrisy if not disingenuousness, because: "Similarly to comparable establishments, Bayreuth as distribution apparatus of select art-wares subjected the festival to the harsh laws of 'industrial' production."[28]

Richard Wagner does appear to have been saying one thing while doing the opposite. Success at any price? Adorno's comparison of Wagner's works to the world of commodities was of course meant as a criticism. As such, Adorno perpetuates the philosophical critique of modern society which Wagner himself articulated. But is it not Adorno who is clinging to an idealistic notion of the artwork which perhaps never was and certainly is no longer true? A more generous reading of Wagner's accomplishments would acknowledge the awareness he demonstrated of the exigencies of the new age. With the *Ring* at its core, the complex modes of selling the Wagner name and product became, after Wagner's death, nothing less than an industry which continues to flourish today.

The Wagner Industry

Among the recollections Wagner dictated to Cosima was an account of the 1846 Palm Sunday benefit concert in Dresden. Against great opposition, he scheduled, rehearsed and conducted Beethoven's Ninth Symphony. Even orchestra members were dismayed at the programming choice; the whole town recalled the disastrous performance of the Ninth a decade earlier; it had confirmed the widely-held belief at the time that Beethoven's later works were strange and unplayable, reflecting the composer's near insanity caused by his irreversible deafness.[29]

Despite all expectations to the contrary, Wagner's concert was an unprecedented musical and financial triumph. But Wagner had not left the question of the concert's success to chance. In a marketing and PR blitz he singlehandedly devised and managed, Wagner posted a series of four anonymous notes advertising the concert and giving readers "up close and personal" glimpses into the spirit and soul of the supposedly mad Beethoven. Wagner took extraordinary care with both the wording and the timing of the notes. They were written in different styles, as if by different persons, and increased in frequency as the concert date approached.[30] Given the image of Wagner as aloof creator, it is telling that he published these notes in the equivalent of today's "gossip" and "personals" section of the local newspaper, the *Dresdener Anzeiger*. The last of the notes invited all Dresdeners to attend the final dress rehearsal, which they did, packing the house already the night before the performance. At the concert itself, Wagner provided explanatory program notes, designed specifically for the uninitiated. Typically for Wagner, these program notes were at once a popular sensation and an aesthetic scandal, providing grounds for academic debate in musical circles well into the twentieth century.

The Palm Sunday concert of 1846 is an exemplary piece of Wagneriana, combining insistence on the highest standards of execution (there were reportedly over 200 rehearsals), meticulous attention to musical-aesthetic detail (twelve rehearsals were set aside for the double bass and cello recitative at the beginning of the last movement), with an instinctive knack for publicity and popularization, including the production and dissemination of tremendous quantities of what we today call "copy"—textual/verbal explanation.

Summing up the episode in his autobiography, Wagner writes: "This experience strengthened the comforting sense in me that I had the ability and strength to push through whatever I earnestly desired with irresistibly fortunate success."[31] What remained was the as yet unrealized goal of turning his own works into similar success: "This was and remained the secret question upon which my life developed long-term."[32]

The "as yet unrealized goal" eventually became what I refer to as the "Wagner industry." The *OED* defines "industry," when "preceded by a personal name or the like" as: "scholarly or diligent work devoted to the study of a particular author or subject; also, the practice of a profitable occupation."[33] *OED*'s examples include the "Shakespeare industry" and the "Joyce industry," as well as the "abortion industry." The "Wagner industry," as I understand it, fits both parts of the definition. The academic study of Wagner was well established already before his death in 1883, and a number of occupations profit from exploiting the Wagner name and line of products: recording, concert and theatrical performance, and the tourist industry of Bayreuth, not to mention the commercial nature of the over 130 Wagner Societies world-wide which, despite their non-profit status, function as a vast apparatus for marketing books, theater tickets, recordings, and a range of events.

There is also a "Mozart industry" and a "Beethoven industry," but the "Wagner industry" is unique because of its history as well as its significantly more diverse and complex structure. More importantly, the "Wagner industry" is different because Wagner himself defined its terms and set it in motion. This was not the case for either Mozart, Beethoven, or any other artistic personality before the twentieth century.[34] Wagner was not alone. Many of his contemporaries were publicity conscious and enjoyed tremendous notoriety during their lifetimes—in the musical world I think of Niccolo Paganini and Franz Liszt. But the pop status these artists enjoyed was tied to their activities as performers and faded after their deaths. Not so with Wagner.

Wagner never uses the word "industry" to describe his own undertaking. Instead, he initially refers to the *Ring*/Bayreuth nexus as his "project" (Vorhaben) and later as his "enterprise" (Unternehmung), a term he uses consistently from the 1860s on.[35] When he does use "industry" it is always meant negatively. Industry, the commercialism and marketing strategies it necessitates, the money-dominated society it creates, and the de-humanization it produces, are all the detestable products of a modernity Wagner begins to critique around 1840 and continues to shun for the remainder of his life, despite all his ideological twists and turns. According to Wagner, art and culture, like humanity itself, have been corrupted, "industrialized" by the forces of modernity. Wagner's enterprise—with the *Ring* as its crown jewel—is conceived and developed as a counter-narrative to the prevailing hegemony of economic necessity. This message dominates Wagner's aesthetics and, as many from G. B. Shaw to Patrice Chéreau have argued, is a compelling interpretation of the *Ring* itself. Although presented as an aesthetic project, Wagner made its sociological stakes clear from the beginning.

It is paradoxical that Wagner used marketing techniques essential to the commercial system he deplored. Like any great entrepreneur, Wagner orchestrated his own publicity campaign, which established him as an immediately identifiable personality and endowed his works with a unique aura. In the crowded field of opera, he packaged his works as products so different from everything else that they could no longer even be called "operas." With the "music drama," Wagner established his own brand name appeal with a distinctive trademark.

He relentlessly engaged in what we today call "spin" by using every available medium of communication — letters, public and private performance, print media including an array of critical and literary forms (reviews, editorials, theoretical essays, autobiographies, novellas) — to overwhelm and thus set the terms of the discourse. His anecdotes, accounts, explanations, and justifications, presented in numerous published and unpublished comments, form what I like to call his "permalore" — the Wagnerian version of permafrost. Like an immovable object, Wagner's own version of the truth continues to be the starting point from which most studies proceed. What we tend to overlook in our effort to grapple with the substance of Wagner's utterances is that so much of what Wagner said or wrote also served this marketing effort.

In the Beginning Was the Word

One of the most electrifying scenes from Goethe's magnum opus finds Faust seated at his desk, intent on translating the famous opening from the Gospel of St. John. With typical Faustian arrogance, he refuses to accept that it could all have begun with a mere "word" and, in a flash of inspiration, settles on a new version: "In the beginning was the deed."

Despairing that he would never live to see the performance of his festival play, Wagner decided to go ahead and publish the text of his *Ring der Nibelungen* in 1862. In the "Preface," he expresses the hope that some royal person will step forth to ensure the festival:

> Wird dieser Fürst sich finden?   Will there be such a Prince?
> »Im Anfang war die That.«[36]   "In the beginning was the deed."

Wagner's conscious echo of Faust sets up the resignation with which he must, for now, be content to begin with "the word" only: words without music, without sound, a situation Wagner concedes is in total contradiction to his declared wishes and vision.

But somewhere, this words-only launch of the *Ring* conforms to a sequence typical for Wagner's career. Almost every significant Wagnerian deed was preceded by the Wagnerian word. These words have historically provided both his admirers and his detractors with ammunition; for the former, a holy text with which to proselytize, for the latter, enough rope to hang him. Wagner would complain life-long that he was misunderstood. But, if there is indeed no such thing as "bad" publicity, Wagner's suggestive, distinctive, colorful, emotive, and often outrageous words continue to keep his name in the public eye.

By 1873, when Wagner wrote that letter to Heckel, the job of selling the *Ring* had long been underway. The existence of the "institutional network" and the physicality of the festival theater were proof of Wagner's success. But when did this effort begin? How did Wagner start "selling the *Ring*"?

Most archaeologies of the *Ring* project, as well as those of the Bayreuth festival, begin in 1848 with Wagner's essay *Die Wibelungen*, which sets out the basic framework of the drama he intended to compose.[37] Descriptions of Wagner's twenty-year project to write text and music usually follow. At the other extreme, Manfred Eger traces the development of both the *Ring* drama and Bayreuth, as uniquely conceived venue, back to Wagner's early childhood.[38]

I think the *Ring's* genesis begins somewhere in between, with Wagner's rhetorical effort to separate himself from the existing world of opera by fashioning his own radical and unique persona along with a brand-new type of operatic product. Marjorie Perloff's observation that for the avant-garde "to talk about art becomes equivalent to making it" points to a syndrome already evident in Wagner.[39] Paul Mann has argued similarly of the avant-garde that "the work's value is defined above all by its power to generate discourse about it.... The real value is circulation itself."[40] What interests me is the narrative Wagner creates and proliferates to introduce, to explain, and in many respects to justify his outrageous aesthetic enterprise. From a marketing perspective, this narrative publicizes, attracts attention, and creates shelf-space for an unprecedented project, where "unprecedentedness" is also a selling point. While it would go too far to suggest that, for Wagner, talking about art was equivalent to making it, he pioneered modernism's penchant for the aesthetic manifesto and the propensity to offer substantial insight into the creative process and the author's intentions.

"Ordinary" vs. "Extraordinary"

Nike Wagner has written that Bayreuth is different because of its mythic dimension.[41] Bayreuth has become its own myth, an extension of the mythic realm portrayed in the tetralogy. But this "mythic dimension" also describes the mystique which lends the *Ring* and Bayreuth a discernible image in the cultural marketplace, an expression of Wagner's successfully demonstrated claim of "extraordinariness." Before he could demonstrate it in 1876, however, Wagner had to argue the claim rhetorically.

"Ordinary" for Wagner meant the repertory theater where — like the department store — a wide array of operas are programmed on successive evenings to keep audiences returning and to maximize box office receipts. The architectural exterior and interior of the "ordinary" theater emphasizes spectacle — both on and off stage — and underscores social stratification. Ostentation and the ceremony of social display was and is as much a part of a night at the opera as any aesthetic enjoyment. So total was Wagner's rejection of conventional opera, its venue and accoutrements, that he declared he would no longer be writing any.[42] Instead, Wagner talked extensively about his "extraordinary" ideas and plans. Since "ordinary" descriptors no longer applied, a new and specialized vocabulary specifically referring to his work came into being.

"Extraordinariness" is central to Richard Wagner's *Der Ring des Nibelungen*, hence his complaint that a performance outside of Bayreuth would render "ordinary" what was "extraordinary." "Extraordinariness" is a quality the work itself conveys, from the audaciously sustained opening note to the virtual apocalypse of the end. But this "extra-ordinariness" goes well beyond the sheer size and scope of the work in the overwhelming range of pleasures and rewards it offers. There is no theatrical experience comparable to attending a full cycle of the *Ring*, an awesome claim maximized when the performance is at Wagner's purpose-built festival theater. The notion of "festival" — a celebration out of the quotidian ordinary — is as much a part of Wagner's idea as is his unconventionally austere design for the theater which focuses all attention on the product. After over 125 years, the Festspielhaus remains unique amongst the opera houses of the world.

Extraordinary, too, is "small, remote, ignored" Bayreuth.[43] Not at all Wagner's "little Paris (petit Paris) outside of France," as Matthias Brzoska suggests, Bayreuth is rather its opposite.[44] If opera exemplifies modernity's aesthetic demise, the metropolis represents its sociological counterpart: site of the estranged daily existence of the masses. Going to Bayreuth constitutes both departure from the ordinary and return to geographic and cultural "heartland." Facing off in Wagner's war of words are two concepts of "ordinary": today's commercialized decadent urbanity versus the pristine genuine ordinariness of bygone rural existence. Wagner and his followers instrumentalized Bayreuth's remoteness to argue for its rootedness in the German folk spirit.[45] While Wagner understood that audiences "suffered" the "monstrous discomfort of Bayreuth,"[46] he also dreamed that its seclusion would enable performers to participate in an artistic undertaking which, in the "ordinary" running of things, was not possible.[47] The notion of sacrifice is a constant feature: audience members would go out of their way to attend; performers would receive little or no pay. Enjoying Wagner's extraordinary offering requires a commensurately extraordinary effort and commitment from all.

According to Boris Voigt, all of these "special circumstances"—the enormity of the work, the separation (physical and conceptual) from regular opera, the design of the festival theater, the specialized vocabulary—can be seen as hallmarks of a typical "charismatic" personality.[48] Certainly the expectation of sacrifice and the willingness of so many to cooperate adds weight to the notion of a Wagner "cult." While methodologically tenuous, Voigt's long-distance psychological diagnosis is confirmed by contemporary sources, and Wagner unabashedly uses religious terminology to describe his theater and work. But these more established ways of looking at the Wagner phenomenon have historically diverted attention from the publicity and, hence, commercial potential reaped by Wagner's uncanny ability to stand out, to be "extraordinary." Leaving aside for the moment Wagner's serious and coherently argued sociological and aesthetic reasons for his rejection of standard operatic forms and repertory theater, the "extraordinariness" of the *Ring*-package also served as a unique and, over time, uniquely successful marketing strategy.

Preview of Coming Attractions

Wagner's 1849 flight from Dresden into exile robbed him of the hope that his newer works would ever be staged. So he felt compelled to write about his plans.[49] The result was a series of theoretical and autobiographical publications, including *Art-Work of the Future*, *Opera and Drama*, and *A Communication with My Friends*. No other creator has left posterity with such a substantial body of explanatory work.

This was not the first time that circumstances "forced" Wagner to write instead of compose. Already ten years earlier between 1840 and 1841, in the midst of his "extremely pitiful condition" in Paris, Wagner wrote reviews, essays, even short stories for the German-Jewish publisher Maurice Schlesinger.[50]

I will not speculate on whether the sense of desperation with which Wagner characterizes the necessity to turn to explanatory prose was genuine or contrived. Either way, the insights Wagner offers concerning his aesthetic taste and creative process are compounded by the opportunity he exploited to publicize his existence, promote his compositions, and fashion himself as a public personality. As early as 1842, Wagner admits "these works helped me considerably to become known and respected in Paris."[51]

With hindsight, I contend that Wagner's writings also anticipate what have become common advertising strategies. An early example is in the novella "A Pilgrimage to Beethoven," first published by Schlesinger in 1841. The novella features an unnamed though thinly disguised "poor German composer" with initial "R..." [Richard] from a town in middle Germany beginning with the letter "L" [Leipzig], who sacrifices all to pay his idol Beethoven a visit.[52] The most significant moment in the story is the discussion between the protagonist and Beethoven about *Fidelio*. Beethoven stipulates that he is no opera composer, and then continues:

> At least, I don't know of any theater in the world for which I would gladly write another opera!
> If I were to write an opera according to my wishes, people would run away; because there
> would be no arias, duets, terzetts, and all the rest with which operas today are patched

together. What I would write instead, no singer would want to sing and no audience would want to hear.[53]

Beethoven despairs that the composer of a real "music drama" (musikalisches Drama) would be considered a fool, but "R..." eagerly picks up on this term and wants to know more. Beethoven imagines that the ideal "dramatic composer" would create a "union of all elements."[54]

The Germanist and eminent Wagner scholar Dieter Borchmeyer has shown that the term "musikalisches Drama" does not originate here with Wagner, but rather in a short story by the romantic author E.T.A. Hoffmann, whose style also serves as Wagner's model.[55] But, *pace* Dieter Borchmeyer, doesn't this miss the point? There is a fundamental difference between Hoffmann's fictitious account of an ideal "music drama," and Wagner's similar description which ultimately results in the realization of the idea. For Hoffmann, the story is the end in itself, for Wagner, it is a blueprint for his future as a composer.

Let me be clear: I am not suggesting that, at the time he wrote the "Beethoven" novella, Wagner had yet conceived of the "music drama" or the *Ring* project as we understand it. I am suggesting that even though he was still trying to get his "conventional" French Grand Opera *Rienzi* performed, Wagner had begun to move on. He knew that, in order to become a success, he would need to make a mark for himself. Since his failure with the Parisian musical establishment was evident, one alternative was to distance himself from it completely, and go solo. This is essentially what his mature career entailed, rhetorically at least. "A Pilgrimage to Beethoven" sets the terms for Wagner's radical break as well as creating the shelf-space and potential demand for a new product. Wagner even has none other than Beethoven endorse it.

Nowadays we call this "product placement": James Bond, played by a well-known actor, drives a car conspicuously showing the BMW trademark, perhaps a model that isn't even available yet.

While it is admittedly only with hindsight that we can appreciate fully the significance of the imagined conversation between Beethoven and "R...," the text serves nonetheless as a "preview of coming attractions." While Beethoven concedes that this new form of opera would currently find no audience, the novella whets our appetite by proclaiming the obsolescence of opera with its set pieces, the necessity to reconceptualize the genre, the dream of uniting all the art forms, the suggestion that author and composer be one person, and the call for a new kind of theater. The title even anticipates the spirit of "pilgrimage" with which audiences have journeyed to Bayreuth. "R..." also models the self-sacrifice Wagner would come to demand of his audience and performers alike. The novella's significance was evidently apparent to Wagner. Only ten years after writing it, Wagner told Liszt of his plans to republish it along with other Paris essays, because they revealed "the beginning of my direction."[56]

If the "Beethoven"-novella inadvertently functions as a "preview of coming attractions," the theoretical treatises written between 1849 and 1853 during the Zurich exile are far more purposeful. By then, both the *Ring* and the idea of the festival had begun to take recognizable shape in Wagner's thoughts. Although the premiere still lay 25 years ahead, Wagner lost no time in writing about it in every form available. The first such announcement comes in the frequently cited 1850 letter to Ernst Benedikt Kietz where Wagner describes his idea in the following terms:

> I am toying with the boldest of plans, which it would require no less a sum than 10,000 thalers to bring out. According to this plan of mine, I would have a theatre erected here on the spot, made of planks, and have the most suitable singers join me here, and arrange everything necessary for this one special occasion, so that I could be certain of an outstanding performance of the opera. I

would then send out invitations far and wide to all who were interested in my works, ensure that the auditorium was decently filled, and give three performances — free, of course — one after the other in the space of a week, after which the theatre would then be demolished and the whole affair would be over and done.[57]

The concision of the letter to Kietz is offset by the long-windedness of *Opera and Drama*, a three-part book, and Wagner's longest single theoretical text, which is dedicated to explaining his distinction between "opera" as it had developed since the late sixteenth century and "drama," an ancient Greek idea, now extinct, which Wagner proposes to reconstitute as the artwork of the future, "since this future is only imaginable as a consequence of the past."[58] But *Opera and Drama* functions no less as an advertisement for Wagner's forthcoming works and for his image as self-anointed artist/creator:

> The creator of the artwork of the future is none other than the artist of the present, who senses life of the future, and yearns to be a part of it. Whosoever nurtures this longing from his innermost being, already now lives in a better world; — but only one person can do this: — the artist.[59]

As a sales tool, *Opera and Drama* missed its mark, finding resistance, incomprehension and disappointment even amongst Wagner's "Friends."[60] Hence Wagner's much more lucid and effectively written *A Communication with My Friends*, which succinctly explains Wagner's new aesthetic principles. At its conclusion, he again announces the creation of the *Ring* cycle and previews the circumstances of its ideal performance:

> I intend to present my myth in three complete dramas with a large prelude. With these dramas I do not intend theater "repertory pieces" in the modern sense, although each one should constitute a self-contained entity, but rather have the following plan for their performance in mind:
>   In the course of three days with a preceding evening, I intend to present these three dramas with the prelude at a festival planned specifically for this purpose: I consider the goal of this performance to be fully achieved, if I and my artistic comrades succeed on these four evenings to convey artistically an emotional (not critical) understanding of our intentions to the audience — who have gathered in order to become acquainted with my intentions. A further result is as irrelevant to me as it is superfluous....
>   With this enterprise, I have nothing more to do with our contemporary theater.[61]

Self-promotion is as integral to *A Communication with My Friends* as any purely intellectual need to clarify the theory. But this is a point many Wagner critics have overlooked. Eckart Kröplin attributes Wagner's "total need for spiritual communication" to a "deep-seated psychological urge," an inborn "pseudo-theatricality" that made him want to be the center of attention at all times, and which accounts for the large quantities of correspondence, as well as the many prose works.[62] But Kröplin's appealing psychological explanation does not account for Wagner's republication of his writings in the multi-volume collected works between 1871 and 1873. The "need to communicate," satisfied with the initial publication, becomes calculated marketing strategy upon a republication timed to coincide with preparations for the Bayreuth festival.

Hartmut Zelinsky describes these writings as examples of Wagner's "mythifying the artistic creative process."[63] But Zelinsky's accusation of mythifying obscures the embedded rationality of Wagner's exercise by banishing Wagner the self-promoter into the same world of the irrational which his dramatic works apparently portray. While marketing may play with mythical images to seduce the consumer, the strategy to do so is highly rationalized.

But Wagner was no ivory-tower scribe. Beyond writing about the cycle and the idea of the festival, Wagner also performed the text on four consecutive evenings between February

16 and 19, 1853, at the Hotel Baur in Zurich.[64] The event, which biographies describe in detail, was intended for a group of invited "friends," and anyone they wished to bring along.[65] Wagner's reading of his text (there was no music) was apparently so captivating that the audience grew over the four evenings.

Ten years later, Wagner was conducting concerts with selections from the *Ring*: The Ride of the Valkyries, Siegmund's aria "Winterstürme," Wotan's Farewell and Fire Music — all of these were "hits" long before the *Ring* was ever performed in its entirety. Theodor Adorno has criticized this practice which Wagner himself initiated, because it undermined the aesthetic integrity of his project by making commodities out of selections which, as complete works, were intended to resist that same process of commodification Wagner considered artistically abhorrent.[66] On the other hand, it is hard to imagine a more effective advertisement for the *Ring* than excerpts like "Siegfried's Journey Down the Rhine." As in the marketing of new films, the "preview of coming attractions" functions to present the best, most intriguing, or memorable moments of a work, consequently suggesting to the audience that the unseen portions of the film are similarly intense or exciting. Success at any price?

Up Close and Personal

One of the best known innovations Roone Arledge brought to television's ABC Sports was an approach to introducing and popularizing athletes, known as "Up close and personal." Short bio-spots were broadcast because, if "people cared about the athletes they were watching," the sporting event would be more meaningful.[67] Arledge evidently understood that being, or at least feeling, more knowledgeable was critical. In the first place, Arledge was of course concerned with audience share and advertising revenue, so any comparison between the marketing imperative informing his programming decisions and Wagner's desire to become known must not be overdrawn. However, Wagner wrote and rewrote his autobiography approximately every ten years. These works are crafted to elicit sympathy and understanding, to offer "the official story," to reveal special insights into Wagner's intellectual and emotional development. At times, they appear no less designed to generate an emotional connection than those reports focusing on hardship overcome and perseverance against all odds which have become standard on television. Wagner grants the reader intimate access into his deepest, innermost feelings: "My true nature, which recoiled from modernity and yearned for the more and most noble...."[68] He becomes the living embodiment of the romantic artist: "I became aware of my extreme loneliness as an artistic person."[69] Wagner brings us "up close and personal," but the confessional tone and all the revelations are highly manipulative, actually serving to justify his aesthetic project. He writes with apparently disarming honesty about his lack of success: "I wrote my death sentence with this work: I could no longer hope to survive in the modern art world."[70] But it is precisely this lack of success that necessitates the radical break. The reader becomes a willing accomplice, a moral supporter — a fan — and it is to each of them, "*to Friends who love me*" (emphasis in original), that the book is dedicated.[71]

Wagner divides the world into two camps: Friends (of his art), and those who are not — a friend-or-foe mentality still evident in Bayreuth today. For Wagner, to be loved and to be understood are one and the same. If you don't love, it is because you don't understand. For Wagner, everything is personal.[72]

Although literary scholars are nowadays at pains to avoid identifying fictional characters and their stories too closely with the autobiographical details of their creators, Wagner's work frustrates that separation. His fiction, as the example of the novellas written in Paris shows, is both a reflection of and a blueprint for his life.[73] Conversely, his autobiographies fictionalize his life and, to repeat Zelinsky, "mythify" his compositional process. For instance, the rough sea passage he survived in 1839 becomes the inspiration for *The Flying Dutchman*. Wagner relates something we have all experienced, or at least can imagine — a rough sea voyage — to something we cannot: creating a complex and compelling piece of orchestral music where there was nothing but a blank sheet of paper before. By relating the one to the other, however, Wagner brings the reader into the creative process, makes it seem more human and understandable. Zelinsky may call it mystification, but the pretence has the effect of reducing the mystery. An even more notable example would be Wagner's "vision" in La Spezia, where the opening E-flat triads of *Rheingold* allegedly came to him in a half-sleep.[74] So powerful is Wagner's description of that moment that even those scholars who have disproved its veracity are nevertheless compelled to repeat it.[75]

Sound Bites

The most enduring evidence of Wagnerian marketing success are the buzzwords, the Wagnerian newspeak, associated with his project. Some of these distinctive terms appear to make Wagner's complex and sophisticated concepts seem readily understandable while others are simply catchy slogans: "Gesamtkunstwerk," "Music drama," "Festspiel," "Zukunftsmusik" (music of the future). Wagner used them sparingly, in some cases not at all. Others, like "Zukunftsmusik," he specifically disavowed. Most have stuck nevertheless. To trace the genealogy and polularization of all these terms would exceed the bounds of this essay, but it is important to acknowledge their role in separating Wagner from the crowd, again making him "extraordinary." The musical equivalents are surely those elemental ideas made recognizable through constant repetition, woven throughout the fabric of the dramas. The device, known as "leitmotiv," is another word Wagner did not invent or use, though it is more closely associated with him and his work than any other.[76] As a compositional technique, Adorno observed compellingly that

> among the functions of the leitmotiv can be found, alongside the aesthetic one, a commodity function, rather like that of an advertisement: anticipating the universal practice of mass culture later on, the music is designed to be remembered, it is intended for the forgetful.[77]

This is a characterization which recalls Adolf Hitler's chilling description of effective propaganda:

> The receptivity of the great masses is very limited, their intelligence small, but their power of forgetting is enormous. In consequence of these facts, all effective propaganda must ... confine itself to a few points and repeat them over and over.[78]

Wagner's leitmotiv is the original sound bite.

If one, admittedly unintended, effect of the leitmotiv was to simplify what is inherently complex, to make easier what is musically difficult, the same can be said for the terminology itself, the Wagnerian newspeak which is integral to the Wagner industry: that quality which gives Wagner the kind of trademark status we associate with a brand name. Most of the specialized Wagnerian vocabulary is associated with the *Ring* cycle. Like the leitmotivs and the popularized musical extracts, these terms function to reduce into manageable packets a work whose indigestible enormity is essentially unmanageable.

Today's commercial world is no less filled with terms to assist the average consumer in coping with the technical complexity of our time: "turbo-charged," "fiber-optic," "Pentium processor," "digitized," "high definition," "DSL"— we don't really understand the technology involved, nor do we need to in order to enjoy the product. But using the terminology makes us feel we are sufficiently informed to make responsible purchasing decisions.

Spreading the Word: An Epilogue

A reasonable criticism of my contention that Wagner was instrumental in founding what became an industry — that he was its master salesman, so to speak — is that his theoretical writings reached a comparatively small readership, his letters only individuals. Neither accounts for the degree of notoriety, sensation, scandal and public visibility which increasingly accompanied Wagner's name, persona, and work from the 1840s on.

Wagner's politics, the warrant issued for his arrest, his public performances, as well as the increasing success of his works — not to mention the scandal of the Paris *Tannhäuser*— compounded by the media attention all of these received, contributed to his fame. But Wagner also had "friends" who went about spreading the word with an aggressive enthusiasm, if not missionary zeal, which Wagner ignited. For instance, Wagner's friend Theodor Uhlig responded on behalf of the composer to charges that the theories described in *Opera and Drama* were incompatible with the works Wagner had composed. In an 1852 essay titled "A Small Protest in the Matter of Wagner," Uhlig no less than Wagner makes use of the "preview of coming attractions" technique as follows: "the theories which Wagner has created are not out of thin air, but are the ideas relating to the artworks which we are yet to see."[79]

Let us further recall that 1873 letter Wagner wrote to his "energetic friend" Emil Heckel with which this essay opened: "throw the matter into the public arena, and indeed with awesome publicity, so that no one can say 'I haven't heard anything about it yet.'" The choice of words bears scrutiny. Notice the aggressive terminology Wagner uses to describe the process of raising public awareness, anticipating the martial similes commonly used by the advertising world today. We speak of a marketing "campaign" and of a media "blitz," both alluding to the precision and coordination — reminiscent of military maneuvers — involved in surrounding and overwhelming the consumer with such speed and effectiveness as to make resistance futile: using more recent military jargon we might speak of advertising as an exercise in "shock and awe." Wagner's music often has just this effect on the listener and, though not trained in marketing, he had a similar ability to overwhelm when it came to publicizing himself and his undertakings.

The missionary zeal has a cult dimension of course, but spreading the word is also a form of marketing. The original statutes of the Wagner Societies founded in the 1870s declare precisely this fundamental obligation of being a Wagnerian: "through discussions and lectures to promote and disseminate knowledge and respect of Wagnerian reforms and accomplishments in music and drama."[80] Back then, all means available were employed to ensure the viability of the Bayreuth festival and secure the performance of the *Ring*. This was the original purpose of the Wagner Societies. But, 125 years later, with Wagner's significance globally recognized and the future of Bayreuth secure, the marketing of Wagner continues. The Internet home page of the Wagner Society of New York proclaims that it is "a not-for-profit corporation devoted to furthering the performance and understanding of the music of Richard Wagner through events such as seminars, lectures, recitals, interviews, films, and assistance to promising young artists."[81] No other composer of the western tradition can claim this kind of organized support.

Institutional and institutionalized endeavors such as these have been accompanied by individual efforts to "sell the *Ring*." The most famous early example is probably Hans von Wolzogen's *Thematischer Leitfaden* (1876) which explained the *Ring* in part by popularizing the concept of "Leit(Motiv)."[82] His best-selling Wagner primer bemoans the widespread "prejudice" that Wagner and the *Ring* are "incomprehensible":

> At first sight, one fears that text and music are, in this case, of such a considerable incomprehensibility, that they might only be somewhat enjoyable with the aid of a course of study in each of the relevant academic disciplines.[83]

However, since the *Ring* is based on myth, it should be "understandable to all without further ado."[84] In an apparent contradiction, Wolzogen then argues that the key to understanding Wagner's self-explanatory work is to understand the motives. And so he launches into perhaps the first, but certainly not the last, book devoted to advice on how to "Enjoy the *Ring*." He even points readers to other books, including Heinrich Porges's *Das Bühnenfestspiel in Bayreuth* and Franz Brendel's *Geschichte der Musik*, which attempt similar tasks.

Already in 1872, Ludwig Nohl had presented "Five popular lectures on the German Music drama" sponsored by the original Wagner Society in Mannheim. The first four lectures were devoted to Gluck, Mozart, Beethoven and Weber, respectively. Only the last lecture concerned Wagner, the last segment being "Das deutsche Nationaldrama: Der Ring des Nibelungen. Die Bühnenfestspiele zu Bayreuth."[85] Wagner in general, and the *Ring* in particular are presented (sold) as the culmination of German cultural development. Even today at the Bayreuth Festival, there are numerous opportunities each day for audience members to become better educated, more suitably prepared for the evening's performance. Being an educated, informed consumer is central to the enterprise, and is in part why the Wagner industry thrives.

While these and other efforts to publicize and explain were under way — an effort which this volume honors and perpetuates — equal and opposite pressure was being applied to limit access to, and, hence, the availability of, that same Wagnerian product. Despite Wagner's claim that the Bayreuth Festival qualified as "a national undertaking" in the "service of German art," the German press was banned from covering the so-called "Grundsteinlegung" (laying of the cornerstone) of the Festspielhaus.[86] Even more, the scarcity of tickets for the Bayreuth festival — artificially maintained, as some suggest — with its 8- to 10-year waiting list, raises the demand, giving ticket-holders the sense that they belong to the chosen. This, too, is part of "enjoying the *Ring*." Wagner and his heirs seem to have understood the laws of supply and demand.

We who enjoy Wagner's music participate in an extraordinary voyage, but the sublime sensory and spiritual experience should not blind us to Wagner's marketing talents, his remarkable ability to generate publicity, awareness, and desire. His entrepreneurial activities constitute the founding impulse of a flourishing industry, as today's "outrageous" stagings and "scandalous" behavior, especially in Bayreuth, serve to sustain the Wagner name and ever-present image.

Notes

1. My thanks to the University of South Carolina for a College of Liberal Arts Summer Study (CLASS) award and to the German Academic Exchange Service (DAAD) for a study grant which funded research trips to the State Library in Berlin and the Wagner Archives in Bayreuth without which this essay could not have been written.

2. Unless otherwise noted, all translations are mine. Letter to Emil Heckel, September 19, 1873. Richard Wagner: *Werke, Schriften und Briefe*, Digitale Bibliothek CD-ROM Vol. 107, ed. Sven Friedrich (Berlin: Directmedia, 2004), 22046–7 (abbrev.: CD-ROM: page number). Originally Richard Wagner, *Bayreuther Briefe* (1871–1883). 2nd

ed., vol. 15 of Richard Wagner's *Briefe in Originalausgaben* (Leipzig: Breitkopf & Härtel, [1907] 1912), 134. Most citations are taken from the new CD-ROM of Wagner's works. In such cases, I will also refer the reader to the printed source.

3. Lore Lucas, *Die Festspiel-Idee Richard Wagners* (Regensburg: Gustav Bosse, 1973), 93.

4. CD-ROM: 4905. Orig. Richard Wagner, *Sämtliche Schriften und Dichtungen*, 16. vols. (Leipzig: Breitkopf & Härtel n.d. [1911]) (abbrev.: SSD) 10: 123.

5. CD-ROM: 4905. SSD 10: 123.

6. Theodor W. Adorno, *In Search of Wagner*, trans. Rodney Livingstone (London: Verso, 1991), 91.

7. Carl Dahlhaus describes Wagner as a "Romantic" who realized his vision "with the dogged, hard-headed persistence of any contemporary business entrepreneur." See John Deathridge and Carl Dahlhaus, *New Grove Wagner* (New York & London: Norton, 1984): 94.

8. See Pierre Bourdieu, *The Rules of Art: Genesis and Structure of the Literary Field*, trans. Susan Emanuel (Palo Alto: Stanford University Press, 1995).

9. Bourdieu, Rules of Art, 21.

10. Paul Mann, *Theory-Death of the Avant-Garde* (Bloomington: Indiana University Press, 1991), 87. See also Robert Jensen, *Marketing Modernism in Fin-de-Siècle Europe* (Princeton: Princeton University Press, 1994), as well as numerous other studies which borrow from and expand upon Jensen's work.

11. Adorno, *In Search of Wagner*, especially p. 83.

12. "Der Bayreuther Patronatsgedanke rückte das Festspielunternehmen Richard Wagners wenn auch ungewollt in die Nähe zeitüblichen Gründertums von Aktiengesellschaften, allerdings mit der reizvollen Variante einer in Aussicht gestellten individuell transzendierbaren künstlerischen Rendite. Wagner hatte solche Gleichsetzung ... selbst provoziert": Michael Karbaum, *Studien zur Geschichte der Bayreuther Festspiele*: (1876–1976) (Regensburg: Bosse, 1976), 19.

13. See also Manfred Wegner, *Musik und Mammon: Die permanente Krise der Musikkultur* (Baden-Baden: Nomos, 1999): "Nicht zufällig ist Bayreuth in den Gründerjahren entstanden. Kein Wunder also, daß die Wagnersche Festspielidee zwischen einem Nation- und einem Aktien-Unternehmen oszillierte" (160).

14. "[D]ieses nationalen Unternehmens ... im Dienste deutscher Kunst," in Richard Wagner, "Aufforderung zur Erwerbung von Patronatsscheinen," Berlin, den 18. Mai 1871, SSD 16: 132–33, here 132. See also Susanna Großmann-Vendrey, *Bayreuth in der deutschen Presse: Beiträge zur Rezeptionsgeschichte Richard Wagners und seiner Festspiele*, Dokumentband 1: Die Grundsteinlegung und die ersten Festspiele (1872–1876) (Regensburg: Bosse, 1977): "War man also geneigt, Wagners Bayreuth als ein suspektes Geschäftsunternehmung ad acta zu legen, so war es doch wiederum beunruhigend, daß nicht nur Wagner und die Wagner-Vereine, sondern auch ein Teil der Presse von den Festspielen als einem höchst wichtigen "nationalen Unternehmen" sprachen. Das Wort national konnte man sich nicht so einfach hinwegsetzen" (17).

15. "[W]ie dies bei Aktienausschreibungen und Staatsanleihen geschiet," Richard Wagner, "An die Patrone der Bühnenfestspiele in Bayreuth" (Bayreuth, 30 August 1873), SSD 12: 317–23, here 318.

16. Grossmann-Vendrey, *Bayreuth in der deutschen Presse*: "[E]ntrüstete Ablehnung des soliden Bürgers, der den ersten großen wirtschaftlichen Aufschwung der Gründerzeit eher argwohnisch betrachtete und von "Actienunternehmungen" vorerst nichts wissen wollte. Neu war in dieser Hinsicht auch Wagners Methode, für sein Unternehmen durch Veröffentlichungen der Wagner-Vere-ine und durch persönliche Konzertreisen zu werben; all das schien seine Festspiele in die Geschäftssphäre herabzuziehen, womit die Kunst-nach dem ungeschriebenen Gesetz des bürgerlichen Idealismus-nichts zu tun haben durfte" (17).

17. Wagner already mentions the idea of publishing his collected works, including a detailed table of contents, in a letter to King Ludwig II dated January 6, 1865. A tenth volume was added in 1883 after the composer's death.

18. SSD 12: 319–20.

19. "[M]einer, jeden Gewinn ausschließenden Unternehmung," Richard Wagner, "Ankündigung der Festspiele für 1876" (28 August 1875), SSD 16: 153–4, here 154. Karbaum observes: "Mit allem Nachdruck wehrte er sich damals gegen jeden Vergleich mit profit-orientierten oder Aktien-Unternehmungen" (21).

20. SSD 12: 320.

21. SSD 12: 321.

22. Richard Wagner, "An den Herausgeber der Amerikanischen Revue" (June 1874), SSD 16: 118–120, here 119.

23. "[I]ch wollte ... Beiträge sammeln zur Verwirklichung einer nationalen Idee." Richard Wagner, "An den Herausgeber der Amerikanischen Revue" (June 1874) SSD 16: 118–120, here 119.

24. Adorno, *In Search of Wagner*, 141.

25. For a comprehensive history of the first festival, see Frederic Spotts, *Bayreuth: A History of the Wagner Festival* (New Haven: Yale University Press, 1994).

26. I borrow the term from Boris Voigt, *Richard Wagners Autoritäre Inszenierungen. Versuch über die Ästhetik charismatischer Herrschaft* (Hamburg: von Bockel, 2003), 208.

27. "In wichtigen äußeren Gesichtspunkten der organisatorischen und betrieblichen Leistung hält das Bayreuther Unternehmen den Vergleich mit zeitgenössischen Industrie- und Wirtschafts-gründungen durchaus stand. Ohne das hochgesteckte künstlerische Ziel aus den Augen zu verlieren," Karbaum, Bayreuther Festspiele, 23.

28. Karbaum, *Bayreuther Festspiele*, 14.

29. For a general account of Wagner's revival of Beethoven's Ninth Symphony, see Andreas Eichhorn, *Beethovens Neunte Symphonie. Die Geschichte ihrer Aufführung und Rezeption* (Kassel: Bärenreiter, 1993), esp. 72–81, as well as Wagner's own account in his autobiography, *Mein Leben*, 341–346.

30. See Helmut Kirchmeyer, *Situationsgeschichte der Musikkritik und muskalische Pressewesens in Deutschland*. Teil 4: *Das zeitgenössische Wagner-Bild*. Bd. 1: *Wagner in Dresden* and Bd. 2: *Dokumente* 1842–45 (Regensburg: Bosse, 1967–1972), here 1: 678.

31. Richard Wagner, *Mein Leben*, ed. Martin Gregor-Dellin (München: List 1969) (abbrev.: ML): "In mir bestärkte sich bei dieser Gelegenheit das wohltuende Gefühl der Fähigkeit und Kraft, das, was ich ernstlich wollte, mit unwiderleglich glücklichem Gelingen durchzuführen" (346).

32. ML, 346: "Das war und blieb die geheime Frage, an welcher sich mein ferneres Leben entwickelte."

33. *Oxford English Dictionary*, 2nd Ed. 1989–1997. Online Version, definition 5c.

34. Interestingly, Dutch author Boudewijn Büch recently published a study of what he calls *De Goethe-industrie: Een Duitse ziekte* (Amsterdam: Uitgeverij De Arbeiderspers, 2002). The book focuses on the ideological appropriation of Goethe (1749–1832), including major sections on communist and national socialist readings.

35. Wagner uses "Vorhaben" and "Unternehmen" throughout his correspondence and works. The earliest example of "Vorhaben" I have found so far that relates

directly to the Ring project is from 1853; see "Vorwort zu der Veröffentlichung der als Manuscript gedruckten Dichtung der »Ringes des Nibelungen« SSD 12: 287. For "Unternehmen," the earliest I have found is from 1860 in "Zukunftsmusik," SSD 7: 136.

36. CD-ROM: 3067; SSD 6:280.

37. For an exhaustive chronological table containing the most important dates in the genesis of the Ring, starting with Wagner's 1848 essay *Die Wibelungen* and ending with the 1876 world premiere of the cycle in Bayreuth, see Richard Wagner, *Sämtliche Werke* Bd. 29,I: *Dokumente zur Entstehungsgeschichte des Bühnenfestspiels Der Ring des Nibelungen*, ed. Werner Breig und Hartmut Fladt (Mainz: Schott, 1976), 12–13. See also Karl Heckel, *Die Bühnenfestspiele in Bayreuth. Authentischer Beitrag zur Geschichte ihrer Entstehung und Entwicklung* (Leipzig: Fritzsch, 1891), 3.

38. Manfred Eger, "Die Bayreuther Festspiele und die Familie Wagner," *Richard-Wagner-Handbuch*, ed. Ulrich Müller und Peter Wapnewski (Stuttgart: Alfred Kröner, 1986): 589–608, here 589.

39. Marjorie Perloff, T*he Futurist Moment: Avant-Garde, Avant Guerre, and the Language of Ruptur*e (Chicago: University of Chicago Press, 1986), 90.

40. Mann, *Theory Death*, 23.

41. Nike Wagner, "Das Theater Wagners und Wagnertheater," *Wagner Theater* (Frankfurt/Main: Insel, 1998): 7–25, here 11.

42. "Ich schreibe keine Opern mehr." CD-ROM: 2185; SSD 4: 345.

43. "[D]as kleine, abgelegene, unbeachtete Bayreuth" CD-ROM: 4672; SSD 9:331.

44. See Katharine Ellis and Matthias Brzoska, "Avant-propos méthodologique," *Von Wagner zum Wagnérisme: Musik, Literatur, Kunst, Politik*, eds. Annegret Fauser und Manuela Schwartz (Leipzig: Leipziger Universitätsverlag, 1999) 35–37, here 36: "il en restera le seul qui achèvera sa carrière en se construisant son 'Petit Paris' hors de la France main néanmoins peuplé par l'élite parisienne." They add, significantly, and quite rightly I believe: "Il est bien évident que le discours Wagnérien aurait pu prendre tout autre chemin si Wagner avait pu achever sa carrière comme tous ses contemporains; c'est à dire sur le pavé parisien." (36).

45. "Ließ ich in den »Meistersingern« meinen Hans Sachs Nürnberg als in Deutschlands Mitte liegend preisen, so dünkte mich nun dem erwählten Bayreuth diese gemüthliche Lage mit noch größerem Rechte zugesprochen werden zu können," CD-ROM: 4673; SSD 9: 332.

46. "Man hat das Opfer der ungeheuren Unbequemlichkeit Bayreuth's einmal-mir zu gefallen (auch zum Theil aus Neugier)-gebracht, schreckt aber vor dem Gedanken der Wiederholung zurück." Letter to Friedrich Feustel, June 14, 1877, repr: *Bayreuther Blätter* 26.7–9 (1903): 211–212, here 211. CD-ROM 22254.

47. "Sie soll zunächst nichts Anderes bieten, als den örtlich fixirten periodischen Vereinigungs-punkt der besten theatralischen Kräfte Deutschlands zu Übungen und Ausführungen in einem höheren deutschen Originalstyle ihrer Kunst, welche ihnen im gewöhnlichen Laufe ihrer Beschäftigungen nicht ermöglicht werden können." CD-ROM 4646; SSD 9: 316.

48. Voigt, *Wagners Autoritäre Inszenierungen*. The whole book pursues this issue. See esp. around p.92.

49. "Seit einiger Zeit bin ich gänzlich aus diesem unmittelbar künstlerischen Verkehre mit ihnen getreten; wiederholt, und so auch jetzt noch, konnte ich mich ihnen nur als Schriftsteller mittheilen: welche Pein diese Art der Mittheilung für mich ausmacht, brauche ich Denen, die mich als Künstler kennen, wohl nicht erst zu versichern," CD-ROM: 2156; SSD 4: 330.

50. CD-ROM: 72; SSD 1: 17–18.

51. "Diese Arbeiten haben mir nicht wenig geholfen, in Paris bekannt und beachtet zu werden," CD-ROM: 72; SSD 1: 17.

52. There has been some discussion of whether Wagner modeled "R..." on Johann Friedrich "R"eichardt or on Ludwig "R"ellstab. The "Reichardt" thesis is proposed by Martin Gregor-Dellin in *Richard Wagner* (München: Piper, 1980), 153, on the basis of entries in Cosima Wagner's diary. See also Dieter Borchmeyer, ed., *Richard Wagner, Dichtungen und Schriften* 10: 298. The "Rellstab" thesis is in Matthias Brzoska, *Die Idee des Gesamtkunstwerks in der Musiknovellistik der Julimonarchie* (Laaber: Laaber, 1995), 174–76, on the basis of greater historical probability, Wagner's assumed familiarity with the Rellstab text, and similarities between Rellstab's and Wagner's texts.

53. CD-ROM 225; SSD 1: 109.

54. CD-ROM 225 & 228 ; SSD 1: 109 & 111.

55. Dieter Borchmeyer, *Das Theater Richard Wagners. Idee-Dichtung-Wirkung* (Stuttgart: Reclam, 1982): 100.

56. CD-ROM: 9567; Letter to Franz Liszt, November, 25 1850. Richard Wagner, *Sämtliche Briefe*, 14 vols. to date, ed. Gertrud Strobel und Werner Wolf (Leipzig: VEB Deutscher Verlag für Musik, 1983), 3: 468 (abbrev. SB)

57. Letter to Ernst Benedikt Kietz, September 14, 1850 (German orig. SB 3: 404–05), in Stewart Spencer and Barry Millington, trans. and ed., *Selected Letters of Richard Wagner* (New York: Norton, 1987): 216–7.

58. "[D]enn diese Zukunft ist nicht anders denkbar, als aus der Vergangenheit bedingt," CD-ROM: 1977; SSD 4: 228.

59. CD-ROM: 1978; SSD 4: 229.

60. See Klaus Kropfinger's discussion of "Aspekte der Rezeption" in his edition of Richard Wagner, *Oper und Drama*, ed. und Kommentiert von K.K. (Stuttgart: Reclam, 1994), esp. 495–533.

61. CD-ROM: 2179; SSD 4: 343–44.

62. Eckart Kröplin, *Richard Wagner. Theatralisches Leben und lebendiges Theater* (Leipzig: Deutscher Verlag für Musik, 1989), 72–76.

63. Hartmut Zelinsky, *Richard Wagner-ein deutsches Thema: Eine Dokumentation zur Wirkungsgeschichte Richard Wagners 1876–1976*, 3rd. ed. (Berlin: Medusa, 1983), 16.

64. For an example of an invitation, see Wagner's February 12, 1853, letter to Hermann Rollett in Zürich, CD-ROM: 10837; SB 5: 194.

65. See e.g. Martin Gregor-Dellin, 370–71.

66. On this important point, see also Adorno, *In Search of Wagner*, 106.

67. John Merli, "Arledge: Technical Achievements Almost Beyond Measure," September 3, 2004 http://www.tvtechnology.com/features/news/n_Arledge_Technical.shtml.

68. CD-ROM: 2069; SSD 4: 279.

69. CD-ROM: 2094; SSD 4: 294.

70. CD-ROM: 2069; SSD 4: 279.

71. CD-ROM: 1991–92; SSD 4: 234.

72. "[E]in Künstler meines Strebens geliebt und seine Kunst somit verstanden werden, wenn dieses Verständniß und jene ermöglichende Liebe nicht vor Allem auch in der Sympathie, d.h. dem Mitleiden und Mitfühlen mit seinem allermenschlichsten Leben begründet ist," CD-ROM: 1986; SSD 4: 231.

73. "Hierin stellte ich, in erdichteten Zügen und mit ziemlichem Humor, meine eigenen Schicksale, namentlich in Paris, bis zum wirklichen Hungertode, dem ich glücklicherweise allerdings entgangen war, dar," CD-ROM: 2040; SSD 4: 263.

74. Wagner, *ML*, 512.

75. See e.g. Martin Gregor-Dellin, 185–88.

76. On the genesis of the term "Leitmotiv," see Thomas Grey, "Leading Motives and Narrative Threads: Notes on the 'Leitfaden' Metaphor and the Critical Pre-History of the Wagnerian 'Leitmotiv,'" *Musik als Text, Bericht über den Internationalen Kongreß der Gesellschaft für Musikforschung Freiburg im Breisgau* 1993, Vol. 2: Freie Referate, eds. Hermann Danuser & Tobias Plebuch (Kassel: Bärenreiter, 1998): 352–58.

77. Adorno, *In Search of Wagner*, 31.

78. Adolf Hitler, *Mein Kampf*, tr. Ralph Manheim (Boston: Houghton Mifflin, 1971), 182 & 184.

79. "...die Theorien, welche Wagner allerdings nicht aus der Luft gegriffen, sondern aus den Ideen zu seinen erst noch zu erwartenden Kunstwerken geschöpft hat," Theodor Uhlig, "Ein kleiner Protest in Sachen Wagner's," Neue Zeitschrift für Musik 36 (1852): 277–78, here 278.

80. "[D]ie Kenntniss und Würdigung der Wagner'schen Reform-Ideen und Leistungen in Musik und Drama durch Besprechungen und Vorträge zu fördern und zu verbre-iten," Akademischer Richard-Wagner-Verein zu Berlin, *Aufruf u.Statuten* April 1872. Archiv Nr.: A2584/VII–1, Nationalarchiv der Richard-Wagner-Stiftung Bayreuth (abbrev: Wagner Archiv).

81. Accessed 3 September 2004 http://www.wagnersocietyny.org/.

82. Hans von Wolzogen, *Thematischer Leitfaden durch die Musik zu Richard Wagner's Festspiel "Der Ring des Nibelungen,"* 2. verbesserte Auflage (Leipzig: Edwin Schloemp, 1876).

83. Wolzogen, *Thematischer Leitfaden*, 1.

84. Wolzogen, *Thematischer Leitfaden*, 2.

85. Poster announcement: (Wagner Archiv Nr.: A2584/IV–5).

86. Richard Wagner, "Aufforderung zur Erwerbung von Patronatsscheinen" Berlin, May 18, 1871, SSD 16: 132–33, here 132. See also Grossmann-Vendrey, 19 and "Protokoll der 7. Verwaltungsratsitzung 4 May 1872" (Wagner Archiv Nr.: RWG Hs. 94 II).

Bibliography

Adorno, Theodor W. *In Search of Wagner*. Trans. Rodney Livingstone. London: Verso, 1991.

Borchmeyer, Dieter. *Das Theater Richard Wagners. Idee — Dichtung — Wirkung*. Stuttgart: Reclam, 1982.

Bourdieu, Pierre. *The Rules of Art: Genesis and Structure of the Literary Field*. Trans. Susan Emanuel. Palo Alto: Stanford University Press, 1995.

Brzoska, Matthias. *Die Idee des Gesamtkunstwerks in der Musiknovellistik der Julimonarchie*. Laaber: Laaber, 1995.

Deathridge, John, and Carl Dahlhaus. *New Grove Wagner*. New York and London: Norton, 1984.

Eger, Manfred. "Die Bayreuther Festspiele und die Familie Wagner." *Richard-Wagner-Handbuch*. Eds. Ulrich Müller and Peter Wapnewski. Stuttgart: Alfred Kröner, 1986. 589–608.

Eichhorn, Andreas. *Beethovens Neunte Symphonie. Die Geschichte ihrer Aufführung und Rezeption*. Kassel: Bärenreiter, 1993.

Ellis, Katharine, and Matthias Brzoska. "Avant-propos méthodologique." *Von Wagner zum Wagnérisme: Musik, Literatur, Kunst, Politik*. Eds. Annegret Fauser and Manuela Schwartz. Leipzig: Leipziger Universitätsverlag, 1999. 35–37.

Gregor-Dellin, Martin. *Richard Wagner: Sein Leben, sein Werke, sein Jahrhundert*. München: Piper, 1980.

Grey, Thomas. "Leading Motives and Narrative Threads: Notes on the 'Leitfaden' Metaphor and the Critical Pre-History of the Wagnerian 'Leitmotiv.'" *Musik als Text, Bericht über den Internationalen Kongreß der Gesellschaft für Musikforschung, Freiburg im Breisgau 1993*. Vol. 2: Freie Referate. Eds. Hermann Danuser and Tobias Plebuch. Kassel: Bärenreiter, 1998. 352–58.

Großmann-Vendrey, Susanna. *Bayreuth in der deutschen Presse: Beiträge zur Rezeptions-geschichte Richard Wagners und seiner Festspiele*, Dokumentband 1: *Die Grundstein-legung und die ersten Festspiele (1872–1876)*. Regensburg: Bosse, 1977.

Heckel, Karl. *Die Bühnenfestspiele in Bayreuth. Authentischer Beitrag zur Geschichte ihrer Entstehung und Entwicklung*. Leipzig: Fritzsch, 1891.

Hitler, Adolf. *Mein Kampf*. Trans. Ralph Manheim. Boston: Houghton Mifflin, 1971.

Jensen, Robert. *Marketing Modernism in Fin-de-Siècle Europe*. Princeton: Princeton University Press, 1994.

Karbaum, Michael. *Studien zur Geschichte der Bayreuther Festspiele (1876–1976)*. Regensburg: Bosse, 1976.

Kirchmeyer, Helmut. *Situationsgeschichte der Musikkritik und muskalischen Pressewesens in Deutschland*. Teil 4: *Das zeitgenössische Wagner-Bild*. Bd. 1: *Wagner in Dresden* and Bd. 2: *Dokumente 1842–45*. Regensburg: Bosse, 1967–1972.

Kropfinger, Klaus, ed. *Richard Wagner: Oper und Drama*. Stuttgart: Reclam, 1994.

Kröplin, Eckart. *Richard Wagner. Theatralisches Leben und lebendiges Theater*. Leipzig: Deutscher Verlag für Musik, 1989.

Lucas, Lore. *Die Festspiel-Idee Richard Wagners*. Regensburg: Gustav Bosse, 1973.

Mann, Paul. *Theory-Death of the Avant-Garde*. Bloomington: Indiana University Press, 1991.

Merli, John. "Arledge: Technical Achievements Almost Beyond Measure," September 3, 2004 <http://www.tvtechnology.com/features/news/n_Arledge_Technical.shtml>.

Oxford English Dictionary, 2nd Ed. Online Version. 1989.

Perloff, Marjorie. *The Futurist Moment: Avant-Garde, Avant Guerre, and the Language of Rupture*. Chicago: University of Chicago Press, 1986.

Spotts, Frederic. *Bayreuth: A History of the Wagner Festival*. New Haven: Yale University Press, 1994.

Stewart, Spencer and Barry Millington, trans. and eds. *Selected Letters of Richard Wagner*. New York: Norton, 1987.

Uhlig, Theodor. "Ein kleiner Protest in Sachen Wagner's." *Neue Zeitschrift für Musik* 36 (1852): 277–78.

Voigt, Boris. *Richard Wagners Autoritäre Inszenierungen. Versuch über die Ästhetik charismatischer Herrschaft*. Hamburg: von Bockel, 2003.

Wagner, Nike. "Das Theater Wagners und Wagnertheater." *Wagner Theater*. Frankfurt/Main: Insel, 1998. 7–25.

Wagner, Richard. *Mein Leben*. Ed. Martin Gregor-Dellin. München: List, 1969.

_____. *Sämtliche Briefe*. 14 vols. to date. Eds. Gertrud Strobel und Werner Wolf Leipzig: VEB Deutscher Verlag für Musik, 1979–.

_____. *Sämtliche Schriften und Dichtungen*. 16 vols. Leipzig: Breitkopf and Härtel, n.d. (1911).

_____. *Sämtliche Werke*. Vol. 29, I: *Dokumente zur Entstehungsgeschichte des Bühnenfestspiels* Der Ring des Nibelungen. Eds. Werner Breig und Hartmut Fladt. Mainz: Schott, 1976.

_____. *Werke, Schriften und Briefe. Digitale Bibliothek* CD-ROM Vol. 107. Ed. Sven Friedrich. Berlin: Directmedia, 2004.

Wegner, Manfred. *Musik und Mammon: Die permanente Krise der Musikkultur*. Baden-Baden: Nomos, 1999.

Wolzogen, Hans von. *Thematischer Leitfaden durch die Musik zu Richard Wagner's Festspiel "Der Ring des Nibelungen."* 2nd verbesserte Auflage. Leipzig: Edwin Schloemp, 1876.

Zelinsky, Hartmut. *Richard Wagner — ein deutsches Thema: Eine Dokumentation zur Wirkungs-geschichte Richard Wagners 1876–1976*. 3rd. ed. Berlin: Medusa, 1983.

II. INTERPRETATIONS

3. Gold Rules: The Politics of Wagner's *Ring*

Neil K. Friedman

> *Both capitalism and communism acknowledge a basic truth expressed by the popular aphorism, "He who has the gold rules."*
> — David C. Korten, *When Corporations Rule the World*

Introduction

"I have been told that Wagner's music is better than it sounds," quipped Mark Twain. Fortunately, the same is true for the plot of *The Ring of the Nibelung*. The story of gods, giants, dwarves, valkyries and heroes is not as far-fetched as it seems. Richard Wagner's great music drama tells us more about nineteenth-century Europe than about ancient gods and gnomes. It is a story of class conflict in Europe with a message to Wagner's contemporaries, although it draws upon ancient Nordic and Germanic mythology for characters and themes.

While almost all admirers of Wagner's work recognize references to his own era, no one has published a full-scale interpretation of the *political* meaning of this operatic cycle. The best-known attempt is by George Bernard Shaw, a major dramatist in his own right, in *The Perfect Wagnerite: A Commentary on the Niblung's Ring*. Despite the title, Shaw must be declared an imperfect Wagnerite. His political analysis peters out frustratingly after three of the four operas, whereupon he adds, in what seems forced reasoning, sections like "Collapse of the Allegory" and "Why He Changed His Mind." Despite its shortcomings, Shaw's explication had a lasting influence. The centennial *Ring* at the 1976 Bayreuth Festival produced by Patrice Chéreau and conducted by Pierre Boulez took off from Shaw and costumed the characters in modern clothing that indicated their social class positions, the doom of the gods thus signifying the downfall of the old ruling class in an industrializing society. This departure made the production highly controversial, heresy in the eyes of self-appointed guardians of Wagnerian purity who booed and walked out despite fine performances. Still, that production released a flood of modern theatrical approaches, some of them bizarre, especially in Europe. A sound political analysis, however, should be based on the original work and the composer's life and thought.

Wagner's own experience as a fervid revolutionary who narrowly escaped into exile after his visible part in the violent 1849 upheaval in Dresden, having consorted in those events with the anarchist Bakunin, has been described in the biographies. When the barricades

Götterdämmerung, Saxon State Opera: Kurt Rydl as Hagen. (Photograph: Matthias Creutziger)

went up, Wagner, then in his mid-thirties, was on the revolutionary side. His immersion in the politics of the period is usually understated, including by Wagner himself in the auto-biography he dictated later in life at the behest of King Ludwig II. Newman recaptures Wagner's state of mind in 1848–49, when the inspiration for the life-work that would become the *Ring* bloomed from a cross-fertilization of his exploration of ancient myth, his intolerable financial difficulties, and the revolutionary atmosphere that he was breathing. That the plan for the *Ring*, at first called *Siegfried's Death*, took shape at this historical juncture is far from coincidence. "In some strange way or other, the Hoard became symbolical, for him, of the factors in modern society to which he attributed most of his own troubles" (Newman II, 20).

Das Rheingold

The prelude sets the historical background to the social upheavals taking place in Wagner's era. Like Marx, Wagner understood that the causes of the social transformations that threatened to overturn the whole order of society stemmed from material bases. He deliberately started *The Ring* at the substructure of the economy and then shifted to the commanding heights — the gods who represent the ruling aristocracy. For an analysis of the work informed by the thesis that the "mythical" beings correspond to social groups in Europe — especially in the German lands — and confronting a roster of mythical characters ranging from gods to dwarves, we need a picture of German society at the time Wagner conceived the *Ring of the Nibelung*. The best source is Marx and Engels' *Revolution and Counter-Revolution in Germany*, a series of articles that focus on the 1840s with the purpose of explaining the failure of the 1848–49 revolutions. Marx and Engels identified a complex class structure and process of change, breaking down the propertied class into different sectors:

> History showed to the Communist party, how, after the landed aristocracy of the Middle Ages, the monied power of the first capitalists arose and seized the reins of Government; how the social influence and political rule of this *financial* section of capitalists was superseded by the rising strength, since the introduction of steam, of the *manufacturing* capitalists, and how at the present moment two more classes claim their turn of domination, the petty trading class, and the industrial working class. The practical revolutionary experience of 1848–49 confirmed the reasonings of theory, which led to the conclusion that the democracy of the petty traders must first have its turn, before the Communist working class could hope to permanently establish itself in power and destroy that system of wages-slavery which keeps it under the yoke of the bourgeoisie [*Selected Works* I, 389].

Thus in the *Ring* we find a class structure with at least the following components. The upper class: aristocrats of noble birth who are hereditary rulers of society ("Gods"). Next, a big bourgeoisie consisting of powerful industrialists ("Giants"). Under them, a petty bourgeoisie (lower middle class) that Marx and Engels refer to as "petty traders" and which includes others engaged in small-scale manufacturing, crafts, or services ("Dwarves"). These petty bourgeois outnumber the big bourgeois, and ambitious members aspire to become the latter. Forming the lower class ("Nibelungs") are industrial workers, increasingly concentrated in larger factories owned by capitalists, but many employed in smaller shops. Key to analysis is the distinction between big capitalist and petty bourgeois — the two components of the European "middle class"— which explains the size gap between giants and dwarves.

Where could an ambitious small businessman look for a source of power that would let him compete with the big players? In the material forces of production or finance. Alberich the dwarf steals the Rheingold and makes from it a ring that has magical powers so awesome that he threatens not just the giants but the very hegemony of the gods. A Rhinedaughter lets slip the secret of the gold when Alberich, scrambling along the river bottom, questions its value. (All quotations from the libretto are Stewart Spencer's translation in Spencer and Millington 1993.)

> The world's wealth
> would be won by him
> who forged from the Rheingold
> the ring
> that would grant him limitless power.

Yet Alberich hears from them that no one can take that gold and make it into a magic ring unless he "renounces love," an act thought to be impossible.

> Only the man who forswears
> love's sway,
> only he who disdains
> love's delights
> can master the magic spell
> that rounds a ring from the gold.

Male and female characters in the *Ring* have somewhat different allegorical functions. Male characters usually represent classes of people in European society, whereas female characters tend to express cultural principles. The Rhinedaughters innocently express the way of thinking that prevailed before the industrial revolution and was looked back upon nostalgically by the Romantics of Wagner's generation: enjoy the beauty of nature without trying to exploit it. To "renounce love" in Wagner's allegory means to give up that romantic view of nature and look at it in the cold light of reason, as an object to be manipulated and exploited. The reigning aristocracy, in spite of— or *because of*— its superior education, was incapable of this intellectual feat. It was the underestimated petty bourgeois tinkering in their workshops who were able to implement the new engineering and financing that would remake the world. They were prompted to do so by being rebuffed in their attempts to join in the pleasures of the romantic world, as Alberich's advances toward the Rhinedaughters are ridiculed.

Alberich has *stolen* the Rheingold. The key to interpretation of this action is in the French socialist Proudhon's 1840 book, *What Is Property?* Proudhon answered his own question on the first page with the famous aphorism, "Property is theft." According to Wagner biographer Gregor-Dellin,

> During the year just ended, 1840, in which Wagner had experienced the total dependence of the penniless artist on the affluent, Pierre-Joseph Proudhon's *Qu'est-ce que la Propriété?* had been published in Paris. Wagner first became acquainted with Proudhon's basic principle — that property connotes theft — through Samuel Lehrs, who always had his finger on the literary pulse. He found it so thought-provoking that he never forgot the author's name; but he had no gift for the patient, painstaking assimilation of economic, scientific, and political theories. Most of what he retained consisted of slogans — conclusions devoid of reasoned argument [104–05].

If Wagner lacked the patience for economic analysis, he showed infinite patience in crafting a musical-dramatic portrayal around Proudhon's seminal slogan. Thanks to multiple references Wagner makes in his own writings and in utterances reported by acquaintances, we know that Proudhon's book impressed him; in his autobiography he recalls taking it "in a spirit that afforded me singularly rich consolation for my position" (*My Life*, 420). Sandra Corse in *Wagner and the New Consciousness* likewise finds Alberich's theft of the gold to be a dramatization of the Proudhonian principle, and she extends this interpretation to include Valhalla:

> Wagner was perhaps influenced by Proudhon's slogan, "Property is robbery," which he called the "signal of revolutions." The ring obviously symbolizes property as theft — Alberich steals the gold from the Rhinedaughters and Wotan steals it in turn from Alberich. But the musical connection between the ring and Valhalla reminds us that Valhalla too is property — and Wotan intends, in fact, to steal it from the giants by robbing them of payment for their labor [83].

The institution of private property became for Wagner the root of all evil in the world, and he tended to shape his perception of history, fading back into ancient myth, around it.

Scene two of *Rheingold* rises to aristocratic heights, where the gods dwell and Valhalla, their castle, has just been completed. Wagner managed to avoid the basic mistake of bourgeois ideologists that Marx and Engels had criticized in *The Holy Family* in 1844:

> As it separates thinking from feeling and the soul from the body, so also does it separate history from natural science and industry, and regards the birthplace of history as being in the hazy cloud formations of heaven rather than in the raw, material production on earth [Quoted in Mehring 100].

No, he was careful to start the *Ring* cycle with the material transformation of nature, only then shifting to "the hazy cloud formations of heaven" to show how the gods dealt with the consequences of material developments down below. Wotan, awakened to face the question of how to pay for Valhalla, looks like a portrayal of Prussian King Friedrich-William IV who, as described by Marx and Engels, was awakened to "some stern and startling realities which interrupted his poetic dreams. Alas, that romanticism is not very quick at accounts..." (I, 312). On a deeper level, Wagner was conscious that the historical origin of mankind's belief in gods could be traced back to human authorities who in ancient times combined secular with religious roles and in more recent history claimed to rule with the grace of God. It is crucial to an understanding of the *Ring* to bear in mind Wagner's intellectual position, influenced by Feuerbach, that gods were created by men and religion utilized to back up political authority. That is why he could portray the European nobility in its dying days as troubled "gods" who seem "human, all-too-human" (to quote Wagner's onetime disciple Nietzsche).

If the dwarves represent the *petty* bourgeoisie, it follows that the giants are the *big* bourgeoisie: big builders, captains of industry and finance, established and prospering — often from government contracts. When the captains of industry attained the strength to build huge projects (Valhalla), the reigning nobility (the gods) would exploit their productive power yet avoid accepting them socially. This is the second case of social rejection in the opera, the first being the Rhinedaughters' ridicule of Alberich; it too has dire consequences. Wagner's giants are happy to work for the gods, but the price they demand is to be brought into godly society. The best way to get in is to marry in, and such is the contract that the giants have reached with Wotan. Wotan's wife Fricka, who reminds him that he has made an unacceptable bargain by agreeing to betroth to one of the giants her sister, the goddess Freia, epitomizes traditional values. It is Fricka who strives to keep society stable while Wotan intuits that unprecedented deeds are required in altered historical circumstances — much as Wagner must have felt when he joined in the 1848–49 revolution to his wife Minna's dismay. It is a shrewd bargain the giants have struck, because with Freia their kind will live on and inherit the earth while the gods will be fated to extinction without Freia's golden apples to keep them young and vigorous.

As the European nobility had to deal with bankers and industrialists to get cities and monuments built, so the gods in *Rheingold* deal with giants. However, when it comes to yielding their future as a ruling class to uncouth monsters, the price seems prohibitive. Instead of payment, deception and trickery are employed to make the builders believe they have been accepted by the nobility when in fact they are viewed as an inferior, uncultured breed. The once almighty god who upheld lofty principles stoops to base means to bolster his regime. Loge, Wotan's chief adviser, who is not of the gods but has made himself indispensable to them, is called upon to get them out of the predicament. Loge, who may represent the clergy or the bar, is supposed to be clever enough to fool the giants into taking something other than what they contracted for. We find out later, when he leads Wotan down to Nibelheim, that Loge is related to the lowly Alberich yet has attained a high-level position as adviser to the ruling elite. Both are parvenus striving to break out of the lower-middle class, each by his own strategy.

When the two giants thump onto the stage to claim their reward, they are dismayed to find that Wotan does not intend to honor the original contract. Although the giants modestly call themselves "dull-witted," Fasolt actually lectures the chief god on the importance of contract law in maintaining legitimate authority — the essence of the feudal system:

> What you are
> you are through contracts alone
> your power, mark me well,
> is bound by sworn agreements.
> Though you are wiser
> than we in our wits,
> you bound us freemen [*uns Freie*]
> to keep the peace....

The self-reference to "freemen" clearly places the giants in the European middle class. Fasolt is infatuated with Freia's beauty, while his cynical brother Fafner wants only to remove Freia's powers of rejuvenation from the gods. This reflects two attitudes prevalent among the industrialists of Europe: some longed to join the aristocracy, others wanted to sweep it out of the way. The god Donner ("thunder"), wielding a hammer that can spark lightning bolts, is held back by

Wotan when he begins to swing it at the giants. Wotan lays down the law by interposing his great spear on whose shaft are carved contracts and treaties. As ruler of the kingdom, he is bound to maintain law and order.

> Nothing by force!
> My spearshaft
> safeguards contracts:
> spare your hammer's haft.

Rulers like Wotan cannot allow dunderheads like Donner to use force arbitrarily, since that would undermine their legitimate authority. European feudalism was based on a contractual relationship in which rights and duties of lord and subject were written. Both parties were bound by contracts enforceable in the king's courts.

The giants have been anxiously viewing Alberich the dwarf as a potential competitor even before Alberich comes to Wotan's attention. Big capitalists are aware of the threat posed by ambitious entrepreneurs. When Loge reports Alberich's theft of the Rheingold, Wotan does not immediately see its relevance, but for Fasolt and Fafner it is disturbing news. Loge explains more about the gold, saying that "once it is forged to a rounded hoop, it helps to confer unending power and wins the world for its master," and now Wotan recalls that he too has heard of the gold. Suddenly this prize seems more attractive to the giants than what they originally bargained for, so they agree that the gods may keep Freia and pay them in Rheingold. True, the gods don't own the gold, but Loge advises Wotan how get it — "What a thief stole you steal from the thief."

The musical transition leading to Scene Three may be the first rendering of the industrial revolution into musical form. It is disturbing even to us who have grown up with a musical beat driven by technology and amplified to ear-splitting levels. As Wotan and Loge descend into the bowels of the earth, blacksmiths' hammers bang on anvils. That hammering is enlarged as if into machines pounding the rhythm when Wotan and Loge enter a noisy, smoky work site. Wagner designed the scene to suggest the coal-fired smog of the industrial zones that he detested. Cooke concludes that "it is clear that Wagner ... poured all his detestation of the evils of capitalism into the creation of Alberich, and particularly into the creation of Alberich's actions in the Nibelheim scene in *The Rheingold*— symbols which could speak so much more powerfully for him than his political prose" (*I Saw* 270–71).

Wotan and Loge find Alberich gloating over his new-found power derived from the ring and using it to enslave other dwarves. "The third scene of the opera, with Alberich wielding the master's whip and the helpless Nibelungs mining gold in the dark shafts of Nibelheim, is a somber, frightening picture, obviously an allegory of the slaves of capitalism, the sweated labor, and the foul working conditions that did exist in many a factory and mine" (Downes xi). One of the terrifying powers he has gained is the ability to make himself invisible. As Shaw interprets this, Alberich's workers "never see him, any more than the victims of our 'dangerous trades' ever see the shareholders whose power is nevertheless everywhere, driving them to destruction" (3–4). Particularly victimized is the skilled dwarf, Mime. At Alberich's command Mime has fashioned a magical helmet, the Tarnhelm, that lets its wearer change shape at will. Shaw has a clever interpretation of the Tarnhelm, likening it to the top hats worn by the bourgeois of the period: dignified dress that made ruthless capitalists appear respectable members of high society. Working conditions in Nibelheim are appalling. Craftsmen who used to find joy in labor have been turned into prisoners of the mines and factories under Alberich's relentless drive. Mime vividly describes the change in their lives from artisans to wage-slaves:

Carefree smiths,
we used to fashion
trinkets for our womenfolk,
delightful gems and
delicate Nibelung toys:
we cheerfully laughed at our pains.
Now the criminal makes us
crawl into crevices,
ever toiling
for him alone.
Through the gold of the ring
his greed can divine
where more gleaming veins
lie buried in shafts:
there we must seek
and search and dig,
smelting the spoils
and working the cast
without rest or repose,
to heap up the hoard for our lord.

"To heap up the hoard" is what the Marxists call "capitalist accumulation." Transformation of the economy from craft to mass production was a wrenching social change in Europe. Not being first to industrialize, the Germans were faced with the task of catching up, not only economically but also socially and politically. As Thorstein Veblen explains:

> In industrial matters Germany was still at the handicraft stage.... Measured by the rate of progression that had brought the English community to the point where it then stood, the German industrial system was some two and a half or three centuries in arrears — somewhere in Elizabethan times; its political system was even more archaic; and use and wont governing social relations in detail [were] of a character such as this economic and political situation would necessarily foster [64–66].

A process that took a couple of centuries in Britain, the world's industrial pioneer, was compressed into a couple of generations in Germany, and into a couple of hours in *Rheingold*.

Alberich is tricked by Loge's flattery and captured. Up on the aristocratic heights, he is informed that his hoard, including the Tarnhelm, is the ransom for release. When Wotan demands the ring too, Alberich is crushed. He tries to resist, but Wotan "seizes Alberich and tears the ring from his finger with terrible force" (stage directions). As soon as Alberich is set free he pronounces a vengeful curse:

Each man shall covet
its acquisition,
but none shall enjoy
it to lasting gain;
its lord shall guard it without any profit,
and yet it shall draw down his bane upon him.
Doomed to die,
may the coward be fettered by fear;
as long as he lives,
let him pine away, languishing,
lord of the ring
as the slave of the ring:
till the stolen circlet
I hold in my hand once again!

This is the curse of capitalism, where everyone is subordinated to the endless quest for profit — most of all the capitalists themselves.

When the giants demand not only the gold and Tarnhelm to redeem Freia, but also the ring that Wotan has come to treasure, Wotan is stubbornly unyielding, until a new figure appears out of the ground: Erda, the earth mother, who counsels him to yield up the ring:

> All things that are — end.
> A day of darkness dawns for the gods:
> I counsel you: shun the ring!

She refuses Wotan's entreaties to explain more, and disappears back into the ground. The all-knowing Erda represents the earthy wisdom of the agricultural society on which the feudal civilization of the nobility was based, a society in which status came primarily with land ownership. Erda symbolizes a land-based value system in its last stage. Eventually Wotan will come to realize that he and the Gods must follow the course of history. The real drama of the *Ring* cycle comes from the developing *consciousness* of its main characters; the events take place almost inevitably given the limitations of the characters' understanding at each stage.

As soon as the giants have the ring, the curse claims its first victim. The two Giants quarrel over division of the loot; Fafner in a fit of rage slays his brother Fasolt and with no apparent regrets gathers up the hoard. Big businessmen, while they may have fraternal relations and cooperate on major projects, are locked in deadly competition. The more ruthless (Fafner) drive out the more tender (Fasolt). Alberich's curse will resound through the cycle, leaving death and destruction.

In the triumphant yet foreboding conclusion to *Das Rheingold* the Gods parade into Valhalla across a rainbow bridge, while the Rhinedaughters below wail over the loss of their treasure: Nature has been violated. Only Loge is able to sense that the gods are headed for disaster, but after some equivocation he seems to go along. At this stage of the drama Loge is the character with the best grasp of the course of events, made possible no doubt by his position suspended between ruling and subordinate classes. But Loge does not come on stage again in the *Ring*; only his fire will be invoked. Other characters have to learn through bitter experience.

Die Walküre

The storm music opening Act One of *Die Walküre* is derived from the "spear motif." As Wotan's spear stands for the rule of law and sanctity of contract, it follows that the storm out of which Siegmund emerges seeking shelter is a breakdown of law and order and he a fugitive. Cooke has pointed out that Siegmund being an outlaw, his motif is opposite that of Wotan's spear (*An Introduction*). Siegmund is an exhausted radical agitator escaping after a defeat at the hands of his class enemies — the way Wagner had to flee to avoid a possible death sentence after his part in the abortive 1849 revolution in Dresden. Siegmund collapses at the home of master Hunding, whose domain is comparable to another state, where Hunding represents the ruler and his wife Sieglinde the oppressed subject. Unhappy Sieglinde shows immediate sympathy for Siegmund, drawn to him by an irresistible attraction. Hunding, returning home, is suspicious of the uninvited guest and struck by a family resemblance to his wife; he inquires as to the visitor's identity. Siegmund calls himself "Wehwalt":

> Friedmund I may not call myself;
> Frohwalt fain would I be:
> but Wehwalt I must name myself.

The root of his name cannot be peace or joy, but woe. From a musical motif (the Valhalla theme) listeners know what Siegmund does not — he is a child of Wotan, a product of one of that god's earthly escapades. The not-unusual phenomenon of aristocrats producing illegitimate children through liaisons with humble women (maidservants, peasant girls, etc.) and then abandoning the kids reflects an autobiographical element, for Wagner believed that his mother, Johanna, was actually an illegitimate daughter of a prince.

Hunding identifies Siegmund as the enemy of his kin, and dictates that the next morning Siegmund must fight him to the death. That night Sieglinde, having given Hunding a sleeping draught, returns to Siegmund and shows him a sword buried deep in a tree standing in the house. Siegmund has been promised a powerful weapon in his hour of need by his father. In fact, the music recalls that it was Wotan who, in disguise, plunged the sword into the tree. The sword that Siegmund names "Nothung" (Needful) represents the force needed to prevail in a crisis. Wagner said in his autobiography that by 1848 he "had arrived at the conclusion that in matters concerning the people there was no point in relying on reason or wisdom, but rather solely on the real power to act, such as is aroused only by enthusiasm or the dictates of necessity" (363). The concept of *Not* [or *Noth*] is expanded in Wagner's *Art-Work of the Future* where, according to Boucher, it signifies the distress or need felt instinctively by the people: "But that word distress must be understood in the dual meaning it has in German: *die Not* — both distress and necessity" (Boucher 46).

Thus the world-shaking significance of the drama in Hunding's hut, where Siegmund and Sieglinde realize they must be long-lost brother and sister, the Walsung twins. Once she states his real name, Siegmund pulls out the sword with a mighty motion. Viewing the *Ring* as a story of *political* "adultery" and "incest" makes the Walsungs' behavior forgivable: The revolutionary agitator, persecuted in one country, seeks refuge in another land where the people are likewise oppressed. That the proletariat of all nations are brothers (and sisters) was the most subversive idea in Europe. That they should get together — "Workers of the world, unite!" — across national boundaries instead of patriotically supporting their respective rulers (the Hundings), was an intolerable threat to the traditional order.

In Act Two, Wotan is armed with his spear, and Brünnhilde — his favorite Valkyrie daughter — is in battle dress. Brünnhilde sings the Valkyrie war cry, joyous at the prospect of carrying out Wotan's will, to take Siegmund's side in his hour of need in the fight against Hunding. The name Valkyrie (*Walküre*) meant "chooser of the slain-in-battle." Valkyries are agents from on high who carry mortal heroes from the battlefield to the gods' domain, Valhalla. In political allegory Valkyries represent the ability of the ruling class to intervene in society and control social mobility. The power of the rulers to co-opt selectively capable members of the lower classes into the aristocracy was essential to maintain hegemony. Feudal societies had honors such as knighthood for commoners of exceptional achievement, often achievement in war. Co-opting heroes from below not only invigorates the ruling class; equally important, it also deprives the lower orders of leadership. However, to intervene on the side of an outlaw who committed political "adultery" and "incest," in disregard of the expected loyalty to local rulers, would be far beyond accepted practice. In no European country did anyone have knighthood bestowed on him for valor in a revolutionary insurrection!

Thus Fricka storms onto the scene and reproaches Wotan for failing to maintain standards of godly decency. She insists that unless Siegmund and Sieglinde are punished, the gods' claim to moral superiority will be worthless; their regime will be undermined. Wotan, the monarch, is forced to concede. Sadly he promises to reverse his judgment, take away the magic of Siegmund's sword, let Hunding win. In the domestic quarrel between Fricka and Wotan, Fricka reminds him that "No nobleman battles with bondsmen," one of the rare places where the analogy is made explicit in the libretto: Gods are likened to human beings of the noble class.

Brünnhilde comes back to confirm her marching orders and is stunned by the sudden reversal. Wotan pours out his heart to her, explaining events back to Alberich's theft of the gold. Audiences who are bored by Wotan's long monologues and tend to doze off until the action picks up again are missing an important history lesson, told from Wotan's viewpoint. The conclusion is that only Alberich, who has renounced love and made the ring, is a real threat to the regime. The emerging bourgeoisie can mobilize the power of capital to attract forces away from the ruling class. That is the outcome Wotan fears most of all for his world, because it is what Wagner, following Proudhon, feared was happening in the European world.

Fafner, having become a dragon sitting on the gold and not wielding the ring aggressively, is not an immediate threat. Still, Wotan would be constrained from taking back the ring from him, as it was given by formal contract: To violate a lawful agreement would call into question the gods' ostensible basis of authority. There is, however, one slim hope. A free agent, operating outside the legal order, could liberate the ring from Fafner. Potentially the hero Siegmund could accomplish this task; but the paradox is that Wotan must now let Siegmund (who, Fricka argued, is not really free) be destroyed in order to preserve the traditional order. In Wotan's unsolvable dilemma Wagner has portrayed the agony of Europe's aristocrats watching helplessly as their world crumbles. They are incapable of establishing a new order based on modern rationality — they cannot "renounce love" in favor of economic rationality, nor can they repudiate the feudal order — yet they covet the benefits of an advancing economy, make deals with industrialists (giants), and try to block threatening entrepreneurs (dwarves). Wotan, once the mighty emperor, is a constrained observer of events, increasingly so as the *Ring* cycle progresses. Wotan finally relates that Alberich has engendered a son who portends the doom of the Gods. Though not named yet, the son is going to be Hagen, who will carry on Alberich's campaign in *Götterdämmerung*. The whole tragedy of the vulgar materialistic class inheriting the world has been forecast.

Brünnhilde shows the youthful idealism that can occur among those in the upper classes. In a pre-revolutionary situation, some radical sons and daughters of the privileged break with their class and go over to the progressive side. Because of her development towards wisdom as the *Ring* cycle advances, Brünnhilde cannot be assigned a simple political significance, however. Following our hypothesis that the female roles in the *Ring* refer to cultural principles, a working hypothesis about Brünnhilde is that she represents the best legacy of the nobility, the high art that the people should inherit from the old order. That would include Wagner's revolutionary art, especially the *Ring*, which he wrote for the masses and, he thought for a long time, could only be staged after a revolution. Avant-garde artists breaking with the ruling class are an indicator of revolutionary times.

Wotan senses Brünnhilde's potential for rebellion and warns her strictly. In a crucial turning point, Brünnhilde will turn against Wotan's command — against the values of Fricka — and forfeit her godhood and privileges as a member of the ruling elite. Yet she will feel that she has done right — what Wotan deep in his heart would have liked to do — and Wotan will comprehend her action although he cannot condone it. Overcome with sympathy, Brünnhilde makes the choice to protect Siegmund; but Wotan himself intervenes and breaks Siegmund's sword on the mighty spear that signifies legal authority. What happened in European history was that the full force of the state was brought down to prevent masses from arming themselves and owning the field — Wagner's reason to flee Dresden. Hunding then finishes off the disarmed Siegmund, and Wotan in a rage slays Hunding with one motion and turns to look for Brünnhilde, who has fled with Sieglinde.

Die Walküre, Seattle Opera: Jane Eaglen as Brünnhilde. (Photograph: Chris Bennion)

Die Walküre, Bavarian State Opera: John Tomlinson as Wotan, Majana Lipovsek as Fricka. (Photograph: Wilfried Hösl).

The third act takes us up to a rocky height where the Valkyries are gathering fallen heroes before taking them on to Valhalla. In political terms, these "heroes" are failed revolutionary leaders who are to be co-opted into the ruling circles after their radical fervor is burned out, and Wagner has a bit of fun with them. When one Valkyrie asks another which slain hero she has hanging from her saddle, the second answers "Sintolt the Hegeling," surely a playful allusion to the intellectual tendency that formed one of the main streams of German radical politics, "Young Hegelians." The other Valkyrie in this vignette carries "Wittig the Irming," a reference which is more obscure — perhaps the "Wittig" who was editor of the radical paper *Dresdener Zeitung.* In any case, Wittig represents another faction among the disputatious revolutionaries; as one Valkyrie says, "Only as foes saw I Sintolt and Wittig." Ironically, the rivals are both being co-opted into the establishment.

Brünnhilde arrives at last, and to her sisters' surprise is bearing not a slain hero but a woman still alive. Without Siegmund, Sieglinde wants only to die, but Brünnhilde convinces her she must escape into the forest, bear the child in her womb, name him "Siegfried," and give him the shattered sword that belonged to his father Siegmund: preserving the revolutionary heritage in a time of repression. With Wotan approaching in stormy wrath, Sieglinde is sent to the eastern forest which Wotan shuns, where Fafner guards the hoard. In Europe, political refugees escaped to other countries seeking asylum, as Wagner fled from the German state of Saxony after the 1849 uprising. Wotan decrees Brünnhilde's punishment, terrifying the Valkyries: she shall be cast out of godly society, made a mere mortal, and put to sleep on the mountain; the man who finds her may take her as wife. Brünnhilde will be turned into a common housewife, a cruel fate indeed. The other Valkyries plead with Wotan to reconsider his harsh sentence, but he chases them off. Then in a touching scene his anger gradually melts under his daughter's entreaties. Brünnhilde explains that she could not but take

Die Walküre, **Act III, Seattle Opera. (Photograph: Chris Bennion)**

pity on Siegmund and in so doing was really carrying out Wotan's inner will. In their extended dialogue the severe, lonely role of the monarch is laid bare. While Wotan cannot retract her banishment, he does grant her one urgent request: let her sleeping place be surrounded with fierce fire so that the man who comes to possess her can be only the bravest hero. Shaw's interpretation of the magic fire is one of his cleverest: "the fires of hell," religious intimidation used by governing classes to keep ordinary people in line. Such fires are threatening only to those who fear them. If Brünnhilde represents the cultural legacy of noble society that would be inherited by the victorious proletariat if all went well in a changing Europe, that culture was surrounded by the religious intimidation of the church: it was for the initiated alone. And if the magic fire represents religion as Shaw suggests, then Loge, who lights it at Wotan's command, could be seen as the high priest of a church that has been brought under state control. Church and state are united to control the population; only a heroic rebel not intimidated by the state or religion (who does not know fear) can break through.

In the next opera Siegfried, who embodies the hopes of the people for a better future (and the hopes of Wagner for a new art not confined in the church but for all the *Volk*), has moments of triumph. In the end, as the "Twilight of the Gods" approaches, the course of events departs from the hopes of the young Wagner and other progressives of his generation. It is not so much that Wagner "changed his mind" as Shaw would have it, youthful radicalism giving way to middle-aged moderation, but rather that he portrayed what was actually happening. High culture was expiring, pushed out by the vulgar; the masses were drawn to mediocrity; idealistic leaders were either co-opted or destroyed; successive revolutions were put down.

Siegfried

Siegfried is a man without a country, a free spirit who recognizes no borders or social constraints. Sieglinde gave birth to him in a great forest and died in the process. Mime, the crafty Nibelung dwarf, found her there, assisted at the birth and undertook to raise him. The child grew to be an unruly youth of formidable strength who wandered in the forest and played with wild animals. If dwarves represent petty bourgeois, and if the character Mime is (as some writers allege) an attempt at a Jewish caricature, then Wagner's symbolism is at least consistent, European Jews typically being lower-middle class artisans, merchants, and such. In any case, Mime is portrayed as a slightly sympathetic and humorous, but calculating and grasping character. Mime raises Siegfried with dedication for the ultimate purpose of getting hold of the treasure and ring for himself by using the lad's strength to kill Fafner. When the opera opens, Mime is hammering away, trying in vain to forge a sword strong enough for Siegfried to use without shattering it. This sword symbolizes the revolutionary force that Siegfried the proletarian can wield to slay the big capitalist, Fafner the giant-turned-dragon. However, the petty bourgeois Mime is incapable of forging the sword of revolution. When Siegfried comes home leading a large bear that terrifies Mime, he says he brought the bear home "to ask you, you scoundrel, about the sword." Wagner perhaps had in mind Bakunin, his Anarchist accomplice in the violent revolution of 1849, whose picture in Gutman's biography of Wagner is captioned "A great bearish itinerant revolutionary, Bakunin cast a powerful spell over Wagner with his inflammatory harangues on the glories of popular revolution" (133). Interpreting Siegfried's bear as the Russian "bear" Bakunin is more precise than Shaw's attempt to depict Siegfried as a Bakunin type. As observed by Wagner, Bakunin's role in events leading up to the Dresden insurrection was precisely to ask where was the sword *Nothung*— the needed revolutionary force (Gregor-Dellin 171–72).

Another autobiographical aspect is found in the quest for knowledge about parents lost in early childhood. Siegfried's persistent questioning eventually brings out the fact that Mime is not his real "father and mother," a claim he always doubted. Mime reluctantly tells the story about Sieglinde, and to prove it takes out the sword fragments. In political terms it is the revolutionary legacy of the masses, gained through costly defeats. Siegfried is excited by the prospect of obtaining the true sword and demands that Mime reforge it immediately. As Mime faces the task of which he is by nature incapable (a petty bourgeois instigator cannot forge the weapon of class struggle for the masses; they must do it for themselves), Siegfried goes off and a stranger drops in.

The awesome stranger is Wotan, in disguise as a Wanderer. He claims to offer wisdom in exchange for hospitality, but Mime is leery. The Wanderer proposes a question-and-answer contest and says he will answer any three questions. To an audience unaware of the political significance, this may seem a trivial game. In fact, it is a deadly serious political discussion of the type Wagner could have heard in the coffeehouses of Leipzig or Dresden. The discussion focuses on the proper analysis of social classes and sources of political change. Mime's three questions refer to the major social classes but are unimaginative, calling for stock answers. First he asks, "What is the race that trades in the depth of the earth?" In other words, who make up the lower orders? The Wanderer answers that it is the Nibelungs, and reviews how Alberich used the ring to dominate the "toiling people." Next Mime asks what race dwells on the earth's surface, and the Wanderer replies that it is the giants, telling how Fafner ended up guarding the hoard. This explains the affluent middle class, the capitalists. Finally Mime asks, "What is the race that dwells on cloud-covered heights?" That is, who composes the upper class, half-hidden from the masses? The obvious answer is that "gods" dwell there, and

Siegfried, Saxon State Opera: Jukka Rasilainen as the Wanderer. (Photograph: Matthias Creutziger)

Wotan is their ruler. Whoever holds his spear (state power) governs the world, the Wanderer explains. Mime's questions were routine academic ones — typical of a petty bourgeois intellectual.

When it is the Wanderer's turn, his first question is "What is the race which Wotan acted badly towards and yet which is dearest of all to him?" Mime carefully answers that it must be the Walsungs. Then the Wanderer asks the name of the sword Siegfried must use to kill Fafner and gain the ring. Mime responds, correctly, that it is "Nothung" and shows that he knows its history and significance. The third question, however, stumps Mime: "Who do you think will forge Nothung, the sword, out of these mighty fragments?" Mime, most skillful smithy, who has been heating and hammering the fragments of the sword over and over, cannot imagine who else could do it. Bourgeois leaders could not admit that anyone but themselves could equip and direct the masses toward revolution. Claiming Mime's head as prize (a sentence to be carried out later), the Wanderer tells Mime the correct answer: "Only he who never knew fear will forge the sword anew," and departs.

Siegfried returns and is exasperated to find that Mime still has not forged the sword. Mime realizes that he has forgotten to teach Siegfried the meaning of fear, and tries hopelessly to explain it, but still fails to make the connection that it is the fearless one who must forge the sword; he admits only that "no dwarf's resources can master the stubborn spell." Siegfried, having lost all trust in Mime's ability, grabs the fragments and decisively begins to forge the sword himself using more radical methods. Each generation has to relearn its revolutionary heritage through practice, not just theory. The reforging of the sword is an allusion to the uniting of revolutionary forces, unity being the source of strength.

As Act Two opens, Alberich is keeping a jealous watch outside Fafner's cave. Wotan, still disguised as the Wanderer, approaches but Alberich recognizes him as the chief god. "I came to watch and not to act," Wotan assures the dwarf. Alberich knows that Wotan dare not take back the treasure and ring from Fafner by force, for that would mean breaking the bond made with the giants. Were the ruling class to repudiate the sanctity of contract, the basis for law and order would disintegrate. By the time Mime brings Siegfried to the entrance of Fafner's lair, Siegfried is ready to declare independence from his foster parent. The proletarian has been educated and goaded to the point of action, but now must act on his own. In "the final conflict" (to quote from the *Internationale*) petty bourgeois allies will be of no help. Mime, getting out of the way, mutters to himself,

> Fafner and Siegfried —
> Siegfried and Fafner —
> if only each might kill the other!

Not intimidated by the dragon's threats, Siegfried slays him with a stab to the heart. But why is Fafner, former giant, now a dragon? L. J. Rather finds that Siegfried slaying the dragon stems from Proudhon, just as Alberich's theft of the Rheingold dramatizes Proudhon's "Property is theft" (*Reading Wagner*, 249). A key element is Proudhon's notion that the proletarian through confrontation with the beast would understand the mystery. The slaying of Fafner begins a rapid enlightenment for Siegfried. First, the dying dragon fills in what has happened, including how the giants got the cursed gold from the gods, brother slew brother, and Fafner "the last of the giants" (monopoly capitalism, the final stage of capitalism), turned into a dragon guarding the treasure. But the greatest enlightenment is yet to come, for as Siegfried tastes the dragon's blood, the singing of a forest bird becomes intelligible to him. The bird expresses the laws of Nature (society), always there but never well understood until revolutionary action makes them comprehensible. Wagner has dramatized the axiom that the masses

Siegfried, **Metropolitan Opera: Siegfried Jerusalem as Siegfried. (Photograph: Winnie Klotz)**

attain wisdom through experience. Bolshevik cultural leader Anatoly V. Lunacharsky was astute enough to penetrate Wagner's symbolism and wrote that Siegfried "had discovered the key to the 'bird's songs,' the prophetic songs of the laws of social order and the means of reviving life" (348).

The contrast between Siegfried's indifference to the treasures and the two Nibelungs' greedy desperation to acquire them could not be sharper, dramatically or musically. Alberich

Siegfried, Act I, Bavarian State Opera. (Photograph: Wilfried Hösl)

and Mime dispute who will take over the prizes Siegfried has won but is presumably too naïve to keep. Neither wins the argument; Alberich leaves, and Mime schemes to take the loot. The Forest Bird, however, warns Siegfried to "not trust the treacherous Mime" and tells him that "the rogue's hypocritical words" will no longer fool him because Siegfried will "be able to understand what Mime means in his heart." After that, Mime's efforts to drug and dispatch Siegfried are transparent, and Siegfried in disgust finally strikes Mime dead. Instigators of revolution are often destroyed by the forces they set in motion. Siegfried is alone, but now he has another guide. Siegfried asks the Forest Bird where he can find a friend, and the bird's song gives him great hope: a glorious bride sleeps on a mountaintop. Siegfried jumps up in exultation and, confirming with the bird that he, who hasn't learned fear, will be able to pass through the fire, heads for Brünnhilde's rock. Brünnhilde asleep on the mountain represents the legacy of the aristocracy, dormant as that class lost vigor yet the heritage of civilization that must pass on to those who will lead the next stage of history. The fire, again in Shaw's interpretation, symbolizes "fires of Hell" or religious mystification that made this culture inaccessible to common people. Now the untutored Siegfried will break through superstition and find true wisdom, no longer godly but in the form of a humanized Brünnhilde.

In the debunking of religion Wagner was deeply influenced by the philosopher Ludwig

Siegfried, **Act I, Bavarian State Opera: Stig Anderson as Siegfried. (Photograph: Wilfried Hösl)**

Feuerbach. It must be from the name Feuerbach (literally "fire-brook" or "stream of fire") that Wagner settled on the magic fire to protect the heroine. Marx had made the name-association in an 1842 essay where he advised theologians and philosophers:

> Free yourselves from the concepts and prepossessions of existing speculative philosophy if you want to get at things differently, as they are, that is to say, if you want to arrive at the *truth*. And there is no other road for you to *truth* and *freedom* except that leading *through* the stream of fire [the *Feuer-bach*]. Feuerbach is the *purgatory* of the present times [Hanfi 41–42].

This connotation spread in leftist circles and likely was picked up by Wagner's ears, alert to dramatic images. If from no one else, Wagner could have heard it from Bakunin, who worked with Marx before 1849. Gregor-Dellin calls Feuerbach "the author who, after Proudhon, most decisively influenced the basic idea of the *Ring*" (110). Finally, the name-association adds credence to Shaw's "fires of Hell" interpretation.

Wotan's spear, symbol of authority, is about to be broken — a historical turning point. At the opening of Act Three, Wotan (still wielding his legal weapon) calls upon Erda to awaken. The last gasp of the feudal agricultural society, Erda now is a fading apparition who can hardly stay awake; yet Wotan still hopes to find in her a fount of knowledge. Erda expresses incomprehension of Wotan's plight and falls back into sleep, leaving the god to use his own judgment. Apart from Brünnhilde's enlightenment at the end of the cycle, Wotan is the only character who comes close to grasping the course of history. He is in a position to observe nearly everything, although the loss of one eye shows his limited perspective. Wotan becomes a tragic figure by trying to intervene and control events which have their own inexorable logic. A noble monarch who resorts to base means in a vain attempt to avert disaster, he has the consciousness of a ruling class that realizes its time is up but cannot relinquish its role easily.

Wotan finds psychological comfort only by accepting the inevitable as his own will. He hopes to turn over his realm not to grasping materialists like Alberich, but to an uncorrupted hero, Siegfried, "free from greed."

After breaking Wotan's spear, triumphant Siegfried marches through the fire to awaken Brünnhilde and claim her as bride. The bold hero who could not be taught the meaning of fear by Mime, by Fafner, even by Wotan, now stands in awe of Brünnhilde. The love duet between Siegfried and Brünnhilde, beautiful in musical rendition, gains even more from allusions to the daunting educational project the two face. The proletarian introduced to the heritage of civilization is at first confused, and so is the bearer of culture encountering her new master. Brünnhilde at one point says, "My senses grow clouded, my knowledge falls silent: is my wisdom to forsake me now?" Through their extended duet, Brünnhilde expresses fears and doubts of the consequences, for both of them, of their impending union. In the end she succumbs, repudiating her aristocratic past and celebrating the end of an era. For the climactic love duet, Porges reports, Wagner's performance instructions were, "At the beginning of their final, heroic hymn of praise the lovers should not be looking at each other: 'they are addressing the whole world'" (114). Many performances do follow this convention, having the hero and heroine put some distance between them, face the audience and sing out to the world.

Götterdämmerung

In the foreboding Prologue of the final opera in the *Ring*, three Norns are trying to spin out theoretical strands to explain events unprecedented in world history. In stage directions they are described as "tall female figures in long, dark veil-like garments." Some believe that they represent scholars, and that an idea for an avant-garde production would be to dress them in academic caps and gowns and set this scene on a college campus. The scholar-Norns are experiencing more and more difficulty. Looking for places to attach their rope, they bemoan the fact that the World Ash Tree has been destroyed, a process traced far back to the time when Wotan broke off a branch to make a spear; upon its shaft he carved laws and treaties, and he held it to rule the world. Ages later, after that spear was shattered by the hero Siegfried, Wotan ordered the World Ash chopped up and stacked like kindling around Valhalla. When they try to incorporate into their discourse Alberich's theft of the gold and all the consequences, their ropes slip, fray, and finally snap. The three Norns cry out at the fragments of rope and resign themselves:

> An end to eternal wisdom!
> Wise women no longer
> tell the world their tidings.

Bernard Shaw's theoretical threads likewise snapped at this juncture. He states that "the ultimate catastrophe of the Saga cannot by any perversion of ingenuity be adapted to the perfectly clear allegorical design of *The Rhein Gold*, *The Valkyrie*, and *Siegfried*," and concludes that "at the point where *The Ring* changes from music drama into opera, it also ceases to be philosophic and becomes didactic.... In the didactic part the philosophy degenerates into the prescription of a romantic nostrum for all human ills" (48, 56). Yet Shaw was never comfortable with this interpretation. In a later edition of *The Perfect Wagnerite* he added a chapter, "Why He Changed His Mind," which tried to use historical changes between Wagner's conception of the *Ring* during the 1848–49 revolution and its first staging in 1876 to justify the composer's supposed philosophical change. By that time, wrote Shaw, "the Siegfrieds of 1848 were hopeless political failures, whereas the Wotans and Alberics and Lokis were conspicuous political successes.... To put it in terms of Wagner's allegory, Alberic had got the ring back again, and was marrying into the best Valhalla families with it" (79–80). Shaw went off the track; Wagner carried the political allegory through to the end.

The sun rises and the heroic figures of Brünnhilde and Siegfried come onto the stage. The audience is reassured as the two recount their deeds of glory with familiar musical motifs. But the Norns' gloom can not be ignored: the situation is not the same in the world. Hero and heroine reaffirm their love and unity of purpose, but there are different nuances, unlike the heady hopefulness at the close of *Siegfried*. Brünnhilde realizes that Siegfried must go on to perform heroic deeds on his own, and regrets that she has little more to offer him:

> What gods have taught me
> I gave to you:
> a bountiful store
> of hallowed runes;
> but the maidenly source
> of all my strength
> was taken away by the hero
> to whom I now bow my head.
> Bereft of wisdom
> but filled with desire;
> rich in love
> yet void of strength,
> I beg you not to despise
> the poor woman
> who grudges you naught
> but can give you no more!

Götterdämmerung, Kirov Opera: Olga Sergeyeva as Brünnhilde, Sergei Lyadov as Siegfried. (Photograph: Natasha Razina)

It might seem strange for a daughter of the chief God to feel unworthy of a husband raised in the woods and a smithy's cave; but the passage makes sense. Brünnhilde has offered venerable wisdom to the proletarian Siegfried — although she now doubts its worth. Her enthusiastic student has learned much since slaying the capitalist dragon, but his capacity to absorb traditional wisdom is limited by the need to create new norms for new situations. While her heritage is lofty and distinguished, in the end it is too elusive for a plebian to grasp and not fully relevant to his new world. That is why Brünnhilde is about to lose Siegfried despite his protestations of loyalty.

The society Siegfried now enters and the characters he meets are new to the *Ring* but not entirely unfamiliar. The Hall of the Gibichungs is populated by descendants of Alberich's type, now grown too big to be portrayed as dwarves: the next generation of the (formerly petty) bourgeoisie, wealthy and with pretensions of being pillars of society. Gunther is master of the hall, but his half-brother Hagen is the clever one, as Gunther readily admits. Hagen is none other than the son of Alberich. Neither is satisfied with his current status. Gunther wants to marry well to solidify his position as a nouveau riche, and Hagen shrewdly suggests the availability of Brünnhilde, who throughout the *Ring* cycle has offered upward social mobility. From the perspective of a Gibichung, Brünnhilde — although cast out of the godly realm — is the noblest (*herrlichste*) wife one could aspire to. However, Hagen cautions, not being a hero like Siegfried, Gunther is incapable of passing through the fire to her lofty abode. At the same time, Gunther's sister — the glittering Gutrune — needs a suitable husband, and mention of Siegfried arouses her interest. His feat in capturing the Nibelung treasure and his prospects for ruling the world with it make him eminently eligible. Hagen hatches an intricate plot by which Siegfried will be tricked into falling for Gutrune and delivering Brünnhilde to Gunther. The method involves giving Siegfried a magical potion to disorient him. Drugs (especially liquor, the bane of the working class) will help, but the fact that Siegfried is susceptible to such manipulation is the important lesson. Although the European masses had tested their political strength, they were distracted from revolutionary goals by the materialistic lures of bourgeois society. If Brünnhilde symbolizes the best heritage of aristocratic culture offered to the masses, then Gutrune exemplifies the vulgar culture of the new rich taking over European cities in Wagner's time. In our day, Gutrune would be shopping malls, television commercials and Hollywood movies — manifestations of materialism that divert citizens from "higher" cultural pursuits. Siegfried arrives at the Gibichung hall, gulps down the potion, and falls into the trap. Under Hagen's approving gaze he seals a blood-brotherhood oath with Gunther. The powerful proletariat has been won over to an alliance with the new capitalists, and the consequences will be far-reaching. Indeed, it is portrayal of these results that was Wagner's main purpose in writing the *Ring* cycle. Wagner foresaw the tragic outcome but had to protest. If only there were a way to stop the inexorable course of history driven by lust for wealth and power!— that is the central message of the *Ring*.

Siegfried, disguised by the Tarnhelm, follows the plot agreed to with the Gibichungs and claims Brünnhilde in the name of Gunther. Brünnhilde's shock at the image of Gunther expresses the outrage Wagner felt as he saw the vulgar bourgeoisie usurping arts that had been the province of aristocracy. It would have been all right if the uncorrupted *Volk*— Siegfried before swallowing the potion — could have been educated to assume the role of cultural leaders. Such a historical outcome was what he had counted on to make possible the new theater where he could properly stage his dramas for the people. But the innocent masses were corrupted by materialistic values and tricked into yielding leadership to the rising business class. When Siegfried returns to the hall, he has already handed Brünnhilde over to Gunther and claims Gutrune as wife. Hagen prepares the final stages of the conspiracy: an ostentatious double wedding, ultimate betrayal of Siegfried, and capture of the ring. As part of the wedding ritual Hagen calls for animals to be slain on the altars of the gods Wotan, Froh, Donner and Fricka, so that the gods will bless the marriages. As the commercial class gained hegemony and married upward, it utilized traditional rituals to legitimize its status.

Dragged to the double wedding ceremony, Brünnhilde doubts her own sanity until she spots upon Siegfried's finger the very ring that "Gunther" seized the night before. It is clear that terrible deceit has been perpetrated, and Hagen slyly suggests that he can help her get revenge. He pumps her for any hint of a weakness in Siegfried, and she lets out that the hero is vulnerable only from the back. The proletariat cannot be defeated in a straight-on battle, least of all by weak and cowardly bourgeois forces; it can be destroyed only by being stabbed in the back by its supposed friends. Gunther, from the respectable section of the business class, regrets that Siegfried has to be murdered but goes along. Hagen, a gangster with no scruples, will do the dirty work. In Act Three during a hunting trip organized by Hagen, Siegfried is temporarily separated from the party and encounters the Rhinedaughters at riverside. They warn him that he will die this day unless he throws the ring back in the water, but he does not take them seriously. The hunting party stops to rest, and Siegfried offers to tell his life story, from childhood with Mime to the victory over the dragon-giant Fafner and the march through the flames to Brünnhilde. After Hagen pours him a second potion that counteracts the first, Siegfried reverts to the truth and relates his loving meeting with Brünnhilde. At the moment of revelation, Hagen plunges a spear into Siegfried's back. Dying, Siegfried has visions of the true Brünnhilde once more. Historically, the masses realize they have made a fatal mistake only when it is too late. Soon Alberich's curse claims yet another victim: Hagen demands the ring, but Gunther defends it for Gutrune. Hagen strikes down his half-brother, just as Fafner slew Fasolt in an earlier fratricidal conflict between capitalists. However, when Hagen reaches for the ring on the dead hero's finger, Siegfried's arm rises menacingly, causing Hagen to draw back in terror. Such is the power of the proletariat that at any sign of movement (a demonstration or strike, for example), its betrayers fear it is not completely dormant.

As *Götterdämmerung* reaches a tragic conclusion — Siegfried's funeral pyre and the conflagration that engulfs Valhalla, the final enlightenment of Brünnhilde and her decision to return the ring to nature by leaping into the flames, and Hagen's desperate plunge after the ring (he drowns from his own greed) — Wagner's deep philosophy finds full expression. the *Ring* ends with a cleansing fire to clear the way for a better world. The ring is returned to the Rhine. The masses are left standing around the stage to ponder what happened. The *Ring* cycle is a warning about what will happen if the forces let loose — industrial rape of nature and greed run rampant — are allowed to prevail. Not only will the nobility with its glorious cultural accompaniments be doomed, but the innocents in society, the sincere Siegfrieds who deserve to inherit what is left, are fated to be pushed aside by striving capitalists.

In his political forecast Wagner was all too prescient when we look at his homeland in the first half of the following century. That the aristocracy was doomed to fade was obvious in his time; the castle-building spree of King Ludwig II of Bavaria, Wagner's patron, was the final fling of an obsolete ruling class. But Wagner's allusions to how the proletariat would be lured into accepting bourgeois values and then fatally betrayed, while the emerging capitalists would struggle among themselves to control the fruits of industry and inherit the trappings of aristocracy, are perceptive socio-historical commentary. Hitler, deluded into thinking himself a Wagnerian hero, would come to play the role of Hagen — the Nazis betraying the proletarians they pretended to champion ("Socialist" in the oxymoronic "National Socialist") and suppressing the respectable businessmen (the Gunthers) who financed their rise to power.

Dresden, city of Wagner's revolutionary adventures, would go up in flames like Valhalla, under Allied firebombing.

No one who analyzes the *Ring* can ignore the fact that, while it expresses universal values, it was designed to enlighten Europeans of the nineteenth century. The composer's grandson Wieland saw this combination of timelessness and timeliness as the key. "For me it is, firstly a revival of Greek tragedy; secondly, a return to mythical sources; and thirdly, moralistic drama in the manner both of Schiller and of Brecht. The *Ring* is the mirror which Richard Wagner holds up to humanity. 'This is how you are,' he says, 'and this is what will happen to our world if humanity does not radically change.'" Wieland's biographer adds that "Wagner's moralistic challenge was addressed to the people of his own time, the society of rationalism and the industrial revolution, which had forgotten its mythical roots. But its message was more than ever applicable to the society of today" (Skelton 178). Humanity still has not learned the lesson.

Bibliography

Bekker, Paul. *Richard Wagner: His Life in His Work.* Trans. M. M. Bozman. Freeport: Books for Libraries, 1970.
Boucher, Maurice. *The Political Concepts of Richard Wagner.* Trans. Marcel Honeré. New York: M & H Publications, 1950.
Bramsted, Ernest K. *Aristocracy and the Middle-Classes in Germany: Social Types in German Literature 1830–1900.* Chicago: University of Chicago Press, 1964.
Carr, E. H. *Michael Bakunin.* London: Macmillan, 1937.
Chancellor, John. *Wagner.* Boston: Little, Brown, 1978.
Cooke, Deryck. *An Introduction to* Der Ring des Nibelungen. 2-CD set. Decca/London, 1995.
_____. *I Saw the World End: A Study of Wagner's Ring.* London: Oxford University Press, 1979.
Corse, Sandra. *Wagner and the New Consciousness: Language and Love in the Ring.* Rutherford: Fairleigh Dickinson University Press, 1990.
DiGaetani, John Louis, ed. *Penetrating Wagner's Ring: An Anthology.* New York: Da Capo, 1983.
Downes, Edward. Introduction. *The Ring of the Nibelung.* Trans. Stewart Robb. New York: E. P. Dutton, 1960.
Gregor-Dellin, Martin. *Richard Wagner: His Life, His Work, His Century.* Trans. J. Maxwell Brownjohn. London: Collins, 1983 (A slightly abridged translation from the German).
Gutman, Robert W. *Richard Wagner: The Man, His Mind, and His Music.* New York: Time-Life, 1972.
Hanfi, Zawar, ed. and trans. *The Fiery Brook: Selected Writings of Ludwig Feuerbach.* Garden City: Anchor, 1972.
Hamerow, Theodore S. *Restoration, Revolution, Reaction: Economics and Politics in Germany, 1815–1871.* Princeton, N.J.: Princeton University Press, 1966.
Hobsbawm, Eric. J. *The Age of Revolution: Europe 1789–1848.* New York: Barnes & Noble, 1996.
Josserand, Frank B. *Richard Wagner: Patriot and Politician.* Washington, D.C.: University Press of America, 1981.
Lunacharsky, Anatoly. *On Literature and Art.* Moscow: Progress, 1965. Chapter "Richard Wagner" (pp. 340–54).
Marx, Karl, and Frederick Engels. "Revolution and Counter-Revolution in Germany." In Marx and Engels, *Selected Works,* Vol. I, pp. 300–393. Moscow: Progress, 1969.
Mehring, Franz. *Karl Marx: The Story of His Life.* Trans. E. Fitzgerald. Ann Arbor: University of Michigan Press, 1962).
Newman, Ernest. *The Life of Richard Wagner.* 4 vols. New York: Knopf, 1976.
Porges, Heinrich. *Wagner Rehearsing the 'Ring': An Eye-Witness Account of the Stage Rehearsals of the First Bayreuth Festival.* Trans. Robert L. Jacobs. Cambridge: Cambridge University Press, 1983.
Proudhon, Pierre-Joseph. *What is Property?* Trans. Benjamin R. Tucker. New York: Dover, 1970.
Rather, L. J. *The Dream of Self-Destruction: Wagner's Ring and the Modern World.* Baton Rouge: Louisiana State University Press, 1979.
_____, ed. *Reading Wagner: A Study in the History of Ideas.* Baton Rouge: Louisiana State University Press, 1990.
Robertson, Priscilla. *Revolutions of 1848: A Social History.* Princeton: Princeton University Press, 1967.

Shaw, Bernard. *The Perfect Wagnerite: A Commentary on the Niblung's Ring*. New York: Time-Life Records, 1972.

Skelton, Geoffrey. *Wieland Wagner: The Positive Sceptic*. London: Victor Gollancz, 1971.

Spencer, Stewart, Barry Millington (and others), trans. and comment. *Wagner's Ring of the Nibelung*. New York: Thames and Hudson, 1993.

Taylor, Ronald, *Richard Wagner: His Life, Art and Thought*. New York: Taplinger, 1979.

Veblen, Thorstein. *Imperial Germany and the Industrial Revolution*. New York: Viking, 1939.

Wagner, Richard. *My Life*. Trans. Andrew Grey. New York: Da Capo, 1992.

_____. *Richard Wagner's Prose Works [RPRW]*. Trans. William Ashton Ellis. Lincoln: University of Nebraska Press, 1993–95.

_____. *Selected Letters of Richard Wagner*. Trans. and ed. Stewart Spencer and Barry Millington. New York: W. W. Norton, 1988.

4. Romanticism in the *Ring*

Barbara J. Guenther

Experiencing Wagner's *Ring*, whether for the first or the fortieth time, is a revelation. Like any great work of art, whether long or short, the *Ring* reveals layer after layer of meaning and suggests a number of approaches. But unlike a *lied* by Schubert or a sonnet by Shelley, the *Ring* is a monumental work, creating even more avenues for the enthralled listener, the professional musician, and the scholar.

The introduction to a perceptive article by M. Owen Lee aptly expresses why the *Ring* invites such a richness of interpretation:

> The subject of Wagner's *Ring* is not much less than the world itself, the world as projected in myth and music. All of external nature is in the cycle — pure, timeless nature and nature crossed and confounded. And our inner human nature is there too — all the storms and calms that we know within us, in our consciousness and unconscious selves. I know no other opera, or set of operas, perhaps even no other work of art, that looks outward and inward so astonishingly [28].

To illustrate the multiple approaches to the *Ring*, consider just one idea that informs Wagner's cycle: nature. One way that commentators can illuminate Wagner's use of nature in the *Ring* is to point out how he uses cycles in nature to underscore his overriding theme of the cycle of development in the vast mythic history of this work: "the passing away of the old polytheistic order and the rise of a new age of human accountability" (Richards 52). Several writers approaching the *Ring* in this way have begun by noting philosophic influences on Wagner: Hegel, who held that the universe was constantly developing, and the early eighteenth-century philosopher Giambattista Vico. Vico held that all nations invariably (though at different rates) followed the "eternal ideal history," with a three-part cycle recurring over and over, though each time on a higher level. Although Vico's ideas were not widely known when Wagner was composing his music-dramas, Wagner may have been familiar with them by way of Goethe. Certainly these ideas were congruent with Wagner's conviction that German art and culture could elevate all of Western civilization (Aberbach 329). Examining Wagner's use of the cycles of nature against the backdrop of these ideas has provided valuable insights into the operas.[1]

A second approach to considering nature in the *Ring* is to examine how Wagner uses elements of nature in an atmospheric way — as metaphors and as indicators of emotional tone — in virtually every scene of the entire cycle. The dramatic appearance of spring immediately following the embrace between Siegmund and Sieglinde in *Die Walküre*, for instance, underscores the couple's rush of feeling, as do Sieglinde's metaphors sung a few moments after the literal and emotional gloom of Hunding's dwelling suddenly yields to the moonlit spring night:

You are the spring,	Du bist der Lenz,
the spring I have longed for	nach dem ich verlangte
in time of the winter frost.	in frostigem Winters Frist [Act I, scene 3; Robb 6]

Sun and moon, thunderstorms and lightning bolts, rainbows and mists, fire and water — Wagner's stage directions again and again invest nature with more than mere decorative significance. This second approach to nature in Wagner's works is the basis for a number of discussions, both short (John Culshaw's introductory essays to the libretti accompanying Solti's recorded *Ring*, for instance) and long. A recent dissertation by Walter William Richards explores not only Wagner's symbolic presentation of nature, but also the ways in which nature interacts with Wagner's characters, providing inspiration, punishment, and healing (4–5).

A third approach is to examine how nature in the *Ring* can be seen in the light of Romanticism: arguably the most important shift in Western sensibility for centuries. This essay will discuss the way in which the *Ring* is suffused by the Romantic sensibility — not only the interpretation of nature, but other Romantic ideas as well.

To find correspondences between Romantic thinking and the *Ring* is not to argue for a conscious intention on Wagner's part; to do so would be to fall into the intentional fallacy. Any meaning found in the *Ring* must come from the work itself, and though we do know, for instance, that Wagner read the work of German and English Romantics, that type of scholarship is the purview of the biographer. Nevertheless, at the same time that we acknowledge Wagner's uniqueness, we must also keep in mind that he was writing music at a particular time and in a particular place. Wagner's great compatriot Goethe wrote in the 1830s that vigorous discussions about romantic literature — in fact, "quarrels and divisions" — had "spread over the whole world" (quoted in Hugo, *Reader* 53); twenty years later, looking back on the 1830s, Liszt wrote of "a new school," both in literature and music, that "attracted the attention and interest of all minds. *Romanticism* was the order of the day; they fought with obstinancy [sic] for and against it" (129).

A century later, one scholar succinctly expressed the pervasiveness of Romanticism as a "tidal wave of primitivistic and idealistic sentiment which moved over Europe" (Bush xiv). That Romantic ideas can be found in the *Ring*, then, is no accident. At the same time, the purpose of this essay is not to illuminate facts of history, ideas of theorists and philosophers, or even influences on Wagner. The purpose is, quite simply, to bring together one strand of intellectual history and one great musical creation in order to illuminate the *Ring* from a different angle. The ultimate purpose of such illumination, the discovery of yet another of the many layers of meaning in this monumental work, is to enhance delight.[2]

What, then, is the essence of this "tidal wave" that saturated the Europe of Wagner's time? Some writers claim that Romanticism is too varied — among countries, genres, and individuals — to be defined; if they choose to discuss the phenomenon, they tend to give lists of traits to be found in the music or literature of the period. Carl Dahlhaus centers his discussion of romanticism in nineteenth-century music around three salient traits, maintaining that "we must abandon our hope of capturing 'Romanticism' (writ large) in a single concept" (*Nineteenth-Century Music* 25, 26). The authoritative reference *A Literary History of England* states that "Romantic phenomena vary in different countries, and even within the same country no two writers are necessarily romantic in the same way or to the same degree, nor is a writer necessarily romantic in all his work or throughout his life" (Baugh 1122).[3] In their concern to avoid overgeneralizing, these writers have leaned the other way, almost fragmenting the concept. One perceptive writer has avoided both these tendencies: Northrop Frye's seminal essay "The Romantic Myth" cuts through the surface differences found in Romantic works to illuminate the heart of Romanticism.[4]

Frye sees Romanticism as one of a very few major changes in mythology occurring in Western civilization. Our oldest myths, he notes, were mother-centered, with nature as an earth goddess renewing her vitality every spring. The mother-goddess was, in moral terms, an ambiguous figure, sometimes benign, sometimes ferocious — or, as in Shelley's "Ode to the West Wind," both destroyer and preserver. The "more aggressive" myths of Judaism and Christianity reflected "an urban, tool-using, male-dominated society, where the central figure usually develop[ed] out of a father-god associated with the sky" (6). This sensibility, which reached its highest point of development in the Middle Ages, maintained its strength down to the seventeenth century, at which point it was still "comprehensive enough to unite the theologian and the philosopher with the poet and the scientist." As science developed and took on its own form, however, "it forced poets to look for another construct, and, in doing so, to realize that all myths are poetic in origin" (10).

This realization gave rise to a new way of thinking — Romanticism — that Frye terms "an imaginative revolution" continuing to the present. The ramifications were numerous and significant, affecting how humans viewed nature, society, redemption, the role of the emotions, the hero, the artist, and the source of creativity. Most of the following discussion will examine the ways in which four important ideas of Romanticism — attitudes toward nature, the primitive, incest, and magic — are seen in the *Ring*. The ending segment will move beyond the stage directions and utterances of the characters in Wagner's poem to look at three other features of the *Ring* and its composer in the light of Romanticism: the transmutation of political themes into myth, the visionary role of the artist, and the remarkable artistic innovation.

The Romantic sensibility came very close to espousing the ancient polytheistic attitude: that nature was filled with forces and powers, gods and goddesses. To the prevailing Judeo-Christian mythology, of course, this was a pagan view, elevating "Eros and Dionysus, sexuality and emotional abandon" (Frye 8). Nature, to the Romantics, was informed by a numinous power, shimmering with significance — a power that was mysterious yet capable of being experienced. Goethe's Werther referred to the "bliss" that flooded his heart as he viewed the forms of nature. He saw far more than the picturesque: what was revealed to him was "the inner, glowing, sacred life of Nature" and all her "unfathomable forces." Goethe was writing early in the Romantic period, in 1774, so it is not surprising that at the same time that his protagonist spoke of the transcendental power of nature, he also spoke in conventional Christian terms of "the spirit of the eternal Creator" and "the bliss of that Being who creates everything in and through Himself" (64–65).

Writing approximately two dozen years later, however, as the full spirit of Romanticism animated English poetry, William Wordsworth found in nature a mysterious power that he did not relate to the older, Judeo-Christian myth:

> I heard among the solitary hills
> Low breathings coming after me, and sounds
> Of undistinguishable motion, steps
> Almost as silent as the turf they trod
> [*The Prelude*, Book I, ll. 322–25].[5]

The effect of encountering nature's mysterious power marked the young poet so strongly that, writing eighteen or more years later about his formative childhood encounters with nature, he vividly recalls that

> for many days, my brain
> Worked with a dim and undetermined sense
> Of unknown modes of being; ...
>
> ...

> huge and mighty forms, that do not live
> Like living men, moved slowly through the mind
> By day, and were a trouble to my dreams [Book I, ll. 391–400].[6]

Nature could move the Romantics so much because they saw themselves as intimately connected with the entire animate and inanimate world. Beneath the transient changes as nature moved through the cycles of the days and of the seasons, these artists knew nature "at heart, the mysterious mother of humanity, brooding in omnipresence"— a knowledge and faith producing poems that were "glowing invocation[s] almost to pantheism" (Cobban 135–36).

German philosophy certainly played its part in developing this idea. Friedrich W.J. Schelling, writing in the first half of the nineteenth century, transmuted the lofty idealism of Kant into a philosophy of nature that was to be as influential outside of Germany (especially on such writers as Coleridge, Shelley, and Emerson) as it was in his own country. Schelling believed in a *Weltseele* (World Soul) that embraced all things and was demonstrated most clearly in the visible phenomena of nature. Because the World Soul unified all phenomena, the individual and nature were, in effect, identical (Horton and Hopper 397). One could hardly find any philosophy more appealing to nineteenth-century Romantics than Schelling's pantheistic thrust.

To the Romantics, nature was not only numinous; it was oracular, "dropping hints of expanding mysteries into the narrowed rational consciousness" (Frye 28). Baudelaire's "Correspondances" (in English, "Correlatives") depicts nature as speaking, though the human cannot always understand the message:

Nature is a temple, in which living pillars	La Nature est un temple où de vivants piliers
Sometimes utter a babel of words;	Laissent parfois sortir de confuses paroles;
Mankind traverses it through forests of symbols	L'homme y passe à travers des forêts de symboles
That watch him with knowing eyes.	Qui l'observent avec des regards familiers [61].

Once again it is Wordsworth who pushes the idea further, suggesting that when nature speaks, the human can understand. A major theme of *The Prelude* is the poet's sense of the "Presences of Nature" that, by "haunting" the child raised in the beauty of England's Lake Country, perform a "ministry" (Book I, ll. 464–68). It is in this "haunting" that nature forms the receptive person; this theme of the reciprocity between nature and the human occurs not only throughout *The Prelude* but also in many of Wordsworth's shorter poems.

If, as Romanticism holds, nature is both numinous and oracular, then it follows that the primal sin in this mythology is a fall away from nature and into self-consciousness. As Frye notes, "the alienated man cut off from nature by his consciousness is the Romantic equivalent of post–Edenic Adam" (18). Wordsworth's great Intimations Ode laments the loss of the "celestial light" and the "visionary gleam" experienced by the child once in union with nature, but treats the separation as an inevitable part of the human condition, not sinful. Coleridge's Ancient Mariner, on the other hand, has sinned, cutting himself off from nature by his killing of the albatross. His only way to redemption is to tell his story over and over, "a story whose moral is reintegration with nature" (Frye 28).

In his theoretical works, Wagner often sounds like a Romantic. In "Beethoven," for instance, he states that "it is this inner life through which we are directly allied with the whole of Nature, and thus are brought into a relation with the Essence of things that eludes the forms of outer knowledge" (*Prose Works* 5: 69). In his essay "The Wibelungs," he speculates that the emergence of day from night "may have been the first [idea] to breed in man a moral consciousness" (*Prose Works* 7: 274). But when he composed the *Ring*, he *demonstrated* a correspondence with Romantic ideas about nature: nature as numinous and oracular, with the primal sin being willful separation from nature.

The most numinous aspect of nature depicted in the *Ring* is the gold lying beneath the Rhine. As light falls on it in the very first scene of the entire cycle, Wagner's stage directions establish the gold's significance:

> *[Alberich] is suddenly attracted and spellbound by the following spectacle. Through the waters an increasingly bright light makes its way from above, gradually kindling, on a high point of the central rock, to a dazzling, brightly-beaming gleam of gold; a magical golden light streams through the waters from this point* [Porter 14].

The gold brings delight to the Rhinedaughters, who speak of it as a "golden ornament" ("Goldes Schmuck") emitting a "golden radiance" ("Goldes Schein"). The Romantic poets writing before Wagner composed his poem saw numinousness in all aspects of nature, inanimate as well as animate. So too with the *Ring*'s gold. In fact, Wagner deepens the significance of the gold even further by personifying it; it is "a living mythological being" (Borchmeyer 220) that, Wellgunde sings, "alternately wakes and sleeps" (Cochrane 12).

WOGLINDE	
Look sisters!	Lugt, Schwestern!
The wakener laughs in the deep.	Die Weckerin lacht in den Grund.
WELLGUNDE	
Through the dark green surge	Durch den grünen Schwall
he calls the blest sleeper to wake.	den wonnigen Schläfer sie grüsst.
FLOSSHILDE	
He kisses her eyelids,	Jetzt küsst sie sein Auge,
So they will open.	dass er es öffne.
WELLGUNDE	
See her smiling	Schaut, es lächelt
with gentle light.	in lichtem Schein.
ALL THREE	
Waken friend!	Wache, Freund,
Wake in joy!	wache froh [Robb 4–5]!

The gold lying in the Rhine is pristine, uncorrupted, innocent. Its importance is archetypal, as Robert Donington notes: the gold underneath the Rhine is not "the refined and quintessential gold which is the hard-won culmination of the alchemical transformation. It is gold, but it is virgin gold" (52, 54–55). As the Rhinedaughters lament its loss at the end of *Rheingold* and in the opening scene of the final act of *Götterdämmerung,* they refer to it as "pure" ("reines Gold"). These daughters (töchter) of the Rhine remind us that the gold is intimately connected with nature; it is their father's gold ("Vaters Gold").[7]

Two of Wagner's characters, true to form, do not appreciate the radiance of the gold lying untouched in the Rhine. Alberich asks the Rhinedaughters,

Is the Gold of value	Eu'rem Taucherspiele
only for your diving play?	nur taugte das Gold?
Then it would be little use to me!	Mir gält' es dann wenig [Cochrane 12]!

After he learns that "the world's wealth" will come to one who forsakes love and forges the gold into a ring, he utters the curse and then severs the gold from its natural element, first taunting the Rhinedaughters:

The Niblung's near to your toy!	Der Niblung naht eurem Spiel [Robb 6]!

Alberich's moral limitations leave him unable to see any inherent value in the gold. Its only importance to him is that it can be an agent of power. Similarly, Loge, characterized by

Das Rheingold, **Kirov Opera, St. Petersburg. (Photograph: Natasha Razina)**

cunning rather than wisdom, fails to appreciate the numinousness of the gold. He refers to it as the Rhinedaughters' "glittering toy" ("gleissenden Tand"), and when he answers Fafner's question, "What glory lies in the gold?" he responds,

It is a trinket	Ein Tand ist's
in the depths of the water	in des Wassers Tiefe,
for the delight of laughing children;	lachenden Kindern zur Lust [Cochrane 22];

This idea in the *Ring* leads Walter Richards to point out a striking parallel between Wagner and the great German Romantic writer Novalis. In the latter's 1802 work, *Heinrich von Ofterdingen,* the title character descends into a mine, symbolizing his return to a pre-industrial, ideal "symbiotic relationship with nature." Deep in the mine, Heinrich acts as the Rhinedaughters did, "simply admiring the beauty of metal ore lying far beneath the earth's surface, rather than anticipating what such exploitation of nature might earn him economically." Richards goes on to make the parallel between Wagner and Novalis explicit: "One has only to remember the frenzied lust of Alberich's dwarves hammering on the Rheingold deep in the earth's bowels to appreciate the opposite, almost childlike delight of the poor miner, Heinrich, in his close relationship to the wonders of nature herself" (54).[8]

Although Wagner's poem speaks for itself, it is worth quoting the composer's comments on the meaning of the gold, explained in his long letter to August Röckel of January 25–26, 1854: "the pernicious power that poisons love is concentrated in the *gold* that is stolen from nature and put to ill use, the Nibelung's ring: the curse that clings to it is not lifted until it is restored to nature and until the gold has been returned to the Rhine" (*Selected Letters* 307). It is the stolen gold, the gold wrested from nature by a love-renouncing curse, that is pernicious. The gold in its original form, as the poem makes clear, is an aspect of transcendent nature.

A second aspect of nature as envisioned by the Romantic poets, nature as oracular, is symbolized by Wagner in the figure of Erda. Her description of herself as one who knows all that was, is, and will be (*Das Rheingold,* scene 4) is unchallenged. In speaking to Brünnhilde, Wotan calls Erda the "wisest, holiest Wala" (*Die Walküre,* II, 2), and he addresses her in *Siegfried,* III, 1 as "mother of wisdom" and "all-knowing one." Donington notes that she appears in the *Ring* only at moments of "profound uncertainty and desperate need," but when she does appear, she demonstrates a knowledge of the situation not possessed by the less intuitive characters. She is characterized not by "blind maternity," but by her instinctive wisdom (108–09).

In Romanticism, the main direction of the quest for insight and self-identity tends to be "downward and inward, toward a hidden basis or ground of identity between man and nature" (Frye 33). Subterranean caves and streams, like those in Coleridge's "Kubla Khan," are often the venue for the meeting of man and nature. Although Erda does not emerge from a cave, her rising up from the lower regions of the world surrounded by a blue glow creates the same impression as that of the oracular cave. This type of imagery—so characteristic of Shelley—"is a revival of a pre-Christian mythology that goes back to the old earth-mother myths" (Frye 34). Erda's injunction that Wotan give up the ring is unambiguous, but her warning about the future is cryptic—"concealed sublimity" ("Geheimnis-hehr"), as Wotan calls it. Again we are reminded of Romantic poets and novelists: in the *Ring,* nature speaks, her message is lofty, and some of what she says may remain unclear though the intimations leave an unforgettable impression on the one seeking insight.

Without this instinctive wisdom of nature, humans cannot survive, yet to a significant extent they have been cut off from instinct by the growth of consciousness (Donington 109). Despite a difference in terminology, nineteenth-century Romantics would agree with twentieth-century Jungians, who define the state of nature as "the situation of largely undifferentiated unconsciousness" (Donington 191), a state in which "mind and matter are not yet separated" (Snook 333). In the Judeo-Christian myth, it was Eden that was forfeited, but to the Romantics, what has been lost is the identification of the human with nature. Humans can be said to have fallen "into the original sin of self-consciousness" (Frye 17).

No figure in the *Ring* illustrates this sin of separation more clearly than Wotan. In *Siegfried,* the Wanderer tells Mime that

From the world-ashtree's	Aus der Welt-Esche
sacred branches	weihlichstem Aste
[Wotan] himself created	schuf er sich einen Schaft:
a spear;	
the trunk withered.	dorrt der Stamm [author's translation].

Not until the Prelude to *Götterdämmerung* do we learn more about this incident and its results. As the First Norn elaborates on Wotan's visit to the heart of nature, she describes the World Ash-tree: "lush and thick," its "holy and verdant boughs sheltered a spring that whispered wisdom ('Weisheit raunend')." The price exacted of Wotan for knowledge was one of his eyes. The observer of the *Ring* will be aware of the overt parallel between Alberich and Wotan (who, speaking to Mime, refers to himself as "Light-Alberich"), a parallel that leads Donington to state that these two are "as close and necessary to one another as the obverse and reverse of one coin" (183). Just as Wotan impoverishes nature by his primal act, so does Alberich, since his theft of the gold darkens the Rhine. Each character has renounced something natural in order to gain power; like Alberich, Wotan has "violate[d] his own natural integrity" (Borchmeyer 229).

By this point in the cycle, as the three Norns recall Wotan's days of power, observers are aware that the god's powerful spear is not a symbol of wise, enlightened leadership, but of

Das Rheingold, Bavarian State Opera, Munich, 2002: John Tomlinson as Wotan. (Photograph: Wilfried Hösl)

bad bargains. Promising the life-sustaining Freia to the giants as payment for their construction of Valhalla, a structure described by Wotan as "manhood's honor, eternal power," seems as foolish as Fricka said it was. Wotan's revelation that he never intended to give Freia to the giants — a bargain carved on his spear — hardly redeems him. He is devious, he becomes a thief, and by the end of *Die Walküre*, he has alienated the person closest to him.

Wotan's first act after gaining knowledge from the spring suggests that the Romantics were right in lamenting the separation from nature. Breaking the branch from the World Ash-tree in order to make his spear of power caused the decline not only of the tree, but of the waters of wisdom as well:

The course of time was long.   In langer Zeiten Lauf
Worse grew the wound in the wood.   zehrte die Wunde den Wald;
Leaves fell in their sereneness.   falb fielen die Blätter,
Then, blight took the tree;   dürr darbte der Baum;
Sadly the source of the water failed. traurig versiegte
                                      des Quelles Trank.
                                      [*Götterdämmerung*; Robb 1]

After Siegfried breaks the spear in two, Wotan plans an appropriate penance: he orders that the World Ash-tree be cut down and its branches chopped to pieces and heaped like a wall around the home of the gods, as firewood. The inevitable end of the rule of the gods will be symbolized by the flames consuming the symbol of Wotan's power, Valhalla. The tragedy's root cause is the willful separation from the instinctive life, Wotan's "self-emancipation from nature by his acquisition of consciousness" (Cooke 249), a separation that makes Wotan's closest parallel in the Bible not God, but Adam:

What we have in this stupendous character [Wotan] is the tragedy of conscious, rational thinking. Wotan hoped to rule the world rightly, with the consciousness he had won from nature. But consciousness itself is, in all mythologies, an ambivalent blessing. Wresting it from nature is a kind of sin [Lee 39].

Wagner was fully aware of the tragic consequences of gaining such consciousness. In 1849, only a year after he composed the original prose-sketch of the *Ring* and the text for *Siegfried's Death*, he explained the symbolism of Wotan's primal act:

From the moment when Man perceived the difference between himself and Nature, and thus commenced his own development as *man* by breaking loose from the unconsciousness of natural animal life and passing over into conscious life,— when he thus looked Nature in the face and from the first feelings of his dependence on her, thereby aroused, evolved the faculty of Thought,— from that moment did Error begin, as the earliest utterance of consciousness. But Error is the mother of Knowledge, and the history of the birth of Knowledge out of Error is the history of the human race, from the myths of primal ages down to the present day ["The Artwork of the Future," *Prose Works* 1: 70].

Just as Wotan's separation from nature has tragic consequences, so does Siegfried's. As soon as the hero enters the world of men scheming for power, he is in trouble, no longer heeding what nature can tell him. In *Götterdämmerung*, he meets the Rhinedaughters, who, though lacking Erda's wisdom, are nevertheless elemental creatures of nature. When they counsel him to return the ring to the Rhine, he sees them only as sly and deceitful ("listigen"). Another set of voices from nature that Siegfried no longer heeds is that of the Forest Birds, as he tells Hagen:

HAGEN
I've heard it told me, Siegfried,
you understand the meanings
of birds when they sing.
but can this be so?

SIEGFRIED
It's ages now
since I heeded their chirps.
....

HAGEN [speaking of Brünnhilde]
(*softly to Siegfried*)
He [Gunther] cannot read her mind
the way you do with birds.

SIEGFRIED
Since hearing the songs of women
my mind has forgot the birds.

HAGEN
Ich hörte sagen, Siegfried,
der Vögel Sangessprache
verstündest du wohl:
So wäre das wahr?

SIEGFRIED
Seit lange acht ich
des Lallens nicht mehr.

Verstünd' er sie so gut
wie du der Vögel Sang!

Seit Frauen ich singen hörte,
vergass ich der Vöglein ganz [Robb 24].

Unlike Alberich and Wotan, Siegfried is naïve and uncalculating. He and Brünnhilde "embody the integrity of the primordial state of nature" (Borchmeyer 231), a state in which power does not yet exist, only natural love. Siegfried abandons this world that had protected and educated him when he leaves his beloved Brünnhilde to carry out (in her words) new achievements, fresh feats ("neuen Taten"). Despite the idealistic aspirations of the lovers, Siegfried's departure from nature to enter "the world of courtly convention" (Borchmeyer 232) will have tragic consequences.

Seen in the context of Romanticism, Siegfried illustrates the perils of separating oneself from nature. Even more, he exemplifies the Romantic idea of primitivism, an idea revived in eighteenth-century Europe and reflected in the works of a number of nineteenth-century

Romantic writers. Jean-Jacques Rousseau articulated the idea more fully than any of his contemporaries, contending that humans are born noble and good in a state of nature. Close to the primitive beauty of nature, humans are healthiest, most virtuous, and most free. Primitivism places the highest premium on the natural, or innate, instincts and passions, on spontaneity and the free expression of emotion.[9]

The popularity of these ideas was mirrored in the enthusiasm with which readers in the later eighteenth century greeted literature whose authors, turning from the Graeco-Roman tradition, found inspiration in Celtic and Norse mythologies and literature. The English poet Thomas Gray translated two Norse poems (*The Fatal Sisters, The Descent of Odin*) and found inspiration in Welsh poems for *The Triumphs of Owen* and *The Death of Hoel*. In 1760 James Macpherson published *Fragments of Ancient Poetry Collected in the Highlands of Scotland*, whose "instant success ... lighted a poetic fire that for a half-century was to rage throughout all Europe" (Baugh 1016). Macpherson followed this success with epic poems, set in early Scottish-Celtic-Erse days, that he attributed to the third-century Irish epic bard, Ossian (*Fingal, Temora*). More important than the fact that the Ossianic poems were probably fabricated by Macpherson is the passion with which they were received, first in England, then in Germany.

The Ossianic poems were translated by the Austrian M. Denis in 1768–69 and became one of the chief influences on the *Sturm und Drang* (Storm and Stress) period of German literature (Horton and Hopper 387). Goethe's Werther, after stating that the "sublime" poet Ossian has replaced Homer in his heart, elaborates by writing of what Ossian suggests to his imagination: howling gales, flowing mists, moonlight, a maiden lamenting her fallen hero, a bard surrounded by "the helpless shades of his dead companions"—all the trappings of heroic myth (110–11). In his *Life of Chopin*, Liszt echoes those sentiments, referring to Ossian and "the mountains of Scotland, with their heavy veils and long wreaths of mist" (48–49).

In English literature, the influence of such atmospheric references to the past is seen in many of the works of Sir Walter Scott and in the novels of Charlotte and Emily Brontë. The influence of Rousseau's primitivism on English poetry was considerable, most notably on Wordsworth's revolutionary *Lyrical Ballads*. His expanded *Preface* to that collection, published in 1802, explained his object in the poems: "to choose incidents and situations from common life," using simple language ("language really used by men"), "throw[ing] over them a certain colouring of imagination," and thereby "tracing in them ... the primary laws of our nature" (734). The protagonists of his ballads include an old leech-gatherer, the child in "We Are Seven," an idiot boy, and the unspoiled Lucy, who was shaped by nature in a reciprocal interchange. Though Wordsworth's use of primitivism was highly individualistic—instead of longing for a golden age to be found in the remote past, he wrote of figures in his contemporary society—it was primitivism nonetheless.[10]

To what extent was Wagner receptive to the value of primitivism that had so captured the European imagination? Throughout his prose works he imagines a past state of perfection that has been effaced by the corrupting influence of social structures. In "Art and Climate" (1859), for example, he maintains that the civilization he lives in is "violently debarred from Nature"; humanity "shall first reach Art when we completely turn our backs on such a civilization and once more cast ourselves ... into the arms of Nature" (*Prose Works* 1: 258–59). In his oft-quoted letter to August Röckel (January 25–26, 1854), he writes of having contemplated two years earlier "'a life in the country,'" visiting a spa with the hope of changing the way he lived. With his customary dramatic flair, he tells Röckel, "I was prepared to give up my art and everything else if only I could return to being a child of nature," but then dismissed the idea as "this naïve wish of mine" (*Selected Letters* 311). Nevertheless, he recognized the appeal of primitivism, and in fact we find the idea reflected in the character of Siegfried.

Siegfried, born in Mime's cave and raised by the dwarf, knew no other human beings as he grew up. The only other persons he encounters during *Siegfried* are Wotan, disguised as the Wanderer, and Brünnhilde. What he knows he has learned from observing nature's creatures. The boy angrily rejects Mime's claim of being both father and mother to him ("ich bin dir Vater / und Mutter zugleich"), noting that nature is filled with fathers and mothers, and each young creature resembles its parents. As one growing up in isolation, unfamiliar with the structures and human interactions found in a social group, Siegfried knows no fear. Thus he is easily manipulated by Mime, who leads him to kill Fafner, the first step in the dwarf's plot to gain possession of the ring.

The stage directions for Siegfried's first entrance specify that he enter boisterously ("mit jähem Ungestüm"), in joyful high spirits ("mit lustigem Übermute"). From that point until he meets Brünnhilde at the end of the opera, he energetically charges his way through events: teasing Mime with a bear from the forest, forging the sword unconventionally and with fierce eagerness ("mit ungestümem Eifer"), slaying Fafner with a single leaping bound ("Siegfried ... springt mit einem Satze"), killing Mime with a swift blow ("einen jähen Streich"), impatiently defying Wotan and breaking his spear with one blow; and, after enthusiastically entering the wall of flame, reaching the sleeping Brünnhilde. His words just before plunging into the fire encapsulate not only his fearlessness, but also his energetic high spirits:

Ha! Gladdening glow!	Ha, wonnige Glut!
glorious light,	leuchtender Glanz!
lighting my pathway	Strahlend nun offen
clearly before me!	steht mir die Strasse.
I'll bathe in the fire!	Im Feuer mich baden!
I'll go through the flames	Im Feuer zu finden die Braut!
to my bride!	
Ho-ho! Ha-hei!	Hoho! hahei!
Again let me call you mate!	Jetzt lock' ich ein liebes Gesell [Robb 33]!

We next see him, in the Prologue to *Götterdämmerung*, as he is about to leave Brünnhilde in order to carry out great deeds. Though he has learned fear, he is inspired by his bride:

You select my fights for me,	Meine Kämpfe kiesest du,
and my victories come from your will.	Meine Siege kehren zu dir [Robb 3].

His natural gifts and guileless nature, however, are no match for characters well schooled in a world of bargains, alliances, manipulation, deceit, and the lust for power and prestige. Tricked by the Gibichungs and their half-brother Hagen, he unwittingly betrays his beloved Brünnhilde and ends up literally stabbed in the back by Alberich's son. As noted above, he had ceased to listen to nature's Forest Birds, his only trustworthy guide in *Siegfried*; and, in the final opera of the cycle, he rejects the advice of the Rhinemaidens, prompting them to say of him:

Come sisters!	Kommt, Schwestern!
Fly from this numbskull!	Schwindet dem Toren!
He fancies himself	So weise und stark
so strong and so wise,	verwähnt sich der Held,
but he's fettered and utterly blind!	als gebunden und blind er doch ist [Robb 23]!

Siegfried's spontaneous naïveté is with him to the end. As Hagen's drugged drink reverses the loss of memory caused by Gutrune's potion, Siegfried relates the story of his life; he is unable to reflect on the consequences of telling his tale.[11] He could not have lived in any case.

Götterdämmerung, Bavarian State Opera. (Photograph: Wilfried Hösl)

Raised in the forest with nature as his trusted guide, his "archaic naïveté" left him without craftiness and duplicity. Because of his innocence, he could not avoid being ensnared in the machinations of a society he could never understand (Borchmeyer 223).

Stage directions, actions, and words — all underscore the Siegfried as an innocent, as a child of nature unsuited for the realities of society. Virtually every character in *Siegfried* who encounters the future hero uses the words *child* (*Kind*) or *boy* (*Knabe*). In his duel of wits with Wotan/the Wanderer, Mime calls his young charge "a daring stupid child" ("ein kühnes dummes Kind"). Speaking to Alberich, Wotan calls Siegfried "the boy" ("der Knabe") and — even when describing his strength — "the child" ("Kühn ist des Kindes Kraft": bold is the child's power). Speaking to Erda, Wotan refers to Siegfried as "a daring boy" ("ein kühnester Knabe"); experiencing Siegfried's rude impatience, Wotan calls him a "raving child" ("rasendes Kind").

When threatened by Siegfried, Fafner taunts him with "Come, boastful boy" ("Komm, prahlendes Kind"), and, after having been mortally stabbed by the hero, refers to him three times as "boy" ("Knabe"), as one with a child-like will ("Kindes Mut"). In the following scene, Alberich calls Siegfried's slaying of Fafner "the boy's deed" ("des Knaben Tat"). Even Brünnhilde calls her future husband a "delightful child" ("wonniges Kind") and " glorious boy" ("herrlicher Knabe").

In *Götterdämmerung*, however, when Siegfried is no longer in touch with nature, he is referred to several times as "Mann" or "Manne." The word signifies either *husband* or *man*; in some of those references (by both Brünnhilde and Gutrune), the context suggests that *husband* is the better translation. In the highly charged scene of recrimination between Brünnhilde and Siegfried, however, it is best translated as *man*:

Be aware, everybody:	Wisset denn alle:
not he [Gunther]	nicht ihm —
but — that man there [Siegfried]	dem Manne dort
married me.	bin ich vermählt [II, 4; author's translation].

In depicting this boy tragically turned man, Wagner wrote that he intended to present "the most perfect human being," characterized by "immediate vitality and action" (*Selected Letters* 309). The hero of *Siegfried* and *Götterdämmerung* is just that — but woefully unable to live in a corrupt society. The only way out, as Rousseau himself held, was for society to progress from decadence and weakness to justice and virtue. Wagner was not so far from Rousseau in this regard, for the ending of the *Ring* brings about the downfall of the Gibichungs, the death of Hagen (though not of his father), the end of the reign of the gods — symbolized by the burning of Valhalla — and the restoration of the gold to the Rhinedaughters.

Siegfried, it is clear, truly exemplifies the Romantic notion of primitivism. One might be tempted to say the same of his father. Though Siegmund knew his parents and twin sister, he was left as a boy with only his father — Wotan in the guise of Wolfe. After finding the mother killed and the sister carried away, father and son moved to the woods. But spending most of one's childhood in the woods is not enough to make a character a true primitive. Siegfried loses his connection with nature *as a result* of entering the courtly world of the Gibichungs; Siegmund *first* loses his love for the woods (when his father is no longer there to hunt with him) and *then* enters the world of men and women:

Then my wish, shunning the woods;	Aus dem Wald trieb es mich fort;
now drew me to menfolk and women.	Mich drängt' es zu Männern
	und Frauen [*Die Walküre;* Robb 3].

Siegfried and his father differ not only in their relationship to nature, but in their level of awareness. Siegfried, as we have seen, does not know what he is doing; in his "immediate vitality and action" he forges ahead, unafraid and heedless of consequences. Not so with his father:

> When Siegmund takes possession of Nothung, he does so as a sign of futurity.... His son is driven instead by a restlessly energetic ignorance, a sense of everything he does not know. The counterpoint provided by Mime's gleeful plotting during the forging scene is more than just a comic effect; the dwarf's tyrannical plans highlight very precisely the extent to which Siegfried acts without understanding what lies ahead of him [Treadwell 98].

Though the character of Siegmund does not exemplify the Romantic notion of primitivism, he and his twin sister Sieglinde are clear personifications of another Romantic idea: incest.

A heightened interest in the theme of incest, like the vogue of primitivism, began in the eighteenth century and by the century's end was widespread in plays and novels (Praz 177). Of those many novels, perhaps the most popular was Chateaubriand's *René* (1802), which chronicled the incestuous love between brother and sister. Mario Praz states that by the time that Byron was writing, in the early nineteenth century, "the subject of incest was in the air" (90).

The subject found its way into Shelley's *Prometheus Unbound*, which celebrated the union of the Titan Prometheus and his sister Asia. Writing of Shelley's great epic, Northrop Frye states that "the symbol of the sister-bride has a scandalous and incestuous sound" (133), and indeed it does. Byron's incestuous relationship with his half-sister so scandalized England that he was driven out of the country forever. Shelley's often quoted statement that "incest is, like many other incorrect things, a very poetical circumstance" implies an important distinction:

incest by a flesh-and-blood contemporary—no matter how famous and lionized—is scandalous, but incest set in a mythological context is something different.[12]

In her discussion of German mythology, Jessie Weston describes an early set of deities, the Vans, as "a kindly race who seem to have been practically the powers of Nature personified" and who held marriage between brother and sister to be lawful. This is consistent with the development of Northern mythology, whose deities seem originally to have been considered bisexual, then at a later time as a pair "existing side by side as male and female counterparts of the same idea," both brother and sister, husband and wife. In one of Wagner's sources, the Völsunga-saga, Siegmund and Signy were regarded as such a divine pair, who in addition were twins (Weston 346).

Since the parents of Wagner's sister and brother are a mortal woman and a god (Wotan), the twins are less divine than, for instance, Isis and Osiris. Weston notes that in representing them as mortals, as in fact Wagner does, there is a real risk of our not being able to be sympathetic toward them. To insure that we care about their troubles, it is important that they be influenced "by some force extraneous to themselves, be it Passion, or be it Fate, the irresistible power of which we ourselves as spectators acknowledge." Only then can we "cordially accept and sympathise with them" (Weston 346). Fate certainly does propel these two characters, allowing Wagner to present incestuous characters who nonetheless engage our sympathy.[13]

One technique that Wagner uses to prepare us for the relationship between Siegmund and Sieglinde is extensive foreshadowing. Wagner puts words into the mouths of various characters speaking before the incest (or in Wotan's case, speaking of events transpiring just after the incest) that, to anyone knowing the complete story of the brother and sister, carry an additional reverberation.

When Siegmund speaks to Hunding and Sieglinde, for instance, he says,

Whatever I thought right	Was Rechtes je ich riet,
others looked on as wrong.	andern dünkte es arg,
What looked evil to me was	schlimm immer mir schien,
others favored as right!	andere gaben ihm Gunst [*Die Walküre*; Robb 3].

He continues with a theme he had raised earlier in the scene, that he and his father were outlaws ("Geächtet"):

No matter where I went	In Fehde fiel ich, wo ich mich fand,
there was strife.	
Wrath found me, go where I would.	Zorn traf mich, wohin ich zog;
When I sought pleasure	gehrt' ich nach Wonne,
Sorrow was found.	wecht' ich nur Weh [Robb 3–4].

During this same conversation, Hunding reinforces the theme of Siegmund as an outsider when he says he has heard "dark stories" ("dunkle Sage") about Siegmund and his father. After hearing how Siegmund fought to rescue a young girl from an unwanted marriage—a fight that, unknown to Siegmund but not to Hunding, was against Hunding's family—Hunding comments,

I know a riotous race:	Ich weiss ein wildes Geschlecht,
it does not revere	nicht heilig ist ihm,
what others do.	was andern hehr [Robb 4].

Wotan, speaking to Brünnhilde in the following act, acknowledges that he brought up his son to "flout the laws of the gods" ("gegen der Götter Rat / reizte kühn ich ihn auf"; Robb 13). All of this exposition establishes Siegmund as an outsider, a condition that he feels deeply.

Wagner does not allow us to forget this, for even as Siegmund embraces Sieglinde, he once more refers to his status among men and women of society:

though I was outlawed	war ich geächtet
...	...
joyful vengeance	freudige Rache
calls now the joyous ones!	ruft nun den Frohen [author's translation]![14]

In addition to foreshadowing, Wagner uses two other techniques to make us care about the twin lovers: the mythic suddenness with which they realize the deep affinity between them, and the contrast of Sieglinde's feelings toward her husband and her brother. From the very first scene of *Die Walküre*, Wagner's stage directions emphasize the fascination between the twins and the fact that they are compelled to act as they do by a force greater than their own wills:

> *Siegmund takes a long draught, while his gaze rests on her with growing warmth. Still gazing, he takes the horn from his lips and lets it sink slowly, while the expression on his face tells of strong emotion* [Porter 88].

At the end of the scene, after Siegmund has fixed his eyes on Sieglinde "with calm and steady sympathy," Wagner directs the two to gaze into one another's eyes, during a long silence, "with an expression of the deepest emotion." When Hunding enters, at the beginning of the next scene, Wagner directs Sieglinde to "involuntarily" turn her eyes again to Siegmund; as Siegmund begins to tell his story, his sister fastens her eyes on him "with evident sympathy and intentness." Later in the scene the stage directions direct Siegmund to indicate his awareness of his sister's feelings ("He turns his eyes to Sieglinde and observes her sympathetic glance"), and after the Walsung has finished his story, Wagner writes that "Sieglinde, pale and deeply stirred, lowers her eyes."

The scene ends with another lengthy stage direction underscoring the attraction between the brother and sister:

> *she turns her eyes on Siegmund so as to meet his gaze, which he keeps unceasingly fixed on her. She perceives that Hunding is watching, and goes at once to the bedchamber. On the steps she turns once more, looks yearningly at Siegmund, and indicates with her eyes, persistently and with eloquent earnestness, a particular spot in the ash-tree's trunk* [Porter 96].

In the following scene, when the two embrace, Sieglinde makes explicit what was already conveyed by the couple's almost mesmerized gazing:

I knew you	dich kannt'ich
distinct and clear:	deutlich und klar:
when my eyes saw you,	als mein Auge dich sah,
you were my own;	warst du mein Eigen [author's translation];

In addition to the foreshadowing and mythically immediate recognition of affinity—underscored by the music itself and the visual appearance of spring—Wagner also helps mitigate the effect of incest by Sieglinde's contrasting reactions to Hunding and Siegmund. In the mundane, non-mythic world, we would expect a wife to feel shame at sleeping with her brother but not with her husband. In *Die Walküre*, this is reversed, as we learn when an agitated Sieglinde speaks to Siegmund of the two men with whom she has been intimate. So distressed is she that she can scarcely even refer to herself and to her brother except in the third person:

May winds blow her away,	Der Wind mag sie verwehn,
The foul one who followed the fair!	die ehrlos dem Edlen sich gab!

For he has given her love,	Da er sie liebend umfing,
And blessedest joy was hers.	da seligste Lust sie fand,
...	...
Groanings and shudders	Grauen und Schauder
of shame and of terror	ob grässlichster Schande
fastened their grip	musste mit Schreck
and filled her with horror	die Schmähliche fassen,
to think she once had obeyed	die je dem Manne gehorcht,
a man she loved not at all!	der ohne Minne sie hielt!
...	...
An outcast am I,	Verworfen bin ich,
bereft of grace!	der Würde bar!
I now must leave him	Dir reinstem Manne
the purest of manhood,	muss ich entrinnen,
I dare not be yours	Dir Herrlichem darf ich
In love and obedience:	nimmer gehören.
Shame would fall on my brother,	Schande bring ich dem Bruder,
scorn on rescuing friend!	Schmach demm freienden Freund!

[III, 2; Robb 15]

Sieglinde's unhappiness with her husband is understandable: there is nothing attractive about him. Siegmund's fight with Hunding's kinsmen on the day he stumbled into Hunding's dwelling reminds us of an earlier conflict, when those same kinsmen witnessed Sieglinde being married to Hunding against her will. Although Hunding himself had not raided Sieglinde's childhood home and killed her mother, he clearly believed that forcing a woman to marry was defensible. Earlier in the day that opens *Die Walküre*, he had arrived too late to help his kinsmen, and only that fact precluded his fighting Siegmund.

By presenting Siegmund and Sieglinde as figures who, despite their troubles, are superior to the established members of society, Wagner skillfully deals with their incest. They, after all, are to bring forth the hero, Siegfried. One of the signs of a mythological hero is that his birth and upbringing are not those of other men. We have already seen the role that Siegfried's upbringing has played in making him heroic; his birth is no less the mark of a hero. The incestuous character of his begetting is a sign that "no mere human procreation was in progress, but a heroic mystery" (Donington 178).[15]

A different type of mystery arises in connection with another Romantic theme found in the *Ring*: magic. Like the other Romantic themes discussed above, the nineteenth-century fascination with magic can be traced to the preceding century, when the Gothic novel and romance came into vogue. In those works, horror and mystery invested the world of ordinary shapes and forms with supernatural implications, leaving early nineteenth-century readers "unusually receptive to ghosts, witchcraft, occultism, and other eerie phenomena." French critics have coined the phrase "low" or "black" romanticism to describe such tastes (Hugo, "Masterpieces" 255), which were satisfied by the popular Gothic and romantic novels significant today only to scholars of literary history.

However, the element of the supernatural was not limited to these once-popular productions; it found its way into works of genuine literary merit. Among the English Romantic poets, Coleridge used this aspect of the supernatural, most notably in *The Rime of the Ancient Mariner*, *Christabel*, and "Kubla Khan." Years after his collaboration with Wordsworth on the *Lyrical Ballads*, Coleridge described the different aims of the two poets. Wordsworth was to choose characters and incidents from ordinary life, whereas Coleridge would use "the modifying colours of imagination," selecting "incidents and agents [that] were to be, in part at least, supernatural." Unlike his predecessors in prose, Coleridge's aim was not simply to create horror; instead, he wished to show "the dramatic truth" lying beneath the magic of the events. To the extent that a reader had "at any time believed himself under supernatural agency," Coleridge maintained, the poems animated by this supernatural thrust would strike deep chords (*Biographia Literaria* 168).

Of all the English Romantics, Coleridge was the most conversant with what was happening in German philosophy and art, and it was the Germans, more than any other group, who had a "nihilistic delight in being detached from life" as well as a strong belief in hallucination and magic (Bowra 4). In fact, the Germans writing Romantic tales of terror far surpassed the English novelists who had inspired them (Prawer, *Frankenstein's Island* 16). Like the best of the English Romantics, the best German writers went far beyond merely catering to popular taste. E.T.A. Hoffmann, for instance, probed into the enigma of the human mind so hauntingly that Heinrich Heine called his work a "cry of terror in twenty volumes" (Hugo, "Masterpieces" 256). One scholar speculates that German Romantics of Hoffmann's generation wrote as they did more out of necessity than inclination, seeking new directions from earlier writers such as Goethe and Schiller, whose achievements threatened to overshadow theirs. Whatever the cause, the younger generation of German Romantic writers, who were contemporaries of Wagner, were concerned with "the darker side of nature and the human mind, ... search[ing] for new *frissons*" and exploring "the frontiers of human consciousness and beyond" (Prawer, *Heine* 282).

This German predilection for the sense of mystery, or magic, is a notable feature of the *Ring*, which is filled with magic: Freia's golden apples maintaining the gods' strength and youth, Valkyries on horseback flying between earth and Valhalla, the magic fire surrounding Brünnhilde, the dragon's blood allowing Siegfried to understand the Forest Birds and Mime's thoughts, Brünnhilde's charm ("Zauberspiel") protecting Siegfried from harm.[16] Let us focus on four of the magical objects that play an important role in the *Ring*: the Tarnhelm, the ring, the Walsung sword, and Wotan's spear.

The Tarnhelm — literally the "disguise-helmet" — was forged by Mime, but it was

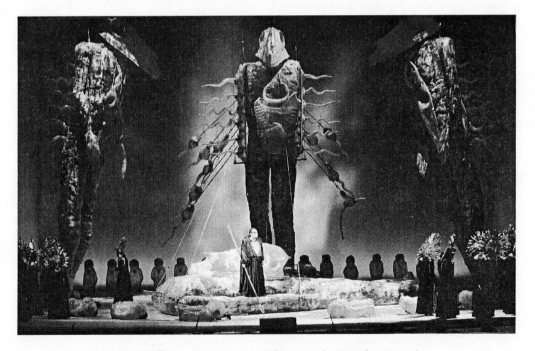

Die Walküre, Kirov Opera. (Photograph: Natasha Razina)

Götterdämmerung, **Kirov Opera. (Photograph: Natasha Razina)**

Alberich's cunning ("List") that invested the object with its power. As Alberich first places the Tarnhelm on his head, in the third scene of *Das Rheingold,* he wonders if its magic ("Zauber") will make him invisible. It does, as Mime learns to his considerable pain, leading the duped brother, shortly after, to tell Wotan and Loge of its magic. Later, when Alberich enters, he boasts of what the Tarnhelm can do:

Fast it transforms me	schnell mich zu wandeln,
just as I wish	nach meinem Wunsch
to a form that is different.	die Gestalt mir zu tauschen,
Thus the helm.	taugt mir der Helm [Robb 19].

Alberich's desire to show off, combined with his underestimation of Wotan and Loge, leads him to be tricked out of owning the Tarnhelm, just as Fafner later loses the helmet because he underestimates Siegfried. Unlike Alberich and Fafner, Siegfried will not be tricked out of the Tarnhelm; more insidiously, he will be manipulated into using it to betray his beloved Brünnhilde. In *Götterdämmerung,* initially unaware of the helmet's power, Siegfried learns of its magic from the treacherous Hagen:

SIEGFRIED
(pointing to the steel network that hangs in his girdle):

[I took] Just this piece, which	Dies Gewirk, unkund seiner
I cannot use.	Kraft.

HAGEN

The Tarnhelm, truly,	Den Tarnhelm kenn' ich,
The Niblungs' most wonderful work!	der Niblungen künstliches Werk;
It serves, when set on your head,	er taugt, bedeckt er dein Haupt,
to transform you to any shape.	dir zu tauschen jede Gestalt.
And if you would travel far,	Verlangt dich's an fernsten Ort,
it transports you in a trice.	er entführt flugs dich dahin [Robb 6].

Perhaps because the Tarnhelm is an object of deceit, it brings no one good fortune. It certainly is not the kind of "morally benevolent" magic that brings about "a lost rapport with the 'sublunary' part of the physical world" (Frye 98). What then of another magical object, the ring?

Again and again Wagner reminds us the ring has magical powers. In the second scene of *Das Rheingold,* after Loge tells Wotan that a magic spell ("ein Runenzauber") was necessary to change the gold stolen from the Rhine into a ring, the god replies with ill humor that Alberich had already uttered the curse, mastering the magic power ("des Zaubers Macht"). In the following scene, Mime tells Loge about a detail of the ring's magic ("Zauber"): it allows Alberich to see where gold lies buried underground. Later in that scene, the ring enables Alberich to summon the Niblungs from the depths of the mines; he needs only to put the ring to his lips and secretly murmur a command.

In *Die Walküre,* II, 2, Wotan — well aware of the ring's magic ("des Ringes Runen") — confides his fear to Brünnhilde that Alberich will conquer Valhalla forever. In the battle of wits between the Wanderer/Wotan and Mime in *Siegfried,* Wotan refers to the coercive energy ("zwingende Kraft") of the magic ring ("Zauberring"). After Wotan leaves and Siegfried returns, Mime uses the same phrase — "coercive energy" — of the ring, imagining how it will make him a Nibelung prince. Throughout *Götterdämmerung,* as Alberich speaks of the ring to various characters — Wotan, Mime, Hagen — he refers to the energy ("Kraft") and magic ("Zauber") that was worked into it, and to its power ("Macht").

Though the ring is powerful, it is not all-powerful. If it were, we would have not a cycle of operas, but a comic-book story — and a short one at that. Despite owning the ring, Alberich cannot prevent Wotan from taking it from him, Fafner cannot keep it or his life, and Brünnhilde finds it useless to her when she most needs it. At the end of the first act of *Götterdämmerung,* a despairing Brünnhilde is accosted by Siegfried, disguised as Gunther:

BRÜNNHILDE
(threateningly stretching out her finger on which is Siegfried's ring):

Stand back! Flee from this token!	Bleib' fern! fürchte dies Zeichen!
You cannot take me by force,	Zur Schande zwingst du mich nicht,
while yet this ring stands on guard.	solang' der Ring mich beschützt.

SIEGFRIED

This is a token for Gunther:	Mannesrecht gebe er Gunther:
he will wed you with this ring.	durch den Ring sei ihn vermählt!

BRÜNNHILDE

Go back, you robber!	Zurück, du Räuber!
Villainous thief!	Frevelnder Dieb!
Don't venture, you rogue,	Erfreche dich nicht, mir zu nah'n!
to come near!	
This is my strength,	Stärker als Stahl
stronger than steel.	macht mich der Ring:
This — cannot be robbed!	nie — raubst du ihn mir!

SIEGFRIED

Why then you shall teach me	Von dir ihn zu lösen,
how it is mine.	lehrst du mich nun!

(He presses toward her. They struggle. Brünnhilde tears herself free and flees. Siegfried pursues her. Again they struggle. He seizes her and plucks the ring from her finger. Brünnhilde shrieks violently. She utters a loud scream and sinks exhausted on the rocky seat in front of the cave) [Robb 12].

The magic of the ring, like that of the Tarnhelm, is important in advancing the inexorable momentum of fate. The strength of the magic of two other objects, the Walsungs' sword and Wotan's spear, depends on the trajectory of the *Ring's* unfolding saga.

When Siegmund first sees the hilt of Nothung, his eyes are blinded by the lightning ("ein Blitz") flashing from the ash-tree. Wotan's magic insured that none of the many warriors who tried to pull the sword from the tree, not even the strongest ("die stärksten") of Hunding's guests, could succeed. Soon after Siegmund makes the sword his own, Wagner underscores the magical nature of Nothung. Fricka, determined that Wotan stop helping his son, berates her husband for having made the magical ("zauberstark") sword available to Siegmund. She prevails, forcing Wotan to counter the magic of Nothung with the more potent magic of his spear, a magic emphasized by Wagner's stage directions. As Siegmund, protected by Brünnhilde, wields Nothung in his fight with Hunding, Wotan intervenes:

> *BRÜNNHILDE*
>
> Slay him, Siegmund!   Triff ihn, Siegmund!
> Trust in your sword!   Traue dem Schwert!
>
> *(Just as Siegmund aims a deadly blow at Hunding a reddish glow
> breaks through the clouds, heralding Wotan, who stands above
> Hunding and points his spear at Siegmund.)*
>
> *WOTAN*
>
> Get back from the spear!   Zurück vor dem Speer!
> In pieces the sword!   In Stücken das Schwert!
>
> *(Brünnhilde, with her shield, has recoiled in terror. Siegmund's
> sword is shivered on the outstretched spear)* [*Die Walküre*; Robb
> 19].

Even the shattered pieces of the sword retain the magic, however. In the following opera, *Siegfried*, Mime, who was so skillful in forging the Tarnhelm (albeit under the direction of Alberich), cannot solder the pieces of Nothung together; he cannot master its energy ("Kraft"). Just as it required a heroic figure to draw the sword out of the tree, so it requires another hero to waken the sword to life. No patching or soldering will do; Siegfried grinds the pieces of the broken sword into shreds, melts them down, and triumphantly recreates his father's sword, singing

> Needful! Needful!   Nothung! Nothung!
> Conquering sword!   neidliches Schwert!
> Again I've waked you to life.   zum Leben weckt' ich dich wieder [Robb 15].

When Siegfried's father and Wotan encountered each other, it was the god who defeated the Walsung; in *Siegfried*, however, it is the magic of the sword of Siegfried — the hero in ascendancy — that breaks the spear of the Wanderer/Wotan — the god in decline. Wagner's stage directions underscore the magical heroism of Siegfried's act, for Wotan's spear is not without its own magical energy:

> *Siegfried with one blow strikes the Wanderer's spear in two: a flash of lightning darts from it
> towards the summit, where the flames, glowing dully before, now break out more and more brightly.
> The blow is accompanied by violent thunder that quickly dies away. The fragments of the spear fall
> at the Wanderer's feet. He quietly picks them up* [Porter 254].

Ever the gifted dramatist, Wagner invests figures and objects with magic in order to drive the plot forward and develop the themes of the *Ring*, particularly the overriding theme of fate. Like Coleridge, Wagner intended to show the dramatic truths beneath the magic.

Looking at the text of the *Ring*, then, we see Romantic themes permeating the action, characters, and even objects. Turning our gaze to the creator of that great work, we see how much Wagner the artist had in common with his Romantic counterparts: transmuting political concerns into mythic artworks, ascribing to the ideal of the visionary artist, and creating radically innovative works of art.

Most of the Romantics, especially in their early years, were strongly political. The first-generation English Romantic poets, for instance, were intoxicated by the prospects created by the French Revolution. In *The Prelude*, Wordsworth was explicit about his euphoria while living in France at the beginning of the Revolution:

> Bliss was it in that dawn to be alive,
> But to be young was very Heaven!
> ...
> The inert
> Were roused, and lively natures rapt away!
> ...
> [All] Were called upon to exercise their skill,
> Not in Utopia,— subterranean fields,—
> Or some secreted island, Heaven knows where!
> But in the very world, which is the world
> Of all of us — the place where, in the end,
> We find our happiness, or not at all!
> [Book XI, ll. 108–9, 123–24, 139–44]

His extravagant claim that he "had given twelve hours thought to the conditions and prospects of society, for one to poetry" could have been made by Coleridge and Shelley, among others (quoted by Abrams, "English Romanticism" 101). With major political upheavals occurring in 1775, 1789, 1830, and 1848, it is not surprising to find Romantic artists in various European countries being charged by political events, and Wagner was no exception.

Wagner was enough of a political activist that he endured a long exile from Saxony, and he wrote extensively about the interaction of politics and art. When he began the *Ring*, he envisioned it as animated by ideas of class, economics, and the state. The fact that Alberich and Wotan are "symbolic of greed for wealth and power" (Kobbé ii) is consonant with the idea in a speech Wagner delivered in 1848: that "the demonic idea of Money" is "*the root of all the misery in our present social state*," "stunting the fair free Will of Man to the most repulsive passion, to avarice" (Vaterlandsverein [Fatherland Club] Speech, *Prose Works* 4: 139, 138).

As idealistic as these sentiments are, they cannot explain the complexity and richness of Wagner's great work. Already in 1854, in a letter to Röckel, Wagner indicates a deepening of this thinking: he writes that the "most profoundly tragic situation of the present day" is the lack of the human longing for love, "a longing to be understood instinctively, a longing that modern reality cannot yet satisfy" (*Selected Letters* 306). As Wagner revised the *Ring* over and over, he became more and more aware of the importance of intuition to the creative process — another important Romantic value. Writing to Röckel in the summer of 1856, he admits that what he had consciously intended in shaping the moral of his music-dramas had become changed and even reversed because as he wrote, he was "unconsciously following a quite different, and much more profound, intuition" (*Selected Letters* 357–58). As a result, the *Ring*, begun as "a parable of Europe's evolution toward a classless, progressive society," eventually became "a parable of a voluntary death that brings a transformation" (Lee 44). Wagner's earlier, political, concept of the *Ring* reflected Romantic thinking, which placed a high value on the individual and freedom. Even more central to Romanticism, however, is the acknowledgement of the power of the intuition and the imagination.

Two distinguished analysts of Wagner's aesthetics go even further in minimizing the importance of politics to the *Ring*'s composer, distancing the political writing and activism from the composition of music. Stressing Wagner's aesthetic autonomy, Deathridge and Dahlhaus maintain that "political convictions meant nothing to Wagner except in relation to the idea of musical drama, the measure of all things for him." Wagner became a revolutionary, they assert, when he saw that the only means of bringing art to the forefront in the theatre was social upheaval. In his preface to the text of the *Ring*, he asked for a princely patron because he did not think the middle class would take art seriously. When the foundation of the German Empire in 1871 caused national pride to swell, he represented music drama as a national work of art, hoping to gain support from the change in public mood (95).

This analysis sees the composer as an opportunist rather than an idealist; he was probably a little of both. Certainly Wagner, like the great Romantic poets, was well aware that existing social structures were corrupt, but politics in the narrow sense was not what animated the Romantic artist. Even Blake, outraged by the social, economic, and political injustices of his time, went far beyond political commentary or satire: his outrage generated a complete mythology. Like Blake, Wagner went beyond the political underpinnings of the *Ring* to produce his own complete mythology — based on Germanic and Norse materials, it is true, but adapted to his own vision.

In the art works of the Romantics, then, politics becomes transmuted into "'the politics of vision,' uttered in the persona of the inspired prophet-priest" (Abrams, "English Romanticism" 102). Such a visionary figure emerges in the ending of Coleridge's "Kubla Khan," a dream-vision of the inspired poet:

> And all should cry, Beware! Beware!
> His flashing eyes, his floating hair!

Die Walküre, Act III, Saxon State Opera. (Photograph: Matthias Creutziger)

> Weave a circle round him thrice,
> And close your eyes with holy dread,
> For he on honey-dew hath fed,
> And drunk the milk of Paradise [*Poetical Works* 298].

No one has written more eloquently of this conviction — that society is held together, nourished, and advanced by its creative power, incarnate in the artist — than Shelley. In his *Defense of Poetry*, he maintains that "a poet participates in the eternal, the infinite, and the one," producing an "electric life which burns within [poets'] words." He ends the essay with these ringing statements:

> [Poets] measure the circumference and sound the depths of human nature with a comprehensive and all-penetrating spirit, and they are themselves perhaps the most sincerely astonished at its manifestations; for it is less their spirit than the spirit of the age. Poets are the hierophants of an unapprehended inspiration; the mirrors of the gigantic shadows which futurity casts upon the present; the words which express what they understand not; the trumpets which sing to battle and feel not what they inspire; the influence which is moved not but moves. Poets are the unacknowledged legislators of the world [297].[17]

Wagner's letters to Röckel express his ongoing recommitment to a divine artistic mission. Writing in 1856, he states, "I am solely an artist: and that is my blessing and my curse ("Ich bin nur Künstler: und das ist mein Segen und mein Fluch"; *Richard Wagners Briefe* 69). "Otherwise," he continues, "I should gladly become a saint and know that my life was settled for me in the simplest way" (*Selected Letters* 359). In his long letter discussing his ideas in the *Ring* (January 1854), he reiterates his dedication to art: "I can no longer exist except as an artist: everything else ... disgusts me, or else is of interest only inasmuch as it has a bearing on art." When he states that "ordinary peace and quiet" is abnormal to his temperament, whereas his "normal condition" is "a state of exaltation" (*Selected Letters* 311), he implies what Shelley made explicit: the creative artist lives with a heightened consciousness, duty-bound to make incarnate the promptings of the creative imagination.

In a well-known passage from his autobiography, Wagner writes of one such prompting:

> I stretched myself, dead tired, on a hard couch, awaiting the long-desired hour of sleep. It did not come; but I fell into a kind of somnolent state, in which I suddenly felt as though I were sinking in swiftly flowing water. The rushing sound formed itself in my brain into a musical sound, the chord of E flat major, which continually reechoed in broken forms; these broken chords seemed to be melodic passages of increasing motion, yet the pure triad of E flat major never changed, but seemed by its continuance to impart infinite significance to the element in which I was sinking. I awoke in sudden terror from my doze, feeling as though the waves were rushing high above my head. I at once recognised that the orchestral overture to the *Rheingold*, which must long have lain latent within me, though it had been unable to find definite form, had at last been revealed to me [*My Life* 603].

Some commentators believe Wagner's account: Lee (36), for instance, and Donington, who is struck by the rebirth imagery in the passage (42). Others interpret Wagner's dream differently. Tanner calls it "another piece of mild mythology" (216); Borchmeyer sees it as "yet another myth that [Wagner] invented in a spirit of mythopoeic fantasy" (362). Treadwell also believes that the story was fabricated, but offers a more thoughtful analysis:

> [In *My Life*] moments of origin are touched by myth. All the well-known stories of sudden inspiration — the *Rheingold* prelude appearing in a waking dream at La Spezia, the inspiration for *Meistersinger* arriving as Wagner stood in front of Titian's *Assumption* in the Frari church in Venice, *Parsifal* conceived on waking one fine Good Friday morning near Zurich — have an appropriately numinous air. Finding beginnings is a magical kind of storytelling.... Narrative, not prophecy, is where meaning is found [112].

The "meaning" of which Treadwell speaks is that it does not really matter whether the dream was actual or whether the composer made it up. What is important is that Wagner saw himself as a Romantic artist: aware of the power of the imagination and dedicated to producing art because the summons to do so came from beyond. When Wordsworth described his first feeling of being called to dedicate himself to poetry, he used the language of religious conversion:

> I made no vows, but vows
> Were then made for me: bond unknown to me
> Was given, that I should be, else sinning greatly,
> A dedicated Spirit... [*The Prelude*, Book IV, ll. 334–37].

Later in *The Prelude* (Book XIII), Wordsworth wrote of discovering that the specific vocation to which he felt dedicated was to be the agent of a new kind of poetry. The Romantics, whether in poetry or music, produced new forms — and once again Wagner's achievement parallels what the Romantic poets were doing.[18]

As nineteenth-century music sought alternatives to the legacy of classicism, "a strange jumble of trends, toward intimacy, monumentality, and virtuosity" emerged (Dahlhaus, *Nineteenth-Century Music* 24–25). Wagner, however, was not consciously seeking to be radical. Rather than calculated attempts to revolutionize a genre, his innovations were true examples of organic form: intuition was given primacy, the emotional intensity so characteristic of Romanticism was given full rein, form emerged from feeling. As M.H. Abrams points out in his perceptive study of Romantic theory, *The Mirror and the Lamp*, art before Romanticism — from Aristotle through the eighteenth century — could be seen as mimetic, best symbolized by the mirror that the artist held up to reality; whereas Romantic art was expressive, best symbolized by a lamp. Wordsworth's definition of poetry as "the spontaneous overflow of powerful feelings" encapsulates this important aesthetic shift. To the Romantic, form does matter, but instead of being a kind of template, it is the result of the artist's feelings and intuitions. Hence, the startling innovations seen in the *Ring* can be described as "technical manifestations" of Wagner's "habitual urge towards expressive intensity" (Treadwell 116).

It is no overstatement to say that the *Ring* made opera into "something that had never been imagined before" (Treadwell 133). Wagner took a genre "previously half ceremonial pomp, half entertainment, and declared it to be the *ne plus ultra* of art," raising for opera the same lofty claims that Beethoven had achieved for the symphony (Dahlhaus, *Nineteenth-Century Music* 195). Dahlhaus points out that Kant and Hegel, as well as the educated classes subscribing to their philosophies, had doubted the artistic credentials of theater. Wagner proposed that his music dramas were not simply theatrical works whose substance resided in a musico-literary text; instead, the theatrical event itself constituted the work of art, with literature and music serving as handmaidens. Wagner's redefinition created nothing less than "an aesthetic revolution that challenged not only the century's credence in texts but its social prejudices as well" (196).

We can identify discrete levels of innovation in the *Ring*. First is the verse form of Wagner's great poem, following the principles set forth in *Opera and Drama*. One noticeable feature of the *Ring*'s text is its alliteration, Wagner's recreation of the *Stabreim* that was an essential feature of Old Germanic poetry. An artistically significant extension of this is the way that the sounds of language are organically fused to meaning, most notably in the opening of the entire cycle. The Rhinedaughters' names are integral: Woglinde, from *wogen*: to billow; Wellgunde, from *Welle*: wave, and Floßhilde (Flosshilde), from *fließen*: to flow. The language of their opening utterance is not a succession of nonsense symbols, but "an approximation of speech in which words are not yet intelligible concepts but musical sounds from the dawn of time" (Borchmeyer 218):

Weia! Waga!	Weia! Waga!
Woge, du Welle,	Billow, you wave,
Walle zur Wiege!	flow round the cradle!
Wagalaweia!	Wagalaweia!
Wallala weiala weia!	Wallala weiala weia [author's translation]!

Wagner was certainly aware of the etymological relationship between *Wiege* (cradle) and *Woge* (wave); he told his wife that the song of the waves was "like the world's lullaby" (Cosima Wagner, diary entry for July 17, 1869, 127). Though Wagner's critics refused to accept his mythological conception of language, ridiculing in particular the Rhinedaughters' "Wagalaweia," critics today understand what Wagner accomplished in using this evocation of speech.

A further level of innovation is the remarkable synthesis of the poetry and the music, which Wagner used throughout the *Ring*; initially, to establish characters, and subsequently, to deepen the delineation. This "intimate fusion of poetic and melodic line," surpassing anything Wagner wrote before the *Ring* (Stein 87), is a prime illustration of the organic form so prized by the Romantics.

In literature, lyric poets had always been concerned with the artistic interaction between meaning and form, even in a set form such as a sonnet, manipulating consonant and vowel sounds, internal rhymes, pauses within lines, and repeated words. However, Romantic theorists and creative artists were so concerned with the unity represented by organic form that they would modify a set form whenever doing so would enhance the poem's meaning. Using the traditional ballad form, for instance, Wordsworth added a line to the final stanza of "We Are Seven" to emphasize the speaker's exasperation, and Keats truncated the final line of each stanza of "La Belle Dame sans Merci" to create a haunting effect in that evocative ballad. Wagner probably had not read Coleridge's discussions of unity and organic form, but the *Ring* stunningly exemplifies the aesthetic synthesis described by the poet. A particularly powerful example is the beginning of Alberich's curse in the final scene of *Das Rheingold*. Musical elements — melody, rhythm, pauses, dynamics — interact with vowel sounds and meaning to create a remarkable word-tone synthesis. Wagner pulls together every aspect of word and music in order to emphasize the bitter sarcasm, ominousness, and increasing intensity of the curse (Stein 84–85).

This remarkable synthesis can be seen in light of the Romantic concern with reconciling subjective and objective, specific and universal. From the finale of Beethoven's Ninth Symphony onward, composers saw the unifying of words and music as one solution to this concern, a solution that was most extensively envisaged in Wagner's *Gesamtkunstwerk*: the ideal union of music, words, and theatrical realization. This synthesis, culminating in the *Ring*, "could be taken as the *ne plus ultra* of Romantic synaesthesia" (Bone 132), an accomplishment that should never be underestimated:

> There is nothing in opera preceding Wagner, or indeed even in Wagnerian opera itself before *Opera and Drama* [completed by Wagner in 1851], that approaches the subtlety, the fullness, the exactness of character portrayal that is now possible through Wagner's invention of this kind of dialogue. The sinister force of Alberich, Mime's bungling stupidity, Loge's slyness, and the characterizations of the other chief personages bring a new dimension to the lyric drama [Stein 87].

An even more striking compositional innovation than the verse form and the musical-poetic synthesis is "the inexhaustibly subtle and fertile use of leitmotif" (Treadwell 114). In bringing the system of leitmotif to culmination in the *Ring*, Wagner moved beyond "'symphonic' form, in which the 'web' of motifs is the basis of the inner cohesion" to what may be called "'architectonic' form, consisting of a discernible grouping (using contrast and repetition) of

Siegfried, Saxon State Opera: Luciana De Vol as Brünnhilde. (Photograph: Matthias Creutziger)

distinct components" (Deathridge and Dahlhaus 98). This "successful mediation between the symphonic and the dramatic" was a "qualitative leap in the history of leitmotif technique" (Deathridge and Dahlhaus 108, 152).

Other operatic composers had used motifs, of course. In "mad" scenes, for example, like those in Handel's *Orlando* or Donizetti's *Lucia di Lammermoor*, "the motifs and the border-line between static and dynamic forms are ... deliberately confused" (Deathridge 7), but no one had used this strategy for an entire opera — let alone a cycle of operas. Until *Lohengrin*, Wagner himself had used the technique of reminiscence motifs, adopted from Weber. These reminiscence motifs were repetitions, quotations, or echoes, whereas the motifs in the *Ring* form a dense web. The *Ring*'s leitmotifs are derivable from each other: Erda's theme, for instance, is a variation of the Rhine-Nature theme, and the leitmotif of the downfall of the gods is the Rhine-Nature theme progressing downward instead of upward. The result is a configuration instead of an accumulation, with the leitmotifs "linked into a contextual system" (Dahlhaus, *Nineteenth-Century Music* 199–200). Wagner had set himself a problem and solved it, working out how music could "reflect, reminisce, and hint at what is to come as well as tell a story directly" (Deathridge 7). The result of this compositional innovation is as imaginative and inventive as any innovation in Romantic poetry:

> What the *Ring* does away with entirely is the conventional notion that musical drama proceeds from moment to moment, event to event, aria to duet to finale, the music at each point expressing or characterizing whatever stage the drama has reached.... Instead it creates a kind of four-dimensional theatre, where each moment in the plot lives alongside other moments and overlaps with them, the orchestra opening pathways between nows and thens. Moving from creation to cataclysm, the tetralogy embraces the whole of time, and treats the element as if it were as fluid as water [Treadwell 124].

Discussing Wagner in the context of the history and development of music leads writers into superlatives:

> Every now and then the creative impulse of man suddenly erupts and produces something so extraordinary, so incalculable, that from the moment it comes into being the history of an art is irrevocably changed. The past can no longer look the same; the future trend can no longer *be* the same. Such a work is Wagner's *Der Ring des Nibelungen* [Culshaw 8].

To irrevocably change the history of music is more than most composers can expect, but placing Wagner in an even larger context — Romanticism — underscores what the *Ring* contributes to the world:

> If a society has ever existed which is completely content with what it has and asks for nothing else, it would not need such comfort as the Romantics have to offer. But to all who are dissatisfied with a current order or a conventional scheme of things, this spirit brings not an anodyne but an inspiration. From discontent it moves to a vision of a sublime state in which the temporal, without losing its individuality, is related to the timeless, and the many defects of the given world are seen to be irrelevant and insignificant in comparison with the mysteries which enclose it [Bowra 292].

Shelley, as aware as any of "the defects of the given world," spoke of the human's infinite insatiability as "the desire of the moth for the star." One can experience a temporary cessation of this longing by entering the world of the Romantic, whether it be by way of literature — Coleridge's mariner, Shelley's skylark, Keats's grecian urn — or by way of Wagner's sublime *Ring*.

Notes

1. A number of commentators have mentioned the possible influence of Vico on Romantic thinking (Frye 14, for instance) and on Wagner in particular. The most extended treatment of Vico and Wagner occurs in John DiGaetani's study *Wagner and Suicide.*

2. Some writers classify Wagner as *Romantic*, while others term him *neo–Romantic. The New Grove Wagner*, for instance, refers to the "'neo–Romanticism' of Wagner and Liszt" (Deathridge and Dahlhaus 9). In another publication, one of those writers explains his choice of the term *neo–Romantic.* Carl Dahlhaus terms the music immediately preceding that of Wagner — early nineteenth-century music — as "romantic in an age of romanticism, which produced romantic poetry and painting and even romantic physics and chemistry." In contrast, he notes, "the neo-romanticism of the later part of the century [when the *Ring* was composed] was romantic in an unromantic age, dominated by positivism and realism" (*Between Romanticism and Modernism* 5).

Using an extra-musical rationale, then, Dahlhaus terms Wagner a neo-romantic while maintaining that his music is indeed romantic.

3. Some writers go even further. A.O. Lovejoy's essay "On the Discrimination of Romanticisms" (*PMLA*, 39 [1924]: 229–53) argues that the variations in Romanticism are so great that one should think of the term in the plural. A more recent commentator, Mary A. Cicora, goes beyond Lovejoy, basing her interpretation of the *Ring* on Jacques Derrida's notion of deconstruction (*Mythology as Metaphor: Romantic Irony, Critical Theory, and Wagner's* Ring). Whether or not Cicora was familiar with Drummond Bone's essay "The Question of a European Romanticism," her thesis can be seen as an outgrowth of his.

4. Although Frye's essay opens a book entitled *A Study of English Romanticism*, it deals with the essence of romanticism in "all Western literatures [beginning] around the later part of the eighteenth century" and coming to fruition in the following century (4). Because Frye's ideas come from literature, they can legitimately be applied to Wagner's great poem of the *Ring*. Additionally, Dahlhaus notes that "the musical notion of romanticism derives from literature" (*Nineteenth-Century Music* 16).

5. Unless otherwise noted, all references to *The Prelude* are from the 1850 version.

6. Wordsworth had just turned 30 when the first part of *The Prelude* was published in 1799. He greatly expanded it and continued to revise it until his death in 1850, so it is not surprising that this lifelong revision of the poem reflects his increasing conservatism. The 1805 lines "I worshipped then among the depths of things / As my soul bade me ... / I felt and nothing else ..." (Book XI, ll. 234–38) became, in the 1850 version, "Worshipping then among the depths of things / As piety ordained ... / I felt, observed, and pondered ..." (Book XII, ll. 184–88; Bloom 149). Nevertheless, our interest here is with the early Wordsworth, writing at the height of his powers and, in collaboration with Coleridge, virtually jump-starting Romanticism in English poetry.

7. The Rhinedaughters themselves ("Nicker," or nixies) are manifestations of nature. Water sprites of Germanic folklore, they come from a long mythological tradition that each place in nature has an attendant spirit, a residing genius or *genius loci.*

8. A further passage from the work by Novalis expresses Wagner's earlier, more political interpretation of his own narrative:

Nature does not wish to be the exclusive property of any single individual.	Die Natur will nicht der ausschliessliche Besitz eines einzigen sein.
As property she transforms herself into a wicked poison	Als Eigentum verwandelt sie sich in ein böses Gift,
which destroys peace and attracts the destructive desire	was die Ruhe verscheucht, und die verderbliche Lust,
to appropriate everything within the circle of its possessor	alles in diesen Kreis des Besitzers zu ziehen,
with a host of endless cares and wild passion.	mit einem Gefolge von unendlichen Sorgen und wilder Leidenschaft herbeilockt.
Thus, it secretly undermines the ground of the owner and soon buries him	So untergrabt sie heimlich den Grund des Eigentümer und begräbt ihm bald
in the collapsing abyss.	in dem einbrechenden Abrund [Quoted in Richards 55].

9. The simplistic idea of the "noble savage," too often taken to be Rousseau's ideal though never mentioned by him, does not figure in the discussion above. In fact, Rousseau believed that a return to nature was neither possible nor desirable.

10. For ten years Wordsworth's sister, Dorothy, accompanied the poet in his walks around the Lake Country, keeping journals that included detailed prose accounts of many of the incidents that her brother later turned into poetry. Holding to his own definition of poetry as "recollection in tranquility," Wordsworth composed the poems later than the experiences that gave rise to them, sometimes as long after as a year and a half.

Not all of Wordsworth's poetry reflects the Rousseauean ideas discussed above, but much of it — including most poems in the groundbreaking *Lyrical Ballads*— does.

11. For a thorough analysis of Wagner's "art of time" — how the music underscores the process of Siegfried's narrative turning into a re-enactment — see Treadwell, 120–24.

12. Gustav Kobbé, writing close to the time of the first performances of the entire *Ring* cycle, maintains that the power of the music alone can make spectators forget about the incest between the Walsung twins. He writes, "For all we know, in those moments when the impassioned music of that [love] scene whirls us away in its resistless current, not a drop of related blood courses through their veins. This is a sufficient answer to the sermons that have been preached against the immorality of this scene. Moreover ... the people of today can imagine that the lovers were strangers or second cousins or anything else" (vi–vii). Though the music of the love scene between Siegmund and Sieglinde is just as "thrilling" and "rapturous" as Kobbé says, Wagner was too good a dramatist to expect the music alone to create meaning.

13. Donington's Jungian reading of the *Ring* stresses the twins as animus and anima. This leads him to remark that the "mythological rightness underlying the symbolism of Siegmund's incest with Sieglinde" accounts for our sympathy for the pair. "Whatever our ingrained resistance to the idea of incest in the ordinary outside world, we are completely on the side of the lovers as we sit watching them in the opera-house. We share in Wagner's own feeling that the world has blossomed into warmth and fruitfulness after

the strained, inhibited congestion of Wotan's plotting and Alberich's hatred in *Rheingold*" (123).

14. Though fate, not vengeance, is the determining factor in the *Ring*, Siegmund's mention of vengeance is interesting. Jessie Weston points out that Sieglinde's counterpart in the Völsunga saga, Signy, was "practically embodied revenge." Signy's actions went far beyond incest, but, Weston holds, we are not simply repulsed by her since, like Wagner's twins, she is influenced by a force outside herself (346–47).

15. Drummond Bone distinguishes several functions of incest in Romantic works, noting that it could be seen as either a liberation from the world ("an in-gathering of the resources of self") or as "an escapist retreat from the human duty to reach out to the world." He notes that "the image of the Ideal as a mere projection of self flits around incestual themes in Byron and Shelley ... whereas Wagner in the *Ring of the Nibelungs* uses incest as a gathering of the powers of the individual against the established social order" (286).

Certainly Wagner was aware of this social theme when he shaped the character of Siegmund, but as he progressed in his work on the cycle, his emphasis moved much more toward the mythic dimension than the social.

16. The potions concocted by Gutrune and Hagen to affect Siegfried's memory are more natural than magic; stage directions specify that Hagen squeeze the juice of an herb into the drink he prepares for Siegfried near the end of *Götterdämmerung*.

17. *A Defense of Poetry* was completed in 1821. Many of the sentences quoted above also appeared in an essay published a year earlier, *A Philosophical View of Reform* (240).

18. Not everything that the Romantic poets wrote was formally innovative, of course. Almost all the English Romantic poets continued to write sonnets, for instance, and Wordsworth and Coleridge used the ballad form. However, the formal innovations were considerable. Though the radical departure from meter would come later, with the American Romantic Walt Whitman, Wordsworth's aesthetics of poetic diction was revolutionary and widely influential.

Bibliography

Aberbach, Alan David. *The Ideas of Richard Wagner: An Examination and Analysis.* 2nd ed. Lanham: University Press of America, 2003.

Abrams, M.H. "English Romanticism: The Spirit of the Age." *Romanticism and Consciousness: Essays in Criticism.* Ed. Harold Bloom. New York: Norton, 1970. 90–119.

_____. *The Mirror and the Lamp: Romantic Theory and the Critical Tradition.* New York: Norton, 1953.

Bate, Walter Jackson. *From Classic to Romantic: Premises of Taste in Eighteenth-Century England.* New York: Harper, 1946.

Baudelaire, Charles. *The Complete Verse.* Trans. Francis Scarfe. London: Anvil, 1986.

Baugh, Albert C., ed. *A Literary History of England.* 2nd ed. New York: Appleton, 1967.

Bloom, Harold. *The Visionary Company: A Reading of English Romantic Poetry.* Garden City: Anchor-Doubleday, 1961.

Bone, Drummond. "The Question of a European Romanticism." *Questioning Romanticism.* Ed. John Beer. Baltimore: Johns Hopkins University Press, 1995. 123–32.

Borchmeyer, Dieter. *Drama and the World of Richard Wagner.* Trans. Daphne Ellis. Princeton: Princeton University Press, 2003.

Bowra, C.M. *The Romantic Imagination.* New York: Oxford University Press, 1961.

Bush, Douglas. *Mythology and the Romantic Tradition in English Poetry.* New York: Norton, 1963.

Cicora, Mary A. *Mythology as Metaphor: Romantic Irony, Critical Theory, and Wagner's Ring.* Westport: Greenwood, 1998.

Cobban, Alfred. "The Revolt Against the Eighteenth Century." *Romanticism and Consciousness: Essays in Criticism.* Ed. Harold Bloom. New York: Norton, 1970. 132–46.

Cochrane, Peggie, trans. *Das Rheingold.* By Richard Wagner. Decca Records, reprinted for the Chicago Symphony Orchestra performances, 1983.

Coleridge, Samuel Taylor. *Biographica Literaria.* 1817. Ed. George Watson. London: Dent, 1975.

_____. *Poetical Works.* 1834. Ed. Ernest Hartley Coleridge. Oxford: Oxford University Press, 1969.

Cooke, Deryck. *I Saw the World End: A Study of Wagner's Ring.* London: Oxford University Press, 1979.

Culshaw, John. "Götterdämmerung." [CD booklet; Solti's *Ring*]. London: Decca, 1997.

Dahlhaus, Carl. *Between Romanticism and Modernism: Four Studies in the Music of the Later Nineteenth Century.* Trans. Mary Whittall. Berkeley: University of California Press, 1980.

_____. *Nineteenth-Century Music.* Trans. J. Bradford Robinson. Berkeley: University of California Press, 1989.

Deathridge, John. "The Ring: An Introduction." *Der Ring des Nibelungen* [DVD Booklet]. Hamburg: Deutsche Grammophon, 2002. 2–9.

Deathridge, John, and Carl Dahlhaus. *The New Grove Wagner.* New York: Norton, 1984.

DiGaetani, John Louis. *Wagner and Suicide.* Jefferson: McFarland, 2003.

Donington, Robert. *Wagner's Ring and Its Symbols: The Music and the Myth.* New York: St. Martin's, 1963.

Frye, Northrop. *A Study of English Romanticism.* New York: Random House, 1968.

Goethe, Johann Wolfgang von. *The Sorrows of Young Werther* and *Novella*. 1774; 1826. Trans. Elizabeth Mayer and Louise Bogan. New York: Random, 1971.

Horton, Rod W, and Vincent F. Hopper. *Backgrounds of European Literature: The Political, Social, and Intellectual Development Behind the Great Books of Western Civilization*. New York: Appleton, 1954.

Hugo, Howard E. "Masterpieces of Romanticism." Introduction. *The Continental Edition of World Masterpieces*. Ed. Maynard Mack. Vol. 2. New York: Norton, 1966. 239–67.

_____. *The Portable Romantic Reader*. New York: Viking, 1957.

Kitcher, Philip, and Richard Schacht. *Finding an Ending: Reflections on Wagner's Ring*. New York: Oxford University Press, 2004.

Kobbé, Gustav. *Wagner's Ring of the Nibelung*. 7th ed. New York: Schirmer, 1896.

Lee, M. Owen. "Wagner's *Ring*: Turning the Sky Round." *The Opera Quarterly* 1 (1983): 28–47.

Liszt, Franz. *Life of Chopin*. Trans. M. Walke Cook. London: Reeves, 1877.

Lovejoy, A.O. "On the Discrimination of Romanticisms." *PMLA* 39 (1924): 229–53.

Mahoney, John L. Introduction. *The English Romantics*. Prospect Heights: Waveland, 1978. 1–22.

Porter, Andrew, trans. *The Ring of the Nibelung*. By Richard Wagner. New York: Norton, 1976.

Prawer, S.S. *Frankenstein's Island: England and the English in the Writings of Heinrich Heine*. Cambridge: Cambridge University Press, 1986.

_____. *Heine: The Tragic Satirist*. Cambridge: Cambridge University Press, 1961.

Praz, Mario. *The Romantic Agony*. 2nd ed. London: Oxford University Press, 1970.

Richards, Walter William. "Nature as a Symbolic Element in Richard Wagner's Treatment of Myth." Diss. Florida State University, 1997.

Robb, Stewart, trans. *Das Rheingold*. By Richard Wagner. New York: Schirmer, 1960.

_____. *Die Walküre*. By Richard Wagner. New York: Schirmer, 1960.

_____ *Götterdämmerung*. By Richard Wagner. New York: Schirmer, 1960.

_____. *Siegfried*. By Richard Wagner. New York: Schirmer, 1960.

Shelley, Percy Bysshe. *Shelley's Prose: or The Trumpet of a Prophecy*. Ed. David Lee Clark. Albuquerque: University of New Mexico Press, 1954 [corrected ed. 1966].

Snook, Lynn. "Richard Wagner's Mythic Models." *Penetrating Wagner's Ring: An Anthology*. Ed. John Louis DiGaetani. New York: Da Capo, 1978. 325–39.

Stein, Jack M. *Richard Wagner and the Synthesis of the Arts*. Detroit: Wayne State University Press, 1960.

Tanner, Michael. *Wagner*. Princeton: Princeton University Press, 1995.

Treadwell, James. *Interpreting Wagner*. New Haven: Yale University Press, 2003.

Wagner, Cosima. *Cosima Wagner's Diaries*. Ed. Martin Gregor-Dellin and Dietrich Mack. Trans. Geoffrey Skelton. New York: Harcourt, 1976.

Wagner, Richard. *My Life*. Authorized trans. New York: Dodd, 1931.

_____. *Richard Wagners Briefe*. Vol. X-XIII. Leipzig: Breitkopf, 1910.

_____. *Richard Wagner's Prose Works*. 8 vols. Trans. William Ashton Ellis. New York: Broude, 1966.

_____. *Selected Letters of Richard Wagner*. Trans. and ed. Stewart Spencer and Barry Millington. New York: Norton, 1987.

Weston, Jessie. "The Valkyrie." *Penetrating Wagner's Ring: An Anthology*. Ed. John Louis DiGaetani. New York: Da Capo, 1978. 345–53.

Wordsworth, William. *Poetical Works*. 1850. Ed. Thomas Hutchinson, rev. Ernest De Selincourt. Oxford: Oxford University Press, 1969.

5. The *Ring*: An Italian Dream Set in Switzerland

John Louis DiGaetani

Wagner died in Venice on February 13, 1883, and it was appropriate on some level that the composer died in Italy since the country had been such a major source of inspiration for him. After Ludwig II became his patron and he could afford many luxuries thanks to the generous king, Wagner often went to Italy, especially in the winters, when the cold climate in Bayreuth was hard on his heart. Wagner repeatedly wrote in his correspondence how much he enjoyed being in Italy, especially Venice, Naples, and Sicily. Indeed, his daughter Blandine (legally his daughter, though biologically she was probably Hans von Bülow's daughter) married Count Biagio Gravina, a Sicilian nobleman, and spent most of her life in Sicily. At the Albergo delle Palme in Palermo there still exists the Salone Wagner where the composer stayed whenever he was in Palermo.

Wagner also wrote most of the music for *Tristan und Isolde* in Venice, and being surrounded by water undoubtedly added to the undulating quality of most of the chromatic music in that opera. Wagner said he got the whole idea for his *Ring* cycle while dreaming on a boat off the coast of Spezia in Italy. He reported that Titian's great painting of the Assumption of the Virgin Mary in Venice inspired him to write the Liebestod at the end of *Tristan und Isolde*. He also wanted the Temple of the Grail in *Parsifal* to be modeled on the beautiful medieval cathedral in Siena, and the garden at the Palazzo Rufalo on the Amalfi coast inspired his vision of Klingsor's magic garden in Act II of *Parsifal*.

Water symbolism occurs often in Wagnerian opera, especially in *Die Fliegende Holländer, Tristan und Isolde,* and the *Ring* cycle. Wagner occasionally went to spas in Germany to find a water cure for his many health problems, but Germany, except for its north coast, is a land-locked country. While cities like Dresden and Munich have rivers, to view a great ocean Wagner repeatedly made the journey to Italy.

While in Italy the mighty cycles of the tides of the ocean would have been constant reminders to him of the powerful cycles of nature. Even in Venice Wagner would have been reminded of the oceanic tides as he looked out on the Grand Canal from his hotel window; the sides of the Venetian canals are marked with water lines from those tides. Wagner probably absorbed Vico's theories about the cycles of nature, and the power of those cycles of nature on human experience, from his reading of his favorite German writer, Goethe. Goethe knew Vico's works, and Goethe's own writings reflect Vico's theories about the cycles of nature. Goethe's greatest work, his play *Faust,* begins with angels singing about the cycles of nature, and those very cycles become a dominant theme in his great play.

In addition to Italy, Switzerland was central to the life and works of Wagner, and he often said to his second wife, Cosima, that the only times in his life that he was really happy were his years in Switzerland, especially at the Villa Tribschen on Lake Lucerne, which is now a Wagner museum. Switzerland began as a refuge for him after his political trouble in Germany, caused by his involvement in the Dresden Revolution of 1848–1849. Most German states forbade Wagner to live within their territories, so he fled to Switzerland, and he was most comfortable where he could use the German language since he was no linguist.

Ernest Newman, in his four-volume biography of Wagner, reports on his arrival in Switzerland in May of 1849 at the home of a friend called Mueller:

> Mueller being at a picnic in the country that day, Wagner had to spend the night of the 28th–29th in the Hotel 'Schwert,' where, by the way, Goethe had more than once stayed. Frau Henriette Hesselbarth, Mueller's daughter, has told us how her father, in answer to the ringing of the house bell on the night of the 29th, put his head out of the window (he had only that evening returned from the picnic), and cried, 'Who is that, so late as this?' 'It is I, Richard Wagner: open quickly!' was the reply. Wagner threw his arms around Mueller and said, 'Alexander, you must give me shelter. I am safe only here. I have fled from Dresden, leaving my wife and property behind me.' As Mueller was out teaching or rehearsing all day, and Wagner felt lonely, he used to invite the two little girls of the house into the room that their father had placed at his disposal: they went rather unwillingly, for they had to sit quite still, not being allowed even to turn the leaves of a book. Wagner would play to them pieces out of his operas, and ask them 'Do you like that?' 'Like the stupid children we were," said Frau Hesselbarth in later years, "We would say 'NO!'" Then he would say, 'In that case you must listen to it until you do." He would often say to us, 'When anyone asks you who your teacher was, say Richard Wagner'" [Newman, II 114–115].

This comic quotation says something of Wagner's rather tyrannical personality, but also his sense of humor. In his autobiography, *Mein Leben*, Wagner writes about his arrival in Zurich and his stay with the Muellers:

> I arrived at Mueller's house, requested a room of some kind as my refuge, and handed over to him the rest of my fortune — twenty francs. I was soon obliged to note that my old acquaintance was a bit embarrassed by my open trust in him and became worried as to what to do with me. At once I voluntarily gave up the large room with piano he placed at my disposal in the impulse of the moment, and retired to a modest little bedroom. The only troublesome matter was my participation in his daily meals, not because they were distasteful to me, but because my digestive organs couldn't cope with them. Outside my friend's house, on the other hand, I enjoyed what was, by the standards of the locality, the most lavish hospitality. The same young men who had been so kind to me during my former trip to Zurich continued to show great pleasure in my company. Before long Jacob Sulzer emerged as the most imposing member of the group.... Whenever I was asked in later years when I had ever in my life run across what is called, in the moral sense, true character and genuine honesty, I could upon reflection name no other than the friend that I made at this time, Jakob Sulzer" [Wagner 423].

Despite his new Swiss friends during this first extended stay in Switzerland, Wagner was often lonely and missed many of his friends in Germany, particularly the Hungarian Franz Liszt, who was in charge of the opera at Weimar and an employee of the Duke there. Many of Wagner's letters to Liszt during this first Swiss period are quite desperate and even suicidal. On March 30, 1853, Wagner wrote from Switzerland to Liszt:

> This cannot go on; I cannot bear life much longer.... Then I shall begin a different life. Then I shall get money how and where I can; I shall borrow and steal, if necessary, in order to travel. The beautiful parts of Italy are closed to me unless I am amnestied. So I shall go to Spain, to Andalusia, and make friends, and try once more to live as well as I can. I should like to fare round the world. If I can get no money, or if the journey does not help me to a new breath of life, there is an end of it, and I shall then seek death by my own hand rather than live on in this manner [Wagner & Liszt].

Such a suicidal letter was followed soon afterwards on May 30, 1853, by another letter to Liszt:

> Dearest friend, have you not yet had enough of Weimar? I must own that I frequently grieve to see how you waste your strength there. Was there any truth in the recent rumor of your leaving Weimar? Have they given in? But all this is idle talk. My brain is a wilderness, and I thirst for a long, long sleep, to awake only with my arms around you. Write to me very precisely, also whether you are inclined, after a little stay at Zurich, to go with me to the solitude of the Grisons; St. Moritz might, after all, do you good, dearest friend; we shall there be five thousand feet high, and enjoy the most nerve-strengthening air, together with the mineral water, which is said to be of beneficial effect on the digestive organs. Think this over, consult your health and your circumstances, and let me know very soon what I may hope for. Farewell, best and dearest of friends. Have my eternal thanks for your divine friendship, and be assured of my steadfast and warmest love [Wagner & Liszt].

There certainly is a homoerotic element to these Swiss letters to Liszt, and also a suggestion of Wagner's loneliness and suicidal thoughts during his first extended stay in Switzerland. These letters and others to Liszt have led some to conclude that Wagner suffered from bipolar illness. There is certainly much evidence of Wagner's depressions in these letters from Switzerland.

In Zurich, his reputation had preceded him and some people already knew his music and his reputation as an opera composer in Germany. Jacob Sulzer, François and Eliza Wille, and other musical people invited Wagner to their houses. He was very soon provided with a residency permit so that he could remain in Switzerland and travel to other parts of Europe if he needed to. While in Zurich, he also met the German silk merchant Otto Wesendonck, plus his lovely wife Mathilde, and they allowed him to stay at their villa near Zurich. While there Wagner wrote his famous *Wesendonck Lieder,* a song cycle on the poems written by Mathilde Wesendonck. Wagner also wrote the first act of *Tristan und Isolde* while in Zurich, though he wrote the last two acts in Venice. The Wesendonck songs were in many ways a trial for the musical themes and harmonies he would develop in *Tristan und Isolde*, which premiered in Munich in June 10, 1865, with Malvina and Ludwig Schnorr von Carolsfeld in the principal roles — conducted by Hans von Bülow.

In order to survive in Zurich, Wagner did much conducting — often of his own music. The main orchestras in Zurich, then as now, were the Algemeine Musik Gesellschaft and the Tonhalle Orchester, and Wagner conducted these groups many times. The first festival of Wagner's music occurred in Zurich, and he envisioned staging his *Ring* cycle and building his festival theater in Zurich, though the thrifty Swiss never provided any financial backing for his mighty project. The Swiss soon got wind of Wagner's mania for spending binges and running up huge debts, and as a result were often suspicious of this spendthrift operatic genius. And Wagner soon learned that it was wise to separate his German friends from his Swiss friends, since they usually did not get along with each other.

Wagner also met the Swiss poet Gottfried Keller in Zurich, and they discussed their concept of art for the people rather than art for the upper classes only. Ultimately Keller and Wagner disagreed on what kind of folk art could be produced: Keller wanted the folk to produce their own art, but Wagner had a different concept of art for the people. He wanted his own art to reflect the common people rather than the aristocracy — a view that had caused him to participate in the Dresden uprising against the Saxon king and aristocracy in 1848–49. But Wagner had an ideological problem here since only the wealthy could afford to contribute to the staging of his revolutionary new operas. He needed the munificence of a king, and eventually found that king in Bavaria's Ludwig II; but in Zurich resided the wealthy Wesendoncks.

Otto Wesendonck and his wife Mathilde lived in the Villa Wesendonck in a suburb of Zurich. That house is now the Rietberg Museum for Oriental and Tibetan art, and now within the city limits of Zurich. On the villa grounds was a little cottage called the Asyl, and that was where Otto Wesendonck suggested that Wagner move with his wife Minna.

The Asyl (Asylum) turned out to be the setting for a series of very emotional scenes and accusations. Wagner and his wife moved into the Asyl in the spring of 1858, and Minna immediately became jealous of Wagner's relationship with the lovely, and much younger, Mathilde Wesendonck. Minna intercepted one of Mathilde's letters to Wagner and went to Otto to accuse his wife of having an affair with her husband. Wagner and Mathilde denied this charge and said they were only working on the Wesendonck poems and songs — and discussing only poetical and musical matters. The biographers are divided on whether or not Wagner had an affair with Mathilde, but their letters are very compromising and seem to suggest that they were indeed lovers. As a result of the scandal caused by Minna's charges, the Wagners left the Asyl and Wagner continued his nomadic journey, going then to Paris while Minna returned to Germany.

Wagner's first Swiss period then, from 1849 to 1858, provided political exile but also artistic stimulation since it was here that he met the Wesendoncks and here that he discovered the philosophy of Artur Schopenhauer. He often discussed Schopenhauer's ideas with the Wesendoncks and his other Swiss friends, though he surely missed his German friends as well. (It was during this first Swiss period that Wagner repeatedly wrote to Franz Liszt, begging him often to visit him in mountainous Switzerland.) In Zurich Wagner finished his text for the *Ring of the Nibelungen* and read it to his Zurich friends. Wagner also composed much of the music for the first two operas in Zurich: *Das Rheingold* and *Die Walküre*. Despite his many personal and financial problems during this first Swiss period, Wagner was always able to write and compose.

As Tamara Evans has summarized:

> His years in Zurich were a productive period. As conductor, Wagner was much sought-after, and he gave Zurich's musical public his very best. He wrote a series of key essays beginning with *Art and Revolution* in 1849, soon to be followed by *The Art-Work of the Future* (1850), *Judaism in Music* (1850), *Opera and Drama* (1851), *A Theater in Zurich* (1851), and *A Communication to My Friends* (1851). Exile did not stifle Wagner's poetic and musical creativity: the texts for *Die Walküre* and *Das Rheingold* were finished in 1852; in late 1853 and 1854, respectively, he had completed both scores. By 1857, while working on the *Siegfried* score and following the Wagners' move to the 'Asylum' adjoining the Wesendonck estate, he devoted his energies in part to the composition of *Tristan und Isolde*, in part to the *Wesendonck Lieder* and to what was to become Zurich's *cause celebre* of the season. Minna's jealousy of Mathilde Wesendonck and the subsequent unseemly encounters between the two women in the summer of 1858 precipitated what had been in the making for quite some time: Wagner fled, some of his belongings were confiscated, and those that were left Minna put up for sale in the local papers. Minna then paid up the debts her husband had accrued with various local merchants and left for Germany [Evans 4].

Wagner was certainly not the only foreigner to find some inspiration in Zurich. Tom Stoppard's very interesting play *Travesties* (first staged in London in 1974) is set in Zurich in the years during and immediately after World War I (1917–18), and he presents Zurich then as another hothouse for revolutions in both the arts and politics. During this period James Joyce, Tristan Tzara, Vladimir Lenin, and other foreign intellectuals lived in Zurich and generated revolutions like Dadaism, the Russian Communist Revolution, and Joyce's interior monologue for his revolutionary novel *Ulysses*. Here, too, Zurich provided a political refuge for foreign artists and political leaders.

Switzerland provided a second political refuge for the ever-political Richard Wagner following the court (and sexual) scandals connected with his stay in Munich in the 1860s under Ludwig II's patronage. Wagner soon asked for more and more money from the Bavarian treasury for his operatic projects, personal debts, and living expenses, and these included the services of Hans von Bülow and his lovely wife Cosima (daughter of Franz Liszt). Wagner's continued financial demands, plus the gossip going around Munich that he was having an adulterous affair with Cosima von Bülow, ultimately made his continued stay in Munich an impossibility, despite Ludwig II's defense of Wagner's irresponsible behavior. Cosima stayed in Munich with Hans, but the composer immediately fled to Switzerland to become a political exile once again, and to find a place to live.

One of the first places he went after the turmoil in Munich was Vevey, and he wrote to one of his former lovers from there: on December 17, 1865, he wrote to Mathilde Maier, telling her how relieved he was to be out of Munich, where he felt he could never work. He felt that his most productive composing usually occurred in a country with beautiful mountain scenery — like Switzerland — and soon afterwards he found Lake Lucerne and Tribschen.

On April 17, 1866, Wagner moved out of a hotel and to Tribschen, on Lake Lucerne, the house that is now a Richard Wagner museum. The museum contains his death mask and his Erard piano, on which he did much composing, plus some of his musical and literary manuscripts. The original spelling of the house's name is Tribschen, but Wagner changed that to Triebschen, because it made a nice pun on the wonderful location of the house on the shores of Lake Lucerne. According to Geoffrey Skelton, "It was the tongue of land on which it stood that induced Wagner to associate the name "Tribschen" with the German verb *treiben* (to drive), or more precisely its past participle form *trieb*, the equivalent of the English word 'drift.' He believed — without any authority beyond his own imagination — that the tongue of land had been formed by currents in the lake, and he changed the name of the house to Triebschen" (Skelton 73). The house also had views of two very tall mountains, Mt. Pilatus and Mt. Rigi, and Wagner repeatedly mentions in his correspondence the Alpine beauty of his new location. He clearly connected Switzerland with both political refuge and wonderful mountain scenery.

Wagner lived in Tribschen during his second Swiss idyll — from 1866 to 1872. These seven years were perhaps the most productive in Wagner's life — on both a personal level and an artistic level — and here the composer does not complain about loneliness and depressions, thanks to his new relationship with Cosima von Bülow, who soon left her husband Hans and moved there with her four children. Both Wagner and Cosima repeatedly referred to this period as the happiest in their lives; Cosima never wanted to leave Switzerland, and did so most reluctantly and only because of Wagner's plans for Bayreuth and the creation of his festival theater there for the staging of his *Ring* cycle.

It was in Tribschen that Wagner got the news that his first wife Minna had died — which must have been greeted with real pleasure; his old friend Anton Pusinelli, Minna's physician, told him this via telegram. It was also while in Tribschen that Cosima divorced Hans, and she and Wagner could finally be honest about their relationship. On June 6, 1869, Siegfried Wagner was born — a very happy occasion of the birth of their final child, and a son and heir, though legally a bastard. On July 18, 1870, the divorce of Cosima and Hans was finalized and in the very next month, on August 25, 1870, Wagner and Cosima were married. It was also in Tribschen that the *Siegfried Idyll* was composed and first performed — for Cosima Wagner's birthday on December 25, 1870.

In addition to all these personal changes, all of which turned out to be very positive for both Wagner and Cosima if not for Hans von Bülow, there were other artistic and intellectual changes as well. Wagner composed *Meistersinger von Nürnberg* and most of the last two operas of the *Ring* cycle, *Siegfried* and *Götterdämmerung*, while living in Tribschen, in addition to the *Siegfried Idyll*. He also wrote some important essays and letters there, and also planned for the Bayreuth Festival there — though that of course necessitated a move to Bayreuth.

Wagner's love of the Swiss Alps certainly enters into his conception for the staging of the *Ring* cycle. Every one of the four operas asks for mountain scenery in its stage directions — the home of the gods, Valhalla, in *Rheingold*; the mountain passes in *Die Walküre*; the final scene of *Siegfried*, with Brünnhilde on the mountaintop, which also appears in the first act of *Götterdämmerung*. In many ways the Ring can be seen as an Italian dream set in Switzerland. Wagner first had his vision of the *Ring* cycle while boating in Spezia; and water appears frequently and symbolically in the four operas. Wagner particularly connected water with Italy because of its geography, being surrounded by oceans, and mountains he particularly connected with Switzerland for its Alpine scenery. Both appear repeatedly and significantly in the *Ring* cycle, particularly the glorious mountain scenery of Switzerland.

Equally important for Wagner's intellectual development, it was at Tribschen that Wagner met Friedrich Nietzsche, the young professor from the University of Basel. He visited Tribschen twenty-three times (according to his count), often staying for long periods, and became devoted to Richard and Cosima. He even helped Cosima close the house when the Wagners moved back to Germany in 1872. Nietzsche also learned much from Wagner, and Nietzsche's essay "The Birth of Tragedy Out of the Spirit of Music" was written while under the influence of the composer. Both men were also very interested in the philosophical theories of Artur Schopenhauer and both discussed his books, particularly *The World as Will and Idea*. Once Wagner moved to Bayreuth and was working to establish the festival theater there, Nietzsche became disaffected and ultimately rejected Wagner and his artistic principles, though he still seemed to love Cosima. Nietzsche's *Contra Wagner* and *The Case of Wagner*, both very hostile to the new Wagnerian enterprise at Bayreuth, appeared during this time. As Nietzsche became older, he undoubtedly grew tired of being a disciple of Wagner, and Wagner certainly loved disciples around him and did not bear criticism of his theories particularly well. Like many artists and writers, there was a paranoid and manic quality to Wagner's personality — perhaps part of bipolar illness.

Some of Wagner's greatest supporters also came from Switzerland, especially the Wesendoncks, and these wealthy friends contributed later to the Bayreuth enterprise. But King Ludwig II insisted that if Wagner wanted to build his ideal theater for the staging of the *Ring* cycle, and he wanted the king to contribute to it, such a theater would have to be somewhere in Bavaria; Bayreuth, in northern Franconia, was as far from Munich as one could be and still be in Bavaria. Wagner clearly preferred living in a small town rather than in a big city, and he came to like living in Bayreuth, though he wanted to leave every winter to avoid the hard winters there. He died in Venice in 1883 while living at the Palazzo Vendramin-Calergi, which still exists and is now the casino of Venice. There is a plaque on the palazzo to indicate that Richard Wagner died there, and a bust of Wagner in the Giardino Pubblico. Thomas Mann's *Death in Venice* contains many references to Wagnerian opera — indeed, its very title refers to Wagner's place of death.

For Wagner, Switzerland meant political refuge and glorious scenery, and that is what Switzerland has meant for many other writers and intellectuals as well. Wagner repeatedly begged Franz Liszt to meet him in the mountains of Switzerland to enjoy its glorious views of nature, and while Liszt did not comply very often since he was busy in Weimar, many others have come to Switzerland before and since then. Switzerland has become a symbol of both wonderful mountain scenery and political refuge for many people before and since Richard Wagner — and of course the country also borders on Italy.

Bibliography

DiGaetani, John Louis. *Wagner and Suicide.* Jefferson: McFarland, 2003.

Erismann, Hans. *Richard Wagner in Zurich.* Zurich: Verlag Neue Zuricher Zeitung, 1987.

Evans, Tamara S. " 'Am Mythenstein: Richard Wagner and Swiss Society" In *Re-Reading Wagner*, edited by Reinhold Grimm and Jost Hermand. Madison: University of Wisconsin, 1993.

Gautier, Judith. *Wagner at Home.* Translated from the French by Effie Dunreith Massie. London: John Lane, 1911.

Newman, Ernest. *The Life of Richard Wagner.* Four Volumes. Cambridge: Cambridge University, 1960.

Skelton, Geoffrey. *Richard and Cosima Wagner: Biography of a Marriage.* Boston: Houghton Mifflin, 1982.

Wagner, Richard. *My Life.* (*Mein Leben*) Translated by Andrew Gray; edited by Mary Whittall. New York: Da Capo, 1992.

_____, and Franz Liszt. *Correspondence of Wagner and Liszt.* Translated into English with a Preface by Francis Hueffer. In two volumes. New York: Greenwood, 1969.

Wille, Eliza. *Erinnerungen an Richard Wagner, Mit 15 Briefen Richard Wagners.* Zurich: Atlantic Musikbuch, 1982.

III. The *Ring* and Germany

6. Wagner's *Ring* and German Culture: Performances and Interpretations On and Off Stage
Steven Cerf

Adjectives that have been used at various times to characterize Wagner's *Ring* cycle have been as diverse and conflicting as epic and national, modernistic and nationalistic, universal and experimental. Certainly, the ways in which German thought and culture have received the *Ring* during different periods since its 1876 premiere as a cycle encompass all of these attributes, and have transformed it into a gigantic mirror of the German society for which it was being staged or artistically evoked or philosophically interpreted. In this six-part essay, I would like to explore the history of reception, the *Rezeptionsgeschichte,* of the *Ring* in German thought and culture over the last one hundred and thirty years. The variety of ways, both on and off stage, that different eras in the German-speaking world have approached this cycle based on pre–Christian myth will be traced. The first portion, covering the years 1869 through 1876, deals with the epic proportions of the tetralogy and the challenges Wagner recognized in the work's first performances in Munich and Bayreuth — a period, not coincidentally, that saw the emergence of the first modern German nation-state. The second portion deals with productions of the Ring, after the opening of Bayreuth, across German-speaking Europe through the First World War and the satirical works inspired by its popularity (1878–1918). The third section deals with both the modernistic path-breaking attempts at staging the Ring and reactions to these during the Weimar Republic (1919–1933). The fourth section examines how the Third Reich (1933–1945) appropriated portions of the cycle for its nationalistic purposes and why so staunch an anti–Nazi Wagnerite as Thomas Mann spent a large period of his exile completing his own humanistic tetralogy, *Joseph and His Brothers*. The fifth section will examine Wieland Wagner as director of the universally mythological *Ring* cycles in Bayreuth from 1951 until his death in 1966. And the final portion will discuss some of the more experimental productions from Patrice Chéreau's Bayreuth centenary staging to other postmodernist productions mounted over the last three decades.

The Ring *as Epic: Its First Performances (1869–1876)*

Every facet of the *Ring* is epic in nature: its almost 15-hour-long duration, the 26 years it took to complete (1848–1874), its 34 scenes, its 36 roles, its one hundred and 24 musical instruments, not to mention its cosmological scope. Wagner, in his 1862 foreword to the printed text of the cycle, voiced his need to have optimal festival conditions to stage all of its four operas as an integrated whole. The nearly catastrophic preparations and the unsettling rehearsals for the very first performance of *Das Rheingold* in Munich in the fall of 1869, which the composer neither conducted nor directed, reinforced his conviction that a *Festspielhaus*, or festival hall, situated in a small town, could be the only venue for his cycle as cycle. Wagner not only felt that a piecemeal presentation created misunderstandings about his tetralogy, but he also strongly believed that the Munich *Rheingold*— mounted despite his opposition and in his absence — had inevitably violated the epic nature of the *Ring*.

When first apprised of the impending production of *Das Rheingold* in Munich, the composer had grave misgivings. Exposing his new cycle to the routine of an urban repertory company was exactly what he had hoped to avoid. In the aforementioned foreword, he had specified an atmosphere in which the artists and audience alike would have no distractions — neither those of city life nor of the spa — to compete for their attention. To wrest *Rheingold* away from a future premiere of the cycle as a whole was particularly galling, as this 1854 work, of all of his operas, best conformed to the revolutionary theories in his seminal tract, *Opera and Drama* (1850–1851). Dispensing with a chorus, concentrating on larger-than-life mythological characters, and employing symphonic interludes to link its scenes, it was the composer's test case for his art-work of the future. Now King Ludwig, who had purchased the opera for a handsome sum from the ever-impecunious composer, was dragging it back to the routinization of a repertory opera company. The *Ring* foreword ends with Wagner's wish that a prince be found to finance this unique artistic endeavor — a prescient wish that would be granted, for it was ironically also King Ludwig II of Bavaria whose support made the first Bayreuth festival, with its performance of three complete *Ring* cycles, a reality.

As Wagner had predicted, rehearsals for the Munich *Rheingold* were a disaster: the originally enlisted conductor and Wotan both resigned after a chaotic dress rehearsal; press attacks and open letters appeared almost daily. Even a parody called *Rhein Blech* (*Rhine Tin* or, colloquially, *Rhine Trash*) drew full houses at a Munich marionette theater. Although intervening rehearsals worked wonders with the production and the actual September 22 premiere was a great success, Wagner was outraged. Three days later, fulminating in an Alberich-like rage, although he had never seen the production, Wagner penned the following curse in his diary, *The Brown Book*:

> You fog-bound dwarves, just try and play with the *Ring*,
> May it pay you justly for your benighted undertaking;
> For, watch out: you'll find the ring your noose;
> You know its curse; see if it lets swindlers profit!
> The curse reaps failure,
> Save for those fearlessly true to the Rhein's gold.
> Your lamentable cardboard and glue spectacle
> Will soon vanish beneath the Nibelung's Tarnhelm
> [*Brown Book*, 173, my modification].

During the six years between Munich's follow-up *Walküre* (June 1870) and the full cycle's Bayreuth premiere, much speculation was generated as to the overall integrated nature of the *Ring*. No less a composer than Johannes Brahms, in a rare cordial 1875 letter to Wagner, voiced his curiosity as to what the next year's opening of Bayreuth would bring: "We have the strange, if stirring, enjoyment of watching this unique work of yours raise itself gradually and come to life — much as the Romans have, when a colossal statue is being dug up. Your less pleasant occupation [is] witnessing our astonishment and disagreement" (Brahms

352). How fitting that Brahms would express his artistic curiosity in terms of excavations of classical antiquities, as Wagner had regarded the celebratory nature of the *Ring*, much as Virgil had regarded the *Aeneid*, as an affirmation of his civilization's past. In addition, hadn't Wagner himself viewed his festival drama in *Art and Revolution* as having its source in classical Athenian tragedy, where an entire citizenry came together to be moved by art?

Wagner was fighting hard for the primacy of the Bayreuth Festival to present his national epic cycle holistically, at a time — 1871 — when Germany itself had finally achieved unification as a civic society — a status that France and England had accomplished, centuries before, as the culmination of the Renaissance. With the Protestant Reformation in the sixteenth century planting the seeds for separation from the Holy Roman Empire (known historically as the First Reich), this empire as a centralizing German force became crippled — a step that brought about the collapse of the fledgling German Renaissance. The Thirty Years' War (1618–1648) in the following century saw overwhelming devastation along with foreign occupation throughout the German lands. Germany was left divided into approximately 300 sovereign states, varying greatly in size and governmental structure, that paid lip service to the Empire but enjoyed de facto independence. Characterized by a disunity created by "particularism" — or what the Germans refer to as *Kleinstaaterei*, a cluster of small states — this vast area in Central Europe, without a centralized government, transportation, or communication, remained a quasi-medieval backwater, subject to war, poverty, and disease, until the middle of the eighteenth century, when a relatively stable economic situation permitted the rise of the middle classes in urban areas. Not until the ghost of the Empire was laid to rest (during the Napoleonic wars at the beginning of the nineteenth century) was the thought of a unified German nation-state possible. Only decades later, in 1871, did the Second Reich emerge, the first centralized modern nation-state on German soil.

With Germany at last having undergone the post–Renaissance transformation from a *Kulturvolk* (cultural federation of states) to a *Staatsvolk* (national and political state), Wagner felt impelled to address his supporters present and German society as a whole at the Festspielhaus cornerstone-laying ceremony in Bayreuth on May 22, 1872, his 59th birthday. As his then staunch ally, the philosopher Friedrich Nietzsche, would later write: "Everything that had happened up to now was a preparation for this moment" (Nietzsche 370). Wagner began his speech by severely criticizing the central German government in Berlin for withholding financial support for his festival: "Of late our undertaking has often been styled the erection of a 'National theatre at Bayreuth.' I have no authority to accept that title. Where is the 'nation,' to erect itself this theatre?" Although Wagner had visited Bismarck, the German Chancellor, that month in Berlin seeking financial support, Bismarck refused to help. Wagner, feeling personally slighted, continued his criticism of Berlin by comparing neighboring France with Germany: "When the French National Assembly was dealing with the State-subvention of the great Parisian theatres a little while ago, each speaker warmly advocated the continuance, nay, the increase of their subsidies, since the maintenance of these theaters was a debt not merely due to France, but to Europe which had accustomed itself to receiving from them its laws of intellectual culture" (Wagner, "Foundation-Stone" 326). This sorry state of affairs led him into a direct appeal to German society and its centralized government officials to support the building of his new festival hall and the staging of the *Ring* for which it was meant. He concluded his talk by ascribing to the cornerstone those talismanic powers that could unseal a cultural national German spirit that builds from within. By referring to his own art and the *Ring* cycle for which the Festspielhaus would now be constructed, he evoked the German spirit "that shouts to you across the centuries its ever young Good-morrow" (327–28).

Not surprisingly it was an article written about this very day by the Prague-born musical editor and Wagnerite, Heinrich Porges (1837–1900), that prompted Wagner to ask the musicologist to be his amanuensis during the 1875 summer rehearsals leading up to the world premiere of the Ring and to provide a detailed written record of them. Porges' *Wagner Rehearsing the 'Ring'* has provided a direct link to the way Wagner ultimately conceived of the cycle for actual stage production.

From Porges' text two facts emerge: Wagner's total directorial hand in these comprehensive rehearsals; and the composer's self-possessed awareness that he was simultaneously working within two dramatic traditions, one of world drama and the other of German national drama. In his introduction to the book-length manuscript, published for the twentieth-anniversary Bayreuth performances of the *Ring* in 1896, Porges summarizes the totality of Wagner's hands-on approach to directing the cycle: "He himself possessed an amazing gift for transformation into any conceivable shape or form — like Proteus, he could, as if by magic, assume at a stroke any role in any situation — indeed, in the rehearsals of the *Ring* he demonstrated these powers so fully that it was as though he himself were the total actor of the entire drama." Continuing, Porges speaks about Wagner's affinity with Shakespeare: "All the directions that he gave pertaining to the action — to the gestures, the positioning, the articulation of sung words — were governed by what he himself has described as the basic principle of Shakespearean drama, namely 'mimic-dramatic naturalness'" (Porges 4). If Wagner recognized this kinship to Shakespeare as a fusion of stylized high art with natural movement and gestures, he also alluded to his affinity with the ancient Greeks. For example, when Fricka bemoans the gods' loss of youth after Freia is taken hostage in *Das Rheingold*, Wagner states that her lament addressed to Wotan "touched the spirit of ancient Greek tragedy" (25).

Wagner's comments referring to Goethe's and Schiller's classical dramas of the late eighteenth and early nineteenth centuries reveal that the composer was consciously working within a national dramatic tradition with which his German-speaking audience could empathize. In particular, the composer's references to the tragic pathos that marked Schiller's most elevated dramas (4) and his comparison of the role of Erda in *Siegfried* with the role of the Mothers in *Faust, Part Two* (37) are telling. That Wagner was aware that he had fashioned a dramatic cycle of the pre–Christian German past that was able to traverse the centuries is evident in Porges' account of the composer's rehearsal of the third scene of Act Two of *Götterdämmerung*, in which the characters have been conjured up from Tacitus' description of the ancient Germans: "The words and the music, charged as they are with defiant self-assertiveness, fearlessness and a strange, almost frightening humor, express the unique character of the German race. These heavy striding phrases should be performed with a tremendous, ruthless energy and no trace of expressive pathos" (130). The word "!Clarity!" — surrounded by exclamation marks — which Wagner posted backstage as his final instruction to the entire *Rheingold* cast just before the actual premiere performance on August 13, 1876, makes sense when one comprehends the detail and immediacy with which Wagner led the crucial 1875 rehearsals. In one word, it summarizes the theatrical viability of his epic work.

From the audience at these first three Bayreuth cycles of the *Ring*, both the international scope of the work and its national underpinning can be gleaned. The royalty of Germany as well as from all over the world marked the transnational importance of the event: not only were Kaiser Wilhelm I of Prussia and King Ludwig of Bavaria in attendance, but the Emperor of Brazil, a variety of Habsburg representatives from the Austro-Hungarian monarchy, and the Grand Duke Vladimir were also present. Wagner's fellow composers attended as well: Liszt, Bruckner, Grieg, Tchaikovsky, and Saint-Saëns, to mention the most prominent. Tchaikovsky called the opening of the *Festspielhaus* "a milestone in the history of Art" and the cycle itself "an event of the greatest importance to the world, an epoch-making work of art" (Hartford 55–56). Grieg, in a similar vein, described the *Ring* as "a great work, full of audacious originality and dramatic merit" (Hartford 69).

But it was Wagner who literally had the last word. Ever since the unification of Germany in 1871, slogans referring to the reawakening of the German national spirit had been used in every realm of German thought and culture. After the curtain fell at the end of the last *Götterdämmerung* performance, the composer, who had felt slighted by Bismarck's lack of financial support from Berlin, saluted the Bavarian King who had come to the front of his box to join in the evening's final flood of applause. Referring to Ludwig as sole benefactor and even co-creator of the *Ring,* he stated his hope that the tetralogy was, indeed, a step toward the creation of a unique and genuine German art (Spotts 69).

The Ring *in Wilhelmine Germany (1878–1918)*

Because of the financial problems incurred by the first Bayreuth Festival, with its deficit of 150,000 marks, Wagner was unable to schedule follow-up performances there. He was thus forced to allow the *Ring* to be performed elsewhere; as a consequence, its exposure and popularity became associated with an ever-expanding German presence in the international political and cultural arena. Once again, King Ludwig came to the composer's financial rescue. By brokering an agreement with the Munich Court Opera, the king saw to it that the opera company would pay royalties on performances of Wagner's operas until the Bayreuth debt could be paid off (Spotts 78).

The man responsible for giving the *Ring* overall national and ensuing continental exposure, which directly led to its enormous popularity, was the director of the Leipzig Opera from 1876 to 1880, Angelo Neumann (1838–1910). In 1878, he produced the first non–Bayreuth performances of the cycle in Leipzig, the city of Wagner's birth — with the staging and costumes based on the official Bayreuth production. That same year saw the complete cycle staged in Munich. Vienna produced the tetralogy in 1879 and Hamburg followed in 1880. As the Court Opera in Berlin had no plans to produce the *Ring,* Neumann's company brought its production to the city's Victoria Theater in 1881, where it enjoyed great success — with the composer himself attending. In 1882, Neumann set up a touring *Ring* company which traveled throughout Germany and Austria, also visiting Holland, Belgium, Italy and Hungary. The company comprised 134 people, including an orchestra of 60, and toured by taking musical instruments and scenery along in five railway cars (Skelton, *Bayreuth* 68). The tour ended in Graz, Austria, in 1883. In 1889, however, Neumann and a newly reconstituted troupe introduced the *Ring* to St. Petersburg.

It was not until 1896 that the *Ring* returned to Bayreuth, for its twentieth-anniversary performances with most of the naturalistic staging from Wagner's day intact and only minor changes approved by the composer's widow, Cosima (Müller and Wapnewski 506–509). Fricka's carriage was now led by two live rams and the "Ride of the Valkyries" was performed by children on wooden horses drawn across the stage in front of a backdrop (Spotts 116). Cosima's approach was, alas, that of an embalmer, as Barry Millington describes it: "[H]er determination to reproduce every gesture, every movement as she remembered it, led to uninspired, over-prescriptive stage choreography. The so-called 'Bayreuth style' (both of stagecraft and *mise-en-sc(ne*) held sway at the Festspielhaus until the 1930s" (375).

The most boldly modernistic staging of the Ring in German-speaking Europe took place, understandably, outside of Germany in turn-of-the-century Vienna, a hothouse of cultural experimentation, at the Vienna Court Opera. The conductor was none other than Gustav Mahler, the director of the Opera. The set designer was Alfred Roller, the president of the Vienna Secession, the most prestigious avant-garde group of visual artists. In 1905, they produced *Das Rheingold* for the first time in Vienna without an intermission, and two years later *Die Walküre*—which was also given uncut for the first time. Theater historians agree that Roller's production was the first actual attempt to break away from the naturalistic Bayreuth style. In *Rheingold*, there was no papier-mâché dragon during Alberich's transformation scene and there was no wooded bridge for the gods to cross over on their way to Valhalla at the end of the opera. In *Walküre*, Grane, Brünnhilde's horse, and Fricka's pair of rams were banned from the stage. And the "Ride of the Valkyries" was abstractly indicated by scudding clouds projected on the backdrop. Although forward-looking critics praised this revolutionary staging, a tradition-minded audience, accustomed to sumptuously realistic stage designs, had a harder time of it, and the second half of the production had to be canceled when Mahler left the opera company in 1908 (Müller and Wapnewski 512). The Viennese powers that be, however, realizing the significance of Roller's productions, kept them stage worthy until the late nineteen-twenties (Prawy 220).

The key to Roller's visually imaginative approach to *Rheingold* was the way he arranged the production's novel two revolving stages: "To ensure that scene shifts could be carried out within the time allotted by the score, he decided to use the revolving stage installed some years previously for *Così fan tutte*. But the size and weight of the sets called for not just one but two circular platforms which turned on themselves 180 degrees, like mill wheels. The new set-up allowed rapid shifting of the three sets needed for the opera's four scenes" (La Grange 79).

An additional futuristic production was designed by Ludwig Sievert and directed by Franz Ludwig Hörth for the Freiburg Opera's 1912 production. For the first time a continuous cyclorama and a revolving stage were used for the entire tetralogy. In *Rheingold*, the gods remained standing on a portion of a globe in an open space not circumscribed by flat painted scenery (Müller and Wapnewski 513).

Walther Rathenau (1867–1922), a distinguished statesman during the early period of the Weimar Republic, looked back in 1918 and summarized the larger-than-life power the *Ring* had taken on, along with Wagner's other operas, for Wilhelmine Germany in the decades prior to the First World War: "It is scarcely possible to exaggerate how deeply the last generation was spellbound by ... Wagner.... There is always someone —... Siegfried, Wotan — who can do everything and knock down everything, ... punish vice and bring general salvation, striking an exaggerated pose, with the sound of fanfares and with lighting effects and staging" (Spotts 130).

To understand the reverence with which most German-speaking operatic audiences approached the tetralogy at a time of expanding prosperity and nationalism there are no better indicators than the contemporaneous parodies of the *Ring*. Two of particular significance were the 1904 operetta by Oscar Straus, *Die lustigen Nibelungen* (*The Merry Nibelungs*), and the 1905 novella by Thomas Mann, *Wälsungenblut* (*The Blood of the Walsungs*). Each of these artists knew his *Ring* well enough to skewer the zealot-like devotion of the perfect-Wagnerite majority.

Although the operetta was premiered in Vienna and Straus himself was Viennese (though no relation to Johann Strauss), the greatest success it enjoyed was in Berlin's famous Theater des Westens. It certainly helped that the outrageous libretto by the Berlin lawyer Fritz Oliven — whose pen name was "Rideamus" or "Let us laugh" — left no stone unturned. When the Kaiser's famous automobile horn, which was set to Donner's invocation of the thunder clouds from

Rheingold, was heard from the orchestra pit and the ancient Teutonic heroes and their relatives performed a presentation reminiscent of the Prussian officers' mess, audiences could not contain their laughter. Everything with regard to the Ring and its craze was parodied: its alliterative verse or *Stabreim*, the dragon in *Siegfried* (there was a dachshund dressed up as a dragon and mention of dragon-blood sausage), and Wagner's serious melodies themselves (Renckhoff 12–18).

The irrepressible melodiousness of the score could not be denied: Siegfried's first-act narrative about what he has done with the Rhein gold ("That is Rhein Gold/that is my Gold") is set to a fetching Viennese waltz tune that is heard again at the end of the operetta, and the overture prominently features a catchy polka which is heard again as part of the Act Two finale when the characters plot to slay Siegfried from behind. Siegfried's betrothal to Gutrune is finalized only after the Gibichungs ascertain that the hero has invested the Rhein gold at 6 percent interest and is running a sparkling-wine factory on the side. At the end of the operetta with the crash of the Rhenish bank and Siegfried's money in it, there is no reason any longer for Hagen to slay Siegfried and, as a consequence, the two become friends.

The publication of Thomas Mann's 1905 novella was delayed until 1921 because of the personal nature of the work: as the title indicates, it is a parody of Siegmund and Sieglinde's incestuous love in *Die Walküre* and, indeed, the two protagonists, also named Siegmund and Sieglinde, are based on Thomas Mann's new bride, Katja Pringsheim and her twin brother, Klaus. In fact, the entire Pringsheim family is satirized. In the novella, the family is tellingly called the Aaronholds. This play on "Aaron" and "Aryan" emphasizes both the Jewish fascination for Wagner — many of Wagner's key musical assistants were Jewish, as were Porges, Neumann, Mahler, and the founder of twentieth-century Zionism, Theodor Herzl — and German Jewry's desire to assimilate within an Aryan society. In fact, the real twins' father, Professor Pringsheim, was not only a zealous Wagnerite but also an early supporter of and contributor to Bayreuth.

In *Blood of the Walsungs*, Mann (1875–1955) evokes the most accessible of the Ring operas in three discrete ways: through actual verbal renderings of the most significant moments in the score; through Wagnerian leitmotific devices associated with different characters, events, and objects; and through a parodic treatment of the opera's plot.

The structure of the brief novella is telling. The first 10 pages deal with a pheasant repast, in the sumptuously appointed town mansion of the Aaronholds, at which the Gentile government official to whom Sieglinde is engaged, von Beckerath, is present. The twins ask his permission to attend that evening's performance of *Die Walküre* for one final time alone together. The middle 10 pages are at the opera house during the performance itself, in which Sieglinde and Siegmund through their holding of hands and other key physical gestures mirror the incestuous longings they behold on stage. The final five pages take place after the operatic performance, with the twins back at their parents' home wildly embracing and physically consummating their passion for each other.

A number of aspects of the turn-of-the-twentieth-century reception of *Walküre* are captured by Mann: the passionate, *frisson*-inducing love music in the final scene of Act One followed by the enthusiastic response of the audience with its "rapturous applause" (*Walsungs* 178–9); Siegmund's emotional response to the heartrending plight of a distracted and operatically "mad" Sieglinde in Act Two (180); the grandeur of the final "Magic Fire" scene of the opera:

> A noble prospect opened out, the scene was pervaded with epic and religious splendor. Brünnhilde slept. The god mounted the rocks. Great, full-bodied flames, rising, falling, and flickering, glowed all over the boards. The Walküre lay with her coat of mail and her shield on

her mossy couch ringed around with fire and smoke, with leaping, dancing tongues, with the magic sleep-compelling fire-music. But she had saved Sieglinde, in whose womb there grew and waxed the seed of that hated unprized race, chosen of the gods, from which the twins had sprung, who had mingled their misfortunes and their afflictions in free and mutual bliss [180–81].

Here in a synchronistic Mannian manner, the gods' and demi-gods' Teutonic status and the Jewish heritage of the Aarenholds are simultaneously invoked.

Humorous descriptions are associated with the performer portraying Hunding, the odd-man-out operatic equivalent of von Beckerath: "Announced by his pugnacious motif, Hunding entered, paunchy and knock-kneed, like a cow.... He stood there frowning, leaning heavily on his spear, and staring ox-eyed" (*Walsungs* 176). It was such parody that allowed Mann to liberate himself from Wagnerian intoxication.

In the years leading up to World War I and during the Great War itself, reception of the now widely popular cycle took on an ugly undertone. The *Ring* was invoked by the reactionary forces popular at Bayreuth, the home during the Wilhelmine era of the "Bayreuth Circle," whose journal, the hyper-nationalistic *Bayreuther Blätter*, became a repository for pan–German and anti–Semitic writings. Under the leadership of Wagner's English-born son-in-law Houston Stewart Chamberlain, this crackpot coterie deemed Wagner's highly problematic prose writings on race and German superiority to be no less important than his music dramas (Müller and Wapnewski 390–91).

In 1911, the noted Indologist Leopold von Schröder published his study, *Die Vollendung des arischen Mysteriums in Bayreuth* (*The Culmination of the Aryan Mystery in Bayreuth*), in which he argued that the highest expression of Aryan symbolism was to be found in Wagner's music dramas and that Bayreuth through Wagner would unite the Aryan peoples who had been separated for 5,000 years. Also in 1911, Reinhold von Lichtenberg published an article in which he viewed the tetralogy as a reflection of German superiority. He viewed the tragedy of the *Ring* as being tied to the avarice of the non–Aryan Alberich and stated that Wotan's force was an innocent one focusing solely on maintaining world order. He concluded: "So we see in all the works of this cycle the final and victorious struggle of the Germanic ideal against foreign — that is, enemy — powers" (Spotts 134–35).

During the war itself, terms from the *Ring* appeared as military plans. "Operation Walküre" became a code name for a military operation and in 1918 the "Hunding Line" became one of the massive defensive lines. Looking back at Germany's surrender, Hitler in his 1925 *My Struggle* (*Mein Kampf*) felt that Germany, as embodied by Siegfried, had been stabbed in the back by a traitorous German parliament (Spotts 156).

The Ring *During the Weimar Republic (1919–1933)*

Ironically, the period during the first half of the twentieth century that saw the greatest artistic innovation and experimentation in all of the performing arts in Germany saw very little in the way of imaginative Wagner productions. On the contrary, during the fourteen years of the Weimar Republic, the first German parliamentary democracy sans monarch, Bayreuth was becoming increasingly the bastion of Nazi thought and culture. As a reaction to the stodgy traditionalist German Romantic Bayreuth style that held sway at the *Festspielhaus*, Adolphe Appia, arguably the most innovative Wagnerian scenic designer and producer, was forced to stage half of a futuristic *Ring* cycle outside of Germany — for Basle, Switzerland during the 1924–1925 season. Appia's emphasis on light and space looked forward to Wieland Wagner's mythologically universal post–World War II Bayreuth productions of the *Ring*. As in the case of Roller's path-breaking productions of the tetralogy that removed nineteenth-century ballast from the stage, Appia's work was conceived for German-speakers outside of Germany.

Adolphe Appia (1862–1928) was a Swiss theorist and designer who was responsible for regenerating operatic scenography. In 1882, he had paid his first visit to Bayreuth and in 1888, after a performance of Wagner's *Die Meistersinger*, he resolved "to reform the art of the theatre." Although he planned an entire *Ring* production for Basle, the project had to be abandoned mid-way after a few performances of *Rheingold* and *Walküre*, as the production was deemed "too revolutionary" (Schumacher 30–31).

The two unique hallmarks of Appia's universalist stage technique were much in evidence in Basle: the replacing of traditionally painted *trompe l'oeil* scenery with non-naturalistic, evocative, symbolically geometrical sets; and the creative use of light (Schumacher 30–31). Appia's sets consisted of "combinations of platforms, stairs, ramps, and a few pillars, with curtains masking the wings, a plain blue-gray backdrop, and the occasional use of a traveler curtain to cut off the upstage area for more intimate foreground scenes" (Carnegy 56). The architectonic elements of these stage structures were sharply defined as their dynamic lines and geometric proportions were highlighted by the stage lighting. Patrick Carnegy has succinctly explained Appia's revolutionary emphasis on lighting:

> The principal agent of change was to be the recently invented electric lighting console with its ability to orchestrate a play of light upon the stage in exact sympathy with the music. For Appia, there was a powerful affinity between music and light in that both expressed what Schopenhauer called the inner essence of phenomena. But light could also imitate phenomena, that is suggest fire, clouds, water, and so on — just as music could. The goal of these reforms was to clear the stage space so that attention would be focused on the singing actor [Carnegy 53].

The only Wagner production of avant-garde starkness in Germany during the Weimar Republic was the 1929 Berlin Kroll Opera's *Flying Dutchman*, which also relied on the effects of lighting on steps, ramps and (primarily block-built) scenery. Not only were the Bayreuth Ring productions steeped in the traditional "Bayreuth style," but many of the events surrounding the post–World War I festival smacked of nationalism and racism. When the Bayreuth Festival reopened for the first time after the war, Siegfried Wagner, the composer's only son and the director of the festival since 1906, refused to fly the flag of the Weimar Republic — instead choosing the old imperial banner as a repudiation of the Weimar Republic. Chamberlain, right up to his death in 1927, turned the *Bayreuther Blätter* from a passively nationalistic house organ into an aggressive instrument crusading for Nazi views on German superiority. Needless to say, Adolf Hitler (1889–1945) felt at home in Bayreuth from his first social visit there in September of 1923 — less than two months before staging the Munich Beer Hall Putsch. He was transported into ecstasy not only by Wagner's music dramas but by their extramusical nationalistic message that paralleled his own political agenda. After Siegfried Wagner's death in 1930, Hitler felt increasingly comfortable at Bayreuth, enjoying the active support of Siegfried's English-born widow, Winifred, who succeeded her late husband as director of the festival.

Even before assuming power in 1933, Hitler regarded the *Ring* as the glorification of the *Führer Prinzip* or "leader concept," viewing Siegfried, the hero of the second half of the cycle, as the prototypical Germanic hero, bent on restoring order in a world dominated by German supremacy. The plot of *Götterdämmerung*, the final opera of the *Ring*, in which Siegfried is stabbed in the back by the Gibichungs, conjured up that aforementioned image of the German parliament's "stab in the back" rather than the Allied military superiority that caused

Germany's military defeat. Hitler saw in Siegfried a kindred spirit, as they were "men ... who were rejected outsiders battling against an entrenched social order." From prison, where he was sent after the Putsch, Hitler wrote a letter of thanks to the Wagner family for their support in which he employed a telling image from the *Ring*, citing Bayreuth as the place "where first the Master and then Chamberlain forged the spiritual sword with which we fight today" (Spotts 141–42).

Propagandistic Use of the Ring *in the Third Reich and a Humanistic Reaction (1933–1945)*

Given Hitler's lifelong devotion to Wagner, it came as no surprise that during his first year in power he attended all six of the first performances of the Bayreuth season, including the four portions of the *Ring*. Needless to say, by emphasizing monumentality, the new 1933 Bayreuth *Ring* production, conducted and directed by Heinz Tietjen, conformed to Hitler's own triumphalist reading of the cycle. Fricka appeared in an oversized chariot in *Walküre* and the Gibichung chorus in *Götterdämmerung* was increased from 26 to 101. Friedelind Wagner, the composer's anti–Nazi granddaughter, observed that Tietjen "was no longer satisfied unless he had at least eight hundred people and a dozen horses milling around on the stage." For her, such grandiosity deprived the tetralogy of its inner emotional meaning (Friedelind Wagner, *Heritage* 149).

Walter Legge, then the music critic of *The Manchester Guardian*, strongly felt that the overall musical and dramatic quality of the Bayreuth performances had been compromised for politically propagandistic purposes. In his pointedly titled review "The Bayreuth Festival 15. VIII. 33 — 'Featuring' Herr Hitler," he observed that book shops that, during previous festivals, had prominently displayed copies of Wagner's autobiography, *Mein Leben*, now sported Hitler's *Mein Kampf*. He continued by voicing his annoyance that "When business detained Herr Hitler in Berlin, 2,000 people were made to wait an hour and a half for their opera [*Siegfried*] until he should take his seat in the theatre" (Legge 190). The political message was simple: Nazi propaganda associated with Wagner was of greater importance than the artistic integrity of the individual music dramas.

Because of Hitler's closeness to Winifred, he made a point of officially attending the Bayreuth festival each summer from 1933 to 1939. Invariably, he would see each of the *Ring* operas of the first part of the season and then return for the final performance of *Götterdämmerung* at the end of the season. Even his preparations for the non-aggression pact with the Soviet Union in August of 1939, and the ensuing partition of Poland which led to the outbreak of World War II, could not keep Hitler away from the festival performances. During the later stages of the war, he reminisced in one of his rambling monologues about those regular visits to Bayreuth: "The ten days of the Bayreuth season were always one of the blessed seasons of my existence.... On the day following the end of the Bayreuth Festival, and on the Tuesday that marks the end of the Nuremberg Congress, I'm gripped by a great sadness — as when one strips the Christmas tree of its ornaments" (Hitler, *Talk* 242). Once again, a work of art is purposely conflated with political propaganda.

Although the Nazis placed great weight on the performance of the *Ring* (at a rehearsal of *Die Walküre* in Berlin, Field Marshal Hermann Goering ran on stage himself to demonstrate to the reigning Wotan of the time, Rudolf Bockelmann, the proper way to wield his spear), their championing of the cycle was by no means limited to the opera house. Fragments of the *Ring* served as aural icons at official occasions. The "Entrance of the Gods into

Valhalla" from *Das Rheingold* was played by the Munich Philharmonic to open the 1937 Party Congress; the Siegfried motif was marched to at rallies (as can be seen in Leni Riefenstahl's propagandistic film *The Triumph of the Will*); and "Siegfried's Funeral Music" from *Götterdämmerung* was played both at the funeral of President von Hindenburg in 1934 and over the radio after Hitler's death was announced.

While the Nazis were appropriating the *Ring* in a fragmented and chauvinistic fashion, Thomas Mann found himself inspired in part by the tetralogy to work on a counter-tetralogy of his own, *Joseph and His Brothers*, which as in Wagner's case would be by far his longest and most ambitious undertaking. The congruencies between the novelist's biblical tetralogy and Wagner's *Ring* are significant. Mann began his novel cycle in December 1926 and did not complete it until January 1942; Wagner's tetralogy occupied him between 1848 and 1874. Mann drew on Jewish sources as Wagner had drawn on Teutonic myth. Mann's project, like Wagner's, began as a relatively small undertaking, assuming gargantuan proportions only gradually. Both works were composed mostly in exile.

As a modernist and an internationalist, Mann took inspiration from Wagner's mythic cycle to champion the universal over the chauvinistic themes the Nazis were mining in the Ring. The presence of a collective consciousness dominates the first work of both Wagner's *Ring* and Mann's *Joseph and His Brothers*. Motifs of timeless waters, covenants and circularity dominate both *Das Rheingold* and Mann's first portion, *The Tales of Jacob*. Like Wotan, Fricka, Loge, and Alberich, Esau, Jacob, and Isaac live in a static world determined by fixed identities.

The second work of each tetralogy deals with the development of the individual. As the titles *Die Walküre* and *The Young Joseph* indicate, Brünnhilde and Joseph emerge as distinct personalities. Both are favorite children, naïve and self-centered, and both Joseph's brothers and Brünnhilde's sisters remain, by contrast, static groups. Ultimately each is exiled from his/her family and undergoes a death-like trial: Joseph is cast down into the well, while Brünnhilde is placed unconscious on a rock surrounded by a ring of fire.

Like a scherzo in a symphony, each third portion, *Siegfried* and *Joseph in Egypt*, is replete with humorous passages surrounding a pair of dwarves. Their greed and calculation serve as a counterpoint to the guilelessness and sexuality of the protagonists. By choosing to remain in Egypt, Joseph surrenders the privileged and divine status of a direct descendant of Abraham. By giving herself to Siegfried, Brünnhilde embraces Eros and completes her separation from Wotan and divinity.

The cycle of events comes to completion in the final sections, *Joseph the Provider* and *Götterdämmerung*. Joseph is finally reunited with his father and siblings and the tribe of Israel is joined together as in the beginning. In *Götterdämmerung*, the ring is reclaimed by the Rhinemaidens, and the cycle ends as it began with the endless flowing of the Rhine. Brünnhilde forgives Siegfried's treachery; Joseph forgives his once-deceitful brothers.

Whereas *Götterdämmerung* is doom-laden, Mann's final installment is joyous and sunlit: he has gone to those ancient Hebraic sources of the Old Testament as an exile from Nazi Germany and as an iconoclastic Wagnerite in bleak times; he has fathomed the universality of Wagner's work to create his own humanistic tetralogy based on material shunned in his former homeland. Mann never denied that "There is a good deal of Hitler in Wagner" (Mann, *Briefe 1948* 115), yet in *Joseph* he creatively showed that Wagner's scope was incomparably wider than that of any racist dictator — that the composer's thematic concerns were universal and even utopian and that his great music dramas were not to be confused with his prodigious anti–Semitic essays. Mann even acknowledged the *Joseph–Ring* connection in a tantalizing snippet in a letter to a reader dated May 1, 1945, in which he states that Wagner's cycle "looms in the back of the *Joseph* tetralogy" (Mann, *Briefe 1944* 145).

Wieland Wagner's Innovative Ring *and Post–World War II Bayreuth (1951–1966)*

In breaking Wagner out of a nationalistic mold and associating him with world mythology, Mann anticipated Wieland Wagner's revolutionary postwar Bayreuth staging of the tetralogy, in which the director's stated aim was "to replace the production ideas of a century ago, now grown sterile, by a creative intellectual approach that goes back to the origins of the work itself. Starting from this basic core, the producer must constantly seek new forms for the work by deciphering the codes and hieroglyphs which Wagner bequeathed in his scores to future generations. Every new production is a step on the way to an unknown goal" ("Denkmalshutz" 178).

When Richard Wagner's grandsons, Wieland and Wolfgang, reopened the Bayreuth Festival in 1951 following denazification, it is not surprising that one of the new productions unveiled should have been that of the Ring, as the *Festspielhaus* had after all been originally built for producing the cycle whole. What was surprising was that the style that Wieland employed both for the *Ring* and the season's opening production of *Parsifal*, was his first revolutionary foray into abstract stagecraft. No longer would the Bayreuth tradition or style that held Wagner's original productions as exemplary and inviolable be observed. Now, Wieland was able to reconnect with the avant-garde theatrical developments banned by the Nazis. Choosing as his primary source of inspiration Adolphe Appia, whose staging had departed greatly from nineteenth-century flat pictorial tableaux and realistic props, Wieland arrived at a universalist vision that would set the tone for Wagner stagings throughout Europe in the decades following World War II.

Aside from the avant-garde artistic necessity to "modernize" Bayreuth, a further consideration for this abstract approach on the part of Wieland was, simply put, economic. The shaky financial status of the festival in a still-recovering West Germany required the simplest stagings possible. With the postwar *Kahlschlag*— the striking bare of encumbering traditions with the figurative slash of a sword — Wieland had no temptation to restore the costly bombast of the traditional approach taken in the 1930s. He arrived instead at a less pretentious, more all-encompassing rendering of his grandfather's staged myths.

Taking his aesthetic cue from modernist art, with its antipictorial symbolism, Wieland devised abstract sets illuminated by contrasting plays of light. The Bayreuth *Festspielhaus*, spared destruction during the war, was equipped at its reopening with sufficient technical resources to catch up with and transcend Appia-like design. Defending his approach in the 1951 Festival handbook, Wieland wrote: "Basically, the works of Richard Wagner tolerate no change.... The actual staging and it alone — is subject to change. To avoid change is to transform the virtue of fidelity into the vice of rigidity" (Spotts 231). Wieland's last sentence was clearly a criticism leveled at his grandmother, his father, and his mother, the three previous traditionalist directors of the festival.

This new Bayreuth style flabbergasted its first audiences. Scenes were presented behind scrims; stage properties were reduced to the barest essentials or replaced entirely by light and shadow; actions and physical gestures of the plainly costumed singers were kept to a minimum.

Geoffrey Skelton has summarized most clearly the role of the dominating *Scheibe* or disc, or circular platform, on which most of the action of the new Ring production took place:

  - The end of this *Ring* was already apparent in its beginning, where in the second scene of *Rheingold* one became conscious of the circular platform, symbolic of the ring itself, on which the whole action of the cycle was to be played out.... In the course of the cycle the symbolic circular platform became increasingly obscured, as Wotan's own ambition became increasingly obscured by the unforeseen complications that beset his way to it. Only at the very end, ... did the circle appear once more in its complete state, alone and empty and bathed in a dim blue-green light like a ring lying submerged in deep water. It was a symbol not only of the fatal ring but of the drama of greedy power come full circle [Skelton, *Bayreuth* 159–160].

As Frederick Spotts has pointed out, this Ring production was a radical break from the past. Even though at its premiere certain realistic accouterments of the tetralogy were included in the production — Valhalla, the rainbow bridge, the ash tree in Hunding's hut, the Valkyries' rock and Mime's forge — none of these appeared as they had before. Indeed, by 1954, Wieland had rid the production of many of these naturalistic objects, giving the impression that he was directing a saga not of the Nordic gods but of Greek mythology. Both *Parsifal* and the *Ring* began with the curtain already raised, thus allowing the gradual illumination of the scene to parallel the gradual unfolding of the drama, a mythological drama that was so universal that its physical and temporal settings were to remain indeterminate (Spotts 215–16).

By 1965 Wieland was prepared to deconstruct his *Ring* even more drastically. This time the giants in *Rheingold* had no clubs and Donner in the same opera had no hammer to strike against the rock. Hunding's hut in *Walküre* was nowhere to be seen. "The sets for *Siegfried* and the first two acts of *Götterdämmerung* were totemistic megalithic objects that looked as though they might have come from a science-fiction film studio." And Gutrune's brief scene in between Siegfried's Funeral Music and Hagen's reentry was regarded as trivializing and therefore cut. Wieland was concerned only with the human essentials (Spotts 227).

Steeping himself in the avant-garde non-representational arts in preparation for these abstract designs, Wieland also read the leading German Wagnerite philosophers of his day and included their work in the house publications for the festival. This intellectual infusion of modernity into the actual festival was a startling departure from the reactionary and racist tone of the *Bayreuther Blätter*— a publication that had held sway during most of the first half of the twentieth century right up to World War II. The idea that the editors of that previous house organ ever would include the likes of such writers as Nietzsche or Thomas Mann would have been unheard of. Two contemporary thinkers in particular figured in Wieland's intellectual constellation: Theodor Adorno (1903–1969) and Ernst Bloch (1885–1977).

Adorno was a musical sociologist, critic, and composer, and a member of Max Horkheimer's Institute for Social Research; most importantly, he was a leading leftist proponent of musical modernism. His elaborate writings on the role of Wotan in the *Ring* are remarkable in the way they influenced Wieland's directorial understanding of the tetralogy. Adorno was fascinated by Wagner's total preoccupation with effecting social change, which "points also to the fact that the universe is an interlocking system in which the more ruthlessly the individual tries to prevail, the less he succeeds. The attempt to change the world comes to naught, but changing the world is what is at issue." Both the active Wotan of the first two operas and the spectral Wotan of the second half of the *Ring* concerned Adorno in much the same way that they fascinated Wieland Wagner. Discussing the first half of the tetralogy, Adorno analyzes Wotan's struggle to act despite being hamstrung by the law: "Wotan is ready for any act of violence as long as he is not bound by codified agreements. Moreover, these very agreements, which impose restrictions on an unenlightened state of nature, turn out to be fetters that deprive him of the freedom of movement and hence help to re-establish chaos" (Adorno 117). In the third opera, Wotan is even denied his name, being referred to as the Wanderer, and his diminution is palpable throughout the final opera by his total physical absence: "Wotan is the phantasmagoria of the buried revolution. He and his like roam around like spirits haunting the places where their deeds went awry, and their costume compulsively and guiltily reminds us of that missed opportunity of bourgeois society for whose benefit they, as the curse of an abortive future, re-enact the dim and distant past.... He has lost his name and his home. Hence like a ghost, he turns up unexpectedly, the spectral image of his own past omnipresence" (Adorno 134).

Ernst Bloch, the German philosopher, was best known for his espousal of the post–Marxian utopian philosophy of hope and, like Adorno, was both a Leftist and a Jew. He also would become a personal friend of Wieland Wagner and was one of the invited speakers at the director's funeral. As Geoffrey Skelton has pointed out, "Bloch's researches into Wagner's use of the *Leitmotive* opened up to [Wieland] new production possibilities" (Skelton, *Wieland Wagner* 198).

In a Bayreuth program-book article, Bloch cited what he felt was Wieland Wagner's uniqueness as a universalist and futuristic operatic director: "Quite unlike C.G. Jung, who was the archaic first stimulator of the new style of production, Wieland introduced an element of Not-Yet, of something fermenting, which fitted Wagner's music absolutely in so far as the *Leitmotive* too not only reminds us of what was, but also anticipates in a mysterious and hidden manner what no one yet knows, what is still coming, generating a complex, interrelated time-structure, with advance intimation of a melos which will not be established until much later" (199).

Postmodernist Approaches to the Ring (1976–2002)

When Wieland Wagner died in 1966 at the early age of 49, his brother and co-director Wolfgang took exclusive charge of the festival. A far better administrator than theater director, Wolfgang displayed little creative energy in his stolid attempts at modernist productions. Aware of his own limitations, he began in 1969 to engage guest directors of international repute. Nevertheless, during the early 1970s, innovations in Ring productions came from other theaters. Striking politically social perspectives marked productions by two leading East German operatic directors, Joachim Herz and Götz Friedrich, both disciples of the great Walter Felsenstein (1901–1975), the original director of the Komische Oper in East Berlin. Joachim Herz's class-conscious Leipzig Ring (1973–1976) set the second act of *Walküre* inside Valhalla as opposed to outside. By placing the scene inside a palatial home, instead of on the traditional craggy pass, Herz, much like Adorno, wanted to remind his audience that Wotan's dilemma arises from his struggle between his natural instincts and the materialistic society in which he finds himself. Götz Friedrich, in his London production of the Ring (1974–1976), used Loge in *Rheingold* as a Brechtian narrator to step outside of the drama and address the audience directly. In employing this stylistic device from Brecht's "Theater of Alienation," Friedrich was asking the audience to think about the social implications of what they were seeing (Millington 377). The stark quality of the platform used throughout the same production — a stage within a stage — recalled, according to Friedrich, "the theater of the Mystery plays and early Soviet revolutionary plays: a theatricalized world order; a theater that provides the world with order" (Burian 61).

Wolfgang Wagner's great challenge now was to secure a director capable of a 1976 centenary Ring production that would restore the primacy of Bayreuth as the center for Wagnerian innovation. After being turned down by three prominent directors in succession — Ingmar Bergman, Peter Brook, and Peter Stein — he invited Patrice Chéreau, a director exclusively of spoken drama, who claimed that his only previous contact with the Ring had entailed sleeping through a *Walküre* performance in Paris. What Chéreau achieved was nothing less than Bayreuth's first postmodernist production. Turning away from both Wieland Wagner and his grandfather, Chéreau fashioned his own deconstructed *Regietheater* (directorial theater) grounded in G.B. Shaw's audacious *The Perfect Wagnerite.* He began the action of the cycle during the nineteenth-century Industrial Revolution and ended it at the present. His characters became more human than divine to underscore their mortal foibles. The opening scene was no longer the free-flowing Rhine but an imposing hydroelectric plant, and the Rhinemaidens were Yukon Gold-Rush prostitutes. Wotan seized a gyrating pendulum to signal the cessation of time. In the second half of the cycle, Siegfried operated a mechanical hammer to forge Nothung. The dragon in this production became an elaborate super-sized antique toy on wheels. And in *Götterdämmerung,* both Siegfried and Gunther wore stylish tuxedos for their double wedding.

This was a highly energized production rich in raw emotion, with much overt sexual behavior and many tender emotional moments, along with violent histrionics and humor, as when Mime mounts a stepladder and crowns himself with a kitchen pot while triumphantly waving a wooden spoon at the end of Act One of *Siegfried.* Though greeted by vociferous boos at the opening nights, the Chéreau production took on an iconic status in the ensuing three seasons, as the most animated and insightful post–Wieland Wagner production at Bayreuth. Its path-breaking postmodernism could not be ignored for it transformed the *Ring*'s previous political and social subtexts into metatext.

After a disappointing naturalistic 1983 Ring production, Bayreuth once again came to the forefront a year before the fall of the Berlin Wall with Harry Kupfer's 1988 Ring. Kupfer, like Herz and Friedrich a disciple of Felsenstein, evoked a world devastated by nuclear catastrophe. By implication, like his two East German colleagues, Kupfer was showing that territorial and materialistic self-aggrandizement at the expense of basic human emotions and needs can only lead to disaster (Millington 378). The Chernobyl disaster in Ukraine, which had occurred while Kupfer was working out his interpretation, seemed so palpably evoked that the production was labeled by some as the "Chernobyl *Ring*" (Spotts 300).

If a postmodernist political and social critique informed the productions mentioned above, it also characterized the recent Stuttgart Ring production (1999–2003), in which each of the four installments was directed by a different stage director and the cast for each opera was different — a first in Wagner production. Klaus Zehelein, the ambitious director of the Stuttgart opera house, chose this approach to highlight the uniqueness of each of the cycle's portions and to compare and contrast the similarities and differences of the four segments.

In Joachim Schlömer's *Rheingold* production, Wotan is a calculating businessman and Fricka, his wife, has a seat on the board. As the production eschews symbolism, Alberich's Tarnhelm, or magic cap, is ignored in favor of a mirror which literally reflects each character's self-deception. Using only one set, the director has the characters garbed in 1920s evening apparel. (À la Thomas Mann's *Magic Mountain*, they are surrounded by mineral springs, classical columns, and marble handbasins. Wherever they might be, hotel or tuberculosis sanatorium, their institutionalization only adds to their stark claustrophobic predicament.

In Christopher Nel's production of *Walküre* there is no ash tree or craggy mountain pass or magic fire tableau; instead, there is the passionate interconnection of the characters: Siegmund grabbing Sieglinde between the legs and Wotan passionately kissing Brünnhilde on the mouth. The human dimensions are seen in the sets as well, from the faded shower curtain in Hunding's hut to the garden dwarf–size gnomes that illustrate Wotan's army of dead heroes during his monologue in Act Two. That the all-powerful god is in a tank suit resting on an air mattress in this scene underscores his predicament. Once again lowering the mythic dimensions of the opera, a wobbly table on which flickering candles can be seen stands in for Brünnhilde's traditional bed of fire.

The characters in *Siegfried*, directed by Jossi Wieler, are once again contemporaries: Mime is in a diner clanking plates and silver instead of forging the sword; Siegfried, wearing a T-shirt with the words "Sieg Fried," is a chubby fifty-year-old and forges his sword on an old cooker; Wotan as the Wanderer slouches around in a baseball cap and a biker jacket threatening everyone with a small revolver. The dragon Fafner sits behind a concentration-camp fence until Siegfried stabs him and hangs his corpse on the fence. Brünnhilde, instead of waking after Siegfried's kiss, knocks him flat and falls asleep again on his paunch. The two romantic leads simply sing past each other in not uncomic fashion.

Because Peter Konwitschny's *Götterdämmerung* production, like the other three, stands on its own, it has its own propulsive drive to the finish — from Siegfried's licking a cook's bowl clean, to the ferocity of a vengeance-ridden Brünnhilde tearing a cake to pieces, and to the heroine in the final scene stepping out of the action to address the audience directly in a formal red dress. For the very final moments of the music drama, Konwitschny has Wagner's original stage directions projected on a screen — only the words and music remain at the end. Clearly, a production such as the variegated Stuttgart Ring, where the multiplicity of styles dominates, fills the creative bill in a postmodernist age.

The quest for the ring quite literally continues to be played out among the Wagner family, not unlike the gods and Gibichungs in *Götterdämmerung*. Each summer during the festival period, journalistic speculation is rife: Should the Wagner family itself continue to serve as the directors or should experienced artistic and managing directors be appointed from outside? Two of Wagner's great-great-grandchildren — Nike Wagner, Wieland's daughter, and Gottfried Wagner, Wolfgang's son — have recently written telling memoirs, from which it is clear that either would eagerly succeed their uncle or father, respectively, as the next director. Wolfgang, however, would like to see his second wife and their daughter succeed him. About this contentiousness, not unlike the tetralogy's power play surrounding the ring, we might only ask, Does art imitate life, or life imitate art? In the case of the Wagner family, the answer is probably both.

Bibliography

Adorno, Theodor. *In Search of Wagner.* Trans. Rodney Livingstone. London: NLB, 1981.

Brahms, Johannes. "To Richard Wagner." June 1875. Letter 245D of *Letters of Composers Through Six Centuries.* Ed. Piero Weiss. New York: Chilton, 1965. 352.

Burian, Jurka. *Svoboda: Wagner.* Middletown: Wesleyan University, 1983.

Carnegy, Patrick. "Designing Wagner: Deeds of Music Made Visible?" *Wagner in Performance.* Eds. Barry Millington and Stewart Spencer. New Haven: Yale University Press, 1992. 48–74.

Cerf, Steven R. "Mann and Wagner." *Approaches to Teaching Mann's Death in Venice and Other Short Fiction.* Ed. Jeffrey B. Berlin. *Approaches to Teaching World Literature.* 43. New York: The Modern Language Association of America, 1992. 49–56.

Hamann, Brigitte. *Winfred Wagner oder Hitlers Bayreuth.* Munich: Piper, 2002.

Hartford, Robert, ed. *Bayreuth: The Early Years.* Cambridge: Cambridge University Press, 1980.

Hitler, Adolf. *Hitler's Table Talk: 1941–1944.* Trans. Norman Cameron and R.H. Stevens. Ed. Hugh Trevor-Roper. New York: Enigma, 2000.

_____. *Mein Kampf.* Trans. Ralph Manheim. Boston: Houghton Mifflin, 1971.

Köhler, Joachim. *Wagner's Hitler: The Prophet and His Disciple.* Trans. Ronald Taylor. Cambridge: Polity, 2000.

Konwitschny, Peter, dir. *Götterdämmerung.* TDK, 2003.

La Grange, Henry-Louis de. *Gustav Mahler: Vienna: Triumph and Disillusion (1904–1907).* Oxford: Oxford University Press, 1999.

Lee, M. Owen. *Athena Sings: Wagner and the Greeks*. Toronto: University of Toronto Press, 2003.

Legge, Walter. "The Bayreuth Festival 15.VIII.33: 'Featuring' Herr Hitler." 1933. *Bayreuth im Dritten Reich*. Ed. Berndt W. Wessling. Weinheim: Beltz, 1983. 189–92.

Mann, Thomas. *Blood of the Walsungs*. Trans. H.T. Lowe-Porter. Ed. Frederick A. Lubich. New York: Continuum, 1999, 162–85.

_____. "To Alan J. Ansen." May 1, 1945. *Briefe von 1944 bis 1950*. Eds. Hans Bürgin and Hans-Otto Mayer. Frankfurt am Main: S. Fischer, 1982. 145.

_____. "To Emil Preetorius." December 6, 1949. *Briefe:1948–1955*. Ed. Erika Mann. Frankfurt am Main: S. Fischer, 1965. 115.

_____. *Essays of Three Decades*. Trans. H.T. Lowe-Porter. New York: Alfred A. Knopf, 1948.

_____. *Joseph and His Brothers*. Trans. H.T. Lowe-Porter. New York: Alfred A. Knopf, 1974.

Millington, Barry, ed. *The Wagner Compendium: A Guide to Wagner's Life and Music*. New York: Schirmer, 1992.

Müller, Ulrich and Wapnewski, Peter, eds. *Wagner Handbook*. Trans. John Deathridge. Cambridge: Harvard University Press, 1992.

Nel, Christoph, dir. *Die Walküre*, TDK, 2003.

Nietzsche, Friedrich. "Richard Wagner in Bayreuth." Ed. Karl Schlechta. *Unzeitgemässe Betrachtungen*. Munich: Carl Hanser, 1966. 367–434.

Porges, Heinrich. *Wagner Rehearsing the "Ring."* Trans. Robert L. Jacobs. Cambridge: Cambridge University Press, 1983.

Prawy, Marcel. *"Nun sei bedankt...": Mein Richard-Wagner-Buch*. Munich: Wilhelm Goldmann, 1982.

Renckhoff, Dorothea. "Oscar Straus and his 'Merry Nibelungs.'" Essay and Plot Synopsis in CD recording. See entry for Oscar Straus, below. 12–18.

Schlömer, Joachim, dir. *Das Rheingold*, TDK, 2002.

Schulze, Hagen. *Germany: A New History*. Trans. Deborah Lucas Schneider. Cambridge: Harvard University Press, 1998.

Schumacher, Claude. "Appia, Adolphe." *The Cambridge Guide to Theatre*. Cambridge: Cambridge University Press, 1995. 30–31.

Shaw, George Bernard. *The Perfect Wagnerite: A Commentary on the Nibelung's Ring*. New York: Dover, 1967.

Skelton, Geoffrey. *Wagner at Bayreuth*. New York: George Braziller, 1965.

_____. *Wieland Wagner: The Positive Sceptic*. New York: St. Martin's, 1971.

Spotts, Frederic. *Bayreuth: A History of the Wagner Festival*. New Haven: Yale University Press, 1994.

Straus, Oscar. *Die lustigen Nibelungen*. Cond. Siegfried Köhler. Capriccio, 1996.

Wagner, Friedelind and Cooper, Page. *Heritage of Fire: The Story of Richard Wagner's Granddaughter*. New York: Harper & Brothers, 1945.

Wagner, Gottfried. *Twilight of the Wagners: The Unveiling of a Family's Legacy*. New York: Picador, 1997.

Wagner, Nike. *The Wagners: The Dramas of a Musical Dynasty*. Trans. Ewald Osers and Michael Downes. Princeton: Princeton University Press, 1998.

Wagner, Richard. *The Diary of Richard Wagner. 1865–1882: The Brown Book*. Trans. George Bird. Cambridge: Cambridge University Press, 1980.

_____. "The Festival-Playhouse at Bayreuth, with an Account of the Laying of the Foundation Stone." Trans. and ed. William Ashton Ellis. *Actors and Singers*. Lincoln: University of Nebraska Press, 1995. 324–28.

_____. "Vorwort zur Dichtung des Bühnenfestspieles 'Der Ring des Nibelungen.'" Ed. 'Dietrich Mack. *Ausgewählte Schriften*. Frankfurt am Main: Insel, 1974. 164–75.

Wagner, Wieland. "Denkmalschutz für Wagner." *Das Festspielhügel: Richard Wagners Werk in Bayreuth, 1876–1976*. Ed. Herbert Barth. Munich: DTV, 1976. 175–78.

Wagner, Wolfgang. *Acts: The Autobiography of Wolfgang Wagner*. Trans. John Brownjohn. London: Weidenfeld & Nicolson, 1994.

Wieler, Jossi, dir. *Siegfried*, TDK, 2003.

7. Wagner's *Ring* Premiere in Munich
*Brigitte Heldt**

With the *Ring* tetralogy Wagner created a unique work that could not be compared with nor resembled any precedent. He required a new scenic concept, but the understanding was missing then: theaters of the nineteenth century were not understood as a scenic space, but resembled a picture with naturalistically painted decorations. The *Ring*, with its mythic symbolism, had to collide with a scenery of its period's historic backgrounds. Wagner himself gave exacting instructions for sets and costumes, and he clearly preferred a realistic style, even if the indications in the scores speak of another language in his visions. Wagner's myth of the beginning and end of the world is not made visible through elaborate scenic miracles and illusions — a stage that copied real events stood in the way of the imagined world of the Ring.

But it was not only the controversy over the inadequacies of existing stage techniques that troubled the relations between Wagner and Ludwig II and led to deep discords during the preparations for the first performances of *Das Rheingold* and *Die Walküre*, but also the different expectations each had of the performance: Wagner wanted to see exemplary performances that showed the scope of his concept of music drama, while the king only wanted to live in his dream world, to flee from his present unpleasant reality into enraptured imaginary worlds. He imagined the perfect illusion with the best possible stage effects.

Wagner in Munich (1864–65)

At their very first meeting on May 4, 1864, in the Munich Residenz King Ludwig assured the composer he would do everything to enable Wagner to finish his current project, the *Ring*, under his patronage. This meeting with the then 18-year-old king was the decisive turning point in Wagner's life. When the Councilor von Pfistermeister brought Wagner the summons to come to King Ludwig II on May 3, he found Wagner in a desperate situation: he had fled from his creditors in Vienna, was facing financial ruin, and hoped for a miracle.

That miracle happened in the person of the young king, who had ascended the throne barely a month before, on March 10, 1864, succeeding King Maximilian II of Bavaria. He had read Wagner's writings on "The Art-Work of the Future" and "The Music of the Future" with enthusiasm. The decisive experience for the 15-year-old prince had been a performance of *Lohengrin* at the Munich Court Opera. In the preface of the first edition of the *Ring* text in 1863 Wagner explained his imagined festival theater where his works would be performed, detached from the

*Translated by Gregory D. Kershner

standard operatic repertory, financed by private means or a princely patron who would want to support the development of German art. Wagner ended with the question: "Will that prince be found?"—and Ludwig was immediately attracted to such a mighty project.

The king and the destitute composer were immediately attracted to each other; each was fascinated by the aura of the other and felt confirmed in his life's meaning. Ludwig enabled Wagner to pay off his debts and paid him generously for his upkeep. First Wagner lived in a house near the English Garden in Munich, and then in a house on Lake Starnberg which Ludwig had rented, and they visited each other daily with the king residing close by at the Berg castle.

Wagner sketched a "Program for the King," in which he planned the "Grand Performance of the Whole Ring of the Nibelung for 1867–68," in a special festival theater in Munich, and the foundation of a music school where performers would be prepared. On September 26, 1864, Wagner asked the king officially in writing to give him the commission to finish the tetralogy, to be prepared and performed in Munich. When Ludwig gladly accepted, Wagner promised the finished work for his patron for his 22nd birthday.

In anticipation of the great work, the king commissioned Michael Echter in 1864 to create frescoes from the *Ring*, according to Wagner's poem, for the Residenz in Munich. The theater painter Christian Jank was commissioned to paint the preliminary scenery for *Das Rheingold* and *Die Walküre*, copies of which would later hang in Wagner's Villa Wahnfried in Bayreuth.

Wagner presented the orchestra score of *Das Rheingold* to Ludwig for his 20th birthday in 1865, and for his birthday in 1866 the score of *Die Walküre*. And *Siegfried*, too, was being composed up to the second act, but that opera and the last one were finished later. However, Wagner did not observe the original time plan, and Ludwig continued to send the composer considerable funds beyond the original agreed-upon sums. Wagner was to be free of daily financial worries and dedicate himself completely to his compositions.

Already in 1864 Ludwig was determined to build the festival theater for the first performance of the tetralogy. In the preface to his *Ring* poem Wagner speaks of a visionary theater, an amphitheater design for the audience, where he would perform the new work with the best singers, and a covered and thus invisible orchestra. Gottfried Semper, a friend of Wagner since his Dresden days, was asked to draw up sketches and a model for this revolutionary new theater.

But the period leading up to Wagner's banishment from Munich was troubled by scandals and intrigues, to which Wagner's opulent lifestyle, his influence on the king, and not least the gossip about his sexual relationship with Cosima von Bülow, the wife of the conductor of the first performance of *Tristan* on July 10, 1865, at the Court Opera, contributed. On the day of the first orchestra rehearsal for *Tristan und Isolde*, Cosima gave birth to her first child fathered by Wagner, named Isolde. Ludwig considered Cosima to be Wagner's muse and publicly defended her honor. Wagner attacked the court rumors in an anonymous article in a Munich newspaper and advised the king to fire some members of the parliament, which then threatened to dissolve, and Ludwig was finally obliged to banish Wagner.

The project of the festival theater in Munich was not pursued, despite the fact that Semper's plans were finished in May of 1866 and the king had fixed the groundbreaking for March of 1867. The general atmosphere at the court and among the citizens of Munich had turned against both Ludwig and Wagner. In addition, Ludwig himself had considered the building rather too opulent, and Wagner's own idea was to present the Ring in a plain, practical building. Semper got the message on September 7, 1867, that the opera house would be not realized.

Model, Festspielhaus for Munich, by Gottfried Semper, architect; never built.

Preparation for the Premiere of Rheingold *in Munich*

Before Wagner arrived in Munich, the Royal Theater (or Court Opera House) there had performed *Tannhäuser* (1855), conducted by Franz Lachner and *Lohengrin* (1858), also conducted by Franz Lachner, and again in 1864 in a new production. In 1864 *The Flying Dutchman* was included in the performance schedule under the direction of Richard Wagner, and this was followed in 1865 by the premiere of *Tristan und Isolde* under the supervision of Hans von Bülow. In 1867 another new production of *Lohengrin* was staged, and in 1868 the premiere of *Meistersinger* occurred under the musical supervision of Hans von Bülow. The king, who owned the score of *Das Rheingold* and *Die Walküre*, also wished to see these works performed on stage. The transcriptions for piano for these two operas were available in 1861 and 1864, and since 1863 Wagner had conducted parts of the *Ring* in concerts. On Feb. 5, 1868, in a letter to the court secretary Lorenz von Düfflipp, Wagner himself suggested that in case the king wished it, these works should be performed at the Royal Theater sequentially from year to year to bring the Ring to completion. And in this connection he pointed to the necessity of improving the technical mechanisms of the stage. The director of the Royal Theater, Karl Freiherr von Perfall, discussed with Wagner the details of the renovation of the stage of the theater.

A year later, in February of 1869, the king ordered that *Das Rheingold* be given a premiere and at the same time that the theater be renovated, which was to be completed a few months before the premiere. In the meantime Wagner had changed his opinion and he distanced himself from these first performances. During the rehearsals for *Meistersinger* in the early summer of 1868, he fell into a dispute with Perfall and decided as a result never again to participate in any repertory performance of one of his works in Munich or anywhere else. There were also disagreements during the rehearsals for *Lohengrin*, and Wagner also was in dispute with the king, who wished to give the title role to sixty-year-old Franz Tichatschek (he preferred him to Wagner's choice of tenor). As a result, Wagner sought to persuade the king not to mount *Das Rheingold*, adding that, because Wagner was in medical treatment at a spa, he would be unable to participate—and without his participation "such a performance would be a disaster" (letter to King Ludwig, Oct. 14, 1868). But Wagner then learned that the premiere would occur despite his objections, and that he could no longer stop the reconstruction of the stage; he yielded to the king and agreed to the performance under the condition that all the participants meet with him at Tribschen. However, he had to desist in becoming personally involved in the production in Munich. Finally, the king pressured Wagner to allow the king "the entire undisputed permission to perform my works and their performances as I see fit." Wagner insisted four weeks later that Ludwig could only perform his pieces before a closed (invited) audience and without a paying public and not in usual opera performances, but opera festivals and royal performances only. Respecting the wishes of the composer, Dr. Reinhard Hallwachs was assigned to direct the performances, but Perfall found him very disagreeable, and the contract for conducting the performances was offered to the court musical director, Hans Richter. Stage hands and singers were also employed at that time.

In his Swiss domicile in Tribschen near Lucerne, Wagner held rehearsals, beginning in April of 1869, with his artistic friends who had traveled from Braunschweig, Berlin, Vienna, and Dresden. He then received Richter and then Hallwachs, and the theater director Friedrich Carl Brandt—brother of the Grand Duke of Court Theater machinists, Karl Brandt. The theater painters Heinrich Döll, Christian Jank, and Angelo Quaglio also journeyed to Tribschen and they provided the original sketches for the scenery. Sketches of the costumes for the characters were designed by Franz Seitz and Wagner annotated them with his own hand. The singer Franz Betz was to be Wotan, Max Schlusser was Loge, and Otto Schelper was to sing Alberich, and they all arrived at Tribschen on August 18, 1869, with Richter in order to rehearse with Wagner.

When the main rehearsals in Munich began the machinery and gas lighting had been completely renovated—and the proscenium was renovated as well and had acquired a new frame; plus the orchestra pit was enlarged and sunk, and the auditorium had been renovated as well. However, the technical rehearsals under Seitz did not go well, and between the brothers Brandt and the stage hands there arose many disagreements.

Also in Munich, Richter submitted his resignation only a few days before the dress rehearsal because the shortcomings of the stage sets were, according to him, catastrophic. This step was made with Wagner's approval and was to be understood as a threat that would force the king to postpone the premiere of the opera—which was scheduled for August 29, 1869.

The main dress rehearsal, conducted by Richter, was performed on August 27 in the presence of the king and between 400 and 500 guests from throughout Europe. Among the guests were Franz Liszt; Camille Saint-Saëns; Felix Draeseke; Peter Cornelius; the writer Ivan Turgenev, accompanied by the singer Pauline Viardot-Garcia and her brother the singer Manuel Garcia; the later Bayreuth conductor Hermann Levi; the violist Joseph Joachim; and the pianist and Liszt pupil Karl Klingworth, who was author of the piano transcription of the opera. Wagner did not attend—neither did Hans von Bülow, the conductor for the premieres of *Tristan* and *Meistersinger*. Shortly before the final dress rehearsal, von Bülow submitted his resignation and left Munich; his wife Cosima had finally separated from him in order to live with Wagner.

The next few days saw a series of tumultuous events. In Tribschen Wagner learned that all sorts of inadequacies in the sets and scenery changes were absurd and impossible. On the other hand the orchestra was wonderful, but Judith Gautier and other French friends told him the stage effects were terrible and that Wagner and Richter should make a most desperate plea to the king to postpone the premiere; Wagner also gave Betz a note to pass to the king in which the singer explained that such a performance under especially unfortunate circumstances would be laughed at for having committed a crime against the work, and that this mad chaos should suffice to stop the performance. The main reason for this disaster Betz identified as the incompetence of Seitz and Trinkmeier, who had designed the scenery in place of Brandt. On August 28, Richter requested that, if the performance were to occur, he be relieved of his duties. The director of the Royal Theater then communicated to the king that the shortcomings had been eliminated and the performance could take place. However, Richter refused to conduct. Perfall subsequently refused to participate in the premiere and felt compelled to dismiss Richter immediately.

Theater Rabble: Messy Affairs of the Theater

Richter's behavior evoked public ire, especially from the guests — and the press — who had arrived on the announced day to find the premiere had been postponed. Ludwig was very angry about this outrage of Richter's, and in addition the king expected his personal changes for the scenery to be respected. In the meantime Wagner telegraphed Düfflipp, Brandt, and the ballet mistress Lucile Grahn; he also handed an executive order to Brandt and ordered Richter not to conduct the performance as long as his conditions were not met.

The situation worsened dramatically between Wagner and Ludwig and no compromise could be found. Most of the artists saw the catastrophe coming but did not understand why a compromise could not be reached. The king then heard from Wagner that Perfall had ignored their agreements, and that Perfall was trying to cause an argument with Hallwachs and the machinists Brandt and Penkmayer, an employee of the theater. The letter that Ludwig composed to Düfflipp testifies to his helplessness and his bitterness. Inapproachably sharp, the king used his royal prerogative and wrote of the theater rabble who were trying to damage this premiere. He spoke of a public revolt against his orders caused by the disgusting intrigues of Wagner, and of an unnecessary lack of submission by Wagner and his rabble. One day later, the king ordered that the premiere be scheduled for the following Sunday, that Richter be dismissed, and that Wagner make himself available. Should he not appear, his income would forever end and never again would the Munich stage perform one of his works. On the first of September Wagner hurried to Munich, wishing to participate in the rehearsals, and in a telegram to the king again demanded that Richter, who in the meantime had moved to a hotel in Munich, conduct the performance; but the king did not respond to Wagner's telegram. The king ordered the premiere, "In order to force to a conclusion the horrible activities of this impossible Rheingold affair in absolute defiance to my will. Wagner must appear in Munich — I have had enough" (*Briefwechsel*).

On the morning of September 2 Wagner arrived in Munich, but soon returned to Tribschen without having accomplished anything in Munich. The *Rheingold* rehearsal in the evening was discontinued because Betz, after a disagreement with Perfall about the contents of his letter from Wagner, left the rehearsal — and on the following morning he too departed. Richter's position and the role of Wotan must be decided upon yet again, according to the will of the king. Despite the strengths of the Munich premiere, Betz felt that he could not participate in the performance because the disagreements were now being discussed in public and would result in a major loss of his professional prestige. The press took the side of

Perfall and the decision of the king and condemned the position of Richter and Wagner. *Das Rheingold*, prior to its first appearance, was called, among the people in Munich, "Rhine Tin." (*Rhein Blech*) Wagnerian opera had once again become one of the main civic actions in the most public area of political life in Munich. Perfall responded publicly to Richter's refusal to conduct the premiere despite a royal order with an immediate dismissal, which moved Wagner once again to insist that Richter remain at the podium, after which Perfall then submitted his own resignation. The local newspapers fully reported the series of operatic scandals.

Finally, Perfall assigned the director of the royal choir, Franz Wüllner, to conduct the premiere, though he until then was not familiar with any of the works of Wagner. The composer responded with a letter to Wüllner — "I warn you, sir, hands off my score — or you shall go to hell. Mind your own business and stick to singing groups, and if you must work with opera scores, do so with your friend Perfall!" (*Saïntliche Schinften*)

The Premiere of Das Rheingold *in 1869*

On September 9, 1869, Wüllner assumed the musical direction of the rehearsals. On September 22, 1869, the premiere of *Das Rheingold* took place before a packed house in the presence of the king — but Wagner was conspicuously absent. Because of the resignations of many of Wagner's chosen singers, all the major male roles were given to Munich singers, so August Kindermann now sang Wotan. To everyone's surprise, there was no fiasco at the premiere — although the scenery and production itself appeared unfinished. The whole affair seems to have been an example of the inappropriateness and egoism of Wagner and Wagner's followers, but the king and his munificence seemed to win the day. In no justifiable way did the occasion become an example of the emancipation of an artist who did not wish to be loyal servant to a prince, who rather wished to have nothing more to do with the theater rabble but wanted only his own demands to be met and put into place.

The main interest of the public at the premiere was in the scenery on stage and the new stage machinery; musically and dramatically, something new and very unusual had occurred, but the most clever instrumental coloring and very unusual harmonies were not entirely appreciated by the public. The excitement and the scenic success were nonetheless a result of the musical innovations, according to a review in a local Munich newspaper. Peter Cornelius wrote in a local musical journal that the scenic aspects of the production were unfortunately placed in the forefront of the public's attention rather than the musical innovations.

The scenery for the premiere of *Das Rheingold* was too much determined by the new technology of this theater and too little by the painted imagery of the sets, and the whole production was aimed at the public's greed for scenic novelty. In *Das Rheingold* Wagner for the first time demanded that all scene changes were to occur before the eyes of the public. The new style of composition of the music seemed ignored by the public, who were engaged only in the visual novelty of this production.

The success of a scene is determined by the extent to which it is able to deceive, to present a fictional reality, which is accomplished by the assistance of the stage technology. The following illustrations of the scenes for *Das Rheingold* by the painter Theodor Pixis testify that the production team closely adhered to Wagner's directions. The first picture is based on a sketch by Heinrich Döll, based on sketches by Christian Jank and Angelo Quaglio. For the rainbow bridge and the free terrain on the mountaintops the entire depth of the stage was employed and was so designed that by means of depth perspective the illusion of spatial distance was cleverly evoked in the minds of the audience. On the surface of the stage, about in the middle of the depth of

Das Rheingold, **the rainbow bridge to Valhalla; drawing by Theodore Pixis, 1871.**

the stage, and seeming free and approachable, the rainbow bridge to Valhalla is represented by a rock in the background through a backward perceptive and a separate piece of scenery.

The subterranean cavern in the third scene of the opera was represented by three stone bridges and a backward perspective. The transformations from the second to the third scenes and finally back to the fourth were achieved by a vertical colored screen that was illuminated. The visual realization of the first scene at bottom of the Rhine with its flowing waters, and the fogs and clouds in the later scenes of the opera, were all captured through screens and special

Das Rheingold, **the Rhinemaidens from the back of the stage; drawing by Theodore Pixis, 1871.**

lighting effects. The pleasant swimming movements of the Rhinemaidens as they circled about the set were achieved by ballet dancers, with the singers in the orchestra pit. Large rocks at the bottom of the river were placed in the front of the stage, and behind them the ballet dancers cavorted on specially constructed swimming carts while the singers sang from the pit.

The costumes were designed by Franz Seitz in consultation with Wagner; Seitz also consulted with the literary historian Hyazinth Holland, who was the consultant to the king and the designer of the picture cycles at Neuschwanstein Castle. The gods appeared in costumes based upon the traditional costumes of noble Germanic singers. On September 22, 24, and 26, 1869, the first performances of *Das Rheingold* were staged; it was presented again in 1870 with *Die Walküre*. The king attended all the performances, and two days after the third performance, he ordered the performances for the premiere of *Die Walküre* for December of 1869, without having informed Wagner of this fact.

The Premiere of the Die Walküre, 1870

The order of the king to begin as soon as possible the preparations for the premiere of *Die Walküre* was issued on September 28, 1869, but finally set for February of 1870 as the earliest possible date. Many postponements occurred because of the stage painters Jank, Quaglio, and Döll, who also were involved with the plans for the new castle at Linderhof. The king insisted that they stick to the planned deadlines because he wanted to see *Siegfried* performed in the summer of 1870. When Wagner communicated in January of 1870 that he also wished to see *Die Walküre* performed, he wrote that he hoped that he would be given the power to execute the performance as he had in 1865 the preparations for the premiere of *Tristan und Isolde*.

Die Walküre, Act III, the Ridge of the Valkyries; drawing by Theodore Pixis, 1871.

The sketches and the completion of the scenes were done by Christian Jank (the first act) and Heinrich Döll (the second and third acts). The cloud formations of the second and third acts were completed according to directions by Angelo Quaglio. The costumes and properties were prepared by Franz Seitz, and the responsibility for the stage machinery lay in the hands of the brothers Brandt. The illusionary effects were especially successful, particularly the storm-and-lightning scenes with their colorful and illuminative cloud formations, which traveled across the stage. For the Ride of the Valkyries, stable boys wore costumes and could be seen riding on real horses, a scene which made people in the audience gasp. The horses were being ridden upon a bridge in the background which was covered in clouds. Later at the Bayreuth premiere in 1876 the Laterna Magica (magic lantern) was employed for this scene. For the Magic Fire scene at the end of the opera the Munich premiere employed burning alcohol, which was conducted through pipes below the stage and behind the scenery. The high flames in time with the crackling sounds from the orchestra placed the audience in fear and horror rather than in astonishment. The music conceded all its effects and at most served an accompanying function to the picture on stage.

The critics have always stressed that the scenic special effects of *Die Walküre* were achieved with great care and thus demonstrated a respect for the work, so Wagner's complaints are not easily understood and indeed seem unjustified. Despite the Wagnerian disapproval, Perfall had achieved a great deal in this particular production.

Insofar as Wagner demanded strict adherence to his stage directions and that costumes and properties be created according to illustrations from Germanic history, should this in any way stand in place of a deeper understanding of his stage works? The dimensions of the failure to comprehend and realize all his theatrical ideas first became apparent to him after the first performance of the complete tetralogy in 1876 in Bayreuth, for which the technical novelties, scenery, and costumes from Munich served as models. "After I have created the invisible orchestra, I want to create the invisible stage" were his bitter words, as related by Cosima (*Tagebücher*). Everything that occurred on stage that invoked an awareness of theater must become invisible, the composer insisted. For Wagner only those media were used which he could employ to produce a natural, historical scenic image. For the subtle dramaturgy of Adolphe Appia, for Alfred Roller's symbolic color and lighting effects, the time had not yet arrived. Three-dimensional rather than two-dimensional design of the stage, the creation of the "plastic stage," which developed decades later, made possible the formative use of lighting in harmony with the rhythmic movements of the performers.

The Tetralogy in Bayreuth

The king waited impatiently for the completion of the *Siegfried* score, though Wagner communicated that he had not completed it, which was actually not true. Wagner completed the score on February 5, 1871, but he wanted to spare that opera the fate of the first two *Ring* operas. Before even receiving the score, Ludwig issued an order for the preparations for the premiere of *Siegfried* for the fall of 1870, and he assigned Franz Seitz the supervision of the production.

Several months before the *Die Walküre* premiere in Munich, Wagner began thinking about the complete staging of the whole *Ring* in a festival theater in Bayreuth. After visiting the old opera house in Bayreuth, whose Baroque stage would not permit his style of opera, Wagner found a hill in the small town on which to fulfill his long-harbored wish for his own festival theater for his own works. The foundation stone was laid May 22, 1872, on Wagner's

59th birthday, and on August 2, 1873, the celebration occurred for the completion of the building. On May 30, 1874, he moved into his new residence, the Villa Wahnfried in the Court Garden, which he had erected with the financial assistance of Ludwig II.

The Munich Premieres of
Siegfried *and* Götterdämmerung *(1878)*

The king was especially keen to see that in the future all of Wagner's works had their definitive productions in Munich. However, Wagner distanced himself from such plans because the continuation of his festival was hindered by a huge deficit of 150,000 marks. His suggestion that in the future a yearly festival in Bayreuth be funded by Munich's Royal Theater, where he was promised a large income, was turned down by Ludwig for financial reasons. Wagner then turned to the supervisor of the Leipzig City Opera and the Court Opera of Vienna. Because both opera houses wanted to perform the complete *Ring* cycle, Wagner conceived of future performances of the Bayreuth festival to be achieved by the working together of the three theaters — Munich, Leipzig, and Vienna — in which each opera house would produce the Ring according to his own performance restrictions, and the costs would be borne by the patrons of the opera.

In the meantime Wagner considered emigrating to America because of the festival's growing deficit. Perfall suggested, in respect to these financial problems and in consultation with the king, that the *Ring* performances occur with the staff of the Munich opera house, and be performed in Bayreuth in order to cover the costs of the deficit, which then subsequently could be made up in funds from further performances in Munich. Ludwig insisted that the *Ring* be staged in Munich in 1878, and indeed, as separate performances, all the operas were given in Munich.

Since the *Rheingold* affair in 1868, Ludwig's decision stood fast that the complete *Ring* was to be performed in Munich. The premiere of *Siegfried* in Munich could be hindered only by Wagner's denial that he had completed the score. In the summer of 1876 Hermann Levi, the court conductor since 1872, was assigned the musical direction of the planned Munich *Ring*, a disappointment to Franz Wüllner, who had been responsible for the premiere of the first two operas.

The first complete performance of the *Ring* outside Bayreuth did in fact occur in Munich in 1878. *Das Rheingold* and *Die Walküre*, which had not been performed in Munich since 1872 and 1874, were ordered prepared for performance by Levi together with the director Karl Brulliott. The performances of *Die Walküre* took place on October 20 and 25, 1878; *Das Rheingold* was also given a new staging in the context of the Munich *Ring* premiere on November 17, 1878. On November 19, *Die Walküre* was performed, on November 21, *Siegfried*, and on November 23, *Götterdämmerung*. The Munich *Ring* became the first complete cycle outside Bayreuth, where the festival performances took place in the course of a week (as Wagner wanted) and were enthusiastically received. The interest in these performances focused on the differences with the Bayreuth premiere in 1876. Everything that Ludwig ordered to be changed from Bayreuth had to be altered for the Munich performances, and what displeased him had to be improved. He indeed admired the sketches by Hofmann; however, the drawings by the brothers Brandt he considered to be less successful. His suggestions for improvements were directed at everything that appeared to be unnatural. For example, the green of the forest in Act II of *Siegfried* the king wanted to be a particular shade of green so as not to limit the imagination of the audience. So he did away with many of Wagner's suggestions and improved the *Ring* for its Munich premiere.

The Munich performance and sets were produced in the Royal Theater's own studios and workrooms and most felt that these performances improved upon the Bayreuth premiere. In conclusion, we must maintain that the two first complete productions of Wagner's *Ring* are closely intertwined with each other. The first compete performance in 1876 in Bayreuth is based on the performances in 1869 and 1870 in Munich. In the first complete *Ring* in 1878 in Munich, the experiences of Bayreuth were learned from and improved upon. Hans Richter, who in 1869 conducted the rehearsals for the premiere of *Das Rheingold*, was Wagner's conductor in 1876 for the *Ring* in Bayreuth. Franz Betz, who played the original Wotan in the Munich rehearsals, continued to sing the same role in Bayreuth. Singers of the Munich Court Theater, who were present at both premieres, were contracted to perform in Munich, and were trained by Herman Levi, who was a close associate of Wagner's during the rehearsals, and who two years later was on the podium in Munch to conduct the *Ring*. Levi also conducted the premiere of Wagner's last opera, *Parsifal,* in 1882, the year before the composer's death. The Munich premieres of *Das Rheingold* and *Die Walküre* were performed in opposition to Wagner's wishes but proved to be preliminary studies for the first Bayreuth festival and its *Ring* premiere. With the first execution of the entire work outside Bayreuth, Munich assumes an important place in the history of *Ring* performances.

Bibliography

Bauer, Oswald Georg. *Richard Wagner: Die Bühnenwerke von Uraufführung bis heute.* Frankfurt: Ullstein, 1982.

Gregor-Dellin, Martin. *Richard Wagner.* Munich: R. Piper, 1980.

König Ludwig II and Richard Wagner. *Briefwechsel.* Karlsruhe: Braun, 1939.

Mack, Dietrich. *Der Bayreuther Inszenierungstil.* Munich: Prestel, 1976.

Petzet, Detta and Michael. *Die Richard Wagner-Bühne König Ludwigs II.* Munich: Prestel, 1970.

Wagner, Cosima. *Die Tagebücher.* Munich: Piper, 1976.

Wagner, Richard. *Sämtliche Schriften und Dichtungen.* Leipzig: Breitkopf & Härtel, 1911.

8. Transgression and Taboo: Eros, Marriage, and Incest in *Die Walküre*

Gregory D. Kershner

The incestuous relationship between Sieglinde and Siegmund in Wagner's *Walküre* is as magnificent as it is disturbing. It is certainly one of the most perplexing re-occurring conundrums in the body of Wagner's operatic oeuvre. Indeed, why is it that Wagner situates the most beautiful of love affairs in the morally reprehensible context of incest? What meaning are we to attach to this fact? How is it to be interpreted? This essay will explore the idea of incest and suggest a possible interpretation of its relevance for Wagner.

In a word, the introduction of incest, perhaps the most repugnant topic in the eyes of Wagner's bourgeois contemporaries, is rooted in an aesthetics of *frisson*, the decadent thrill of crime.[1] It in no way forecloses the protagonists' doom, nor mitigates Siegfried's final demise. To the contrary, the horror of incest, as Freud called it,[2] serves to enhance the aesthetic pitch of the opera, elevating the theme of sibling incest love into a holy realm by transgressing the static system of moral injunction and taboo. It opens a passageway to the sacrosanct world of otherness, i.e., that 'outside' of lawlessness. However, it nevertheless presupposes an order of taboo, whose transgression must be repeatedly crossed, as George Bataille insists.[3] In this way, Wagner is deeply indebted to the dialectics of Hegel, which, I shall argue, he translates into drama and opera. In a sense, Wagner creates a narrative of perversion in the pathological sense of the term, one whose texture and dramatic structure are built around transgression and taboo. Let us now turn to a discussion of the incest theme in literature and psychology.

The persistence of the incest theme in literature and opera can hardly be a surprising phenomenon, for during the last two centuries incest and its prohibition have taken a central position in our interpretations of the growth of private and social life. Sociologists led by Emile Durkheim, whose *Incest: The Nature and Origin of the Taboo* appeared in 1898, began by arguing that incest taboos have the social consequences of binding a social group together behind common rituals and sentiments. Anthropologists, led by Frazer, whose *Totemism and Exogamy* was published in 1910, began by insisting on the universality of the incest prohibition and the great importance that primitive societies attached to it. The work of Freud pointed to the central role incest played in psychic development, in particular in the Oedipus complex, which implied that all individuals have incestuous fantasies, and in *Totem and Taboo* (1913), which outlined its prohibition in the growth of society. Later, Lévi-Strauss made still greater claims for the centrality of incest. In *The Elementary Structures of Kinship* (1949), he identified the development of the incest prohibition with the development of culture: "[T]he incest prohibition is at once on the threshold of culture, in culture, and in one sense

163

... culture itself.... It is the fundamental step because of which, by which, but above all in which, the transition from nature to culture is accomplished."[4]

A contemporary of Lévi-Strauss, Georges Bataille, in *The Accursed Share* (1947), situated the problem of incest within the framework of taboo and transgression and its relationship to death and desire. In Bataille's works the incest taboo creates a desire for transgression. Discussing sexual transgression, Bataille comments, "[I]t seems to me that the object of the prohibition was first marked out for coveting by the prohibition itself: if the prohibition was essentially of a sexual nature it must have drawn attention to the sexual value of the object (or rather, its erotic value)."[5] Bataille's understanding of taboo and transgression is especially insightful because it does not posit transgression as an act that undermines taboo. To the contrary, he argues that the transgression of taboos serves to enhance sexual *jouissance*. He has claimed that the notion of transgression is intimately linked to the one of taboo, and argued in *Eroticism* (1957) that "men are swayed by two simultaneous emotions: they are driven away by terror and drawn by an awed fascination. Taboo and transgression reflect these contradictory urges. The taboo would forbid the transgression but the fascination compels it."[6] Bataille considers sexuality as pure expenditure. He has pointed out that Christianity, with its stress on reproductive sexuality, has denied and morally condemned transgressive aspects of sexuality.[7]

Since the prohibition of incest, a form of castration, is found in numerous societies, Jacques Lacan in *The Function of Language in Psychoanalysis* (1956) employs it as an argument for the universality of the Oedipus complex. In doing so he relies heavily on the concept of the prohibition of incest developed by Lévi-Strauss in *Elementary Structures of Kinship*. Lacan writes:

> This is precisely where the Oedipus complex — insofar as we continue to recognize it as covering the whole field of our experience with its signification — may be said, in this connection, to mark the limits that our discipline assigns to subjectivity: that is to say, what the subject can know of his unconscious participation in the movement of the complex structures of marriage ties, by verifying the symbolic effects in his individual existence of the tangential movement towards incest which has manifested itself ever since the coming of a universal community.
>
> The primordial Law is therefore that which in regulating marriage ties superimposes the kingdom of culture on that of nature abandoned to the law of copulation. The interdiction of incest is only its subjective pivot, revealed by the modern tendency to reduce to the mother and the sister the objects forbidden to the subject's choice, although full license outside of these is not yet entirely open.[8]

If incest has seized an unprecedented position in critical thinking, moreover, its significance in nineteenth-century literature has long been acknowledged. Beyond its universality, the theme takes on a special significance in late and post–Romantic literature.[9] The meaning of incest varies still further, of course, when individual authors and works are taken into account, but in Richard Wagner's *Die Walküre* a pattern of significance can be traced which reveals as much about bourgeois culture as it does about the theme itself. Though it may at first seem an incidental feature of the opera, I will suggest that the development of the incest theme takes place at the heart of Wagner's *Walküre*. Jean-Jacques Nattiez and Robert Donington have done much already to advance an understanding of incest in *Die Walküre*, by repudiating the reductive biographical approach and stressing the importance of brother-sister or sibling incest.[10] But the limited scope of these studies has left much still to be done.

Before turning to the specific instance of sibling incest in *Die Walküre*, we need to consider the early history of the composition of the *Ring*. The myth of the Nibelungs is starkly objectified in the first sketch of 1848. In it, Siegfried is born of the incestuous bond of Siegmund and

Sieglinde, both descendants of the race of Walsung. In starkly objective terms, Wagner recounts the story relating to Siegmund and Sieglinde:

> In the race of the Walsungen this hero at last shall come to birth: a barren union is fertilized by Wotan through one of Holda's apples, which he gives the wedded pair to eat: twins, Siegmund and Sieglinde (brother and sister), spring from the marriage. Siegmund takes a wife; Sieglinde weds a man (Hunding); but both their marriages prove sterile: to beget a genuine Walsung, brother and sister wed each other.[11]

The confessional character is less derived from Wagner's need for creating an aesthetic doctrine than conceived as laying the groundwork for a world-view. Wagner's original intention is succinctly expressed by Thomas Mann in a lecture about the *Nibelungenring* delivered in Zurich in 1937:

> Man muß sich darüber klar sein, daß ein Werk, wie *Der Ring des Nibelungen*, das Wagner nach dem *Lohengrin* konzipierte, im Grunde gegen die ganze bürgerliche Kultur und Bildung gerichtet und gedichtet ist, wie sie seit der Renaissance herrschend gewesen war, daß es sich in seiner Mischung aus Urtümlichkeit und Zukünftigkeit an eine inexistente Welt klassenloser Volklichkeit wendet.[12]

Wagner utilizes the *Ring* to pave a way to the *Volk*, conceived unhistorically as an absolute value, as an eternal, invariable social substance. In his mythic world-view, all specific historical references are irrelevant; the trans-historical and pre-historical suffices. Moreover, this pre-historical social mass (*das Volk*), in his view, is primitive and uncivilized. In his depictions of Wotan, and later Siegfried, it is characterized as lawless and these figures transgress the practical ordinances governing normal civil society, and in the context of this study, the taboo prohibiting incest.

Fully embracing the sociological category of the "folk" (true to his reading of Proudhon and his acquaintance with Röckel and Bakunin), Wagner's concept of myth necessarily assumed a social-theoretical function in the *Ring*.[13] From his point of view, the "folk" represents the unconscious realm of collective desire and instinct, a folk "governed by the instinctive laws of nature.... Un-nature's rule ... and by force of its own Want to annihilate what is for nothing but annihilation."[14] Indeed, incest is a part of nature's instinctual drive, and it is a condition of utopia, in Wagner's revolutionary sense of the term. Hence, the *Ring* is not a political mythology, similar to the one he created in *Wieland*, but it constitutes a social mythology, one longing for a return to a utopian society based upon instinct and necessity.

In Wagner's world of ideas in 1848, the Nibelungs symbolize the world of conventional bourgeois capitalism:

> From the womb of night and death was spawned a race that dwells in Nibelheim, that is, in gloomy subterranean clefts and caverns.... [W]ith restless nimbleness they burrow through the bowels of the earth, like worms in a dead body; they smelt and smith hard metals.[15]

The feudalism of the giants, who are unproductive, rests heavily upon the laboring masses, the folk: "But the giants do not understand to use their might; their dullard minds are satisfied with having bound the Nibelungen."[16] The natural forces of instinct and sexual perversion represented by the Nibelungen have been nullified. Therefore, Wotan devises a plan: "only a free will, independent of the gods themselves, and able to assume and expiate itself the burden of all guilt, can loose the spell." The spell of Christian guilt, that is — a system of taboos and prohibitions, which in the course of the plot is subverted by perverse desire.

The subsequent order of events related in the sketch in broad outline trace the events in the tetralogy. The proximity to, and Wagner's intimate understanding of, the ideals of the utopian socialists is indisputable. Whether following the doctrines of Saint-Simon, Fourier or Proudhon, Wagner's ideas without exception rotate around the opposition between the productive and unproductive strata in bourgeois society, specifically the opposition between the working and middle classes. Wagner in his unique way remained indebted to the ideals of utopian socialists. Indeed, the Nibelungs alone are productive, but they are incapable of self-government; therefore, it is Wotan's task to replace Alberich's governance with one devoid of prohibition and taboo. However, it is a world not entirely irrational, but one built upon the natural order of the folk, which is the 'commonality' of humanity, as Wagner put it.[17]

The Young German (*Junge Deutschland*) ideals of sexual liberation make themselves felt in the sibling incest between Siegmund and Sieglinde, which alone can guarantee the perpetuation of the Walsungs.[18] Moreover, Siegfried and Brünnhilde are Young German protagonists, as well; and the anarchist component is also present. The 'free will' in Siegfried, who is naïve and an outlaw, is motivated by raw desire; he is the genuine descendent of Wotan, the inveterate adulterer. These characters represent the victorious and liberating tenets of 'egoism' found in contemporary theories of anarchy.[19]

It is well known that Wagner occasionally regarded marriage as a constricting burden, which to him — especially in his early years — was an expression of bourgeois ideas about property and economic security rather than of love — again, ideas that Wagner acquired through his reading of Hegel and the Young Germans. Shortly before his death, as Cosima Wagner conveys in her diaries, he commented on the splendor of Venetian palaces: "This is property! The basis of all corruption, and property decides marriages...."[20] We see that to the very end of his life Wagner remained indebted to the ideas of anarchists, socialists, and Young Germany; indeed, he remained thoroughly a rebel. It is a point of view that is pervasive throughout the *Ring*. Hence, we can see that even in advanced age he was suspicious of the bourgeois institution of marriage. It comes as no surprise that stable marriages are hard to find in the Ring, and wherever they appear they are destructive. Hunding marries Sieglinde without her consent, won from thieves against her will; she is his private property, objectified, and love cannot serve as the basis of their relationship. Wotan and Fricka live in continual strife and whatever Wotan does meets with Fricka's utter displeasure: "Though it delights you, I am afraid!"[21] The brief marriage between Siegfried and Gutrune is ascribable to Siegfried and Gunther's deceit, and it ends tragically with the slaying of Siegfried. All the other marriages, moreover, are fruitless, even that of Fricka, the divine guardian of marriage.

In "Opera and Drama," a work imbued with the radical ideas of Proudhon, Saint-Simon, Bakunin and Feuerbach, Wagner expresses his displeasure with the social system of prohibitions against free love:

> In the terrible demoralization of our present social system, revolting to the heart of every veritable Man, we may see the necessary consequences of asking for an impossible virtue, and a virtue which eventually is held in currency by a barbarous Police. Only the total vanishing of this demand, and of the grounds on which it has been based, — only the upheaval of the most un-human inequality of men, in their stationings towards Life, can bring about the fancied issue of that claim of self-restriction: and that, by making possible free love.[22]

Under the current social system of bourgeois convention and prohibitions, free love cannot be realized or experienced, for love and marriage represent irreconcilable differences.[23] And so it follows that the few marriages in the *Ring* appear forced, marriages governed by bourgeois convention and legal provisions: Hunding represses Sieglinde, to such an extent that when Sieglinde encounters Siegmund she develops ideas of fleeing. Fricka on the other hand constantly fights for Wotan, bewails his promiscuity, and chides his infidelity. In scenes saturated with petty-bourgeois melodrama she promises him the bliss of humble family life:

For I wished you faithful and true; / My thoughts were for my husband, / How to keep him beside me / When he was tempted to roam: / Safe in our castle, / Calm and contented, / There I might keep you / In peaceful repose.[24]

But Wotan is anything but a loving husband. He who begot Brünnhilde with Erda, and the twins Siegmund and Sieglinde with an unknown woman, the father of eight extra-marital Valkyrie daughters, Wotan epitomizes the lawless philander and adulterer, and promotes incest in *Die Walküre*. He hopes that Siegfried, the offspring of sibling incest, will redeem the world, become the liberator from bourgeois egoism, and create a society based upon free love.

As we can see, the incestuous relationship between Siegmund and Sieglinde, instigated by Wotan, is an acrimonious critique of the bourgeois institution and a negation of marriage. As mentioned above, the prohibition of incest is not only essential to the social function of marriage in society, but is also a taboo upon which all culture evolves (according to Lévi-Strauss); transgression of this taboo is among the greatest 'sins' that can be committed in bourgeois society. Family and marriage provide the decisive basis of society, the defense of which constitutes a common thread in nearly all significant and important concepts of bourgeois-liberal thought.[25]

Special mention must be made here of Georg Wilhelm Friedrich Hegel, who greatly influenced Wagner's thinking at the time he was composing *Die Walküre*. For Hegel, marriage and family were the moral bases of society and state, marriage being the "immediate type of ethical relationship" that comes about as the result of the "free consent of the persons, especially in their consent to make themselves one person, to renounce their natural and individual personality to this unity of one with the other. From this point of view, their union is a self-restriction, but in fact it is their liberation, because in it they attain their substantive self-consciousness."[26] Like other thinkers of his generation, Hegel viewed marriage as an institution that guarantees the upbringing of children, and later, when they are grown up, encourages their departure from their parents' home so that they in turn will be able to found new families.

For the bourgeois institution of marriage (and with it the family), which was emerging at this time as a legal entity, the prohibition of incest played a central role, though it was seldom overtly dealt with in connection with marriage and the family. This was so because its prohibition was self-evident and it was strictly forbidden. The reason for so strict a prohibition can be found in the fact that incest would lead to a lasting and ultimately destructive destabilization of the family.

In *Die Walküre* Wagner not only introduced and developed the incest theme, but attributed to it and its consequences a central role in determining the opera's subject. Wagner referred to Siegfried, the product of incest, as the "noblest hero in the world," who — in the words of an oft-quoted letter to his friend Uhlig — "is the man of the future, desired and willed by us, but who cannot be created by us and who must create himself through our annihilation."[27] The introduction of Siegfried symbolizes more than deliberate negation of the sacred bourgeois institution of marriage and therefore a corruption of its stabilizing function in society; it has a more profound psychological significance, as well.[28] Wagner provides us with a revealing psychological reading of incest as exemplified in the Oedipus myth, set forth in the theoretical works he composed at the time he was writing *Der Ring des Nibelung*.

Initiating his discussion of Greek drama in the third part of "Opera and Drama," Wagner opens with this enigmatic but telling observation: "The Greek Fate is the inner Nature-necessity, from which the Greek — because he did not understand it — sought refuge in the arbitrary political State."[29] Here the Greek idea of fate is unequivocally linked to the notion of instinctual drive,[30] as something beyond control, beyond the subject's restraint. Admitting this lack of mastery, the Greek erects in its place a substitute in the form of State and its derivative forms of substitution, such as marriage and family. These forms of disavowal Wagner refers to collectively and singularly as "an outer necessity for the maintenance of Society,"[31] as a reaction to the horror of fate or, in psychoanalytic terms, to unrepressed instinctual drive. Wagner continues and asserts that the *Lebenstrieb* is inexhaustible and eternal, but that the essence of State and hence marriage is utilitarian and mediated, based upon custom. Wagner's reading of Hegel is especially evident here; however, he abandons him by defining the family as repressive and shackling.

Analogously, Hunding and Sieglinde find themselves in a repressive marriage, one Wagner would insist is typical of the bourgeoisie. But Sieglinde, as a descendent of Wotan, the symbol of unrestrained *Lebenstrieb*, is driven to battle against the repressive institution of marriage; and this she does:

> And oh, have I found / today that friend, / come from the distance to end my grief? / Then all I have suffered / in pain and distress, / yes, all I have suffered in sorrow and shame, / all is forgotten, / all is atoned for! / Regained all things / I thought I had lost; / my fondest desires / gain their fulfillment, / if I have found that friend, / and hold that hero to me![32]

Sieglinde commits a crime, in Hegel's terms, against ethical custom by finding redemption in Siegmund instead of her husband. Similar to Madame Bovary in Flaubert's novel of the same name, in the eyes of bourgeois society she has ruined herself.

In "Opera and Drama" Wagner investigates whether Oedipus had committed incest when he married his mother and begot children; Wagner responds with an emphatic denial of this claim. But to understand why, we must first note the distinction he makes between instinct and social convention. Because Oedipus falls in love with his mother, Jokasta, prior to knowing he had transgressed social interdiction, he and his mother did not commit a crime. However, from society's viewpoint his actions must be condemned and punished whether he was aware of it or not.

In Wagner's celebrated letter to Röckel of January 25, 1854, the subject of moral repulsion in *The Ring* is addressed. Wagner rhetorically queries: "Where, then, can we locate the root of the matter?" His response to this question is that in order to better understand the incest motif and the second act of *Die Walküre* we must first of all examine the dialogue between Wotan and Fricka, the goddess of family values. She intervenes at a decisive moment in *The Ring*; in the second act of *Die Walküre*, she attacks Wotan's support of the adulterous and incestuous Walsung twins. She not only forces him to abandon his son, but also stipulates Siegfried's demise. Wagner has intentionally made Fricka, the advocate of bourgeois family values, unsympathetic. She represents the juridical order of societal repression. Indeed, she must at all costs sustain and enforce the law, as Wagner writes:

> The necessity of prolonging beyond the point of change the subjection to the tie that binds them [Wotan and Fricka] — a tie resulting from an involuntary [*unwillkürlich*] illusion of love, the duty of maintaining at all costs the relation into which they have entered, and so placing themselves in hopeless opposition to the universal law of change and renewal.[33]

Fricka resolutely upholds the sanctity of marriage and, by extension, the rule of law. Although Siegmund and Sieglinde's incestuous relationship is beyond reproach in the eyes of Wagner, the pair must nevertheless be punished for their transgression from the viewpoint of Fricka, the principal supporter of bourgeois morality. Her ideal of domestic bliss is conveyed in Love's Enchantment theme: "safe in our castle, / calm and contented, / there I might keep you / in peaceful repose."[34]

Freud used the hypothesis of a primal transgression to explain the original guilt — the sons combined against the primal father, murdered him, and the females whom he reserved for himself they divided among themselves. They felt and passed on to their descendents their guilt at having committed incest. Guilt, in psychology, is the emotional feeling that follows the infringement of a moral injunction, as Freud asserted.

Let us now return to the key passage in "Opera and Drama" where Wagner explains incest in the Oedipus myth and thereby elucidates its meaning in his other works.[35] As mentioned before, Wagner distinguishes between two modes of thought that, echoing his reading of Hegel's dialectics, find their materialization in social and political realities as well. His argument proceeds from the Greek notion of *fatum*, which he defines as 'inner necessity'; elsewhere he calls it unconscious 'instinctual drive.' This instinctual drive, well illustrated in Wotan's unbridled licentiousness, is opposed to the law of custom and convention, as embodied in the character of Fricka. Tapping the resources of the unconscious mind is the driving force behind change and revolution; however, it is constrained by normative systems based upon taboo and law. But one cannot exist without the other; it is their productive interaction, their dialectical contradiction that propels history forward. This is pure Hegel; and ultimately, *The Ring* is a political drama. Like Hegel, Wagner regards the state as the most total embodiment of custom, and therefore, of norms and taboos. Whereas the individual is motivated by instinct, which in Wagner's eyes is completely 'natural,' the state is motivated by policy, i.e., politics, and politics is the purpose of modern art.[36] This is by no means a novel interpretation of Wagner's *Ring*, but original in its linking the incest motif with politics and the unconscious.[37]

In the myth of Oedipus, Wagner asserts, the public feels horror at the fact that Oedipus has wedded his own mother and begotten children by her:

> Oedipus, who had espoused his mother and begotten children of her, is an object that fills us with horror and loathing, because he unatonably assaults our *wonted* relations towards our mother and the views which we have based thereon.[38]

But as explained above, they are not guilty of incest, because their first attraction was sexual, and hence, instinctual. It was only later, after public opinion made them aware of their transgression, that they became conscious of their guilt.[39] As is the case with Siegmund and Sieglinde, Oedipus and Jokasta are now saddled with the "irremovable curse of that Society." The same curse weighs upon their offspring, as well — namely, Siegfried in the *Ring*. They must all be annulled for their crimes of incest:

> The hapless pair, whose Conscience stood within the pale of human Society, passed judgment on themselves when they became conscious of their unconscious crime: by their self-annulling, for sake of expiation, they proved the strength of the social loathing of their action, — that loathing which had been their own through Wont, *even before* the action itself; but in that they had done the deed, despite this social conscience, they testified to the far greater, more resistless might of unconscious individual Human Nature.[40]

For the dramatic (dialectical) development of the plot, the contradiction described here provides the underlying motivation of the opera. From Schopenhauer, Wagner borrowed the tragic and pessimistic theme; from Hegel, he derived the more important dramatic and dialectic structure, that between consciousness and unconsciousness, between state and individual, between transgression and taboo. That the incestuous siblings continue in their relationship after consciousness of their crime assures both their and Siegfried's ultimate destruction; but at the same time it extols the strength of instinctual drive — the unconsciousness of freedom.

Notes

1. Charles Baudelaire, a fanatical follower of Wagner, who was profoundly influenced by him, discussed the aesthetics of *frisson* in "Projet de preface" for *Les Fleurs du mal.*

2. Siegmund Freud, *Totem and Taboo* [1913], trans. James Strachey (New York: Routledge, 1950) 152–55.

3. Georges Bataille, *The Accursed Share*, Vol. 2: The History of Eroticism, trans. Robert Hurley (New York: Zone, 1991) 89–94 and 213–23.

4. Claude Lévi-Strauss, *The Elementary Structures of Kinship*, rev. ed., trans. James Ball et al. (Boston: Beacon, 1969) 12, 24.

5. Georges Bataille, *The Accursed Share*, Vol. 2: 48.

6. Georges Bataille, *Eroticism: Death and Sensuality*, trans. Mary Dalwood (London, New York: Marion Boyars, 1987) 68.

7. See Michael Richardson, *Georges Bataille* (New York, London: Routledge, 1994) 102–107.

8. Jacques Lacan, *The Function of Language in Psychoanalysis*, trans. Anthony Wilden (Baltimore: Johns Hopkins University Press, 1968): 40.

9. For early discussions of the incest motif in late and post–Romantic literature, see Mario Praz, *The Romantic Agony* (London: Oxford University Press, 1933) and A. E. Carter, *The Idea of Decadence in French Literature 1830–1900* (Toronto: University of Toronto Press, 1958); for more recent accounts, see Erwin Koppen, *Dekadenter Wagnerismus* (Berlin: de Gruyter, 1973), Jean Pierrot, *The Decadent Imagination 1880–1900* (Chicago: University of Chicago Press, 1981), and Bram Dijkstra, *Idols of Perversity: Fantasies of Feminine Evil in Fin-de-Siecle Culture* (New York: Oxford University Press, 1986). For a general overview of the theme from a psychoanalytical viewpoint, see Otto Rank, *The Incest Theme in Literature and Legend: Fundamentals of a Psychology of Literary Creation* [originally published in 1912] (Baltimore: Johns Hopkins University Press, 1992).

10. Robert Donington, *Wagner's "Ring" and its Symbols: The Music and the Myth* (London: Faber and Faber, 1963); Otto Rank, *Das inzest-Motiv in Dichtung und Sage: Grundzüge einer Psychologie des dichterischen Schaffens* (Leipzig: Deuticke, 1926) 587–595; L. J. Rather, *The Dream of Self-Destruction: Wagner's 'Ring' and the Modern World* (Baton Rouge: Louisiana State University Press, 1979) 43–63; Gail Finney, "Self-Reflexive Siblings: Incest as Narcissism in Tieck, Wagner, and Thomas Mann," *German Quarterly* 56 (1983) 243–256; Marc Weiner, *Richard Wagner and the Anti-Semitic Imagination* (Lincoln: University of Nebraska Press, 1995) 199–205; and Jean-Jacques Nattiez, *Wagner Androgyne: A Study in Interpretation* (Princeton: Princeton University Press, 1993).

11. Richard Wagner, "The Nibelung-Myth as Sketch for a Drama" in *Richard Wagner's Prose Works*, trans. William Ashton Ellis (London: Routledge, 1895–1899) 7: 305.

12. Thomas Mann, *Gesammelte Werke* (Frankfurt: S. Fischer Verlag, 1974) 9: 511.

13. Richard Wagner, "The Art-Work of the Future" in *Richard Wagner's Prose Works* 1: 73–82.

14. "The Art-Work of the Future" 1: 81

15. Richard Wagner, "The Nibelung-Myth as Sketch for a Drama" in *Richard Wagner's Prose Works*, 7: 301.

16. "The Nibelung-Myth as Sketch for a Drama" 302.

17. "'The Folk,' was from of old the inclusive term for *all the units* which made up the total of a *commonality*" ("The Art-Work of the Future" 74).

18. For a discussion of the sexual liberation in the German literary movement known as *Junges Deutschland*, see

Helmut Koopmann, *Das Junge Deutschland: Eine Einführung* (Darmstadt; Wissenschaftliche Buchgesellschaft, 1993).

19. See Max Stirner's *Der Einzige und sein Eigentum* (1845) for an extreme Left Hegelian viewpoint on egoism and anarchy.

20. Cosima Wagner, *Cosima Wagner's Diaries: An Abridgement*, ed. Geoffrey Skelton (New Haven: Yale University Press, 1997).

21. Richard Wagner, *The Ring of the Nibelung*. Trans. Andrew Porter (New York: W. W. Norton, 1977) 19.

22. Richard Wagner, "Opera and Drama," in *Richard Wagner's Prose Works* 2: 352–353.

23. For stimulating accounts of mid-nineteenth century family life, including incest, see Eric Hobsbawm, *The Age of Capital 1848–1875* (London: Weidenfeld & Nicolson, 1975) and Michelle Perrot, "La familie triumphale" in *Histoire de la vie Privée*, vol. 4 Aries & Duby, eds., (Paris: Editions du Seuil, 1987).

24. Richard Wagner, *The Ring of the Nibelung*, 20.

25. For a discussion of liberal concepts of family in nineteenth-century Germany, see Ingeborg Weber-Kellermann, *Die deutsche Familie: Versuch einer Sozialgeschichte* (Frankfurt am Main: Suhrkamp, 1974).

26. Georg Wilhelm Friedrich Hegel, *Philosophy of Right*, trans. T. M. Knox (Oxford: Oxford University Press, 1952) 111.

27. Richard Wagner, *Sein Leben in Briefe: eine Auswahl aus den Briefen des Meisters*, ed. Carl Siegmund Benedict (Leipzig: Breitkopf & Härtel, 1913) 308 (Jan. 25–26, 1854).

28. It is important to recall that Siegfried was raised like an animal in the forest.

29. Richard Wagner, "Opera and Drama" 2: 179.

30. Wagner's notion of inner fate is an English rendition of the German *Lebenstrieb*, which would be translated into post–Freudian English as "instinctual drive."

31. "Opera and Drama" 179.

32. Richard Wagner, *The Ring of the Nibelung*, 89.

33. A translation of Richard Wagner's letter to August Röckel, reprinted in Richard Wagner, *Wagner on Music and Drama: A compendium of Richard Wagner's Prose Works*, eds. Albert Goldman and Evert Sprichorn (New York: Dutton, 1964) 290–291.

34. Richard Wagner, *The Ring of the Nibelung*, 20. Deryck Cooke, in *An Introduction to Wagner's "Der Ring des Nibelungen"* (New York: Time Inc., 1972) labels this theme "Domestic Bliss." The German is more explicit in "domestic" detail: "herrliche Wohnung, / wonniger Hausrat / sollten dich binden / zu säumender Rast." For the location in the score of the cited passage, see Richard Wagner, *Die Walküre: Vocal Score*, trans. (New York: G. Schirmer, 1986) 61, staves 1–2.

35. Wagner experimented with the incest theme in a number of other works, as well. It is suggested in *Tannhäuser* and *Lohengrin*, barely disguised in the mother-son consummation in *Tristan und Isolde*, and an even a more overt evocation in *Siegfried*.

36. "Thus the Poet's art has turned to *politics*: no one now can poetise, without politising" in "Opera and Drama" 178; "So ist die Kunst des Dichters zur *Politik* geworden: Keiner kann dichten, ohne zu politisieren" in "Oper und Drama" in *Sämtliche Schriften und Dichtungen* (Leipzig: Breitkopf & Härtel, 1912) 4: 53.

37. For another, albeit different, political interpretation of *The Ring*, see Hans Mayer's *Portrait of Wagner: An Illustrated Biography*. New York: McGraw-Hill, 1972.

38. Richard Wagner, "Opera and Drama" 182. Again, the German is clearer and more explicit: "Oidipus, der

seine Mutter ehelichte und mit ihr Kinder zeugte, weil sie unsre *gewohnten* Beziehungen zu unsrer Mutter und die durch sie gebildeten Ansichten unversöhnlich verletzt" in "Oper und Drama" 56.

39. A similar conclusion is reached by Freud in *Totem and Taboo*. He notes: "If I am not mistaken, the explanation of taboo also throws light on the nature and origin of *conscience*. It is possible, without any stretching of the sense of the terms, to speak of a taboo conscience or, after a taboo has been violated, of a taboo sense of guilt" in Sigmund Freud, *Totem and Taboo* 85.

40. Richard Wagner, "Opera and Drama" 182–83. In German, these ideas are expressed still more clearly: "Das betroffene Paar, das mit seinem Bewußtsein innerhalb der sittlichen Gesellschaft stand, verurteilte sich selbst als es seines unbewußten Frevels gegen die Sittlichkeit inneward: dadurch, daß es sich um seiner Büßung willen vernichtete, bewies es die Stärke des sozialen Ekels gegen seine Handlung, der ihm *schon vor* der Handlung durch Gewohnheit zu eigen war; dadurch, daß es die Handlung dennoch trotz des sozialen Bewußtseins ausübte, bezeugte es aber die noch bei weitem größere und unwiderstehlichere Gewalt der unbewußten individuellen menschlichen Natur." "Oper und Drama" 57.

Bibliography

Ariès, Philippe and Georges Duby, eds. *A History of Private Life*. 4 Vols. Cambridge: Harvard University Press, 1990. Trans. of *Histoire de la vie Privée*. 4 Vols. Paris: Editions du Seuil, 1987.

Bataille, Georges. *The Accursed Share*. Trans. Robert Hurley. 3 Vols. New York: Zone, 1988–1991.

_____. *Eroticism: Death and Sensibility*. Trans. Mary Dalwood. London: Marion Boyars, 1987.

Baudelaire, Charles. *Oeuvres Completes*. Ed. Y. G. Le Dantec. Rev. ed. Claude Pichois. Paris: Gallimard, 1961.

Carter, A. E. *The Idea of Decadence in French Literature 1830–1900*. Toronto: University of Toronto Press, 1958.

Cooke, Deryck. *An Introduction to Wagner's* Der Ring des Nibelungen. New York: Time, 1972.

Dijkstra, Bram. *Idols of Perversity: Fantasies of Feminine Evil in Fin-de-Siecle Culture*. New York: Oxford University Press, 1986.

Donington, Robert. *Wagner's 'Ring' and its Symbols: The Music and the Myth*. London: Faber and Faber, 1963.

Finney, Gail. "Self-Reflexive Siblings: Incest as Narcissism in Tieck, Wagner, and Thomas Mann." *German Quarterly* 56 (1983): 243–256.

Freud, Sigmund. *Totem and Taboo: Some Points of Agreement between the Mental Lives of Savages and Neurotics*. Trans. James Strachey. London: Routledge, 1950.

Hegel, Georg Wilhelm Friedrich. *Philosophy of Right*. Trans. T. M. Knox. Oxford; Oxford University Press, 1952.

Hobsbawm, Eric. *The Age of Capital 1848–1875*. London: Weidenfeld & Nicolson, 1975.

Koopmann, Helmut. *Das Junge Deutschland: Eine Einführung*. Darmstadt: Wissenschaftliche Buchgesellschaft, 1993.

Koppen, Erwin. *Dekadenter Wagnerismus: Studien zur Europäischen Literatur des Fin de Siècle*. Berlin: de Gruyter, 1973.

Lacan, Jacques. *The Function of Language in Psychoanalysis*. Trans. Anthony Wilden. Baltimore: Johns Hopkins University Press, 1968.

Lévi-Strauss, Claude. *The Elementary Structures of Kinship*. Trans. James Ball et al. Boston: Beacon, 1969.

Magee, Bryan. *Aspects of Wagner*. 2nd ed. Oxford: Oxford University Press, 1988.

Mann, Thomas. *Gesammelte Werke*. 13 Vols. Frankfurt am Main: S. Fischer, 1960–1974.

Mayer, Hans. *Portrait of Wagner: An Illustrated Biography*. New York: McGraw-Hill, 1972.

Nattiez, Jean-Jacques. *Wagner Androgyne: A Study in Interpretation*. Trans. Stewart Spencer. Princeton: Princeton University Press, 1993.

Pierrot, Jean. *The Decadent Imagination 1880–1900*. Chicago: University of Chicago Press, 1981.

Praz, Mario. *The Romantic Agony*. Trans. Angus Davidson. 2nd ed. London: Oxford University Press, 1951.

Rank, Otto. *The Incest Theme in Literature and Legend: Fundamentals of a Psychology Of Literary Creation*. Trans. Gregory C. Richter. Baltimore: Johns Hopkins University Press, 1992. Trans. of *Das Inzest-Motiv in Dichtung und Sage: Grundzüge einer Psychologie des dichterischen Schaffens*. 2nd ed. Leipzig; Deuticke, 1926.

Rather, L. J. *The Dream of Self-Destruction: Wagner's 'Ring' and the Modern World*. Baton Rouge: Louisiana State University Press, 1979.

Richardson, Michael. *Georges Bataille*. New York: Routledge, 1994.

Stirner, Max. *The Ego and His Own*. Trans. Steven T. Byington. London: C. Fifield, 1912. Trans. of *Der Einzige und sein Eigentum*. Leipzig: Otto Wigand, 1845.

Wagner, Cosima. *Cosima Wagner's Diaries: An Abridgement*. Ed. Geoffrey Skelton. New Haven: Yale University Press, 1997.

Wagner, Richard. *Richard Wagner's Prose Works*. 8 Vols. Trans. William Ashton Ellis. London: Routledge, 1893–99.

_____. *The Ring of the Nibelung*. Trans. Andrew Porter. London: Faber, 1977.

_____. *Sämtliche Schriften und Dichtungen*. 15 Vols. Leipzig: Breitkopf & Härtel, 1912.

_____. *Sein Leben in Briefen: eine Auswahl aus den Briefen des Meisters*. Ed. Carl Siegmund Benedict. Leipzig: Breitkopf & Härtel, 1913.

_____. *Wagner on Music and Drama: A Compendium of Richard Wagner's Prose Works*. Eds. Albert Goldman and Evert Sprichorn. New York: Dutton, 1964.

_____. *Die Walküre: Vocal Score*. New York: G. Schirmer, 1986.

Weber-Kellermann, Ingeborg. *Die Deutsche Familie: Versuch einer Sozialgeschichte*. Frankfurt am Main: Suhrkamp, 1974.

Weiner, Marc. *Richard Wagner and the Anti-Semitic Imagination*. Lincoln: University of Nebraska Press, 1995.

IV. PRODUCTION AND INFLUENCE OF THE *RING*

9. A Select Production History of the *Ring*

Erick Neher

A production history of Wagner's *Der Ring des Nibelungen* is a story as complex as that told by the operas themselves. Perhaps no opera (or, more accurately, music-drama tetralogy) has so dramatically occupied the times through which it has lived. Each era, each opera house, each major artist has created, recreated, rejected, reaffirmed and recycled its own *Ring* staging, often as a tribute to or a direct assault on previous stagings of the work. And each staging seems at once to reflect *and* prescribe the society in which it exists. The power of Wagner's *Ring* undoubtedly lies in its ambiguity. Its meanings are multifarious; they change upon each individual encounter with the work. Wagner seems deliberately to have smudged the epistemological edges of his magnum opus in order to prevent definitive interpretation. For this reason, the *Ring's* fascinations are inexhaustible. Its theatrical manifestations can be sponges soaking up powerful contemporary resonances, mirrors reflecting and flattering the audience, or burning bushes, arguing against the status quo and upsetting the balance of power. Herewith a look at several signature productions of Wagner's *Ring* over its century and a quarter of existence, with an emphasis on productions at the work's birthplace and, still after all these years, primary home, Bayreuth.

The World Premiere

It is impossible to separate the 1876 world premiere of the complete *Ring*, directed by Wagner himself, from the fact that it also served as the opening production of his groundbreaking Bayreuth Festival Theater. Wagner developed the idea of a theater devoted solely to his work shortly after the fiasco of the 1861 Paris premiere of *Tannhäuser*. In a letter to Hans von Bülow, dated December 17, 1861, he stated,

> I need a theater in which only myself can produce. It is impossible to bring about what I need and to find a real footing for my work in the same theaters where other operatic nonsense ... is produced and where everything — the acting, concept, and required effect — is basically diametrically opposed to my work.[1]

Productions at most nineteenth-century opera houses, which looked to the lavish spectacles of the Paris Opera as their model, did not place a high value on dramatic consistency and verisimilitude. Wagner complained frequently of "effects without causes," especially in productions of the grand operas of Meyerbeer and Rossini. House managements and sponsoring governments, rather than artists, dictated performing styles. Although his works had found success and his reputation was high by the mid–1860s, Wagner remained unhappy with what he felt were consistently unsatisfactory presentations of his works. When the young King Ludwig II of Bavaria, obsessed with Wagner's music, offered his patronage, Wagner immediately drafted plans to build a theater in which he could control every aspect of production from design to staging to the architecture of the building itself.

With architect Gottfried Semper, Wagner designed a structure that was revolutionary in its conscious manipulation of the spectator/stage relationship and its use of theatrical aesthetics as a guiding principle. Wagner specifically intended the Bayreuth auditorium, a fan-shaped amphitheater, to evoke ancient Greek stages. He described, in almost spiritual terms, the situation of the spectator confronted with the revolutionary layout:

> His seat once taken, he finds himself in an actual "theatron," that is a room made ready for no purpose other than ... looking straight in front of him. Between him and the picture to be looked at there is nothing plainly visible, merely a floating atmosphere of distance ... whereby the scene is removed as it were to the unapproachable world of dreams.[2]

As an antidote to the ornate, audience-oriented theaters of the mid-nineteenth century, the Bayreuth *Festspielhaus* forced the audience to submit itself completely to the artistic event. Contemporary commentators spoke of a "theater of narcosis" in which the spectator, induced by the hypnotic music and the dark setting into a sort of trance, would form a direct connection with the emotional core of the drama, unhindered by rationalization.

The highly charged atmosphere surrounding the opening of the festival created grandiose expectations. In an appointment hailed as a major coup, Joseph Hoffmann, a noted Viennese artist with minimal theater experience, was chosen as scenic designer. With this choice, Wagner attempted to raise scene-painting to the artistic level of the other components of his music-theater, an idea already expressed in his essay "The Art-Work of the Future." Wagner wrote to Hoffmann: "What I want is to be able to put in front of our most expert scene-painters sketches produced by real artists, in order thereby to stimulate them to nobler efforts."[3] Influenced by the picturesque historical accuracy of the innovative Meningen Theater, Hoffman turned to the art world's then-current vogue for romantic naturalism, typified by the works of Böcklin, von Menzel, and Feuerbach. Wagner and Hoffman's professed interest to get as close to naturalistic illusion as possible was inevitably crippled by their reliance on painted, two-dimensional backdrops instead of three-dimensional set pieces. In fact, a frustrated ambivalence consistently characterized Wagner's scenic ideas. According to theater historian Richard Beacham,

> Despite what would appear to have been a generally literal-minded conception of settings, his advice and instructions to his scene designers at Bayreuth were frequently vague and elusive, in marked contrast to the high precision of his work in other areas of production. This suggested that Wagner desired more than he could visualize — something at any rate other than the romantic naturalism which his craftsmen invariably produced.[4]

In this light, the attempted but compromised scenic naturalism of the world-premiere *Ring* production was probably a frustrated acquiescence to the style of the day — a best alternative.

An elaborate portrayal of nature dominated the scenery in Wagner and Hoffman's *Ring*. Gnarled, twisted trees, boulders, bushes, clouds, and streams filled the background, creating elaborate frames for the action which always took place downstage center. Costume designer Emil Doepler, taking his cue from Hoffmann's pictorial naturalism, employed Gothic historicism, displayed most obviously in the sharp, pointed helmets and spears. Nineteenth-century sensibilities are visible as well, for instance in Brünnhilde's bulky draperies, hardly practical for a horse-riding warrior maiden. Every element of the designs is weighty, filled out. Whereas Wagner's music achieves its effects via unsettled, shifting chromatic frames of reference, the visual look of the Bayreuth *Ring* was solid, unchangeable, conventional. Like the sets and costumes, the lighting at Bayreuth strove for naturalism and, in the process, proved the most innovative visual aspect of the production. Whereas most nineteenth-century lighting aimed solely to illuminate the faces of the artists, Wagner desired realistic effects. A contemporary description by William Apthorp in *Scribner's Magazine* elaborates.

> Shadows are cast *from* the sun and moon, and not *toward* them. The out-of-door scenes are lighted in a manner utterly at variance with theatrical convention. The light seems all to come from one point; not from a point 20, or 30, or 40 feet distant, but from the very sun or moon itself. Trees cast their proper shade.[5]

To expunge the formulaic gestures of the opera singers of his day, Wagner worked incessantly on every detail of blocking. The ultimate goal was movement which looked natural and which rose organically from the demands of the text and music. To achieve this result, Wagner was, ironically, forced to program almost every action, matching it with music composed with the performers' movements in mind. Apthorp noted that

> the actor's by-play is often to be regulated by what music is going on in the orchestra.... The actor is less free to put in what by-play he chooses and, especially, *when* he chooses.... The actor is in duty bound ... to regulate his acting that every change of facial expression, every gesture and movement, shall fall pat with the corresponding musical phrase or accent in the orchestra.[6]

Within this rigid structure, Wagner demanded maximum intensity and commitment, but the tight control of the singers' movements was less an example of authoritarian directorial control than an attempt to break bad habits.[7] Whether the ideal desired by Wagner and described by some commentators was always met was a matter of opinion. George Bernard Shaw remembered of those early *Ring* performances, that "half rhetorical, half historical-pictorial attitude and gesture prevailed. The most striking moments of the drama were conceived as *tableaux vivants* with posed models, instead of as passages of action, motion and life."[8]

The complete *Der Ring des Nibelungen* premiered in August 1876, to a star-studded audience, including Kaiser Wilhelm I. Although observers recognized the event as a milestone in cultural history, most contemporary reports concur with Wagner's disappointment over the inadequacy of the naturalistic visual approach, especially when juxtaposed with the genius and iconoclasm of the music. Wagner admitted to King Ludwig that all of his work precipitated only "the birth of an ordinary child of the theater,"[9] and Wagner's wife Cosima, in her diary, noted that "Costumes, scenery, everything must be done anew for the repeat performances."[10] Shaw concluded that "the Bayreuth experiment, as an attempt to evade the ordinary social and commercial conditions of theatrical enterprise, was a failure."[11] A year after the premiere, Wagner summed up the problem in a telling quip to Cosima: "Oh, I hate the thought of all those costumes and greasepaint.... Having created the invisible orchestra, I now feel like inventing the invisible theater!"[12] This statement became a touchstone for succeeding Wagnerian theatrical innovators.

Cosima's Ring

After Wagner's death in 1883, Cosima Wagner grabbed the artistic reins of the festival, reigning as queen of Bayreuth for the next 20 years and as high priestess of the Wagner cult until her death in 1930. She saw as her mission the perpetuation of Wagner's work in a manner as faithful as possible to his intentions. This meant, in her mind, strict adherence to Wagner's written stage directions and to the physical staging in his own productions. Those precise instructions, devised to break singers of bad stage habits, became, in Cosima's hands, formulas, recipes for performances. For instance, in an attempt to discourage grandstanding and encourage naturalistic acting, Wagner had requested that singers not look at the audience but at each other during dialogues. Cosima turned this preventative measure into a rigid pattern of profiles.[13] She exhaustively trained singers in a fastidious system of movement and gesture, precisely timed to the music. This was the famous "Bayreuth Style," a total integration of dramatic impulses with musical expression, practiced with only slight modifications until World War II. Cosima's daughter and assistant, Daniela, described the style as a complete fusion of action and music: there would be "no theme, no melodic phrase which has not to be given visual expression through gesture, movement, positioning and mime."[14] This style influenced productions of the Ring worldwide for the next fifty years. Cosima taught by imitation rather than by bringing the actors to a deep understanding of their roles so that movement would be spontaneous and organic. She met any challenge to her authority with the rejoinder, "That is what the master wanted."

Because of her dislike for the initial Ring production designs, which she called "small minded and tasteless,"[15] Cosima created a new production of the *Ring* in 1896 with sets by Max Brückner and costumes by Hans Thoms. The new settings provided greater simplicity and clarity for the stage action and featured majestic, brilliantly colored dramatic landscapes with clearly delineated playing spaces, free of the clutter of the Hoffmann designs. Hindsight can accuse Cosima of pedantry, but not of shoddiness. Her production of the *Ring* had a mechanical precision which impressed most observers. Many of her staging ideas were sensible, even progressive, compared to the rest of the operatic world. However, as psychological realism became more prevalent in the theater with the advent of the new wave of modern authors — Ibsen, Strindberg, Chekhov and Shaw — Bayreuth fell inexorably behind the times. In 1906 Cosima suffered a stroke and resigned the directorship of the festival in favor of her son Siegfried.

Outside Bayreuth

A touring production based on Wagner's original Ring production, directed and supervised by Angelo Neumann, spread the Bayreuth aesthetic to Leipzig, Berlin, London, Holland, Belgium, Italy, Vienna, Hungary and Russia during the 1880s and '90s. In each visited city, Neumann laid the groundwork for "proper" presentations of the *Ring* in the local opera houses by providing the example and leaving behind designs and blocking plans.[16] Opera houses, unaffected for the most part by new developments in the theater, looked to Bayreuth as a model for serious, authentic presentations of the *Ring* dramas, despite the widespread understanding that Wagner had considered his original production a failure in theatrical terms. A mere 10 years after the first festival, William Apthorp confidently judged the success of the Bayreuth mission.

> It is by enforced care for details that the Bayreuth Festival-performances of [the *Ring*] still maintain their reason of being.... The importance of Bayreuth in the art-history of this century lies far less in the fact that Wagner's greater music-dramas are performed there than in the peculiar style and conditions in which they are given.[17]

The most important early rumblings of dissent from the standard position on staging the *Ring* came from the Swiss artist, Adolphe Appia. Wagner's music dramas, by emphasizing inner, emotional states, had provided the young Appia with a paradigm for the possibilities of theatrical art. He found the actual contemporary productions of the operas less satisfying, later remarking, "The mise-en-scène in Bayreuth, conceived in the pictorial tradition of the day, impressed me only by its unusual luxury.... Even the careful treatment of the characters left an emptiness because there was no harmony between scenery and acting."[18] Appia's essay "Notes on Staging *Der Ring des Nibelungen*" and his book *Music and the Art of the Theater* included proposed designs for the *Ring* operas. Drawing on Schopenhauer, Appia felt that music should express an interior drama which spoken drama could not reveal. On stage, light became the equivalent of music in expressing what Schopenhauer called "the inner essence of phenomena."[19] Scenery must be subjective, not objective, said Appia. In other words, the audience must see the world of the protagonists as they themselves see it. Appia demanded the abolition of two-dimensional flats, asking instead for a solid playing space with acting areas on various levels. Modifications in lighting, not movement of flats, would indicate scene changes. Appia's set pieces were geometrical, fitting together organically and rhythmically, with all superfluous decoration and detail removed.

"Notes on Staging *Der Ring des Nibelungen*" contains a practical discussion of staging issues for the *Ring* operas and advice to directors and designers. Appia's ideas on mise-en-scène include placement of the players:

> The more the dramatic action turns inward and for that reason loses contact with outward appearances, the more the actor must use the downstage area...; the more the poetic-musical expression turns outward and develops the importance of the environmental qualities of the setting, the more the actor must tend to play upstage within the setting.[20]

Appia encouraged the performers to sing directly to the audience, a break from Wagner's and Cosima's careful construction of the fourth wall. By discarding painted backdrops and paying attention to dimensions, he hoped to prevent the futile attempt to imitate nature which invariably created an imbalance between the flesh-and-blood players and their cloth-and-paint environment. Appia's sketches for *Die Walküre* display the radical simplicity of his designs. Inspired by Japanese painting, and by Schopenhauer's notion that suggestion is more powerful than statement, the tree in the first act becomes simply a column, rising into the flies without branches or leaves, yet still dwarfing the house. The mountain-top in the third act is one large, multi-faceted rock, rather than a series of connected set pieces. The impression is of a place on the edge of space; beyond the tip of the rock nothing is visible. The corners of the stage are empty, creating a sense of openness and wildness. One's eye is led to what lies above and beyond the confines of the playing area.

In 1924, Appia designed a Ring production at the Municipal Theater of Basel. The set pieces, mostly large, three-dimensional boxes, were more geometric than his earlier published sketches, any vestiges of naturalism having disappeared. Cubist art provided the strongest influence here. Unfortunately, rehearsal time and money were short, and the stage size limited. The resulting stage images seem amateurish today, partly because, although the scenery was now completely non-naturalistic, the costumes remained traditional. The setting did not create a sense of spaciousness or weight but instead seemed cramped, lacking in perspective. In Frankfurt in 1925, Ludwig Sievert designed a more successful Ring which gave a sharply angular twist to Appia's abstraction, employing large geometric shapes and stylized stairs.

The Tietjen Productions

When Siegfried Wagner died in 1930 at the age of 61, his 33-year-old widow Winifred assumed control of the festival. The English-born Winifred came to Germany and met and married Siegfried in 1914, becoming a German citizen shortly thereafter, and an enthusiastic supporter of Hitler and the Nazis in the early 1920s. After Siegfried's death, Winifred appointed Heinz Tietjen as Artistic Director of Bayreuth, the first non–Wagner to direct productions there. Tietjen's new productions marked the first wholesale departures from the stagings of Cosima's time. Tietjen, with his designer Emil Preetorius, banished much of the busy, mannered detail favored by Cosima (already a simplification from Wagner's original productions) and replaced it with a cleaner, three-dimensional, monumental neo-classicism, influenced by Futurist art and by the theater work of Max Reinhardt. Preetorius and Tietjen took Wagner's demand for an unobtrusive practical background seriously, working with restraint to bring together traditional illusion and symbolic suggestiveness. Preetorius did not know Appia's work when he began to design for Bayreuth,[21] but similar, albeit much more conservative, aesthetics manifest themselves throughout his designs. Above all, Preetorius and Tietjen introduced a new sophistication to the lighting, using spots and gels to achieve emotional and thematic effects. In 1932, Tietjen appointed Paul Eberhardt as chief lighting designer and brought in a state-of-the-art lighting system to replace the ancient system which had been powered by a discarded locomotive.[22] Preetorius, echoing Appia, spoke of "the medium of light, the element which in its subtle power to change and to create change is of all elements the one most nearly related to sound."[23]

Tietjen and Preetorius' new production of the *Ring* premiered in 1933. The sets were marked by a freedom from obtrusive trees and building façades. Rather than relying on intricate filigree to create a sense of authentic antiquity, Preetorius used stark, straight lines and simple, box-like forms, often hiding half the stage in darkness. A cyclorama depicting a dramatic, cloud-strewn sky dominated the action. A frequently reproduced and influential image was Tietjen and Preetorius' Valkyrie rock in the third act of *Die Walküre*, a remarkably vivid and symbolically expressive image conveying the sense of a fateful place in a high, wild part of the world with minimal, tasteful means. A simple fir tree on the side of the stage was typical of Preetorius' restraint, compared to Hoffman's and Brückner's stage-spanning forests. In this manner, Preetorius took steps toward Wagner's request for an "unobtrusive practical background." Unlike Appia's designs, Preetorius' weightier approach focused attention forward, on the stage action, not outward to a thematic concept beyond the limits of the stage.

Tietjen's most controversial innovation was the expansion and redirection of the chorus. Under Wagner, the Gibichung men in *Götterdämmerung* numbered 26. By the 1920s, the number had grown to 64. In 1933, Tietjen employed 101, arguing that budgetary requirements had constrained the earlier festivals.[24] Wagner, in his stage directions, stressed the importance of treating the chorus as a group of individuals. Influenced by the omnipresent example of Reinhardt, Tietjen abandoned this idea for a more stylized approach, using the chorus in symbolic fashion, often silhouetting them in the front or on the sides of the stage in order to highlight action in the center. Costumes became more uniform and groups were blocked in patterns with no effort made to create a sense of natural positioning. Certain observers read the extravagance of the chorus and the rigid, uniform blocking and lack of individualism as symptoms of fascist or at least reactionary ideology, an opinion given credence by the close ties between Bayreuth in the 1930s and the Nazi party, thanks to Winifred's personal friendship with Hitler.

Tietjen's productions proved enormously influential outside Bayreuth. Opera was slow to follow theater in extricating itself from the days of painted flats and footlights. As late as the 1930s, European and American productions of the *Ring* employed tattered, two-dimensional backdrops with perhaps a few papier-mâché rocks scattered about to suggest depth. By the late 1940s, when the cessation of war allowed opera companies to invest in new stagings, the world looked to Bayreuth for ideas and found them in Tietjen and Preetorius' monumental, geometric naturalism. Photographs of the 1947–8 *Ring* at New York's Metropolitan Opera, directed by Herbert Graf and designed by Lee Simonson, are almost indistinguishable from Bayreuth's 1933 staging. The seeds of avant-garde opera staging, planted by Otto Klemperer's Kroll Opera in pre–Nazi Berlin, did not blossom in a Ring production until well after the war and, once again, Bayreuth led the way.

The Wieland Revolution

Following the Second World War, the reins of the Bayreuth Festival were handed to Winifred and Siegfried's two sons, Wieland and Wolfgang Wagner. In the several years following the reopening of the festival in 1951, Wieland staged the productions while Wolfgang focused on administration. Two imperatives shaped every aspect of Wieland's work in those first years: the need to cleanse the Nazi stain from Wagner's operas and the need to economize, given postwar Germany's initial calamitous economic state. Wieland's genius lay in turning these two negative realities into positive artistic statements; the psychological situations in the operas became the focus of Wieland's attention rather than their exterior settings. Wieland viewed the *Ring* not as a political tract but as a meditation on family relationships, love, and betrayal. He saw the dispute between Wotan and Brünnhilde as equivalent to that between Creon and Antigone: a young woman's conscience struggles between duty to family and the law, while a ruler must go against his personal wishes to maintain his power.

The intellectual foundations of "New Bayreuth" rested on the skeptical, analytical approach of such thinkers as Theodor Adorno and Ernst Bloch, not to mention Freud and Jung. Revered Wagner scholar Ernest Newman's book, *Wagner Nights*, published in 1949, was just one of a growing number of new interpretations of Wagner's work that stressed the composer's fatalism and compassion rather than his celebration of irrationalism, and that emphasized the ideas found in Wagner's operas over those in his prose essays, which Newman denigrated as "sham-intellectual maunderings."[25] Many of these scholars pointed out that the *Ring* operas diametrically opposed Nazi lust for power and conquest. Siegfried, seen as an Aryan superman by the Nazis, blunders on all fronts. Although his funeral oration mourns the death of a hero, Brünnhilde, in her immolation, recognizes that his death was inevitable. Pure, irrational id could not do any good for the world; it must unite in death with her feminine, compassionate ego. As Wieland's sister Friedelind pointed out, "If Hitler had read the *Ring of the Nibelung* with understanding, he could have foreseen his own doom."[26] This seems obvious to us now, but at the time a major reevaluation was necessary.

Wieland focused on the character of Wotan, who had attempted to justify his means with his ends. That the Nazis used this argument to justify their crimes did not escape Wieland's attention. The new, ambiguous approach to the character of Wotan was the strongest interpretative change in the postwar Bayreuth productions. No longer a supreme god, he now appeared fallibly human, a victim of his own weaknesses. A distrust of authority and the dangers of the search for power guided Wieland's interpretation.[27] The fault for the downfall of the gods lay less in the intervention of an unwelcome foreign element, the dwarves, than in the nature of the gods themselves, who refused to renounce the lust for "means of production," the desire for a hierarchical society, and, at the end, the "Will" to live. The old god's last-minute, futile defiance of Siegfried and the resulting destruction of his spear by the very sword which it had shattered, were Wotan's defining moments and the *Ring* became, in this sense, an Ancient Greek drama of retribution. Wagner had already inscribed a self-knowing ambiguity in the text when he had the god refer to himself in *Siegfried* as "Licht-Alberich (light––Alberich)."

The Nazis had emphasized a traditional reading of Alberich and Mime as clichéd Jewish caricatures, emphasizing their stooped stance and greed. Wieland's answer to the anti–Semitic problem was, in simple terms, to make Alberich look as good as possible and Wotan and Siegfried as bad as possible, graying the morality which had been black-and-white in the pre-war productions. Alberich's plight became tragic, similar in fact to Shylock's in *The Merchant of Venice*, a peculiar nobility that finds support in the tragic, imposing musical themes Wagner assigns to the dwarf, as opposed to the shuffling, whining figures that accompany Mime. Although the moral balance between Wotan and Alberich shifted dramatically, Wieland recognized that the Nibelungs could not escape a basically negative reading. For all his tragic pathos, Alberich's goals are incontestably despicable and Mime even lacks his brother's Luciferian dignity. Yet rather than succumb to traditional depictions, Wieland equated the characters with his own generation's model of evil. Alberich, in makeup and action, became a blood-smeared fascist and Nibelheim the world's first concentration camp; the grisly uniformity of the slaves — their slow, joyless movement — made the point.

In the 1951 Bayreuth Festival Program, Wieland published his first manifesto, entitled "*Überlieferung und Gestaltung* (Tradition and Innovation)." The essay begins by quoting Wagner's lament on the need for an invisible stage. Whereas Wagner's music remains permanent, the actual staging of the operas is subject to change, Wieland argues, based on the fact that methods of observation and visual conventions change from year to year. Wieland credits the development of electrical stage lighting with effecting the greatest revolution in modern theatrical history. "Illuminated space has replaced the lighted canvas," he notes. "The remote mystery of the famous [1876] settings would be unmercifully destroyed in the harshness of electric light."[28] Wieland also comments on the futility of competing with Wagner's intensely expressive music, which so vividly paints visual pictures through sound.

> It is music which transmits Wagner's visions in so expressive a language that it is well-nigh impossible to duplicate those visions for the eye.... Today, after 75 years of improving our technical methods to an incredible point of perfection ... we must still admit that the stage can, at its best, provide only a spare reflection of that which is triumphantly conveyed from the orchestra pit.[29]

The solution lies in not trying to compete with Wagner's music but instead providing as unobtrusive a background as possible, as Wagner originally requested.

Whereas Wieland's production of *Parsifal* at the first postwar Bayreuth Festival in 1951 was deemed a triumph, his initial attempts to find a visual representation of the *Ring*'s underlying symbolic quintessence proved more difficult, what with its dragon fighting, sword forging, maiden awakening, oaths on spears, storms and wind. The production underwent radical revisions in the next few years and, in fact, Wieland later completely repudiated the 1951 performances, even attempting to suppress photographs of them. The major problem probably lay in not going as far toward complete abstraction as he had with *Parsifal*. The production veered uneasily from naturalistic realism to stylized abstraction, and ended up disappointing on both ends. Undoubtedly the limited preparation time crippled Wieland's ability to present his best efforts, but his major innovation, the re-evaluation of Wotan, was instantly apparent.

Visually, Wieland built on the view of the operas as extensions of Greek tragedy by returning to Wagner's conscious attempt to evoke the ancient Greek theater, this time placing the evocation on the stage and not just in the design of the auditorium. The centerpiece of his designs was his famous disc-shaped playing areas. "I tried to enlarge the force of the acting in the *Ring*," Wieland said, "by concentrating it in a small space — the ring-disc — and to stylize the Nature which encircles this acting space. This acting space substitutes for the *cothurnus* of the Ancients."[30] In Nibelheim, rather than depict expansive caves and tunnels under the earth, Wieland used his lit disc and surrounding blackness to emphasize the tragically limited world of the dwarves, who lined the rim of the circular playing space as if anxious to escape. The second and fourth scenes of *Rheingold* took place on a disc which seemed suspended in the air. A projection, non-specific as to architectural period, conveyed the castle of Valhalla. The curved playing space suggested an elevated location and symbolized both the curved earth and the ring. As the cycle progressed and Wotan's ambition became increasingly indefinite and complicated, the platform became increasingly obscured.

Wieland's *Walküre* Act II set is influenced by Appia's, but here the cluttered geometric set pieces have disappeared and only Appia's vertical opening at the back of the stage, in which Brünnhilde dramatically appears, silhouetted against a blazing light, remains. Wieland's use of silhouette for the Ride of the Valkyries in *Walküre*'s Act III also recalled Appia. In 1951, Wieland still retained the fir tree on the left and a semblance of rocks and levels with an effect not unlike Preetorius' 1933 Valkyrie Rock, although decidedly more abstract; by the next year these embellishments were gone, the space now corresponding more directly with the gods' mountaintop in *Rheingold* and the blank playing space of the final immolation, creating greater stylistic continuity from scene to scene. The sloping diagonals and claustrophobic, cramped cave of *Siegfried*'s Act I reflected the twisted, limited world view which Mime imparted to the young hero. In Act II, a modified naturalism again predominated in 1951, with tree trunks and even leaves, all simplified in subsequent years. Fafner the dragon, a gruesome 30-foot head which appeared not out of a cave in the ground but out of the blackness at the back of the stage, was the most popular scenic effect in the opera. In Act III, the cyclorama, for the first time in the cycle, shifted from dark black to blazing blue at the awakening of Brünnhilde, producing the most famous image in Wieland's oeuvre: Brünnhilde and Siegfried on a curved, bare platform against the bright sky, as if on the very top of the world. The picture, as Bayreuth assistant Oswald Bauer points out, was a remarkable visual realization of Nietzsche's description of the scene: "Here nature arises — so pure, lonely, inaccessible, without desire, flooded by the radiant light of love."[31] Like the Expressionists, Wieland banished objects from his stage and concentrated solely on seeing the world through the subject's eyes. We don't need to see the trees in Siegfried's forest or the rocks on Brünnhilde's mountaintop. We know they are there — they are part of the pre-understanding which we bring to the theater.

Götterdämmerung began with the three Norns, on a bare stage with a swirling background, holding the rope of fate. Act II of *Götterdämmerung* displayed remnants of realistic stone patterning on the walls and steps outside the Gibichung Hall, elements that disappeared in the following years. In 1951, the chorus crowded onto the multiple available playing areas. The various levels, reminiscent of Appia's sketches of rhythmic stairs, diffused the audience's focus of attention, which should be on Brünnhilde and the spear. In later years, the removal of the levels and the uncomplicated placement of the chorus let Wieland focus all attention on the interplay of the principles, whose relative positions on the stage carried extra meaning because of the simpler circular playing area. The space itself, less cubistic, became a symbol rather than a real, tangible place, a reification of Wagner's use of the musical leitmotiv as a symbol rather than a descriptive element. In the third act, Wieland returned to a more stylized setting for the banks of the Rhine. The final conflagration occurred on a completely bare stage with the cinematic projection of Valhalla going up in flames. Not authentic fire but rather glowing red light suggested the end of the world. The central playing disc, which had appeared in all but the first scene of the cycle, now stood empty, covered in a dim bluish light as if submerged in water.[32] Wieland did not bring on chorus members at the end to watch the destruction of the gods, as Wagner's libretto specifies. His finale did not promise a new order; whether anyone survived the immolation, in fact, remained unanswered. The postwar world could not provide easy resolutions to the problem of man's inhumanity to man.

Wieland deliberately discouraged gesture suggested by the musical line, encouraging instead organically derived, psychologically motivated movement, independent of the music — a return, in essence, to Richard Wagner's ideal. Yet like his grandfather, Wieland did not leave the movement of the singers to chance. In fact, he paid meticulous attention to positioning and to spatial relationships, developing symbolic and thematic concepts through the mise-en-scène while still allowing his singers latitude to create natural movement. His direction of the actors concentrated less on intensely physical, realistic action than on archetypal, psychologically motivated stage images. A bilateral confrontation might occur, for example, with the two characters on opposite sides of the stage, rigidly facing away from each other. In Act II of *Walküre*, Brünnhilde and Wotan stood almost motionless as they locked wills. The stylized blocking heightened the symbolic import of the scene — the confrontation was not between a father and daughter but between two philosophical views, two psychological personas. Wieland freed the singers from Cosima's demand that movement correspond directly to music, allowing for a richer interaction of actor and text. "It is true that the music and what the actors do go together," he said, "but they don't stick together as if one were the cause and the other the effect."[33] Wieland realized that an actor standing still during a frantic, explosive outburst in the orchestra could make as powerful an effect as an actor raging and storming around the stage.

By removing the layers of artifice such as the elaborate sets and the histrionic movement from the staging of Wagner's music dramas, Wieland hoped to find a more direct connection to their spirit. The audience would be able to *hear* the works in a way never before possible. The stage pictures would not interfere with Wagner's desired direct line between the music and the unconscious mind. "[The music's] capacity for expression is so great that often the part added by theatrical business seems ridiculous," Wieland noted in an interview,[34] reinforcing his negative positivism, his success through not trying.

Wieland's style changed over the next decade and a half until his death in 1966. His Bayreuth productions from the first five years after the reopening might be called the "Abstract" stagings. Beginning in 1956, the stages became less bare and the shapes less geometrically regular. By the mid–1960s and his second production of the *Ring*, he had entered his "Symbolic" period. Enormous, totemic structures dominated the designs, derived from Jung's studies of archetypal symbols in primitive cultures and influenced by Henry Moore's sculptures. Wolfgang eventually joined his brother in directing and designing productions. He set his 1960 *Ring* on a split disc which represented the work's break in the natural order. Wolfgang's productions, while functional, lacked Wieland's visionary genius. His talents lay in financial and artistic administration and while his brother lived he continued to devote the bulk of his time to those activities.

After Wieland

Wieland restored Bayreuth to the position in the artistic avant-garde it had lost after Wagner's death. The festival once again became a center of debate and influence, although the influence was no longer musical but theatrical. The worldwide influence of Wieland's style not only on Wagner productions but on opera production in general was staggering. Opera companies, especially the financially struggling European ones, began applying Wieland's style to practically every opera in their repertories. Within ten years, almost every major house had at least one Wieland-influenced production and was well on its way to converting its entire German wing to "New Bayreuth." Herbert von Karajan revealed his seminal self-directed *Ring* production at Salzburg over several years in the 1960s and the Wieland influence was obvious. Abstract panoramas appeared on vast cycloramas, consisting of totemic shapes and sculpted in dark shadows. Characters appeared in hieratic, Greek-influenced costumes and stood very still for long stretches of time. This production became the basis for the Metropolitan Opera production which Karajan began bringing to New York during the company's second season at Lincoln Center. Karajan did not stay to finish the complete cycle although the final result was of a piece stylistically.

Back at Bayreuth, Wolfgang shocked the opera world by assigning the 1976 centennial production of the *Ring* to the brilliant young French director, Patrice Chéreau. Chéreau's production, designed by Richard Peduzzi and conducted by Pierre Boulez, was easily one of the most controversial and, eventually, one of the most admired *Rings* in the work's history. Chéreau abandoned Wieland's style, which had become establishment practice by the mid–1970s. Wieland's *Ring* productions were classic modernist works of art: serious in purpose and tone, spiritual, intellectual, psychological, unified and somewhat stringent in their reliance on minimalist means. Chéreau's approach was classically postmodern in its reaction against the modernist aesthetic. He moved away from high seriousness and relied instead on irony and satire. The theater became not a temple but a playground. Philosophy and psychology were rejected in favor of political and social commentary. Most importantly, he rejected the notion of a work of art needing to be unified and organic in favor of collage, of disunities between text and setting, of picking and choosing from various historical periods and theatrical styles. Nothing was strictly original in Chéreau's *Ring* because everything was ultimately a reference to something that came before it — either in art or in history.

Chéreau set the opera in several times and places, most specifically in Wagner's own century. Sets juxtaposed an industrial world and embattled nature. The first scene of *Rheingold* was set at a hydraulic dam and Siegfried and Mime's hut was dominated by a giant mechanized furnace which Siegfried employed to forge his sword. The world of the Gibichungs in *Götterdämmerung* was a bourgeois nouveau-riche parody, menaced by Hagen's working-class agitations. The gods, dressed as rich aristocrats, wearing luxurious robes and sporting elaborate hair styles, became emblematic of the complacent aristocracy of the era, unaware and not ready for the rise of the underclass that will shortly engulf them.

Chéreau portrayed Wotan as Richard Wagner himself, complete with scruffy facial hair and elaborate dressing gown. The head god was neither a king nor a lawgiver, as he might have been in nineteenth-century productions, nor an avatar of the self or consciousness, as he was in Wieland's hands. Instead, he was a self-reflexive theatrical reference to the very author of the work itself, not necessarily the composer's self-portrait but instead a reminder on the part of the director that the *Ring* is no more and no less than a cultural artifact of its era. By forcing Wagner into the story itself, he disrupted any sense of realism or of organic unity and forced the audience to realize that the *Ring* is not a mysteriously sacred work that exists outside of time and space but instead is only the specific work of a specific man, deriving from a specific social context. This acknowledgment amounted to no less than a wholesale demythologizing of the operas, a process furthered by Chéreau's Brechtian revelation of the means of illusion. For example, the dragon Fafner in *Siegfried* was an obvious stage construction on

***Das Rheingold*, Seattle Opera: The Rhinemaidens. (Photograph: Chris Bennion)**

wheels, maneuvered by visible stage hands. Chéreau's production also relied on a much more physical and naturalistic acting style than had been seen in previous Rings, complementing the relatively contemporary costumes. Most famously and, at first, notoriously, the work's erotic elements were opened up and vividly displayed. Siegmund and Sieglinde did not run into the night at the end of Act I of *Die Walküre* but instead fell to the stage floor in a powerful coital embrace.

Chéreau's *Ring* at Bayreuth was the first internationally successful postmodern opera production and, thanks to its long run and eventual worldwide telecast, it set the tone for opera production for the next thirty years, particularly in Europe. Chéreau's empowering influence was felt throughout Europe in *Rings* directed by a young and radical set of artists, many of them disciples of the great East German director Walter Felsenstein — a sort of anti–Wieland in his day due to his interest in modern settings, highly physical blocking, and social commentary. This group of young Turks included, most prominently, Harry Kupfer, Götz Friedrich, Ruth Berghaus and Nikolaus Lenhoff, all of whom directed *Rings* at major German houses and in London and San Francisco. These productions, like many European opera productions in the 1980s and 1990s, aroused widespread admiration for their vibrant theatricality, radical intelligence and brilliant "touches" as well as widespread condemnation for ignoring Wagner's "original intent" and purposefully provoking the audience merely for the sake of scandal and publicity.

At Bayreuth the pendulum is always swinging, so the follow-up to Chéreau's production was a romantic fairy-tale approach from English director Peter Hall in 1983, then Harry Kupfer's post-nuclear-holocaust *Ring* in 1988, Alfred Kirchner's arty, abstract *Ring* in 1994, and, most recently, the 2000 production directed by Jurgen Flimm, which might be referred to as the Enron *Ring*, with the action taking place at a large multinational capitalist corporation, and the characters all behaving like businessmen who have gotten in over their heads with various agreements, arrangements, and overvaluations of their assets. Additional prominent *Rings* from the last thirty years include Friedrich's futuristic production, first seen at London's Covent Garden in 1974, and a series of stagings in Seattle, most prominently a Chéreau-influenced production directed by François Rochaix that played with the idea of nineteenth-century theatrical illusionism.

The counter-reaction to the domination of postmodernist radicalism in European *Ring* stagings, already visible in Hall's generally poorly received Bayreuth production, found its most successful manifestation in the Metropolitan Opera's immensely popular staging, launched in 1986 and completed in 1989. Director Otto Schenk and designer Gunter Schneider-Siemssen, who had created a triumphant pictorial *Tannhäuser* for the Metropolitan in 1977, took as their mantra the desire to create the *Ring* that Wagner himself would have created had he lived in the era of hydraulic elevators, computerized lighting, and slide projections. Forgoing political, social, philosophical or psychological interpretation, this production instead attempts to bring Wagner's requested stage pictures to elaborate life, glorying in the naturalistic depiction of forests, rivers, and mountains and culminating in an apocalyptic *coup de théâtre*. The goal was to let Wagner's ideas speak for themselves, unhindered by directorial intervention. We know from his writings that Wagner saw the *Ring* as a political parable on the use and misuse of power, a dialectic on the inevitable corruption of capital, an environmental warning against the rape of nature, and a philosophical manifesto on the need to remove oneself spiritually from worldly entanglements. The Met's staging highlights none of these levels for fear of favoritism. Costumes suggest no time or place, so the production is not about a specific era but about every era. The evil characters are conventionally ugly and the good characters conventionally beautiful, thus avoiding any interpretive ambiguities. Schenk, Schneider-Siemssen, and costume designer Rolf Langenfass simply tell the story. The

Götterdämmerung, Metropolitan Opera: Matti Salminen as Hagen. (Photograph: Winnie Klotz)

results, depending upon taste, are either liberating or bland, refreshingly faithful or dismayingly faceless. The Metropolitan *Ring* continues to attract visitors from around the world, many of them eager to see one of the world's only naturalistic *Rings* of the last 50 years, but just as many of them eager to experience a flattering mirror of their own pleasure in conspicuous consumption and display of wealth. The production has now been in the repertory for almost twenty years and shows no sign of going anywhere.

Conclusion

This study merely scratches the surface of *Ring* productions. The cycle has been done in multiple productions in every major opera house in the world and in most of the minor European and American houses. Each production attempts to communicate to its audience in vivid and relevant terms and yet each production employs markedly different visual and theatrical means. The Bayreuth influence dictated a gradual stripping away of scenic excess over the first 75 years of the operas' history, culminating in Wieland Wagner's epochal staging. Since then, directors, empowered by Wieland's successful disregard for the letter of Wagner's stage directions, have employed a legion of approaches from the minimalist to the expressionist to the surrealist. The pendulum has swung to and from the poles of pictorial naturalism and extreme stylization. Only one thing has remained consistent: Wagner's visionary, elemental, inspiring words and music, which manage always to act as the prime communicators of meaning and pleasure in any *Ring* staging.

Notes

1. Letter to Hans von Bülow of December 17, 1861, quoted in Hans Mayer, *Richard Wagner in Bayreuth* (trans. Jack Zipes), Rizzoli, 1976, p. 30.

2. Richard Wagner, "Bayreuth," in *Wagner on Music and Drama*, ed. and trans. Albert Goldman and Evert Sprinchorn, Da Capo Press, 1964, pp. 365–366.

3. Letter to Joseph Hoffman, quoted in Geoffrey Skelton, *Wagner at Bayreuth: Experiment and Tradition*, George Braziller, 1965, p. 43.

4. Richard C. Beacham, "Adolphe Appia and the Staging of Wagnerian Opera," in *Opera Quarterly*, University of North Carolina Press, Autumn 1983, Vol. 1, No. 3, p. 116–7.

5. William Apthorp, "Wagner and Scenic Art" in *Scribner's Magazine*, November 1887, p. 525.

6. Apthorp, p. 528.

7. Skelton, *Wagner at Bayreuth*, p. 37f.

8. George Bernard Shaw, *The Perfect Wagnerite*, Dover, 1967, pp. 129–30.

9. Letter to King Ludwig II of Bavaria of August 25, 1879, quoted in Oswald Bauer, *Richard Wagner: The Stage Designs from the Premieres to the Present*. Rizzoli, 1982, p. 230.

10. *Cosima Wagner's Diaries, Vol. 1*, trans. Geoffrey Skelton, Harcourt Brace Jovanovich, 1976, p. 922.

11. Shaw, p. 127.

12. Quoted in *Cosima Wagner's Diaries, Vol. 2*, p. 154.

13. Skelton, *Wagner at Bayreuth*, p. 84.

14. Daniela Thode, quoted in Skelton, *Wagner at Bayreuth*, p. 81.

15. Quoted in Ronald E. Mitchell, *Opera: Dead or Alive*, University of Wisconsin Press, 1970, p. 137.

16. See Skelton, *Wagner at Bayreuth*, pp. 60–69.

17. Apthorp, p. 516.

18. Appia, "Theatrical Experiences and Personal Investigations," unpublished essay, quoted in Beacham, p. 14.

19. Schopenhauer, quoted in Patrick Carnegy, "The Staging of *Tristan and Isolde*: Landmarks Along the Appian Way," in *English National Opera Guide: Tristan and Isolde*, ed. Nicholas John, Riverrun Press, 1981, p. 32.

20. Appia, "The Work of Living Art," trans. H.D. Albright, University of Miami Press, 1960, p. 90.

21. Ronald Mitchell, *Opera Dead or Alive*, 1970, p. 132.

22. Manfred Eger, *Catalogue and Guide, Richard Wagner Museum in Bayreuth*. Richard Wagner Foundation, 1985.

23. Quoted in Skelton, *Wagner at Bayreuth*, p. 153.

24. Skelton, *Wagner at Bayreuth*, p. 151.

25. Quoted in George Windell, "Hitler, National Socialism and Wagner," in John DiGaetani (ed.), *Penetrating Wagner's Ring*, Da Capo Press, 1978, p. 227.

26. Friedelind Wagner, *The Royal Family of Bayreuth*, Eyre and Spottiswoode, 1948, p. viii.

27. Geoffrey Skelton, *Wieland Wagner: The Positive Skeptic*, St. Martin's Press, 1971, p. 110.

28. "Tradition and Innovation," in *The Music Review*, November 1952, p. 297.

29. Ibid, p. 298.

30. Quoted in Charles Osborne, *The World Theater of Wagner*, Macmillan, 1982, p. 159.

31. Quoted in Bauer, *Richard Wagner: The Stage Designs from the Premieres to the Present*, p. 235.

32. Ernest Newman, "Bayreuth 1951: A Vigorous New Style," *Musical America*, September 1951, p. 19.

33. Quoted in Roy McMullen, "Phantom of the Festspielhaus," *High Fidelity*, November 1966, p. 63.

34. Ibid., p. 62.

Bibliography

Adorno, Theodor. *In Search of Wagner.* New York: Schocken, 1984.
_____. "Wagner and Bayreuth," in *Bayreuth Festival Program,* 1967.
Appia, Adolphe. *Music and the Art of Theater.* Coral Gables: University of Miami Press, 1962.
_____. *Staging Wagnerian Drama.* Trans. Peter Loeffl, Boston: Birkhauser, 1982.
_____. "The Work of Living Art." Trans. H. D. Albright. "Mau Is the Measure of All Things." Trans. B. Hewitt. Ed. B. Hewitt. Coral Galdes, University of Miami Press, 1968.
Apthorp, William. "Wagner and Scenic Art," in *Scribner's Magazine* (November 1887, Volume 2, Number 5). New York: Charles Scribner's Sons, 1887.
Bauer, Oswald Georg. *Richard Wagner: The Stage Designs and Productions from the Premieres to the Present.* New York: Rizzoli, 1983.
_____, and Mack, Dietrich. *The Bayreuth Festival: The Idea, the Building, the Performances.* Bayreuth: Verlag der Bayreuther Fespiele, 1989.
Beacham, Richard C. "Adolphe Appia and the Staging of Wagnerian Opera," in *Opera Quarterly,* Autmn 1983, Vol. 1, No. 3. University of North Carolina Press.
Culshaw, John. *Ring Resounding.* New York: Limelight, 19987.
DiGaetani, John, ed. *Penetrating Wagner's Ring.* New York: Da Capo, 1978.
Donington, Robert. *Wagner's "Ring" and Its Symbols: The Music and the Myth.* Boston: Faber & Faber, 1984.
Eger, Manfred. *Catalogue and Guide, Richard Wagner Museum in Bayreuth.* Bayreuth: Richard Wagner Foundation, 1985.
Gollancz, Victor. "Discussion with Wieland Wagner," in *Bayreuth Festival Program,* 1967.
_____. *The "Ring" at Bayreuth.* Afterward by Wieland Wagner. London: Camelot, 1966.
Haas, Willy. "Richard Wagner and the 'New Bayreuth'" in *Bayreuth Festival Program,* 1961.
_____. "Wieland Wagner," in *Bayreuth Festival Program,* 1967.
Hartford, Robert, ed. *Bayreuth: The Early Years.* Cambridge: Cambridge University Press, 1980.
John, Nicholas, ed. *English National Opera Guide: Tristan and Isolde.* London: Riverrun, 1981.
Mayer, Hans. *Richard Wagner in Bayreuth.* Trans. Jack Zipes. New York: Rizzoli, 1976.
McMullen, Roy. "The Phantom of the Festspielhaus. Interview with Wieland Wagner," in *HighFidelity Magazine,* New York, November 1966.
Mitchell, Ronald E. *Opera: Dead or Alive.* Madison: University of Wisconsin Press, 1970.
Newman, Ernest. "Bayreuth 1951: A Vigorous New Style," *Musical America,* September 1951. New York, 1951.
_____. "Wagner and Bayreuth Today" in *Bayreuth Festival Program,* 1960.
_____. *The Wagner Operas.* New York: Alfred A. Knopf, 1981.
Osborne, Charles. *The World Theater of Wagner.* New York: Macmillan, 1982.
Porges, Heinrich. *Wagner Rehearsing the "Ring": An Eye-Witness Account of the Stage Rehearsals of the First Bayreuth Festival.* Cambridge: Cambridge University Press, 1983.
Schafer, Walter. *Wieland Wagner: Personlichkeit und Leistung.* Tubingen: Rainer Wunderlich, 1970.
Shaw, George Bernard. *The Great Composers.* Ed. Louis Crompton. Berkeley: University of California, 1978.
_____. *The Perfect Wagnerite.* New York: Dover, 1967.
Skelton, Goffery. *Wagner at Bayreuth: Experiment and Tradition.* New York: George Braziller, 1965.
_____. *Wieland Wagner: The Positive Skeptic.* New York: St. Martin's, 1971.
Spotts, Frederic. *Bayreuth: A History of the Wagner Festival.* New Haven: Yale University Press, 1994.
Wagner, Cosima. *Cosima Wagner's Diaries,* Vol. I and II. Ed. M. Gregor-Dellin and D. Mark. Trans. G. Skelton. New York: Harcourt, 1976,
Wagner, Friedelind. *The Royal Family of Bayreuth.* London: Eyre and Spottiswoode, 1948.
_____, with Hess, Paul. "Siegfried Wagner: A Daughter Remembers Her Father," in *The Opera Quarterly* (Spring 1990, Vol. 7, Number 1). Durham: Duke University Press, 1990.
Wagner, Nike. *The Wagners: The Dramas of a Musical Dynasty.* Trans. Ewald Osers and Michael Downes. Princeton: Princeton University Press, 2001.
Wagner, Richard. "Bayreuth." *Wagner on Music and Drama.* Ed. and trans. Albert Goldman and Evert Sprinchorn. New York: Da Capo, 1964.
_____. *My Life,* "Authorized Translation." New York: Tudor, 1936.
_____. *The Prose Works of Richard Wagner.* Vol. 1-8. Trans. William Ashton Ellis. St. Clair Shores: Miami Scholarly, 1972.
Wagner, Wieland. "Tradition and Innovation." *The Music Review.* Nov., 1952.
Wagner, Wolfgand. *Acts: The Autobiography of Wolfgang Wagner.* London: George Weidenfeld and Nicholson, 1995.

10. The *Ring* in America
Joann P. Krieg

Since America, or the United States of America, is a land of all possibilities, it is not outrageous, I hope, to begin this consideration of Wagner's *Der Ring des Nibelungen* in America with a bit of imaginative, thus "possible," dialogue. The time is the winter of 1880, the place Naples, where Richard and Cosima Wagner have fled to recover from the financial failure of the Bayreuth Festival. A door opens and a man strides forward.

> RICHARD: "Cosima, gather up the children and pack our trunks; we're moving to America, to a place called Minnesota."
> COSIMA: (resignedly) "Ach, Himmel!"

Though it seems more than a little incongruous to imagine Wagner living, writing, and producing a *Ring* cycle in Minnesota, the composer was quite serious about his intentions to emigrate. Why this interior province of America held such attraction remains a mystery, but, since he had acquired a map of North America which he pored over, it may be that the sound of the place name held some appeal. Wagner may have felt as did his American contemporary, Walt Whitman, who wrote, "What the strange charm of aboriginal names?–Monongahela–it rolls with venison richness upon the palate" (Whitman 30). Or perhaps it was the surrounding sounds of the Italian language while in Naples that made the vowel-laden "Minnesota" fall musically on Wagner's ear. (One is reminded of Puccini's warm reaction to the name "Minnie" when, with his limited English, he attended David Belasco's *The Girl of the Golden West*.) Cosima Wagner's diaries reveal the intensity of her husband's feelings for America; she quotes him as exclaiming, "What the Greeks were among the peoples of this earth, this continent is among its countries!" (*Diaries* 2:435) Such sentiments may have been nurtured by the very lucrative commission that came his way from the Centennial Committee in Philadelphia, which he honored by composing the Centennial March featured in the opening ceremonies on July 4, 1876. The march, though well received, had little merit, save for the inspiration for the *Parsifal* Grail theme that Wagner claimed he received while composing it. Minnesota, America, the New World, beckoned almost irresistibly to Wagner at this time and for reasons not unlike those of many a nineteenth-century European seeking a new life; he was financially pressured and felt Germany offered him no future possibilities. His plan for America included a Wagner association that would finance his projects and underwrite annual festivals of his works. For this American Bayreuth he would have a new work to offer, his yet unperformed *Parsifal*.

The plan may have been a bit of a ruse, though Wagner seems not to have doubted its plausibility, or even a bit of blackmail designed to make King Ludwig II of Bavaria come to his senses and realize that the composer of his dreams might actually slip away, taking with him a vital part of German culture. Ludwig rose to the occasion, fortunately, and secured the future of the Bayreuth project, the theater and the festival. And so ended Wagner's American adventure. It had not been, however, simply an aberration brought on by the exigencies of the moment. Wagner had seriously contemplated emigrating to America years earlier when his part in the Dresden uprising had brought upon his head exile and near financial ruin. At that time he thought he might make a living in America by conducting while writing the Nibelung operas, which he then intended to have performed on the banks of the Mississippi River (Wagner, *Letters* 243). Had this plan been realized the young Samuel Clemens (later to be known as Mark Twain) might have experienced his first Wagner opera on the makeshift stage of a river boat rather than years later in Bayreuth. As late as August and September of 1879 Wagner spoke directly to the American people through the pages of the country's most prestigious journal, *The North American Review*. In "The Work and Mission of My Life," he offered a biographical sketch and laid out his artistic aims. A review there of his struggles with the German aristocracy and its indifference to his aspirations for a preserved German culture led to a renunciation of hope for fulfillment in his native land and the attachment of future aspirations to the New World where, he concluded, he hoped to someday labor with Americans "as earnest co-workers in the domain of ideal, spiritual progress."

As we know, Wagner's music came to the United States in bits and pieces, one might say. Nineteenth-century Americans knew him first from marches, overtures (the *Rienzi* and *Flying Dutchman* overtures were particular favorites), preludes and other orchestral pieces, which were played as parts of concerts in the nation's principal cities. Cities such as New York and Philadelphia, with large German populations, had symphony orchestras whose performances were highlighted by the works of Mozart, Beethoven, Schubert, Liszt and Schumann, and their patrons were especially eager to become familiar with their native country's latest genius. In the main, these audiences were not the ones who flocked to Italian and English opera, which was not considered by the symphony audience as "serious" music. Italian opera had found its adherents, however, especially in New York, where, until the Civil War interrupted all such activities, it was a viable part of the city's cultural life from the time of its introduction in 1825. Of course, Mozart had written opera in Italian, but, with the exception of Beethoven's *Fidelio*, which was performed in New York City from 1839, and Weber's *Der Freischutz*, opera in German was not a familiar commodity. Thus, there was on average a 20-year lag between the premiere performance of a Wagner opera and its first production in America.

The *Ring* arrivals were very much a New York story, and, with one exception, Metropolitan Opera events. The exception was *Die Walküre*, which debuted at the New York Academy of Music in April 1877, before the Metropolitan Opera existed. From there the opera was taken to Boston for a performance within the same month. It did not take the Metropolitan long to catch up with this precedent and in 1884, just one year after its opening, the company offered *Die Walküre* under the baton of Leopold Damrosch. *Siegfried* came to the Metropolitan in 1887, conducted by Anton Seidl, and *Götterdämmerung* a year later with the same conductor. The Metropolitan premiere of *Götterdämmerung* was part of the first *Ring* cycle in that house, though the cycle was incomplete, *Rheingold* having been eliminated. (Excisions also were made in the other operas, most unforgivably the Norn scene in *Götterdämmerung*.) In 1889 the complete cycle was performed for the first time in America, and the Metropolitan took that production on tour to Philadelphia, Boston, Milwaukee, Chicago and St. Louis, all cities with significant German populations. Ten years later the cycle was taken to San Francisco, marking the completion of the east-to-west trek of the *Nibelungen*.

In what is the major study on Wagner in America, Joseph Horowitz has given us a full picture of the work done by the first two great conductors of Wagner's music in America, Theodore Thomas and Anton Seidl. These two, the latter especially, are the heroes of Wagner's New World acceptance, having ushered in the decade of "Wagnerism" when, from about 1880 to 1890, the American passion for this music reached its apogee. Both men benefited from democratic impulses and institutions peculiar to a time and place, which served to further their efforts. The early decades of the nineteenth century had seen the democratization of European opera that occurred, principally though not exclusively, in New York City, when an art form that originally was viewed as elitist and aristocratic captured the hearts of city dwellers to enjoy in the 1840s and '50s a popularity that ensured its commercial success. This turn of events owed much to a proliferation of theaters and to a competitive press that seized on opera as a kind of blood-sport, with critics on competing newspapers attacking one another via their praise or derision of individual singers.

Symphonic music performances, where Wagner first came to the attention of Americans, remained far more elitist, with each orchestra dependent upon a subscriber base wealthy enough to maintain it. The park movement of the mid-century, however, proved to be a great boon to widening the audience for orchestras, and Wagner's music made its first real advances in popularity at outdoor concerts held in the newly established parks of many American cities. Though not actually situated within the park itself, New York's Central Park Garden, an enclosed auditorium located very close to the city's new recreational oasis, was Theodore Thomas' podium for eight summers. It was here that the city's first all–Wagner concert was held, in 1872, at which the Ride of the Valkyries was heard in America for the first time (Horowitz 58). The audience is said to have showed its enthusiasm by jumping onto chairs and shouting approval. The sound of that performance seems to have burned into the American consciousness from that point, to remain the nation's quintessential Wagner association. For Wagner, too, the concert in the Park Garden had a significant consequence. Theodore Thomas seized the opportunity offered by the public enthusiasm for the Ride to form the first Wagner *Verein* in America to raise money toward the funding of the initial *Ring* cycle in Bayreuth. The following year this group sent $10,000 to Bayreuth, which, together with the $5,000 he received for the Centennial March, must have been a major factor in fostering Wagner's American dream (Horowitz 58).

Some years later another outdoor venue played a large part in furthering Wagnerism in the New York area. This time it involved the other great conducting proselytizer, Anton Seidl. In the summer of 1888 Seidl began a series of summer concerts at Coney Island, an ocean playground located on the shores of Brooklyn. Brooklyn was then a separate city, though in the following year it would combine with New York and other smaller municipalities to form the five boroughs of the City of New York as we know it today. The concerts were sponsored by the Seidl Society, an all-female group whose purpose was to further an appreciation of the music of Richard Wagner. Through the contributions of its members the society was able to offer concert tickets at fifteen and 25 cents, and free tickets were made available to workers, to the poor and to orphaned children. The concerts were enormously popular and, needless to say, the Ride of the Valkyries was a consistent favorite. Seidl continued the programs through the summer of 1896, after which a storm with exceptionally high waves washed away the music pavilion; seemingly only the forces of nature could prevail against the music of Wagner (Horowitz 204).

The Seidl Society had very high democratic ideals which were designed to counter any anti–Wagner arguments and allay the fears of some that Wagner's was an elitist art unsuited to a democracy. These fears were much the same as those that had been expressed early in the century when Italian opera was introduced, but, as already pointed out, democracy quickly absorbed that art form so that by mid-century the more than two thousand barrel-organs that played on the streets of New York rang with the "tunes" of Donizetti, Bellini, and Verdi. Wagner's music, with the exception of the "Ride," resisted such familiarization, but what it offered was a romanticism that could be experienced physically and interpreted spiritually. This interpretation became a major function of the Seidl Society and of many, music critics and others in positions of influence, who promulgated Wagnerism as a counter to the rampant materialism of the Gilded Age.

Transcendentalism, the American form of nineteenth-century romantic idealism, shared that movement's German roots though with a slight detour to New England where it was refashioned by Ralph Waldo Emerson. Emersonian transcendence into realms of spirit via nature informed American landscape art, its largely nature-based poetry and fiction, and its theology. When this cultural base was threatened by the eroding forces of materialism in the latter decades of the century, there were those who sought ways to reinforce it and Wagner's music became a critical part of their arsenal. In this they were helped by the composer's two-part address to Americans in *The North American Review* where Wagner had emphasized his desire to work with Americans "in the domain of Ideal, spiritual progress." With this as a spur, publications at all levels soon featured articles on Wagner's life and art, and analyses of his operas that emphasized their spiritual aspects. *Lohengrin* and *Tannhäuser*, especially, were Christianized, and the saving power of woman's love in the latter and in *Der Fliegender Holländer* played well against the still prevalent notion of "The True Woman," the self-sacrificing paragon of virtue dear to American popular imagery of the time.

The attempt at Christianization and the emphasis placed on the spiritual in Wagner's operas ran into difficulty when the *Ring* operas were introduced, but by then Wagnerism was in full spate, and the success of at least one of the four operas was all but guaranteed by the public enthusiasm for the Ride of the Valkyries. What Americans found in Wagner's operas was "uplift," to use Joseph Horowitz's descriptive word of emphasis, and what they understood of the *Ring* was a parable of redemption where greed is conquered. Further, they saw in the fall of the gods and the promise of a new world an allegory of their own history as it pertained to the old nobility of European society.

Speculation that there was some hesitation on the part of those less susceptible to the sweep of fashion is fed by the comments of Walt Whitman, the poet of *Leaves of Grass,* who in 1882 was just a decade away from his death at the age of 73. Wagner, Verdi, and Whitman were all of the same revolutionary generation, when romantic self-expression led to rebellion against the received traditions of religion, government, and art. The passing of the old gods, which Wagner portrayed in the *Ring*, was a very real occurrence for these men of genius, and is reflected in the works of each. For Whitman, who loved opera, the passage of time and the changes it brought to the operatic scene proved something of a challenge. Whitman had been a great lover of Italian opera, especially *bel canto* opera, and though in his later years he no longer attended performances, he was interested in following musical developments. He had heard some of Wagner's music in concerts and described the experience as having "astonished, ravished me, like the discovery of a new world" (Traubel 116). There was another angle to his interest, however. As he told his young German-American friend Horace Traubel, who was already a Wagner devotee, "So many of my friends say Wagner is Leaves of Grass done into music that I begin to suspect there must be something in it" (116). What these friends were reacting to, of course, was the romantic sweep of Wagner's music, which certainly does parallel that of Whitman's poems. More than this, both the poet and the composer had purposely aimed at a new artistic freedom of content and form, breaking with all earlier conventions.

That each was supremely successful in this aim is attested to by the recognition of their parallelism by their contemporaries.

Whitman's hesitation before making a full commitment to Wagner's music was based, so far as we can tell from his recorded words, on two things: Wagner's retreat, in his operas, from his own time and place, especially in the *Ring* with its mythological setting and what Whitman called "Jack and the Beanstalk stories"; and a fear that "Wagner's art was distinctly the art of a caste–for the few" (Traubel 116). For Whitman, whose belief in democracy was absolute, the central question was the one he put to Traubel: "Do you figure out Wagner to be a force making for democracy or the opposite?" (116). Traubel recorded the question but failed to record the answer. Still, Whitman seems to have been sufficiently convinced by the Wagner enthusiasm of a number of his adherents to overcome his fears, helped no doubt by the composer's severe criticism of German aristocracy. Then too, the composer's anti–Semitism seems not to have penetrated America's shores. As to the "Jack and the Beanstalk stories" (by which Whitman seems to have meant *Siegfried*), Traubel provided Whitman with the libretto of *Die Walküre*, which he returned without having read in its entirety. He was approving of what he did read, presumably the Siegmund and Sieglinde story, which may be an indication of his intuitive grasp of the symbolical, psychological implications of their union. Whatever his final conclusions on the operatic content, he accepted the judgments of others regarding his artistic kinship with Wagner and never rescinded his own judgment that hearing the music was like the discovery of a New World.

While Whitman may have relegated the character of Siegfried to the realm of fairy tales, the character was truly much closer to the figures that peopled American folklore. Though created in the early decades of the century, these figures lingered in the national consciousness as potent reminders of early conquests of natural forces. Robust, larger-than-life figures, the Mike Finks and Davy Crocketts who, though real-life individuals, took on a mythical aura through the medium of their own tall tales, roamed the American wilderness or maneuvered its wide rivers, creating an America of the imagination to rival any of Wagner's created forest environs. Whitman had drawn on these figures in creating the persona who sings the "Song of Myself" in *Leaves of Grass*, merely transporting his speaker from the wilderness setting of folklore to the streets of New York City. Similarly, the giants of *Das Rheingold* had their counterparts in America's folkloric pioneering giants who were hailed as "half-horse, half-alligator" in their strength, and the Nibelungen toiling over their gold hoards could not fail to awaken memories of the stories that emanated from California during that state's Gold Rush years. One music critic, Henry Krehbiel of the *New York Tribune*, saw the folkloric resemblance clearly when he said of Siegfried that he was a "prototype ... of the American people in being an unspoiled nature" (Horowitz 149). Here Krehbiel hits upon the very essence of the connection, for the predominant characteristic of America's nineteenth-century folklore was the quality of innocence, by which the American Adam was distinguished from his European forebears and contemporaries.

Had Mark Twain seen the *Ring* cycle when he visited Bayreuth in 1891, he might have recognized in Wagner's Siegfried the innocence of his own creation, Huck Finn, the boy who defies his father, falls among treacherous companions, and, unlike Siegfried, ultimately achieves his own moral freedom by acting outside the law to gain the freedom of another. But Twain did not see the *Ring*; instead he saw *Parsifal*, *Tannhäuser*, and *Tristan and Isolde*. His comments on Wagner have become the stuff of T-shirts and cocktail napkins (that the music is better than it sounds, etc.) and, indeed, being Mark Twain, he had many a facetious comment to make — on the singing, which he would have preferred not to hear so that he could revel in the orchestral Wagner, and on the audience, which he described as disciples worshiping

"At the Shrine of St. Wagner," the title of his essay account. But the *Tannhäuser* left him "drunk with pleasure," and his description of his internal state at the opening of *Parsifal* is not only perceptive but strongly suggests some of the directorial approaches to staging Wagner's operas that would be taken in the twentieth century:

> Finally, out of darkness and distance and mystery soft rich notes
> rose upon the stillness, and from his grave the dead magician began
> to weave his spells about his disciples and steep their souls in his
> enchantment. There was something strangely impressive in the fancy
> which kept imbedding itself that the composer was conscious in his
> grave of what was going on here, and that these divine sounds were the
> clothing of thoughts which were at this moment passing through his
> brain, and not recognized and familiar ones which had issued from it at
> some former time [Twain 62].

Anyone who has seen the 1982 Jurgen Syberberg film treatment of *Parsifal*, with its myriad representations of Wagner that almost make him a participant in its action, can recognize the prescience of Twain's description. Unfortunately, the comment is too lengthy to fit on a cocktail napkin, so many remain under the mistaken impression that Twain was too boorish (or too Parsifal-like) to comprehend what he saw enacted in the holy temple.

In general, the critical reception of Wagner in nineteenth-century America was rapturously laudatory, with the notable exception of John Sullivan Dwight, the eminent Boston critic and editor of *Dwight's Journal of Music*. Dwight, a Transcendentalist and moralist, disapproved of Wagner on moral and ethical grounds which prevented him from ever appreciating the music. His feelings were intensified when reports of the first Bayreuth *Ring* were filed with newspapers in the States by music critics in attendance. Dwight printed the reports but added his own negative commentary, which when read now often seems similar to comments raised in twenty-first-century America about European opera productions. He questioned whether the *Ring* operas had any meaning, if they touched the emotions of listeners, and ultimately, if anyone could really be interested in such stories (Horowitz 140). But Dwight was out of step with American musical taste and his *Journal* ceased publication in 1881, just when Wagner was poised to become a musical mania in wide portions of the United States.

The spread of Wagnerism in the early 1880s was due in large part to the tireless efforts of Theodore Thomas, who brought his devotion to Cincinnati, where he led that city's first May Festival of choral music in 1873. Later he led a similar festival in New York that drew choristers and instrumentalists from not only surrounding areas but from as far away as Chicago. Critics were hard put to find words to express their delight and admiration, and when Thomas took a Wagner festival on tour to Baltimore, Philadelphia, Montreal, Portland (Maine), Richmond and Washington, the frenzy spread from city to city and from critics to audiences. The most innovative thing about the tour was the fact that it offered not just an orchestra, but chorus and soloists, so that audiences in places where the operas had not yet been produced could hear world-class vocalists, some of whom had been featured in the Bayreuth *Ring*, singing the parts of Sieglinde and Siegmund, Wotan and Brünnhilde.

Another important American music critic who, having begun as a Wagner devotee, turned away from the operas, was James Gibbons Huneker, a figure to be reckoned with in his own time and worthy of remembrance for his wide-ranging application of a keen set of critical values. A trained musician, Huneker was for many years a foremost critic of serious music before branching out to include criticism of drama and art, and to enlarge his reputation still further by writing essays, novels and short stories. In 1886, when he was just beginning his career as music critic, he wrote to Alfred Barili, an old friend and a nephew of Adelina Patti,

"Say what you will there is nobody like Wagner...." Die Walküre I have heard three times and now for me to listen to a namby-pamby Italian opera with its commonplace plot and more than commonplace music would be quite impossible" (Huneker, *Letters* 3). And to Barili a year later, rather grandly, "I am Wagner mad. I know all the leit motives" (Huneker, *Letters* 5).

Huneker later turned away from Wagner, mainly because of his discipleship to the European modernist movement and partly because of a growing disdain for opera. In his essay "The Music of the Future," where he compares Wagner to Brahms, Huneker claims Wagner is "all showy externalizations, a seeker after immediate and sensuous effects..." (Huneker, *Essays* 75).The condemnatory "sensuous effects" is a reflection of Huneker's growing objections to Wagner the man as a decadent immoralist. In his writings he often hinted at a sexual component in the relationship between Wagner and King Ludwig II. That Ludwig was homosexual was a fairly commonly accepted fact in musical circles, but Huneker's insinuations about Wagner, along with his claims that Wagner's music was "effeminizing," seem much of a piece with a homophobic tendency in his criticisms that in the post–Freudian world casts suspicion on him despite his reputation as a womanizer. Huneker carried his moralistic opinions of Wagner over into his fiction writing. *Melomaniacs* (1902), a collection of his short stories, includes three, "Brynhild's Immolation," "Hunding's Wife" and "Siegfried's Death," whose plots offer contemporary parallels of the *Ring*'s morally fraught situations.

In these later years of the nineteenth century Wagnerism pervaded so much of American culture that one finds its influence at various points. There were many individuals possessed of great creativity who, while not necessarily restricting their appreciation to the Nibelungen saga, responded to Wagner's music in ways that proved inspirational to their own art. Among architects of the time, one, Ralph Adams Cram, architect of West Point and New York City's Cathedral of St. John the Divine, found in Wagner a kinship based on his own love of Medieval Gothic structures, while another, Louis Sullivan, found inspiration for his own soaring architectural designs. Sullivan's response to Wagner's innovativeness replicated his earlier response to Walt Whitman, which placed him in the company of others, including the promulgator of atheism Robert Ingersoll and the dancer Isadora Duncan, both of whom intuited the Wagner/Whitman parallels. When the Chicago firm of Adler and Sullivan was given a commission to build the city's opera house in 1886, it was Sullivan who produced the plan that became the Chicago Auditorium Building, opened in 1889. The structure has been termed Wagnerian, by no less an architectural giant than Frank Lloyd Wright, for its spaciousness, its extravagant design, and for the evidence it offers of its builder's own realized powers (Dizikes 256).

In his autobiography we find Sullivan referring to himself in the third person, as if he were a character in a novel or perhaps the protagonist of a great operatic drama. He describes his experiences of hearing *Tristan* and *Die Walküre* in terms that suggest the old folkloric images stirred to new life by Wagner's music: "[H]e saw arise a Mighty Personality–a great Free Spirit, a Poet, a Master Craftsman, striding in power through a vast domain that was his own, that imagination and will had bodied forth out of himself..." (Sullivan 291). Some years later this folkloric Ubermensch was connected more firmly with its background in the American landscape, and, negatively, with the Wagnerian *Ring*, by the art and music critic Paul Rosenfeld in his 1920 *Musical Portraits*. Rosenfeld wrote,

> For nowhere did the forest of the Nibelungen flourish more lushly,
> more darkly, than upon the American coasts and mountains and plains....
> His [Wagner's] regal commanding blasts, his upsweeping marching violins,
> his pompous and majestic orchestra, existed in the American scene....

American life seemed to be calling for this music in order that its vastness,
its madly affluent wealth and multiform power and transcontinental span,
its loud, grandiose promise might attain something like eternal being [Horowitz 292–93].

Like James Huneker, Rosenfeld's sympathies lay with the modernists, and though his critique of American society appears to echo those earlier criticisms of the Gilded Age that saw Wagner as a spiritual alternative, he, in fact, Americanizes Bernard Shaw's Fabian-inspired socialist reading of the *Ring* and locates the roots of American Wagnerism in a Nibelungen-like avarice and desire for conquest.

This view of the *Ring* also pervades the 1877 poetic tribute "To Richard Wagner" by the American poet Sidney Lanier. Lanier was an accomplished musician as well as poet, who wrote seriously on music theory and produced a volume of essays on *Music and Poetry* (1898). His Wagner tribute hails the composer as the bearer of a spiritual message that will counter not only the materialism of his day but the dark forces of capitalism. In its lines the poet foresees a fearful conflict between workers of the world and the giant capitalism until the characters of Wagner's operas rise up to "advance/From darkness o'er the murk mad factories." The concluding stanza looks especially to the *Ring* figures:

> O Wagner, westward bring thy heavenly art
>   No trifler thou. Siegfried and Wotan be
> Names for big ballads of the human heart.
>   Thine ears hear deeper than thine eyes can see.
> Voice of the monstrous mill, the shouting mart,
>   Not less of airy cloud and wave and tree,
> Thou, thou, if even to thyself unknown,
> Hast power to say the Time in terms of tone [Lanier 653].

As the nineteenth century faded, Wagnerism, having made an impression on the cultural scene, gradually made its way into American literature. The most notable author to make use of this material was the novelist Willa Cather, who began her writing career as a writer of articles and reviews for the Pittsburgh *Courier*. Though born in Virginia, Cather grew up in Red Cloud, Nebraska, and spent her formative years in the west. Cities in these states were not able to support opera houses and so were dependent on the Metropolitan Opera tours, which became important events. In June of 1899 the tour included Pittsburgh, where four operas, among them *Lohengrin* and *Die Walküre*, were performed. Cather reviewed all of the operas and was rather harsh (though probably truthful) in her evaluation of Lilli Lehmann's singing as Sieglinde. Lehmann was near the end of her career and Cather judged the voice to be "worn out" (Cather, *World* 2:623–626).

Cather's harshness was no doubt the result of the high standards she brought to the opera house, just as she did to everything in her life. And, as she loved Wagner's music, she revered those singers who truly could meet the composer's demands, a reverence that was given full play in her 1915 novel, *The Song of the Lark*. Perhaps preparatory to this were the two Wagner-themed stories in her first published volume of short stories, *The Troll Garden* (1905). The better known of the two–indeed, one of her most famous stories–is "A Wagner Matinee." The "ladies matinee" to which the narrator escorts his music-loving aunt, who is revisiting her native Boston after long years' absence in the dry and uncultivated regions of the American west, is an all–Wagner orchestral performance that includes "four numbers from the *Ring*, and closed with Siegfried's funeral march" (Cather, *Troll Garden* 114). The aunt's tearful response to a music she has never before heard and her wish not to have to relinquish such beauty, are registered in her fervid plea at the concert's end, "I don't want to go, Clark, I don't want to go! (115). Cather was always divided in her feelings about the places in America which, like Lincoln, Nebraska, where she attended college, were the proving ground for immigrant dreams of a better life but were removed from all cultural sources and became, in that isolation, threats to the spiritual lives of their inhabitants. In "A Wagner Matinee" one senses that Siegfried's funeral march registers in Aunt Georgiana's mind as marking the death of her own musical soul.

The second of the two stories, "The Garden Lodge," concerns a world-famed opera tenor, a Wagner specialist, who has spent a month in the home of Caroline Noble and her husband. They are a well off, culturally active couple, with Caroline the more reserved, one would even say more controlled, of the two. She, as a result of a poverty-driven necessity in her early life, is careful not to follow the example of family members and allow her love of music—or of any one thing — to become a passion. Passion enters her life, however, when she accompanies the tenor in daily rehearsal sessions in the garden lodge. It is a passion unacknowledged by either save for a brief moment when he sings to Caroline Siegmund's words to Sieglinde, "Thou art the Spring for which I sighed in Winter's cold embraces" (60). Caroline faces the choice of whether to allow herself to fully entertain this experience of passion when, after the tenor has left their home, her husband suggests the removal of the lodge to make way for a larger, more commodious structure. His wife's first impulse is to resist the suggestion because the lodge, and the surrounding garden, have been the scenes of her great joy. In one restless night spent alone in the lodge she allows her emotions full sway, playing Wagner's richly moving strains and feeling once again the tenor's touch on her body as he had sung the words. By morning she has decided to accede to her husband's wishes and have the lodge destroyed. The story, of course, is a play on, and reversal of, Act 1 of *Die Walküre* with the tenor as the Siegmund who is the reflection of Caroline's repressed passion. As is so often the case in Cather's writing, the garden setting represents temptation. The symbolism is part of Cather's Medievalism, which, like Wagner's, draws on Christian allegory that associates the female body with the lush natural setting of a springtime garden. Though somewhat neglected because of the attention to "A Wagner Matinee," "The Garden Lodge" is an excellent transcription of Wagner's love story with Cather's added moralization.

In *The Song of the Lark* Cather combines her two favorite subjects, art and the American west. Her heroine Thea Kronberg is of a Scandinavian immigrant family and grows up in the small town of Moonstone, which she leaves in young adulthood to study music in Chicago. During a sojourn in the canyons of the southwestern desert, Thea attains a Brünnhilde-like self-awareness and determination which she resolves to channel into her vocal art. The latter portion of the book details her life as a reigning diva in the opera world, where her greatest achievements are in Wagnerian roles. In one of the final chapters Cather gives a marvelous description of Thea/Sieglinde's emotions in the Nothung and recognition scenes in *Die Walküre* where the Walsung twins yield to each other longingly and exultingly. In this full-length novel Cather quotes Wagner's libretto in the German, rather than in English, as she does in "The Garden Lodge," but again imposes her high moral standards on her heroine. Thea's devotion to her art entails a conscious decision to serve it and it alone, leaving very little time or inclination for personal relationships; it is a sacrifice that Cather demands of her so that the artistic vessel will remain sacred and untouched.

Much has been written of Cather's devotion to the music of Wagner, and in some cases critics have strained to "justify" it since they find the fit of Cather's moralism with Wagner's often licentious romanticism a strange one. Arguments that connect their shared beliefs in the sanctity of art and in a Schopenhauerian philosophy are sometimes convincingly made, but rather than stressing these often extraneous matters it seems more to the point to see in Cather's response to Wagner an emotional release like that of Caroline Noble's, whose "noble" but repressive sentiments Cather herself shared. Present-day awareness of Cather's lesbian nature and her conflicted feelings concerning it make the repression understandable, as well as her fixation for a time on the opera singer Olive Fremstad. Fremstad was one of three divas (Geraldine Farrar and Louise Homer were the others) who were the subjects of an article, "Three American Singers," Cather wrote for the December 13, 1923, issue of *McClure's* magazine. Of the three, it was Fremstad who fascinated Cather most: Olive Fremstad who had set the audiences at the Metropolitan Opera House abuzz with her performance of Kundry in *Parsifal*. Cather was already writing *Song of the Lark*, using Fremstad as her model, when she undertook the article. Through it Cather came to know the soprano and the two began a friendship that lasted many years. Like Cather's heroine, Fremstad sang both Sieglinde and the two Brünnhilde roles, and many of the details of Fremstad's life are mirrored in the novel. However, Mary Cushing, Fremstad's biographer and companion, claimed to have heard the singer tell Cather, after the book's publication, "It wasn't really much like that" (Cushing 244).

Other than these works and a structural parallel to *Parsifal* undergirding her 1922 novel *One of Ours*, Cather's only literary connection to Wagner was the preface she wrote for Gertrude Hall Brownell's book of Wagner redactions, *The Wagnerian Romances* (1925). In the preface she claimed to admire only two of the many books on Wagner, Shaw's *The Perfect Wagnerite* and Hall's. Other writers of her time, though they could not fail to be aware of the Wagner craze, did not choose to make similar use of the topic. Henry James, who we know attended at least one Wagner performance — a *Parsifal* in February 1914 — has been erroneously quoted as casting aspersion on the composer (Edel and Powers 391; Cather, *Song*, xvii). The story that gave rise to the inaccuracy involves a Russian painter and lover of the arts, Paul Joukowsky, whom James knew in Europe from about the spring of 1876, the same year in which James found himself "bored" at hearing selections from "Wagner's Bayreuth operas" when played by a French pianist (Edel, *Letters* 73). On April 25, 1880, James wrote his sister Alice that he had been to stay with Joukowsky in Posilippo, outside Naples. Joukowsky had wanted to take him to visit the Wagners, with whom the Russian was on familiar terms, but James refused since he spoke no German and Wagner spoke nothing else. To Alice, James describes Joukowsky — not Wagner, as has been claimed — as a "ridiculous mixture of Nihilism and bric a brac" (Edel, *Letters* 282). In his preface to the 1909 New York edition of his novel *The Wings of the Dove* (1902), James did, however, pointedly refer to his wealthy heroine Milly Theale as one of "the Rhinemaidens," by which he implied that, like the guardians of the golden ring, Milly sets in motion an economic disaster that leads to tragedy (James, *Wings* x).

While not in the same literary vein as Willa Cather, the enormously popular writer Gertrude Atherton produced an intriguing novelistic treatment of a Wagnerian soprano in her 1910 *Tower of Ivory*. The highly readable story involves a young English aristocrat, John Ordham, who meets and falls in love with Margarethe Styr, an American soprano who, having successfully hidden her sordid early years as Peggy Hill, has surfaced in Europe with a stage name and a title bestowed upon her by King Ludwig II of Bavaria, Wagner's own patron. Wagner does not appear as a character, but it is he who engages Styr to sing Isolde and Brünnhilde at Bayreuth, after which she regularly appears at a Munich opera house. Ordham marries a young American who cannot fail to disappoint him since he is secretly still enamored of the elusive Styr. He begins a love affair with the singer, and when his wife dies in childbirth the way seems clear for their marriage. Instead, rather than become the Countess of Bridgminster and disgrace Ordham in London where the truth of her past has become known, Margarethe goes out in a blaze of glory, choosing to kill herself on stage (by unexplained means) at the moment when as Brünnhilde she leaps into Siegfried's funeral pyre.

The story is melodramatic and comes up short on literary merit, but the author creates some wonderful types of European artists, aristocrats, and poseurs, as well as exciting descriptions of operatic performances, especially the *Ring*. If one does not enter into the reading of it expecting a Jamesian experience, one can find this an engaging tale of Wagnerian opera in Wagner's own time, complete with rather specific references to Ludwig's sexual preference.

Among American artists there are but two who have made significant contributions to the field of Wagnerism; interestingly, both contributions pertain to the Ring. Albert Pinkham Ryder, perhaps the best of the American purveyors of late-nineteenth-century romantic landscapes, created *Siegfried and the Rhinemaidens* (1888–91) under the direct influence of a performance of *Götterdämmerung* at the Metropolitan Opera in the 1888 season. He is quoted as having said that after seeing the opera he went home, began work, worked for 48 hours straight, and "the picture was the result" (Homer and Goodrich 162). The existence of a small sketch indicates otherwise, however, and art historians now believe, on the basis of this and evidence of built-up paint film on the canvas, that the picture was worked on for a longer period of time — perhaps as long as three years since it was first exhibited, at the New York Athletic Club, in 1891.

It has been suggested that Ryder may have been influenced by the Metropolitan's adaptation of the Viennese Josef Hoffmann's original set designs or by illustrations of them published in *Scribner's Magazine* in 1887, but since the Metropolitan's adaptation is lost we cannot know (Homer and Goodrich 162). Ryder's Siegfried, wearing a helmet, is on horseback, not on foot as he is in the opera. He rides along a path adjacent to the river and it is not possible to tell if he is approaching the Rhinemaidens or, having scorned their warnings, is on his way to seek Gunther. An oil on canvas now owned by the National Gallery of Art in Washington, the work is an excellent example of Ryder's style, which typically involves a darkly painted night scene with trees and other natural objects that seem to bend and writhe beneath some force of nature. These elements appear here as well, but the painting's dark tones, which surround Siegfried on one side of the canvas and seem to foretell his unhappy end, are, on the other side, brightly lit by the golden glow of a full moon that casts its light on the river and the maidens. The glow on the water dramatically suggests the river's cache of gold originally in the maiden's protective care. The overall effect of the painting might be described as eerie, but the contrast of dark to golden glow mitigates this and leaves the viewer with an awareness of having looked at a prime example of American painterly romanticism well suited to its inspiration.

The other piece of Wagner-influenced work is not a single painting but fourteen colored drawings by the illustrator Maxfield Parrish. The drawings were done to accompany an article on "Wagner's Ring of the Nibelung" by F. J. Stimson in *Scribner's Magazine* of December 1898. The drawings were made first on paper with wash, ink, and lithographic crayon. These were photographed and the print colored, probably with oil glaze (Ludwig 190). Unfortunately, the result was not permanent and what remains of the drawings shows a disfiguring loss of color so that they no longer are worthy representations of this artist's talent.

Another *Scribner's* article, in 1889, examined "Some of Wagner's Heroes and Heroines" and argued that "Brunnehilde is Woman, *the* Woman, *das Ewigweibliche*, in the fullest sense" (Apthorp 347). The argument was based of course on the full picture of this character given in the *Ring* where Brünnhilde is seen first as a young virgin, loving to her father but capable of "second-guessing" him, one might say, to the point of disobeying him. Her acceptance of her punishment and subsequent awakening to love, marriage, and the role of wife, are all seen by the article's author–a man — as masterful delineations of a noble and heroic character to be seen as inspiration to contemporary womanhood. It is difficult, however, to know the effect of this character on young American women of the time, especially when the character of

Elisabeth in *Tannhäuser* seems to have garnered most of the public's attention. It is possible to view Henry James's novella *Daisy Miller* (1879) as a portrait of a young Brünnhilde-like character whose willfulness leads to tragedy, but at the same time one wonders if the expatriate and determinedly unmarried James is the best source for information on young American women of the time. Joseph Horowitz quotes from a popular 1907 novel, Charlotte Teller's *The Cage*, in which the young, unmarried heroine attends a Wagner concert with her boyfriend and is carried off into a sexual fantasy while listening to the Ride of the Valkyries. "She felt herself strong and vital, astride a horse of Walhalla," Teller writes, but when the music ends the woman feels "as though she had been thrust back and down just before she had reached the summit" (Horowitz 217–18). Teller may be closer to the truth of the American female experience of the time, whether as Elisabeth or Brünnhilde, but one likes to believe that the photographic images of turn-of-the-century American women carrying aloft placards bearing the words "Votes for Women" owed something to the image of Brünnhilde lifting her sword high and sounding her "Ho-jo-to-ho!"

It is that image, of a helmeted Brünnhilde with sword and shield, which has ingrained itself in the American psyche, along with the Ride of the Valkyries, as symbolic of, not necessarily the operas of Richard Wagner, but all opera. For many, Brünnhilde is an icon of opera, instantly recognizable and, unfortunately, emblematic of what is believed to be off-putting about the art. Countless television commercials have made use of the image, as has many a comic film. Russel Myers' comic strip "Broom Hilda," begun in April of 1970, suggests the Wagner character's name but depicts a witch-like troll who bears no resemblance to her. Another comic strip, Dik Browne's "Hagar the Horrible," which began in the King Features Syndicate in 1973, centers on a Viking warrior, Hagar, whose wife Helga fits the stereotypical image of a Valkyrie with long blonde braids and a horned helmet. The now famous Looney Tunes cartoon feature, "What's Opera, Doc?" released July 6, 1957, featured Bugs Bunny and Elmer Fudd, with Fudd taking the Brünnhilde role and singing, to the tune of the "Ride," the never-to-be-forgotten "Kill da wabbit" lyrics. Between 1989 and 1991 DC Comics has given the world the *Ring* in four issues, each issue corresponding to one of the four operas. The very striking art and adaptation were by P. Craig Russell, who also drew *Siegfried and the Dragon* (Marvel Comics, 1980).

More serious use of the Ride of the Valkyries was made by D. W. Griffith in his 1915 silent film *The Birth of a Nation*. Told from the South's point of view, the film offers a favorable depiction of the origins of the Ku Klux Klan. When the robed and hooded Klansmen ride out to do battle with the Carpetbaggers, the action is to the musical accompaniment of the "Ride." For the most part, the film employs an original music score, under the direction of Louis F. Gottschalk, which Griffith later adapted to the 24 frames-per-second running speed needed for sound; but the Wagner melody adds to the dramatic tension of the film's crucial scene. Director Francis Ford Coppola enlarged on Griffith's idea by using the Wagner "Ride" in his 1979 film *Apocalypse Now*. In this updating of Joseph Conrad's novel *Heart of Darkness*, where the American forces fighting in Vietnam represent all the darkness one could imagine, the music forms the background for a helicopter squadron dropping napalm bombs on Vietnam villages. In the 2001 director's cut, *Apocalypse Now Redux*, a longer version of the film, the bombing scene is considerably extended so that the music is repeated many times, in a 70 mm six–Track Dolby sound mix that outdoes in volume any performance ever heard in an opera house. The American-made film trilogy based on J. R.R. Tolkien's *The Lord of the Rings* has elicited critical analysis that, like the Danish author Peter Kjaerulff's *The Ring-bearer's Diary* (1985), links the trilogy to Wagner's *Ring*, but the English origin of the source places the comparison outside the scope of this discussion. Much less well known, but worthy of attention, is a 1999 one-hour documentary, *Sing Faster: The Stagehands' Ring*, which won that year's Sundance Filmmaker's Trophy. A co-production of Oregon Public Broadcasting and the Independent Television Service and available on VHS, it is a marvelously entertaining view of a 1990 San Francisco Opera *Ring* production from the perspective of the stagehands who are responsible for seeing that all the sets and props, including dragons and smoke machines, are in place on time. The necessity to move quickly and quietly is shown to be only a portion of their responsibility; stagehands must familiarize themselves with the music so that they are cued to action in ways that parallel the responses of the on-stage performers. In long stretches of "between" times, they play poker, knit, and discuss the stories of the *Ring* operas.

While these various uses of Wagner's *Ring* made their way into twentieth-century American popular culture, performances of the operas, either singly or in complete cycles, were growing in number and popularity. The story begins, as might be imagined, with the Metropolitan Opera which, following its initial Ring in 1889, offered productions sporadically; but the work came upon hard times during two World Wars and at times suffered neglect from managers who did not care for it or its composer. A cycle was given at the end of World War II, in the 1947–48 season, and not again until 1967 when Rudolph Bing brought the von Karajan/Schneider-Siemssen production from Salzburg. The operas were to be introduced one a season, but the European artistic staff ran afoul of American labor problems when a dispute delayed this plan and the *Siegfried* could not be offered on schedule. Von Karajan, who was to have conducted, left the project but it was finally completed in the 1974–75 season (Robinson 67). The spring of 1989 brought another new Ring, which is still current at the Metropolitan. Sets and stage designs were again by Gunther Schneider-Siemssen, with Otto Schenk as producer and James Levine conducting. A naturalistic, somewhat cluttered production, its Germanic, romantic sets strongly suggest Wagner's own designs.

For a long while the Metropolitan Opera's dominance was absolute, so far as *Ring* cycles were concerned. When one considers that Chicago and Boston only formed their first opera companies early in the twentieth century, the comparative wealth of these cities to that of New York, and the necessity of building audiences to support a costly *Ring* cycle, the slow advance is understandable. Building an audience for Ring performances might have been helped by good professional recordings of the tetralogy, but until Decca's 1997 CD set, the first-ever complete studio recording, under Georg Solti, none was available. But things have changed. In a way, it was again the Metropolitan Opera that provided the stimulus for change when other companies noted its success in marketing *Ring* cycles. Under the artistic direction of James Levine, cycles have been offered at the Metropolitan on a fairly regular basis for the past thirty years, with the current production reproduced on compact discs, VHS tapes, laser discs and DVD. While many find the production boring and unimaginative, and others have simply tired of it, these many reproductions have tended to standardize the Ring for thousands of people who come to each Metropolitan repetition expecting to find the familiar. Even the in-house surtitles, in a highly readable format and thoughtfully optional, are those found on the various video reproductions and proved truly a revelation to many when the production was telecast on public broadcast outlets in 1990.

The Seattle Opera began a tradition of summer *Ring* cycles in 1975, and in 1986, with the encouragement of its director, Speight Jenkins, a Wagner enthusiast, offered a new, visually spectacular production that featured an Immolation scene so fiery that ticket buyers were warned of possible heat discomfort in the front rows of the orchestra. Wagner audiences being a hardy lot, the production has become highly popular and when offered, every four years or so, ticket demand is very high and comes from many foreign countries as well as all parts of the United States. The San Francisco Opera added a cycle in 1990, the subject of the above-described documentary. The Chicago Lyric Opera's centenary celebration included a *Ring* cycle, staged in 2005, and Houston Grand Opera and the New Orleans Opera have begun offering single operas of what eventually will be complete cycles. Placido Domingo, the Los Angeles Opera's general director, had hoped to present there a Ring that would have brought to Wagner's imagining the considerable talents of George Lucas's Industrial Light and Magic, the company responsible for the remarkable *Star Wars* film production, but costs have proved a stumbling block. The company still plans to produce a Ring, but with a different production team (Lacher 5). Such notions of production "teams" are indicative of the American approach to producing opera, whereby a director works in collaboration with the conductor, a set designer, a costume designer, a lighting designer, possibly a choreographer and chorus master. The cost of such a team may be initially higher, but is mitigated by a lowered risk of ending up with a piece of *Regietheater* whose directorial point of view so diverges from public expectations that the production never pays for itself in ticket sales.

New York City has seen (at this writing) half of the first *Ring* cycle sung in English in the United States. (The English National Opera has done the complete cycle in English as part of its mission.) Eos Orchestra, under its conductor Jonathan Sheffer, is bringing to the city, in installments, the arrangement by Jonathan Dove that was done originally by the Birmingham (UK) Touring Opera in 1990. A reduction for chamber orchestra, the production is a reinterpretation of the *Ring* done with vivid staging, in English, and with a dramatic immediacy that often works very effectively, though the lack of a full orchestra is keenly felt. The Eos *Das Rheingold* appeared in New York in 2002 and *Die Walküre* in 2004. At that rate Wagner's four-night offering would extend to eight years, but the Pittsburgh Opera Theatre has announced it will present the first two operas in 2006 and the remaining two the following year.

One of America's foremost composers, Christopher Rouse, has written what he calls "a fantasy" for percussion and orchestra based on themes from *Götterdämmerung*. Titled *Der Gerette Alberich* ("Alberich Saved"), the 1997 work imagines the return of Alberich to the godless post–*Götterdämmerung* world of Wagner's *Ring*, where he is free to work out his evil designs. The 22-minute piece draws on Wagner motifs associated with Alberich, but after a rousing opening in which the dwarf celebrates his good fortune at having survived the *Ring*'s final catastrophe, there follows a slow movement based on the "Renunciation of Love" motif where we see a kinder, more gentle Alberich than Wagner ever shows, and the music suggests a sense of his regret at what has been lost.

The latter years of the twentieth century, when American singers moved into the front ranks on international opera stages, saw such figures as James Morris, Deborah Polaski, Deborah Voigt, and Jessye Norman take on roles in Wagner's *Ring* that brought them worldwide acclaim. But perhaps the foremost American name connected then and now to the *Ring* is that of conductor James Levine. The Cincinnati-born Levine grew up in a place where the first May Festival of choral music, in 1873, featuring the music of Richard Wagner, was under the baton of Theodore Thomas, a position Levine was destined to fill a century later (Marsh 18). Levine is only the third American to conduct in Bayreuth, an honor he shares with Lorin Maazel and Thomas Schippers (Marsh 236). After conducting *Parsifal* there in 1982 he returned in 1994 for his first Bayreuth *Ring* cycle, which was repeated the following four summers. The Metropolitan Opera was the scene of his first conducted complete *Ring*, in 1989, the highly successful Schenk/Schneider-Siemssen production discussed above. In a conversation with music critic Robert Marsh, Levine offered what can be said to be–especially for its reference to Wagner's own willingness to be innovative — the final word on the whole perplexing and controversial matter of Ring interpretations. "The *Ring* is so complex," Levine commented, "and any idea that there is one way to present it is ridiculous. Wagner knew that; it lies behind his statement at the end of the first cycle in 1876 that 'next time it will all be different'" (Marsh 238). While the conversation as recorded by Marsh did not pertain specifically to the Metropolitan, one can hope that when it comes time to retire that company's nearly 20-old production, Wagner's words will be remembered and perhaps work their magic, and the composer's never-realized American dreams for his *Ring* will receive new life.

Bibliography

Ahlquist, Karen. *Democracy at the Opera, Music, Theater, and Culture in New York City, 1815–60*. Urbana and Chicago: University of Illinois Press, 1997.

Apthorp, William. "Some of Wagner's Heroes and Heroines." *Scribner's Magazine*, Vol. 5:3, 1989. 331–348.

Atherton, Gertrude. *Tower of Ivory*. New York: Macmillan, 1910.

Cather, Willa. "Gertrude Hall's *The Wagnerian Romances*." In *On Writing: Critical Studies on Writing as an Art*. Foreword by Stephen A. Tennant. Lincoln: University of Nebraska Press, 1988.

_____. *The Song of the Lark*. Edited with Introduction by Sherrill Harbison. New York: Penguin, 1999.

_____. *The Troll Garden*. Afterword by Katherine Anne Porter. New York: New American Library, 1961.

_____. *The World and the Parish: Willa Cather's Articles and Reviews, 1893–1902*. 2 Volumes. Edited by William M. Curtin. Lincoln: University of Nebraska Press, 1970.

Cushing, Mary Watkins. *The Rainbow Bridge*. New York: Arno, 1977.

Dizikes, John. *Opera in America, A Cultural History*. New Haven: Yale University Press, 1993.

Edel, Leon. *Henry James' Letters*. Vol. 2, 1875–1883. Cambridge: Harvard University Press, 1975.

_____ and Lyall H. Powers. *The Complete Notebooks of Henry James*. New York: Oxford University Press, 1987.

_____. *The Wings of a Dove*. New York: Scribner's, 1909.

Homer, William Innes and Lloyd Goodrich. *Alfred Pinkham Ryder, Painter of Dreams*. New York: Harry N. Abrams, 1989.

Horowitz, Joseph. *Wagner Nights, An American History*. Berkeley: University of California Press, 1994.

Huneker, James Gibbons. *Essays by James Huneker*. Edited by H. L. Mencken. New York: Scribner's, 1929.

_____. *Letters of James Gibbons Huneker*. Edited by Josephine Huneker. New York: Scribner's, 1922.

_____. *Melomaniacs by James Gibbons Huneker*. New York: Scribner's, 1927.

Lacher, Irene. "The Camera Can Wait; The Opera Is Calling." *The New York Times*, Sept. 2, 2004:E1, 5.

Lanier, Sidney. "To Richard Wagner: A Dream of the Age." *The Galaxy*, Vol. 24:5, 1877. 652–653.

Lawrence, Vera Brodsky. *Strong on Music: The New York Music Scene in the Days of George Templeton Strong*. Three Volumes. Chicago: University of Chicago Press, 1988–1999.

Ludwig, Coy. *Maxfield Parrish*. New York: Watson-Guptill, 1973.

Marsh, Robert C. *Dialogues and Discoveries: James Levine, His Life and His Music*. New York: Scribner's, 1998.

Robinson, Francis. *Celebration: The Metropolitan Opera*. Garden City: Doubleday, 1979.

Sullivan, Louis H. *The Autobiography of an Idea*. New York: Dover, 1956.

Traubel, Horace. *With Walt Whitman in Camden*. Vol. 2. New York: Rowman and Littlefield, 1961.

Twain, Mark. *The Complete Essays of Mark Twain*. Edited by Charles Neider. Garden City: Doubleday, 1963.

Wagner, Cosima. *Cosima Wagner's Diaries*. Translated by Geoffrey Skelton. Two Volumes. New York: Harcourt Brace Jovanovich, 1980.

Wagner, Richard. *Selected Letters of Richard Wagner*. Translated by Steward Spencer and Barry Millington. New York: Norton, 1987.

Whitman, Walt. *An American Primer by Walt Whitman*. Edited by Horace Traubel (1904). Steven's Point, Wisc.: Holy Cow! Press, 1987.

11. Wagnerian Opera's Influence on World Literature

John Louis DiGaetani

As Wagner lay dead in Venice in February of 1883, his influence continued especially strongly in literature all over Europe. Today, he is generally credited as one of the founders of the Decadent and Symbolist movements in European literature, which reached a high tide of popularity in the 1880s, 1890s, and around the turn of the century, although Wagner continued to exert his influence well into the middle of the twentieth century, and even afterwards. Wagnerian allusions and Wagnerian themes often occur in Decadent literature, especially the themes of death and suicide. A group of European writers at the time saw Wagner as the avant-garde artist who led by pointing to the inevitability of suicide, and they saw to it that his themes and literary techniques appeared often in their writings.

At the time Wagner died his operas had not entered the standard repertory of any English or American opera house. In an effort to raise funds for Bayreuth, Wagner himself went to London in the spring of 1877, where he conducted a series of eight concerts. Although they failed to make much money for the Bayreuth enterprise, these concerts proved to be critically successful, earning serious attention and widespread approval among the artistic avant-garde. While Wagner was in London he met George Eliot, her companion George Lewes, and Robert Browning, among other important writers. One of the first results of this attraction between intellectuals and artists and Wagner's operas was the appearance in 1881 of the first book on Wagner in English, Francis Hueffer's *Richard Wagner.* Hueffer, Ford Madox Ford's father, had already left his native Germany, but he remained an ardent Wagnerian all his life and usually summered in Bayreuth, often attending performances there. In addition to writing the pioneering book on the composer in English, he started a periodical entitled, appropriately, *Die Meister.* The journal became popular among many avant-garde writers and musicians and it served to further the cause of Wagner's music throughout Europe and America. In May of 1882 Angelo Neumann staged the entire *Ring* in London, where it proved a popular success. Even English royalty helped the Wagnerian cause, as noted by Ernest Newman:

"Neumann was very successful with this first production of the *Ring* in London. Thanks to an introduction from the German Crown Prince he managed to get the Prince of Wales (afterwards King Edward VII) to attend no fewer than eleven of the performances. The Prince had been so charmed by the swimming Rhinemaidens that at one performance of the *Rheingold* he went behind the scenes and expressed a desire to see the apparatus at work; but when he discovered that the occupant of the car was not to be the pretty young Augusta Kraus but one of the male stage hands he turned away with an impatient 'What the devil!'" [Newman, IV, 673].

With the Prince of Wales's help, then, by 1882 London had seen on stage all the standard Wagner operas except for *Parsifal*, which Wagner wanted performed only at his new theater at Bayreuth. With performances available in London and advocates like Francis Hueffer, the operas were becoming popular in England by the end of the nineteenth century.

As the 1890s became increasingly Wagnerian in their musical taste, this influence began to show itself in many of the arts in Britain, and in the increasing volume of critical appreciation of the German composer. In 1898 George Bernard Shaw wrote *The Perfect Wagnerite,* which summarized the complicated plot of the *Ring* and provided a Fabian socialist interpretation that remains today generally sound. Shaw saw the *Ring* as a parable about the corrupting power of money — which causes a loss of both love and life for many of the people who lust after it. Most critics since Shaw have used this basically Marxist interpretation, although changing some of its elements and eliminating most of Shaw's socialist doctrines.

During the Edwardian period in particular, Wagnerian themes appeared in the short stories and novels of some major British writers. Joseph Conrad's first novel, *Almayer's Folly* (1895), includes references to Wagnerian opera and ends with an Immolation scene that imitates the German composer's work. Conrad's story "Freya of the Seven Isles" (1912) also includes allusions to *Tristan und Isolde* and ends with the death of both young lovers. In *Chance* (1913) Conrad uses patterns of imagery and characterization from Wagner's *Der Fliegende Holländer*, and water imagery pervades this novel, as it does the opera.

There are also similarities between Conrad's *Nostromo* and Wagner's *Ring*, and the connection is too close to be coincidental. In the former, it is significant that the San Tomé silver mine is first mentioned while Conrad is describing the young love and courtship of the Goulds in Italy. Early in her married life Emilia Gould becomes aware of an evil shadow darkening her happiness with her husband. The silver mine, ominously connected with death, poses a threat to the Goulds' new love — like the curse and rejection of love necessary for the golden ring to have its power in Wagner's tetralogy. Charles Gould believes that the silver mine had hounded his father to an early grave; that this death should occur while he is first in love parallels the curse in Wagner's *Ring*.

With *Victory* (1915) Conrad also used Wagnerian patterns to help create a suggestively operatic atmosphere, ending again with the death and suicide of the two lovers. Conrad mentioned his indebtedness to Wagner and Wagner's interest in suicide as the best alternative to some of life's very difficult situations, situations which appear in many of Conrad's tragic novels. Wagner's operas provided Conrad with many examples of the union of music and myth, and thereby helped him to give his own fiction what he called "the magic suggestiveness of music" — especially music from Wagner operas.

D. H. Lawrence's early novel *The Trespasser* (1912) has a major character called Siegmund who often quotes verses from Wagnerian opera and who ends the novel by killing himself as a result of a love affair gone wrong. Lawrence's greater novel *Women in Love* (1916) includes even more Wagnerian allusions and ends with the suicide of one of the major characters, Gerald Crich. Lawrence clearly went through an early phase of what can be called Wagnerian decadence, and he used this influence in his writing. Early in his career Lawrence wrote to his friend Blanche Jennings: "I love music. I have been to two or three fine orchestral concerts here [London]. At one I heard Grieg's 'Peer Gynt' — it is very fascinating, if not profound. Surely you know Wagner's operas — *Tannhäuser* and *Lohengrin*. They will run a knowledge of music into your blood better than any criticism." Here too and in a very direct way Lawrence indicates his indebtedness to music and especially to Wagnerian opera. Many of the earlier novels by Lawrence included love, love not reciprocated, and subsequent suicide, and he indicated that he absorbed many of these provocative themes from Wagnerian opera and its own uses of love and suicide.

Wagnerian patterns also exist in all of James Joyce's major works, and Joyce often combined his use of Wagner with his use of Giambattista Vico, having learned about Vico's cycles primarily through Wagnerian opera. While the mature Joyce was not much moved by Wagner's music, he always remained interested in the operas as mythic dramas. His fiction indicates an increasing use of Wagnerian patterns for a variety of artistic effects. In "A Painful Case" in *Dubliners*, Joyce first used Wagnerian material, from *Tristan und Isolde*. The references to the opera in that story comment ironically on the sterility of Mr. Duffy and his cautious refusal of Mrs. Sinico's offer of love, and in that story alcohol becomes the magic potion which the lovers drink. In *A Portrait of the Artist as a Young Man* Joyce uses the Forest Bird motif from *Siegfried* and uses the musical motif thematically in the novel. Stephen's ashplant in that novel is a reference to Wagner's Wotan and the spear he carries and thereby dramatizes Stephen's pretentious desire for power and authority. Also, in *Portrait*, the fourth chapter ends with a vision of woman and water, which is the first of an important series of such allusions in Joyce's fiction.

In *Ulysses* the ashplant cane that Stephen carries has Wagnerian overtones, but they are used in a more complex way. In addition to references to Wotan's spear, as in *Portrait*, a new pattern of allusions to Siegmund's and Siegfried's sword Nothung also appears. They suggest Stephen's desire for a means of defense to assert his own generation and his own sexuality; the sword is a phallic symbol of his young manhood. The fact that the ashplant refers to both Wotan's spear and Siegfried's sword helps Joyce imply that the novel's generational conflict is cyclical rather than progressive — as in Vico. *Ulysses* also employs the symbolic combination of water and the female principle: in Stephen's vision of his mother as the sea, in the Rhinemaiden allusions in the Sirens chapter of the novel, and finally in the water imagery in Molly Bloom's final soliloquy. Joyce shared Wagner's redemptive view of woman; the symbolic connection of woman with the fertility of water exemplifies this. Also in *Ulysses*, a pattern of allusions to *Der Fliegende Holländer* provides the novel with a counterpart of Homer's Odyssey myth. These allusions help Joyce to characterize Bloom's sympathy with the sufferings of the ordinary man.

Finally, in *Finnegans Wake,* the symbolic combination of water with the female principle and redemption figures prominently. Wagner's *Tristan und Isolde* provides a mythic body of allusions in *Wake* and helps Joyce to structure the novel and parody the Tristan myth. But in the process his characters, by their connection with the characters in the opera, have become more mythic. This is especially true of "Mildew Lisa," a name used for HCE's daughter. The Wagnerian pun involved is comic, a pun on the first line of the Liebestod ("Mild und leise"), but it also reminds the reader of the cycle of love, death, and rebirth.

Finnegans Wake contains many other puns — on Wagner's life, titles and theater — that cleverly parody Wagnerolotry. Joyce used Wagnerian patterns for many effects in his fiction, from mythic elevation to mythic parody, but the effects that recur most frequently are comic, varying in subtlety from irony to punning wordplay.

E. M. Forster loved Wagner's operas all his life. He was moved by performances of the complete operas as well as orchestral excerpts at concerts, and for even more performances went to the Wagner Mecca at Bayreuth. What he especially enjoyed in Wagner's music was its specific definition and visual dimension. Forster liked knowing the literal and even verbal equivalents of the music he was hearing, and this of course is one of Wagner's fortes. As a result, Wagner figures significantly in Forster's essay "Not Listening to Music": "With Wagner I always knew where I was; he never let the fancy roam; he ordained that one phrase should recall the ring, another the sword, another the blameless fool and so on; he was as precise in his indications as an oriental dancer. Since he is a great poet, that did not matter." It is interesting here that Forster regarded Wagner's writing, at least his librettos, as highly as his music.

Wagner's leitmotifs are very useful not only for organizing music but also for giving the texts visual equivalents, and with opera, the text should be as important as the music. But Forster also recognized the literary possibility in this technique. In an interview with the *Paris Review*, he was asked, "Do you have any Wagnerian leitmotif system to help you keep so many themes going at the same time?" Forster responded, "Yes, in a way, and I am certainly interested in music and musical methods." We can see this in virtually all of Forster's novels, where Wagner and his operas are directly mentioned.

Howards End (1910) is the Forster novel containing the most Wagnerian allusions, which help to communicate particular meanings and to establish a specifically Edwardian intellectual milieu. Early in the novel Margaret talks heatedly about the confused connections between the arts:

> But, of course, the real villain is Wagner. He has done more than any other man in the nineteenth century towards the muddling of the arts. I do feel that music is in a very serious state just now, though extraordinarily interesting. Every now and then in history there do come these terrible geniuses, like Wagner, who stir up all the wells of thought at once. For a moment it's splendid. Such as splash as never was. But afterwards — such a lot of mud; and the wells — as it were, they communicate with each other too easily now, and not one of them will run quite clean. That's what Wagner's done [Forster, *Howards End*, 39–40].

Margaret is perceptive here in recognizing Wagner's immense influence upon a succeeding generation of artists and thinkers.

Later in *Howards End*, one of the most important passages in the book occurs and clearly states its major theme, using an image of a rainbow bridge derived from *Das Rheingold*: "Margaret greeted her lord with peculiar tenderness on the morrow. Mature as he was, she might yet be able to help him to the building of the rainbow bridge that should connect the prose in us with the passion. Without it we are meaningless fragments, half monks, half beasts: unconnected arches that have never joined into a man. With it love is born, and alights on the highest curve, glowing against the grey, sober against the fire. Happy the man who sees from either aspect the glory of these outspread wings" (186).

As Forster says even more clearly later in *Howards End*: "Only connect! That was the whole of her sermon. Only connect the prose and the passion, and both will be exalted, and human love with be seen at its height. Live in fragments no longer. Only connect, and the beast and the monk, robbed of the isolation that is life to either, will die" (186–87). Clearly here Forster intuited the bipolar quality of much of Wagnerian art and wanted to create a kind of novel which would move beyond polarity into a unified whole.

Wagner's operas also had a pronounced influence upon some of the major novels of Virginia Woolf. *The Voyage Out* (1915), *Jacob's Room* (1922), *The Waves* (1931), and *The Years* (1937) all owe something to Wagnerian opera. These works span most of Woolf's writing career, which implies a prolonged and probably changing influence, and the time gaps between the works also allow for some differences in her uses of the operas. She had a lasting fascination with the person of heroic potential, the influence of such a person upon the ordinary man, the suddenness of death, and the pervasive presence of the dead among the living. All these themes are archetypal rather than social or economic, and they lend themselves to mythic treatment.

Woolf's curiosity abut the artistic uses of myth naturally drew her to Wagner's mythic operas. Since Woolf often went to concerts and operas when she was in London, her lifelong involvement with music would also attract her to the composer, especially given the exalted opinion of his works and the frequency of their performance in London during her formative years. The combination of myth and music, embodied so consummately in his operas, links two of her special interests.

In 1909 Virginia Woolf wrote a long article for the *London Times*, entitled "Impressions of Bayreuth," describing the Bayreuth Festival's season of 1909 for Londoners who were unable to get there. In the process of reporting her reactions to the performances, she demonstrates a profound knowledge of Wagnerian opera and Wagnerian production; this article was written by someone who knew the operas well. She was particularly fascinated by the Bayreuth production of *Parsifal* and says in her article:

> Somehow Wagner has conveyed the desire of the Knights for the Grail in such a way that the intense emotion of human beings is combined with the unearthly nature of the thing they seek. It tears us, as we hear it, as though its wings were sharply edged. Again, feelings of the kind that are equally diffused and felt for one object in common create an impression of largesse and ... of an overwhelming unity. The grail seems to burn through all superimcumbences; the music is intimate in a sense that none other is; one is fired with emotion and yet possessed with tranquility at the same time, for the words are continued by the music so that we hardly notice the transition. It may be that those exalted emotions, which belong to the essence of our being, and are rarely expressed, are those that are best translated by music [23].

While her discussion of the opera's basic dichotomy of emotional appeals is highly perceptive, the desire to verbalize its effect implies an essentially literary response. Her final comment about music and literature sustains this impression of her as a music-lover with literary interests. Although she was fond of the other operas as well, "Impressions at Bayreuth" indicates that *Parsifal* had a special hold on her emotions, a hold that was reflected in references to the opera in several of her novels. Virginia Woolf, according to most of her biographers, suffered from bipolar illness. She may have sensed the bipolarity in many of Wagner's operas, and that may have been part of her attraction to his works.

In France, Wagner's influence was even more pervasive than in England according to Eugen Weber, despite Wagner's notorious Francophobia. As Weber writes: "Wagner's influence was limited by the anti-German reaction of 1870–71 and affected only narrow avant-garde circles for the next decade or two. After 1885, however, and especially in the 1890s, Wagner became the inspiration and touchstone of everything that was bold and new. The *Revue Wagnerienne*, devoted to his gospel, became one of the advance posts of decadence and symbolism" (Weber 144). In addition, many of the French Symbolist poets like Valéry, Mallarmé, and Gautier wrote for this Wagnerian periodical, and they often used Wagnerian themes in their poetry.

Weber also comments on the increasing frequency of the performances of Wagner's music in France:

> The introduction of ... Wagner himself to a broader public owed a great deal to two musical entrepreneurs of genius: Jules Pasdeloup and Jules-Edouard Juda Colonne. The former started his Sunday "popular concerts" in 1861. The latter, once conductor for Pasdeloup, founded his own series in 1873. Here, for the first time, music lovers could actually listen to the great orchestral works so seldom heard by those who lived before the age of the phonograph. And though, in the wake of the Franco-Prussian War, Passdeloup had promised to play no more German music, he soon broke his promise, as did Colonne. When Wagner died, in February 1883, *Le Figaro* noted in passing that fragments of his operas were "now accepted in France and played at the *concert Pasdeloup.*" After 1890 Wagner's works seem to have figured in every Sunday program [Weber 144–145].

Along with the music of Wagner came many of the ideas contained in his operas — especially the attraction to suicide, which recurs in the operas and which influenced the intellectual movement that eventually came to be known as Decadence. As an example of such Decadence of the Wagnerian sort, *Axel*, a play by Villiers de l'Isle Adam, gained a special notoriety. Here, the yearning for death is especially prominent among the main characters. As to normal life, says one of the characters in the play, "our servants will see to that for us." Throughout this play the author uses his characters, especially his main character, to give voice to a cultural yearning for death and suicide — a yearning almost as powerful as that voiced by Wagner's Tristan.

Eugen Weber also discusses Wagnerian influences in the French novel *A Rebours*:

> One of the most forceful expressions of this point of view sprang, fully armed, from the pen of a converted Naturalist as early as 1884. Joris-Karl Huysmans, when he wrote *A Rebours*, was a high civil servant, deputy head of that branch of the Sûreté which kept an eye on anarchist and other subversive activities. The book's conclusion was not that everything was decaying; it was already hopelessly rotten. The aristocracy had been despoiled and cast aside, the clergy was at a low ebb, the bourgeoisie was vile, the people crushed, the crowd turbid and servile, the arts silly at best. "Collapse society: die, old world!" Des Esseintes cries as the book ends and the tide of human mediocrity surges to the heavens. The disgust with humanity, already striking in the writings of the Naturalists, erupts among the aesthetes of the fin de siecle" [Weber 148].

The world-weary despair and longing for death that characterize much of fin-de-siecle literature, especially Villiers and Huysmans, powerfully reflect the depression and suicidal ideation which we have found so frequently in Wagnerian opera. Just as Tristan and Isolde conclude at the end of the opera that they both will be better off dead, so too these later writers echo this Wagnerian theme, which they revive and amplify to create the Decadent period in European literature. Villiers himself visited Wagner several times in Tribschen, Munich, and Bayreuth with his friend Judith Gautier (daughter of the poet Theophile Gautier) and was clearly much influenced by the Wagner operas, especially the *Ring*.

In addition to France and Britain, Italy became obsessed with Decadence and the Decadent writers as well. Gabriel D'Annunzio clearly reflected the death-obsessed movement of Decadence in his *Il Trionfo della Morte*, where death is seen as the ultimate triumph and where life is seen as futile and stupid. D'Annunzio claimed to be one of Wagner's pallbearers in Venice, where the composer died in 1883, and in his writings the Italian poet made personal use of many Wagnerian themes, particularly suicide and death, which must be regarded as recurrent Wagnerian obsessions. For example, D'Annunzio often suggests in his work that the human act of playing with death may well be the principal source of enjoyment in life.

In Germany the leading Decadent writer was Thomas Mann, who wrote about Wagner and Wagnerian opera repeatedly, especially in his famous essay "The Suffering and Greatness of Richard Wagner," (1933), where he confesses his debt to the opera composer. Several Wagnerian themes appear throughout Mann's writings, but especially the themes of futility, frustration, and death. Other critics have noted the connection between *Tristan und Isolde* and Thomas Mann's *Death in Venice*, which is a homosexual variant of the Liebestod theme, with the famous writer Gustav von Aschenbach going to Venice and becoming obsessed with Tadzio, a young boy from Poland. Since Wagner died in Venice, Mann's title is clearly a Wagnerian allusion; and in his novella we have an artistic work about obsessive love and its result, the suicidal death of Gustav at the end of the story. Though he is repeatedly warned about the presence of the plague in Venice, Gustav refuses to leave his beloved Tadzio, though ironically he never speaks a word to him. The final pages of the novella reflect the final fantasy vision of Aschenbach as he imagines the beloved Tadzio in the water and beckoning to him — just as Isolde's Liebestod ends with her vision of Tristan in the water, beckoning to her.

Mann also wrote a famous story called "The Blood of the Walsungs" (1905), which makes use of the incestuous Wagnerian Walsung brother and sister, Siegmund and Sieglinde. By the end of Mann's story, the sibling relationship becomes incestuous as well. Again, as if to underscore Wagner's perceptive portrayal, Mann's story "Tristan" (1902) provides a modern, ironic love story which uses allusions to Wagner's *Tristan und Isolde* for purposes of contrast with a modern absence of a loving relationship.

The last of the great Decadent writers was undoubtedly Samuel Beckett, whose Nobel Prize for Literature in 1962 capped a distinguished career. His chief writings extend the main Decadent themes into mid-century, for in his plays as well as his novels ideas of death and especially suicide play an important role, as the result of a view of life that remains essentially bleak and hopeless. While Beckett never alludes to Wagnerian opera directly, his use of Wagnerian obsessions such as death, suicide, dream-visions, and hopelessness reflect the depressive element in Wagnerian opera.

Beckett's most famous play, *Waiting for Godot* (1953), for example, presents us with an onstage image of two old bums, two old comedians, who are waiting for a "Godot," someone who never arrives. They are killing time until time kills them, waiting for Godot, who keeps sending messengers who promise his eventual arrival. "Godot" sounds like a variant of God, and indeed there are numerous religious references in the play. Yet while Godot can be God, he can also be a symbol of something that people always want but will never find — as is demonstrated by the futile waiting and frustration throughout the play. One of the few bright spots in Vladimir and Estragon's lives is the thought of suicide. They sometimes become excited about the thought of suicide because they hope death by hanging will give them an erection and an orgasm, things very unusual in their sterile existence of futile waiting. To us, their fascination with death and suicide, and their yearning for some fulfillment, some god, who will never arrive, seems very similar to the roles of Tristan and Isolde in Wagner's opera.

Suicide and death, recurrent themes in the novels and plays of Beckett, become a final endorsement, the last and perhaps most brilliant flowering of the Decadent movement in literature, and of the larger artistic movement which clearly began with Wagnerian opera. To die, even to commit suicide, thus becomes the final act of both desperation and hope. For Beckett as much as for Wagner, suicide stands as the ultimate escape and a source of comfort for a long-suffering humanity.

More recently, J. R. R. Tolkien's famous Ring tetralogy of four novels — *The Hobbit* (1937) and *The Lord of the Rings* (three volumes, 1955) — is clearly indebted to Wagner's *Ring*. Although Tolkien claimed that he was not influenced by Wagner's four *Ring* operas, there are too many similarities in the plot for this claim to be credible, and the famous film versions of the Tolkien novels also reflect this Wagnerian influence in their mythic plot, characters, and vision.

In American literature, Willa Cather's *The Song of the Lark* (1915) remains the most obviously Wagnerian of novels, based as it is on the career of the great Wagnerian soprano Olive Fremsted. Her performances as Isolde and Brünnhilde remain the high points of this very Wagnerian novel. More recently, Thomas Pynchon's *Gravity's Rainbow* includes repeated references to Wagner's knight Lohengrin. Clearly Wagner's *Ring* cycle, in addition to his other operas, influenced literature in many countries beyond Germany, and influenced literature in many profound ways. Wagnerian opera reverberates in literature as no other opera has, primarily because of its uses of myth, mythic characters, mythic themes, and mythic symbols.

Bibliography

DiGaetani, John Louis. *Richard Wagner and the Modern British Novel.* Rutherford: Fairleigh Dickinson University Press, 1978.

Forster, E.M. *Howard's End.* 1910.

_____. "Not Listening to Music." (1939). In *Two Cheers for Democracy.* New York: Harcourt Brace, 1951.

Gautier, Judith. *Wagner at Home.* Translated by Effie Dunreith Massie. London: John Lane, 1911.

Newman, Ernest. *The Life of Richard Wagner, Vol. IV.* Cambridge: Cambridge University Press, 1976.

Weber, Eugen. *France Fin de Siècle.* Cambridge: Harvard University Press, 1986.

Woolf, Virginia. "Impressions at Bayreuth," ed. John L. DiGaetani, *Opera News* (August 1976) p. 23.

V. THE LANGUAGE AND MUSIC OF THE *RING*

12. The Language of the *Ring*
Stewart Spencer

We may begin, as the *Ring* begins, on the bed of the Rhine:

> Weia! Waga!
> Woge, du Welle,
> walle zur Wiege!
> Wagalaweia!
> Wallala weiala weia!¹

These lines aroused amusement and incomprehension at least from the time of the first public performance of *Das Rheingold* in Munich in September 1869, with the result that the whole of Wagner's oeuvre came to be dubbed "Wigalaweia-Musik."² The Viennese critic Daniel Spitzer gleefully described the opening moments of *Das Rheingold* as follows when he reviewed the first Viennese performance of the work on January 24, 1878:

> One of the Rhinedaughters, Woglinde, swims to the surface and, with a wriggling movement as delightful as the scenic arrangements allow, circles a rocky ledge at the center of the stage, while at the same time uttering a series of natural sounds, "Weia! Waga! Wagalaweia! Wallala weiala weia!" These sounds have been devised by the Master himself and have achieved considerable notoriety, but since they have never previously been put to use, we are uncertain as to the mood that they are in fact intended to express. The cry of "Weia!" seems to indicate a very disagreeable sensation, the call of "Wallala!," by contrast, a particularly agreeable one, so that the two together may be intended to characterize the feeling of pleasure alternating with displeasure experienced on initially immersing oneself in a cold bath.³

Spitzer was being willfully disingenuous, for Wagner had already sought to defend his neologistic gambit in an open letter to Nietzsche dated June 12, 1872:

> From my studies of Jacob Grimm⁴ I once borrowed an Old High German word "Heilawac" and, in order to make it more adaptable to my own purposes, recast it as "Weiawaga," a form which we may still recognize today in the word "Weihwasser" [holy water]. From this I passed to the cognate linguistic roots "wogen" [to surge] and "wiegen" [to rock], finally to "wellen" [to billow] and "wallen" [to seethe or welter], and in this way I constructed a radical syllabic melody for my watermaids to sing by analogy with the "Eia popeia" [hushabye] of our children's nursery songs.⁵

In other words, the Rhinepersons' *vocalise* is an expression of the sanctity of nature and the childlike innocence of the river's nympholeptic daughters. Having witnessed the birth of the world in the amniotic floodwaters of the Rhine, we hear on the lips of the Rhinemaidens the invention of language itself. It must have pained and puzzled Wagner to find himself so misunderstood, since a belief in the emotional accessibility of both words and music had been central to the work's aesthetic from the outset: the right sound, in phonological and musical terms, ought to evoke a spontaneous response in the listener without any need for the intermediary of rational thought processes.[6]

In his earlier librettos, Wagner had followed Romantic models: *Die Hochzeit* (or at least the surviving parts of it), *Die Feen*, *Das Liebesverbot*, and *Rienzi* largely dispense with end-rhyme and in doing so reflect a process inaugurated by E. T. A. Hoffmann and developed by Georg Döring in his libretto for *Der Berggeist* (1825), for which Spohr specifically requested an unrhymed text.[7] The rejection of end-rhyme was part of a general movement towards heightened prose and a breakdown of formal structures in the interests of psychological realism. If *Der fliegende Holländer* reverts to classical rhyme schemes, this is because of the work's ostensibly more "popular" character and its division into folksong, ballad, and chorus. So adept had Wagner become at writing Romantic librettos that from the vantage point of the 1860s, when he started work on his autobiography, he even claimed that other composers were foolish not to leap at the chance of setting his own discarded texts.[8] Meanwhile Wagner had become interested in the subject matter of the *Ring*, an interest that was to have far-reaching consequences on his development as a librettist.

His decision to tackle an opera on the allegorical tale of the ring and its succession of fatally foredoomed owners appears to have been prompted by a series of articles in the *Neue Zeitschrift für Musik* inviting composers to write a "national opera" based on the late twelfth-century *Nibelungenlied*.[9] At the time of its rediscovery in 1755, this last-named poem was hailed as a German *Iliad* and by the early nineteenth century had come to be seen as the epitome of national aspirations, embodying, as it did, the notion of a united, powerful Germany in contrast to the fragmented, downtrodden nation of the post–Napoleonic era.[10] Other composers who toyed with the idea of writing a Nibelung opera include Mendelssohn, Schumann, Gade, and Liszt, although only in the case of Heinrich Dorn did the project come to fruition.[11]

Wagner started borrowing editions of the *Nibelungenlied* from the Dresden Royal Library as early as January 1845,[12] and he is also known to have owned a further four editions as part of his private library.[13] But the appeal of the poem must have started to wane as Wagner began to develop anarchical leanings and to turn to myth as the expression of a process of necessary revolutionary change. Reluctant Hegelian that he was, Wagner could not use history to predicate the future: myth alone could embody the cosmic struggle between the forces of reaction and a more human and enlightened regime.[14] It was in order to excavate the mythic substratum of the material that Wagner started to delve more deeply into the Scandinavian versions of the legend, versions which in keeping with the scholarly thinking of his time he regarded as more archaic and therefore as more prototypically Germanic.[15] And it was here, in the Old Icelandic Edda, not in the mainland *Nibelungenlied*, that he found the verse form of the *Ring*, a type of alliterative meter that is the work's most striking and notorious linguistic feature. Wagner's decision to turn his back on the classical prosody of the Romantic poets and to look instead to the Germanic meters of the early Middle Ages was probably taken during the autumn of 1848. Although this dating is bound to remain speculative, it is based on the fact that his handling of alliterative verse forms was profoundly influenced by the writings of Ludwig Ettmüller, and we know that it was not until October 21, 1848, that Wagner borrowed Ettmüller's edition of a selection of Eddic poems from the Royal Library in Dresden.[16] Other dramatists, including Friedrich Heinrich de la Motte Fouqué, Gottfried August Bürger and Johann Wolfgang von Goethe, had used alliterative meters in their stage plays, but Wagner was the first to use *Stabreim* in an opera libretto and to use it, moreover, in a way that consistently obeys the rules of alliterative verse forms as formulated by Ettmüller. Eduard Devrient, the Dresden playwright whom Wagner regularly regaled with readings from his latest works, was sufficiently impressed to note in his diary: "The fellow's a poet through and through. A beautiful piece of work. Alliteration, as used by him, is a real find for opera poems and ought to be raised to the level of a general principle."[17] (Conversely, Devrient was frankly alarmed at what he described as the "socialist" pretensions of the 1848 scenario "The Nibelung Legend."[18])

Ettmüller was virtually alone among early nineteenth-century Germanists in realizing that the alliterative verse forms of Old Icelandic, Old High German, and Old English poetry are fundamentally different from Romance meters and that little is to be gained from parsing them in terms of spondees, trochees, dactyls, and the like.[19] Instead, he analyzed the lines in terms of *Hebungen* and *Senkungen*, or "lifts" and "dips" (or "sinkings"), noting that there are typically two, occasionally three, lifts or heavily accented syllables per line, with a variable number of dips or weakly stressed syllables dividing them. In consequence, the number of syllables in a line is extraordinarily fluid and may vary from two to nine or more, as in the following example from the Prologue to *Götterdämmerung*:

> Ihn **geiz'** ich als **ein**ziges **Gut**:
> für den **Ring** nimm nun **auc**h mein **Roß**!
> Ging sein **Lauf** mit **mir**
> einst **kühn** durch die **Lüf**te—
> **mit mir**
> ver**lor** es die **mäch**t'ge **Art**.[20]

The lifts are marked in bold, while the alliterating staves are italicized. Lines of two lifts are distinguished typographically from those with three, the shorter lines being indented further than the longer ones.

In his translation of a selection of the heroic poems from the Elder Edda, Ettmüller noted that lines of two lifts are linked together alliteratively in pairs: the main stave (German *Stab*, hence *Stabreim*) is located on the first lift of the second line of each pair (technically described as a half-line), while the two lifts in the preceding half-line are treated as supporting staves, one or both of which must alliterate with the main stave. In the case of lines with three lifts, any two of the staves may alliterate with each other. A strophe from the *Sigrdrífumál* may illustrate these various points:

> **Hei**ll dagr, *hei*lir dags **syn**ir,
> heil *n*ótt oc *n*ipt!
> óreiðom *au*gomlítiðocrþinig,
> oc gefit *si*tiondom **sigr**![21]

[Hail, day! Hail, sons of day! And night and her daughter now! Look on us here with loving eyes, that waiting we victory win[22]].

It is clear from verbal parallels between Ettmüller's translation of the *Reginsmál* and a passage, later suppressed, in *Siegfried's Tod* that Wagner had access to Ettmüller's 1837 edition while still in Dresden:

Hell wohl lachten
Hundings Söhne,
die Eilimin
des Alters beraubten,
wenn mehr des Fürsten
Muth anreizten
rothe Ringe
als Rache des Vaters.[24]

Wie lachten wohl — sagt' ich — Hunding's Söhne,
hörten sie solch' ein Lied,
daß Siegfried's Waffe mit Würmern focht,
eh' sie den Vater gerächt![23]

The following example juxtaposes parallel passages from Ettmüller's translation of the *Fáfnis-mál* and a speech from Act Two of *Siegfried* in which the Forest Bird warns Siegfried to be wary of Mime's duplicitous words:

*Haupt*es kürzer laß' er
den *haa*rigen Schwätzer
fahren *h*in zur *H*el;
*ih*m dann *ei*gen
wird *al*les Gold,
der *H*ort, den Fafnir *h*egte.[25]

O *trau*te er Mime
dem *treu*losen nicht!
*Hö*rte Siegfried nur *sch*arf
auf des *Sch*elmen *Heuch*lergered':
wie sein *Herz* es *m*eint
kann er *M*ime versteh'n;
so *n*ützt ihm des *Bl*utes Ge*n*uß.[26]

In the Ettmüller passage, the third and sixth lines have three lifts each. It will be seen that Wagner's treatment of the system is extremely free: in particular, he is fond of chiasmic structures alien to Old Icelandic poetry and often links together lines which, strictly speaking, are alliteratively independent. The third and fourth lines are linked by the initial rhyme of *scharf* and *Schelmen*, although, having three lifts each, they ought rather to rhyme internally. For the purposes of alliteration, all vowels and diphthongs may rhyme interchangeably (*Erb'* und *Eigen*, / *ein'* und *all'*)[27]; initial *h* is ignored, as are weakly stressed prefixes such as *ver-* and *Ge-*. (In the last line of the passage from *Siegfried*, for example, *nützt* alliterates with *Genuß*.) Moreover, Wagner's Saxon dialect does not distinguish between voiced and voiceless plosives, so that his characters occasionally lapse into Leipzig regionalisms: "*D*ämmert der *T*ag schon auf?" asks the Second Norn.[28] Finally, Wagner adheres to the rule that consonantal clusters should be treated as discrete sounds: *str*, for example, can alliterate only with *str*, not with *st* or *s*. And so on.

In the winter of 1850–51, in the longest of his aesthetic treatises, *Opera and Drama*, Wagner set out to provide the theoretical foundations for his use of *Stabreim* in the *Ring*. Of course, we need to treat with some caution the composer's *post hoc* rationalization of his artistic method, but the dangers are less acute here, in the case of a more or less contemporary text, than with the earlier Romantic operas. Adopting an essentially Romantic argument that can be traced back to writers such as Rousseau and Herder,[29] Wagner asserts that the earliest language and most immediate expression of individual emotion is music. Heightened emotion is said to have been vented in the form of a melodic vocalization, while accompanying gestures imbued the utterance with a sense of rhythm. The addition of consonants enabled primitive man — and woman — to distinguish between objects in the world of physical phenomena, while alliteration was pressed into service in order to point up relationships between cognate roots. As language developed, so it moved increasingly away from its poetic roots: the need to describe complex relationships in a fragmented society that had lost touch with nature led to the emergence of a language that could express concepts but which was no longer capable of expressing emotions. The iambic pentameter, which Wagner had been happy to use in his Romantic operas, is now derided as a "five-footed monster"[30]; and end-rhyme is deemed to have been a Romantic aberration which the composer now dismisses as a psychological irrelevance and an aesthetic evil that has led to the emotional impoverishment of the language and to an ever-increasing dislocation between form and content.

Wagner's return to his roots presupposes, therefore, a return to Germanic linguistic roots, since it is here that he found what he believed to be the purest expression of the "Reinmenschliche," or "purely human," as embodied in the figure of Siegfried. The interrelationship between the form and content of the poem of the *Ring* is clear from the following passage from *A Communication to my Friends* (1851), in which Wagner writes of his rejection of "merely *conceptualized* modern verse, with its insubstantial and fleeting form,"[31] before going on:

I should straightway have had to abandon "*Siegfried*" had I been able to elaborate it only in this kind of meter [i.e., the Romance prosody typical of Wagner's Romantic operas]. And so I had to think of another speech melody; and yet, in truth, I had no need to think at all but merely had to make up my mind, for at the archetypally mythic source where I found the youthfully handsome human being, Siegfried, I also found, quite involuntarily, the physically perfect linguistic expression in which this man could alone manifest himself. This was *alliterative verse* which, in keeping with genuine speech inflections,[32] can be adapted to suit the most natural and lively of rhythms; which is at all times readily capable of the most infinitely varied expression; and in which the folk themselves once wrote poetry at a time when they were still poets and the creators of myths.[33]

This credulous belief in the poetic abilities of the *Volksseele*, or folk soul, was an essential article of Romantic faith: the common people, being closest to nature, spoke the language of the heart. By recreating that language, Wagner hoped to address a direct emotional appeal to the atrophied hearts of his nineteenth-century listeners and arouse within them a sense of the human emotions that he felt had been stifled by the corrupting influences of modern civilization. Or, as he puts it in *Opera and Drama*:

> Just as we had to remove from the content of the drama all external distortions, all that has to do with the pragmatism of history, with affairs of state, and with dogmatic religious belief, in order to depict that content as something purely human and instinctively necessary, so we must now exclude from its linguistic manifestation all that derives from, and pertains to, these distortions of the purely human and instinctively necessary, removing these features in such a way that only the kernel remains.[34]

By removing all unnecessary "noise"[35] and by compressing the number of weighted syllables in each line of verse, Wagner aimed to produce an emotionally charged language in which the number of heavily accented syllables, linked together by initial rhyme, would reflect the intensity of the feelings expressed. At best, the poem of the *Ring* is a skillful literary pastiche; at its worst, it comes perilously close to parody. Ettmüller had advised against secondary alliteration and the coining of pseudo-archaic expressions.[36] But Wagner had no such inhibitions. Indeed, the premises upon which his argument was based persuaded him that the more insistent the *Stabreim* and the more willfully archaic the language,[37] the more "authentic" the text of the *Ring* would be as an expression of "purely human" emotions.

The poetic diction of the Elder Edda is intensely compact and densely allusive, not least as a result of its strophic form (a feature that it shares with neither Old English nor Old High German poetry, where epic forms are preferred). By transferring an essentially lyric form to an epic drama and by subscribing to his contemporaries' mistaken belief that the conscious and highly elaborate artistry of the Eddic poems is a spontaneous outpouring of the popular spirit, Wagner has counterfeited a style that proves as much of a hindrance as a help in our understanding of the text. Certainly, it has divided critical opinion, with reactions ranging from Eduard Hanslick's dismissive conclusion that "if they were spoken rather than sung, these stammering and stuttering alliterations would excite general irritation not unmixed with mirth"[38] to Thomas Mann's equally iconoclastic assertion: "It has always seemed to me absurd to question Wagner's poetic gifts."[39]

If we judge the poem of the *Ring* by the highest literary standards — and the fact that Wagner thrice published the libretto in advance of the music[40] entitles us to do so — we may be tempted to voice a number of reservations, yet the temptation to question individual aspects of the text soon evaporates in the face of the tour de force that it represents. As long as we accept it on its own terms, we shall be less inclined to subject it to our pitying scorn.

The archaisms, for example, can be justified by reference to Wagner's Rousseauesque theory of language. Here we often need to approach the text from the standpoint of Middle High

German semantic usage. When, at the end of *Das Rheingold*, the Rhinedaughters describe the gods as "falsch und feig," there is, I believe, more than a hint of Middle High German *veige*, a word related to English "fey" and meaning "fated to die." (In modern German, the word means "cowardly.") Similarly, when Sieglinde greets Siegmund as her "Freund," Wagner may have been thinking of Middle High German *vriunt*, meaning "lover." "Fromm," which means "pious" in modern German, is used by Wagner in its older sense of "brave"; "Muth" is closer to its medieval meaning of "mood" than its modern, more limiting, sense of "courage"; and both "Noth" and "Neid" have far wider semantic fields than nineteenth-or twentieth-century usage would suggest. Finally, words such as "Friedel,"[41] "neidlich,"[42] and "freislich"[43] had not been in use for centuries when Wagner revived them. (Here I should like to deplore the modern editorial practice that modernizes Wagner's orthography but leaves his grammar and vocabulary untouched. Let me give an example. In Act Two of *Die Walküre*, Wotan tells Fricka:

> Noth thut ein Held,
> der, ledig göttlichen Schutzes,
> sich löse vom Göttergesetz:
> so nur taugt er
> zu wirken die That,
> die, wie noth sie den Göttern,
> dem Gott doch zu wirken verwehrt.[44]

[A hero is needed who, lacking godly protection, breaks loose from the law of the gods: thus alone is he fit to perform that feat which, needful though it may be to the gods, the god is forbidden to do.]

Modern German prefers the forms *Not*, *tut*, and *Tat*. This change is easily made, of course. But in Wotan's very next speech we find: "Ihres eig'nen Muthes / achtest du nicht" (Have you no heed of their own independence?) Modern German has largely abandoned the use of the genitive with *achten*, so that, logically, we should modernize this too and have "Ihren eignen Mut achtest du nicht." But this is musically impossible. Similarly, Wagner uses the strong declension of the verb *fragen*—"er frägt," "sie frug"—rather than the modern "fragt" and "fragte." And, much to Schopenhauer's irritation,[45] he frequently suppresses weakly stressed prefixes, so that we have *gehren*, *hehlen*, *kiesen*, and so on, rather than *begehren*, *verhehlen*, and *erkiesen*. In short, it seems to the present writer that archaic forms—orthographic, semantic, and grammatical—are such an integral part of the poem that their retention is essential.)

Moreover, not only is the language archaic, it also—and again for ideological reasons—reveals a degree of linguistic purity that no translator can hope to match, based, as it is, on exclusively Germanic roots.[46] Although the line "Ich erschlug einen wilden Wurm" (literally, "I slew a ferocious worm") may raise a smile on the lips of modern German audiences, Wagner's refusal to accept the Greek-based *Drache* obliges him to adopt the German word *Wurm* instead. It may be added in passing that the bantering exchange between hero and dragon in Act Two of *Siegfried* may well strike today's listeners as heavy-handed, but it, too, can be explained in terms of Wagner's belief that the young Siegfried was a popular, *völkisch* fairy-tale hero.[47] Also worth noting in this context is Wagner's elaborate use of wordplay, a penchant for paronomasia apparent on every page of the libretto, just as it is on every page of Cosima's diaries: "Rheingold! Reines Gold!" (literally, "Rheingold! Pure gold!") is only the most obvious instance of a device that is the despair of every translator.[48] Wagner's alliterative language lends itself to punning, adding an element that may be playful or poetically charged, depending on the context. At its best—in Siegmund's Spring Song and Wotan's Farewell—the poetry is undeniable, yet it remains a fact that Wagner later stepped back from so extreme an alliterative position and that in none of his later librettos did he use *Stabreim* to the same extent as he had done in the *Ring*.[49] "I am no poet," he told Cosima on January 22, 1871, only days before completing the full score of Act Three of *Siegfried*, "and I don't care at all if people reproach me for my choice of words, in my works the action is everything. To a certain extent it is a matter of indifference to me whether people understand my verses, since they will certainly understand my dramatic action. Poets are nonentities compared to musicians, painters, and sculptors — it is only dramatists who can compete with them."[50]

If Wagner's self-deprecatory comment was intended as a *captatio benevolentiae*, Cosima failed to rise to the bait. But by now, of course, the composer had converted to Schopenhauerism and subscribed to the Sage of Frankfurt's belief in music's ability to express the "essence" of things without the intermediacy of words.[51] Two decades earlier, Wagner's thinking had still been colored by Feuerbach and the latter's tuist philosophy,[52] allowing the composer to see his text as the male "fertilizing seed" that impregnated the female world of music. At mid-century, Siegfried and *Stabreim* were inexorably interlinked, with Wagner still very much on the side of the young hero. At the end of November 1849, for example, we find him writing to Theodor Uhlig:

> It is not a question of convincing people and winning them over, it is a question purely and simply of extermination; we shall gain the strength to bring this about in the future only if we learn to see ourselves as the disciples of a new religion and consolidate our faith by means of our mutual love: let us stick to the side of youth — and let the older generation rot in hell, they have nothing to offer us.[53]

This is pure Feuerbach, but it reflects a mood that could not last.[54] Whereas Siegfried had initially been the embodiment of the New Man and the *Ring* a lesson in revolutionary thinking, the downfall of the gods meant that Siegfried's death lost its ethical justification[55] and the hero ceased to be the great white hope. "Which is the greater, Wotan or Siegfried?" Wagner asked Cosima on July 2, 1872, and, without waiting for an answer, he went on: "Wotan is the more tragic, since he recognizes the guilt of existence and is atoning for the error of creation."[56] Siegfried is no longer the man of the future but is consigned to a phase in the history of the world's evolution, just as the *Ring* as a whole is now felt to reflect a single stage in the prehistoric past. Cosima again, this time an entry of October 2, 1882: "Then friend Rubinstein arrives and at our request plays us the conclusion of *Götterdämmerung*. R. joins in and sings Brünnhilde's last words, he is pleased with it all, so heathen and Germanic! [...] He recalls Gobineau and the Germanic world that came to an end with this work."[57] The *Ring* — and its language — belonged to a phase in world history that predated the degeneration of the species, reflecting a pristine Germanic paradise that could never be regained.

Notes

1. Quotations from the poem of the *Ring* are taken from *Wagner's Ring of the Nibelung: A Companion*, trans. Stewart Spencer (London 1993), here p.57. This text is based on the first edition of the *Gesammelte Schriften und Dichtungen* (Leipzig 1871–83), v.257–vi.364, emended in the light of the full scores: in the case of *Die Walküre* and *Siegfried*, the first editions of 1874 and 1875 were used. For *Das Rheingold* and *Götterdämmerung* the new critical editions of Egon Voss (Mainz 1988–9) and Hartmut Fladt (Mainz 1981), published as part of Schott's ongoing *Sämtliche Werke*, were preferred.

2. Wilhelm Tappert (ed.), *Richard Wagner im Spiegel der Kritik: Wörterbuch der Unhöflichkeit, enthaltend grobe, höhnende, gehässige und verleumderische Ausdrücke, die gegen den Meister Richard Wagner, seine Werke und seine Anhänger von den Feinden und Spöttern gebraucht wurden* (Leipzig 2/1903), 48. This volume was reset in 1968 under the shorter but no less eye-catching title of *Hurenaquarium und andere Unhöflichkeiten: Richard Wagner im Spiegel der zeitgenössischen Kritik* (Munich 1968), here p.68.

3. "Die erste Aufführung von 'Rheingold,'" *Gesammelte Schriften*, ed. Max Kalbeck and Otto Erich Deutsch

(Munich and Leipzig 1912–14), iii.265–84, here 269–70: "Eine der Rheintöchter, Woglinde, schwimmt auf und umkreist so anmutig zappelnd, als es die betreffenden Vorrichtungen erlauben, ein in der Mitte befindliches Riff, indem sie dabei die zu großer Berühmtheit gelangten, vom Meister ersonnenen Naturlaute Weia! Waga! Wagalaweia! Wallala weiala weia! ausstößt, von denen uns allerdings, da sie bisher noch nicht in Verwendung standen, unbekannt ist, welcher Gemütsstimmung sie eigentlich Ausdruck geben sollen. Der Ausruf Weia! scheint eine sehr unbehagliche, der Ausruf Wallala! dagegen eine besonders behagliche Stimmung anzudeuten, und so dürfte wohl beabsichtigt sein, das zwischen Behagen und Unbehagen wechselnde Gefühl, das man anfangs in einem kalten Bade empfindet, zu bezeichnen." Connoisseurs of Bavarian dialect may also enjoy the following lines, published in the *Münchener Punsch* at the time of the Munich première. (On this occasion the Rhinemaidens refused to use their swimming machines but sang from the wings while their parts were played on stage by extras.) "Wigala wogala weia, / Bleib i auf der Schaukel, so muaß i speia. / Wigala wogala wack, / Fall i abi, so brich i's Gnack." Quoted by Detta and Michael Petzet, *Die Richard Wagner-Bühne König Ludwigs II.* (Munich 1970), 201.

4. Jacob Grimm, *Deutsche Mythologie* (Göttingen 2/1844), 551–57. Although Grimm's text is a ragbag of unassimilated quotations drawn indiscriminately from pagan and Christian sources, references to the practice of drawing holy water "before sunrise" and "young women telling prophecies in spring water" may perhaps have influenced Wagner when the *Ring* began to assume dramatic form. Raymond Furness has also drawn attention to a possible source in *Sir Tristrem*, a 3344-line Middle English romance attributed to the thirteenth-century poet Thomas of Erceldoune: "Sche seyd: 'wayleway!'" See Raymond Furness, "Nymphs and nympholepsy," *Wagner*, vii (1986), 13. Although Furness does not say so, Wagner could have stumbled upon this line in Friedrich Heinrich von der Hagen's edition of Gottfried's *Tristan* (Breslau 1823), ii.126, but the present writer remains unconvinced by the analogy.

5. First published in the *Norddeutsche Allgemeine Zeitung* on June 23, 1872, in response to Ulrich von Wilamowitz-Möllendorff's critique of Nietzsche's *Die Geburt der Tragödie* and reprinted in Richard Wagner, *Gesammelte Schriften und Dichtungen* (see note 1), ix.350–58, esp. 356; see also Richard Wagner, *Gesammelte Schriften und Dichtungen* (hereafter GS) (Leipzig 4/1907), ix.295–302, esp. 300, and *Richard Wagner's Prose Works* (hereafter PW), trans. William Ashton Ellis (London 1892–99), v.292–98, esp. 297. (References to Ellis's translation are included for purely orientational purposes.) "Dem Studium J. Grimm's entnahm ich einmal ein altdeutsches 'Heilawac,' formte es mir, um für meinen Zweck es noch geschmeidiger zu machen, zu einem 'Weigawaga' (einer Form, welche wir heute noch in 'Weihwasser' wiedererkennen), leitete hiervon in die verwandten Sprachwurzeln 'wogen' und 'wiegen,' endlich 'wellen' und 'wallen' über, und bildete mir so, nach der Analogie des 'Eia popeia' unserer Kinderstubenlieder, eine wurzelhaft sylabische Melodie für meine Wassermädchen."

6. See, for example, *Opera and Drama* in GS iv.136–37 (PW ii.274–75) and *"Zukunftsmusik"* in GS vii.104 (PW iii.312).

7. See Siegfried Goslich, *Die deutsche romantische Oper* (Tutzing 1975), 198.

8. Among these composers were Carl Gottlieb Reißiger, Josef Dessauer, August Röckel, Ferdinand Hiller, Jan Bedrich Kittl, Franz Liszt, and Hector Berlioz. Among the works offered to them were *Die hohe Braut*, *Die Sarazenin*,

Die Bergwerke zu Falun, and *Wieland der Schmied*; see John Deathridge, Martin Geck, and Egon Voss, *Wagner Werk-Verzeichnis (WWV): Verzeichnis der musikalischen Werke Richard Wagners und ihrer Quellen* (Mainz 1986), 149–50, 245–46, 247–48, and 342–43. In the event, only Kittl availed himself of the opportunity offered to him. Performed under the title of *Bianca und Giuseppe, oder: Die Franzosen vor Nizza*, his setting of *Die hohe Braut* opened in Prague on February 19, 1848, prompting one local reviewer to comment pointedly that Wagner should stick to writing librettos in future, since this was clearly where his talents lay; see *Bohemia*, xxx (February 22, 1848), quoted in Isolde Vetter, "Wagnerforschung — literarisch. Richard Wagner als Librettist von Johann Friedrich Kittls *Bianca und Giuseppe, oder: Die Franzosen vor Nizza* (1848)," Carl Dahlhaus and Egon Voss (eds.), *Wagnerliteratur — Wagnerforschung: Bericht über das Wagner-Symposium München 1983* (Mainz 1985), 163–79, esp. 173.

9. Anton Wilhelm Florentin von Zuccalmaglio, "Die deutsche Oper," *Neue Zeitschrift für Musik* (hereafter *NZfM*), vi (1837), 191; Louise Otto, "Die Nibelungen als Oper," *NZfM*, xxiii (1845), 49–52, 129–30, 171–72, 175–76, and 181–83; and Franz Brendel, "Vergangenheit, Gegenwart und Zukunft der Oper," *NZfM*, xxiii (1845), 33–35, 37–39, 41–43, 105–8, 109–12, 121–24, 149–52, and *NZfM*, xxiv (1846), 57–60 and 61–64. Elsewhere, Friedrich Theodor Vischer struck a similarly nationalistic note in his *Kritische Gänge* (Tübingen 1844), ii.399–410. Louise Otto even offered to provide Wagner with a libretto on the subject; see Wagner's letter to Gustav Klemm of June 20, 1845, in Richard Wagner, *Sämtliche Briefe*, ed. Gertrud Strobel and others (Leipzig 1967–2000 and Wiesbaden 1999–), ii.438.

10. See Mary Thorp, *The Study of the Nibelungenlied: Being the History of the Study of the Epic and Legend from 1755 to 1937* (Oxford 1940).

11. See Richard Wagner, *Sämtliche Werke: Band 29, I Dokumente zur Entstehungsgeschichte des Bühnenfestspiels Der Ring des Nibelungen*, ed. Werner Breig and Hartmut Fladt (Mainz 1976), 15–16 and 26; see also Adelyn Peck Leverett, "Liszt, Wagner and Heinrich Dorn's *Die Nibelungen*," *Cambridge Opera Journal*, ii (1990), 121–44.

12. See Elizabeth Magee, *Richard Wagner and the Nibelungs* (Oxford 1990), 214. As Magee points out, a question mark hangs over an entry in the Royal Library loan journals for January 1844, when a Herr Wagner borrowed a copy of "Nibelungen von Hagen": it is unclear whether this is a reference to one of Friedrich Heinrich von der Hagen's four editions of the poem or whether it refers to his 1819 study *Die Nibelungen, ihre Bedeutung für die Gegenwart und für immer*.

13. See Curt von Westernhagen, *Richard Wagners Dresdener Bibliothek 1842–1849* (Wiesbaden 1966), 99.

14. See Stewart Spencer, "Engi má við sköpum vinna: Wagner's Use of his Icelandic Sources," *Wagner's Ring and Its Icelandic Sources*, ed. Úlfar Bragason (Reykjavík 1995), 55–76.

15. In *A Communication to my Friends*, Wagner himself uses the term "urdeutsch" in this context; see GS iv.312 (PW i.358).

16. *Die Lieder der Edda von den Nibelungen* (Zurich 1837) was borrowed on October 21, 1848, and returned on January 1, 1849, together with von der Hagen's edition of the *Völsunga saga*; see Magee, *Richard Wagner and the Nibelungs* (note 12), 214. Among the other translations of selections from the Poetic Edda to which Wagner had access during the 1840s were those by Jacob and Wilhelm Grimm (Berlin 1815), Friedrich Majer (Leipzig 1818), Gustav Thormod Legis (Leipzig 1829), Jakob Laurenz Studach (Nuremberg 1829), and Ludwig Ettmüller (Leipzig 1830). But it

was not until Karl Simrock published his complete translation in 1851 that Wagner was able to read the Poetic Edda in its entirety. Of course, all these translators had been aware of the existence of *Stabreim* in the original Icelandic and had used it in their translations, but not in any systematic way. The relative lack of *Stabreim* in the prose draft to *Siegfried's Tod*, which Wagner completed on October 20, 1848, is striking; see Richard Wagner, *Skizzen und Entwürfe zur Ring-Dichtung*, ed. Otto Strobel (Munich 1930), 38–55.

17. Eduard Devrient, *Aus seinen Tagebüchern*, ed. Rolf Kabel (Weimar 1964), i.457: "Der Kerl ist ein Poet durch und durch. Eine schöne Arbeit. Die Alliteration, wie er sie gebraucht, ein wahrer Fund für das Operngedicht; sie sollte zum Grundsatz dafür erhoben werden" (entry of December 2, 1848).

18. Devrient, *Aus seinen Tagebüchern* (note 17), i.451: "Kapellmeister Wagner brachte mir einen Opernentwurf, hatte wieder große sozialistische Rosinen im Kopf" (entry of October 21, 1848).

19. See Hermann Wiessner, *Der Stabreimvers in Richard Wagners "Ring des Nibelungen"* (Berlin 1924), 5–12. As Wiessner points out, Ettmüller derived this insight from *Die Verslehre der Isländer von Erasmus Christian Rask, verdeutscht von Gottl. Christ. Friedr. Mohnike* (Berlin 1830), but Rask's text was theoretical rather than a translation of Eddic poems. Significantly, Ettmüller's 1830 translation of the *Völuspá* still uses classical prosody, but by 1837 his reading of Rask had persuaded him to adopt a different approach to Eddic metres. It was not until Eduard Sievers published his pioneering studies of Germanic metre much later in the century that the rules were properly codified; see especially Sievers's article "Zur Rhythmik des germanischen Alliterationsverses," *Beiträge zur Geschichte der deutschen Sprache und Literatur*, x (1885), 209–314 and 451–545; and xii (1887), 454–82; see also Sievers, *Altgermanische Metrik* (Halle 1893).

20. *Wagner's Ring of the Nibelung* (see note 1), 286.

21. Gustav Neckel and Hans Kühn (eds.), *Edda: Die Lieder des Codex Regius nebst verwandten Denkmälern* (Heidelberg 1962), i.190.

22. *The Poetic Edda*, trans. Henry Adams Bellows (New York 1957), 389.

23. GS ii.219.

24. *Die Lieder der Edda* (note 16), 12.

25. *Die Lieder der Edda* (note 16), 18.

26. *Wagner's Ring of the Nibelung* (note 1), 247.

27. *Wagner's Ring of the Nibelung* (note 1), 275 (*Siegfried*, Act Three, Scene Three).

28. *Wagner's Ring of the Nibelung* (note 1), 280 (*Götterdämmerung*, Prologue). See also "Dort die K<u>rö</u>te, / <u>gr</u>eife sie rasch!" (p.100) and "An seine B<u>r</u>ust / <u>pr</u>eßt' ich mich weinend" (p.303).

29. See Thomas S. Grey, *Wagner's Musical Prose: Texts and Contexts* (Cambridge 1995), 259–63.

30. GS iv.106 (PW ii.241): "als fünffüßiges Ungeheuer."

31. GS iv.328–29 (PW i.375): "der nur *gedachte* moderne Vers mit seiner verschwebenden, körperlosen Gestalt."

32. See A. J. Bliss, "The Appreciation of Old English Metre," *English Medieval Studies presented to J. R. R. Tolkien on the Occasion of his Seventieth Birthday*, ed. Norman Davis and C. L. Wrenn (London 1962), 27–40, esp. 29.

33. GS iv.329 (PW i.376): "Den '*Siegfried*' mußte ich geradesweges fahren lassen, wenn ich ihn nur in diesem Verse hätte ausführen können. Somit mußte ich auf eine andere Sprachmelodie sinnen; und doch hatte ich in Wahrheit gar nicht zu sinnen nöthig, sondern nur mich zu entscheiden, denn an dem urmythischen Quelle, wo ich den jugendlich schönen Siegfriedmenschen fand, traf ich auch ganz von selbst auf den sinnlich vollendeten Sprachaus

druck, in dem einzig dieser Mensch sich kundgeben konnte. Es war dieß der, nach dem wirklichen Sprachaccente zur natürlichsten und lebendigsten Rhythmik sich fügende, zur unendlich mannigfaltigsten Kundgebung jederzeit leicht sich befähigende, *stabgereimte Vers*, in welchem einst das Volk selbst dichtete, als es eben noch Dichter und Mythenschöpfer war."

34. GS iv.118 (PW ii.255): "Wie [...] wir aus ihrem Inhalte alles von Außen her Entstellende, pragmatisch Historische, Staatliche und dogmatisch Religiöse hinwegnehmen mußten, um diesen Inhalt als einen rein menschlichen, gefühlsnothwendigen darzustellen, so haben wir auch aus dem Sprachausdrucke alles von diesen Entstellungen des Reinmenschlichen, Gefühlsnothwendigen Herrührende und ihnen einzig Entsprechende in der Weise auszuscheiden, daß von ihm eben nur dieser Kern übrigbleibt."

35. See John Lyons, *Introduction to Theoretical Linguistics* (Cambridge 1969), 88.

36. *Die Lieder der Edda* (note 16), xiv–xv.

37. See Oswald Panagl, "'Vermählen wollte der Magen Sippe dem Mann ohne Minne die Maid': Archaisches und Archaisierendes in der Sprache von Wagners *Ring*," *Die Programmhefte der Bayreuther Festspiele 1988 – IV: "Siegfried*," 37–65; Engl. trans., 108–29.

38. Eduard Hanslick, "R. Wagner's Bühnenfestspiel in Bayreuth," *Neue Freie Presse* (13 August 1876), quoted by Susanna Großmann-Vendrey, *Bayreuth in der deutschen Presse: Dokumentenband 1: Die Grundsteinlegung und die ersten Festspiele (1872–1876)* (Regensburg 1977), 171: "Ohne Musik, nicht gesungen, sondern gesprochen, würden diese stammelnden und stotternden Stabreime überall eine mit Ärgerniß gemischte Heiterkeit erregen;" trans. by Henry Pleasants as "Richard Wagner's Stage Festival in Bayreuth," *Music Criticisms 1846–99* (Harmondsworth 1963), 132.

39. Thomas Mann, "Richard Wagner und der 'Ring des Nibelungen,'" *Im Schatten Wagners: Thomas Mann über Richard Wagner*, ed. Hans Rudolf Vaget (Frankfurt 1999), 169: "Wagners Dichtertum anzuzweifeln schien mir immer absurd;" trans. by Allan Blunden as "Richard Wagner and Der Ring des Nibelungen," *Pro and contra Wagner* (London 1985), 190.

40. First in a privately printed edition of fifty copies in 1853, then in 1863, and finally in 1872 as part of his collected writings.

41. *Wagner's Ring of the Nibelung* (note 1), 60; MHG *vrídel* = "lover."

42. *Wagner's Ring of the Nibelung* (note 1), 138; MHG *nîtlich* = "hostile, fearsome."

43. *Wagner's Ring of the Nibelung* (note 1), 190; MHG *vreislich* = "terrifying."

44. *Wagner's Ring of the Nibelung* (note 1), 144.

45. See William Ashton Ellis, "Schopenhauer's Private Copy of the Ring-Poem," *The Life of Richard Wagner* (London 1900–8), iv.440–46.

46. Alfred Forman made a heroic stab at doing so and gained Wagner's approval in the process, but the result is often bewildering and makes little sense unless we have the original alongside us as a crib: "The boon thou shalt —/ shalt not forbear from!" Brünnhilde launches her final speech in *Die Walküre*. "Or strike at me now / as I strangle thy knee, / thy darling mangle, / to dust with thy maid, / from her body spill / the breath with thy spear; / but not fiercely unfence / her here to a nameless harm"; Alfred Forman, *The Nibelung's Ring* (London 1877), 165. See also Cosima Wagner's reference to "the Englishman who sent a fine translation of *Die Walküre*" (CT, September 15, 1873).

47. See Wagner's letters to Julie Ritter of May 6, 1857, and Otto Wesendonck of August 28, 1859, in Wagner, *Sämtliche Briefe* (note 9), viii.312 and xi.202; see also CT,

June 25, 1876. For more on the development of Wagner's *völkisch* outlook, see George L. Mosse, *Germans and Jews: The Right, the Left, and the Search for a "Third Force" in Pre-Nazi Germany* (New York 1970), 3–33.

48. Wagner's *Ring of the Nibelung* (note 1), 117. Other examples include Alberich's play on *bürgen/bergen* in the lines "Daß keiner mir müßig / bürge mir Mime, / sonst birgt er sich schwer / meiner Geißel Schwunge" (That none shall be idle Mime shall answer, or else he'll not scape the swing of my scourge) (p.94) and Wotan's wonderfully evocative lines at the end of Act Three of *Die Walküre*: "Denn Einer nur freie die Braut, / der freier als ich, der Gott" (For one man alone shall woo the bride, one freer than I, the god) (p.190). This is as good a place as any to say that I disagree with Rudolph Sabor's claim that "Wagner's characterization does not begin on the stage: it is already planned in the language of the text, where each character is given his or her own distinctive mode of expression." See Rudolph Sabor, *Richard Wagner: Der Ring des Nibelungen. A Companion* (London 1997), 14. Not only do the constraints of the *Stabreim* preclude such differentiation, but, as Adorno rightly points out, it is Wagner's own voice that we hear in each of his characters, who emote on cue, rather than developing internally; see Theodor W. Adorno, *Versuch über Wagner* (Frankfurt 1981), 109; trans. Rodney Livingstone as *In Search of Wagner* (London 1981), 116.

49. See Stewart Spencer, "Wagner as librettist," *The Wagner Compendium*, ed. Barry Millington (London 1992), 264–68.

50. CT, January 22, 1871: "Ich bin kein Dichter, und es ist mir ganz gleich, ob man meiner Diktion Vorwürfe macht, bei mir ist alles Aktion; es ist mir bis zu einem gewissen Grad gleichgültig, ob man die Verse versteht,

meine Handlung wird man schon begreifen. Der Dichter ist neben Musiker, Maler, Plastiker ein Unding, nur der Dramatiker kann da aufkommen."

51. Arthur Schopenhauer, *Sämtliche Werke*, ed. Arthur Hübscher and rev. Angelika Hübscher (Mannheim 1988), ii.304; trans. E. F. J. Payne as *The World as Will and Representation* (New York 1969), i.257.

52. See J. G. Robertson, "Richard Wagner as poet and thinker (2)," *Wagner*, vi (1985), 41–55.

53. Wagner, *Sämtliche Briefe* (note 9), iii.166: "Hier ist nichts zu überzeugen und zu gewinnen, sondern nur auszurotten: dieß mit der Zeit zu thun, dazu erhalten wir die kraft, wenn wir als jünger einer neuen religion uns erkennen lernen, und durch gegenseitige liebe uns im Glauben stärken: halten wir uns an die Jugend, — das Alter laßt verrecken, an dem ist nichts zu holen!"

54. The physiological and psychological reasons for this change are explored by the present writer in "Zieh' hin! Ich kann dich nicht halten," *Wagner*, ii (1981), 98–120.

55. It will be recalled that in *Siegfried's Tod*, Siegfried's death was intended to bolster up Wotan's precarious rule. In the 1848 libretto the gods were destined to survive.

56. CT, July 2, 1872: "Von Wotan und Siegfried, welcher nun am höchsten steht, Wotan der tragischste, er hat die Schuld des Daseins erkannt und büßt den Schöpfungs-Irrtum."

57. CT, October 2, 1882: "Darauf kommt Freund Rub. und spielt uns auf unser Ersuchen den Schluß der Götterdämmerung, R. tritt hinzu und singt die letzten Worte Brünnhilden's, freut sich des ganzen, so heidnisch Germanischen! [...] Er gedenkt Gobineau's, der germanischen Welt, die mit diesem Werk ende."

Bibliography

Ellis, William Ashton. "Schopenhauer's Private Copy of the Ring-Poem." *The Life of Richard Wagner*. London: Kegan Paul, Trench, Trübner, 1900–8. iv. 440–46.

Ettmüller, Ludwig. *Die Lieder der Edda von den Nibelungen*. Zurich: Orell, Füßli, 1837.

Goslich, Siegfried. *Die deutsche romantische Oper*. Tutzing: Hans Schneider, 1975.

Grey, Thomas S. *Wagner's Musical Prose: Texts and Contexts*. Cambridge: Cambridge University Press, 1995.

Magee, Elizabeth. *Richard Wagner and the Nibelungs*. Oxford: Clarendon, 1990.

Panagl, Oswald. "'Vermählen wollte der Magen Sippe dem Mann ohne Minne die Maid': Archaisches und Archaisierendes in der Sprache von Wagners *Ring*." *Die Programmhefte der Bayreuther Festspiele 1988–IV: "Siegfried."* 37–65. Engl. trans. 108–29.

Spencer, Stewart. "Wagner as librettist." *The Wagner Compendium: A Guide to Wagner's Life and Music*. Ed. Barry Millington. London: Thames and Hudson, 1992. 264–68.

Wagner, Richard. *Gesammelte Schriften und Dichtungen*. Leipzig: C. F. W. Siegel's Musikalienhandlung, 4/1907.

_____. *Richard Wagner's Prose Works*. Trans. William Ashton Ellis. London: Kegan Paul, Trench, Trübner, 1892–99.

_____. *Wagner's Ring of the Nibelung*. The full German text with a new translation by Stewart Spencer and commentaries by Barry Millington, Elizabeth Magee, Roger Hollinrake and Warren Darcy. London and New York: Thames and Hudson, 1993.

Wiessner, Hermann. *Der Stabreimvers in Richard Wagner's "Ring des Nibelungen."* Berlin: 1924. (Germanische Studien Heft 30).

13. An Interview with Jane Eaglen

John Louis DiGaetani

Jane Eaglen has become one of the foremost Wagnerian sopranos of our time — the Isolde and Brünnhilde of choice in most opera houses in the world in the early part of the twenty-first century. She has sung around the world, though Seattle is her home base and where she prefers to live. She was born in Lincoln, England (in the Midlands), and attended the Royal Northern College of Music in Manchester. She began studying piano and conducting and wanted a career in music, but a voice teacher there convinced her to sing professionally. She very early decided that she wanted to specialize in the Wagnerian repertory.

She began singing professionally with the English National Opera in London in 1984, singing roles in Gilbert and Sullivan and with a voice flexible enough for coloratura, *bel canto* roles in operas by Rossini and Donizetti, though she wanted most to sing Wagner. By the middle of the 1990s, she was singing her favorite roles, Norma and Brünnhilde. She sang Norma at the Seattle Opera in 1994 with great success, singing this role at other opera houses as well, including the Metropolitan. She first sang Brünnhilde in a complete *Ring* cycle at the Lyric Opera of Chicago in 1996 to very positive reviews; the next year she sang Brünnhilde in the *Ring* in Vienna to great acclaim. In 2000 she sang the same role in the Ring cycle at the Metropolitan Opera in New York, and again in the spring of 2004. Earlier, in 1998 she sang Isolde at the Seattle Opera with Ben Heppner as Tristan, and in the next year they repeated these roles at the Metropolitan Opera. She has specialized in the most difficult of the Wagnerian soprano roles, Brünnhilde and Isolde, and sung them with apparent ease and singular success at opera houses around the world. I spoke with her about her insights into the Wagnerian soprano repertory.

JD: Tell me how your career developed and how you became interested in singing Wagnerian opera.

JE: The first time I heard Wagner, as a teenager, I immediately liked the music. I began by studying the piano and thought I might have a career as a pianist or conductor. I was attending the Royal Northern College of Music in Manchester and I began studying voice with Joseph Ward — and I am still studying with him, by the way.

JD: Is he the one who said you should consider singing rather than piano playing as a career?

JE: Yes. I was only 17 years old at the time, but he heard me sing and immediately said that I would one day sing Brünnhilde and Norma.

JD: It must have been a large voice even back then.

JE: Actually, it was not a large voice back then, but he heard some quality in my voice that told him I had the potential of being a Wagnerian soprano. He was a wonderful voice teacher for me and made my career possible. When I first heard Wagner I was bowled over by the use

Siegfried, **Seattle Opera: Jane Eaglen as Brünnhilde. (Photograph: Chris Bennion)**

of the orchestra — this was clearly symphonic music rather than regular operatic music — but then I noticed his use of the voice and his dramatic characterization and I became hooked.

JD: Why were you drawn to sing Brünnhilde?

JE: I love her character — I love both her music and her personality. I see her as an exuberant teenager in the beginning who is very smart and fearless, but gradually she learns fear. She enters life with a lot of enthusiasm but gradually comes to wisdom over the course of the three operas she appears in. She is a big, fun girl — like me. Every time I sing her I find something new in her character that makes her appear interesting and lifelike in a new way.

JD: Who is the most important man in her life?

JE: Wotan is the most important man in her life. She is the hero Wotan is looking for during his monologue in Act II of *Die Walküre.* Wotan says he is looking for a hero, but he does not know that that hero is sitting right next to him.

JD: What about Siegfried?

JE: Siegfried is very important too because he is her destiny, and through him she becomes a real human being.

JD: Does she love him?

JE: Yes, she does, which explains her fury when she sees him about to marry another woman in *Götterdämmerung.* Siegmund is also important to her; during the second act of *Walküre* she does not understand why he does not want to go to Valhalla with her but instead wants to stay with that sleeping woman, Sieglinde.

JD: Yes, during the Todesverkündigungmusik, she tells him of his own death and that he must leave the earth and leave Sieglinde to come to Valhalla.

JE: Brünnhilde learns from him something about the power of love. From his son Siegfried she learns about the sexual side of love and what being a human being really means. As a goddess she could never know this.

JD: When Wotan takes away her godhood at the end of *Die Walküre,* he is actually doing her a real service since by then he has concluded that the gods are all doomed to death.

JE: And when Brünnhilde is with her sister Waltraute in the first act of *Götterdämmerung,* she is mirroring her old self in the second act of *Die Walküre* because Waltraute can not understand why she is unwilling to give up the ring for some mere mortal. Brünnhilde explains to her uncomprehending sister something of the nature and power of love itself.

JD: Why does Brünnhilde commit suicide? The *Ring* cycle ends with her suicide right after she sings the Immolation scene.

JE: She doesn't have a choice really. This is her destiny. She was wrong to plot Siegfried's murder and she knows that the ring must be returned to the Rhine and the Rhinemaidens.

JD: Is her suicide an attempt to reconnect with Wotan?

JE: Well, she does sing most of the Immolation Scene to her father Wotan. But now her life's work is done and she wants to reconnect with both Wotan and Siegfried in some way, though there is no clear indication of a belief in an afterlife in the Ring.

JD: Her love of Siegfried also contains some hatred, which we see most fully in *Götterdämmerung*.

JE: That is part of her impetuous nature. Love and hate are different sides of the same coin and part of the complex nature of the human experience of love.

JD: Long before Sigmund Freud, Wagner presents the paradoxical nature of love in the *Ring*. Aside from the dramatic challenges, what are the vocal challenges in the role of Brünnhilde?

JE: All three Brünnhildes are in a way different in the three operas of the *Ring* she appears in. In *Die Walküre* it is a low role, except for her opening war cries, of course. The *Siegfried* Brünnhilde is higher but shorter, and I find that the most difficult of the three. She must lie down on an often dirty, dusty set and there is no chance to warm up. I would rather sing five hours in the other Wagner operas; but the love music for Brünnhilde at the end of *Siegfried* is so glorious. She has lost her godhead and she is about to lose her maidenhead so she is naturally afraid but also joyful and excited. The *Götterdämmerung* Brünnhilde is longer but I do not find it as difficult to sing; and the changing nature of her character makes all three roles terrific. I used to sing Turandot but have given it up since I find the character not interesting enough.

JD: Well, she only has one opera after all! Brünnhilde has the whole *Ring* cycle to develop and change. I find it interesting that she threatens suicide in the last act of *Die Walküre*—and of course the *Ring* ends with her suicide.

JE: She is very impulsive and she is very human, but suicide is a ploy and a threat to get what she wants from her father. She is a very rounded character—Turandot seems so one-dimensional in comparison. Wagner certainly knew how to create interesting roles for women. For a man he certainly understood how women change and develop and what they are really interested in. As an opera composer he is absolutely the best—on both the dramatic and musical levels.

JD: Some feminist critics have argued that Wagner actually was interested in torturing women. I have read that the new *Ring* cycle at the English National Opera in London emphasizes this misogynist approach. Would you agree?

JE: Frankly, I find that point of view rather silly. Wagner's women don't just take poison at the end—as in some operas I could mention—but instead they initiate the action. Sieglinde too initiates much of the action in the Ring.

JD: Are you tempted to sing Sieglinde?

JE: I do not find her as interesting as Brünnhilde, frankly. She moans too much and is not as fully rounded.

JD: And she appears in only one of the four operas. Only Wotan, Brünnhilde, and Alberich appear in three of the *Ring* operas.

JE: Yes, and both women are active rather than passive characters.

JD: Yes, and that reminds me of your wonderful Isolde. She too has a complex balance of love and hate for her lover, Tristan.

JE: Tristan is actually quite passive in that opera since it is really Isolde who initiates all the action there.

JD: She tries to murder poor Tristan in the first act, and he knows it. They have actually entered a suicide pact, which she initiates. I also like the fact that your Isolde does not die at the end — Wagner's final stage directions are vague since he doesn't say she dies but sinks on Tristan's body.

JE: Yes, I do not think Isolde should die at the end — just as Ortrud does not die, nor does Elsa die either — she "sinks lifeless," which does not mean that she is dead.

JD: Does the role of Elsa interest you?

JE: Elsa is lighter and higher than Ortrud and I am more comfortable at this point in my career with Ortrud.

JD: What about Kundry? You would be terrific in that role, I think.

JE: That role is too low for me — it is actually a mezzo-soprano voice.

JD: Why do you think the *Ring* cycle is being done so frequently these days, and what do you think are the main themes of the work?

JE: I think the *Ring* deals mostly with personal relationships. People who are afraid of the *Ring* cycle think that it is about gods and dwarves and politics and philosophy, but I think it is really about personal relationships — father/daughter, father/son, husband/wife. The *Ring* is a huge piece — the biggest in all opera — but most of the scenes actually contain only two people in conflict. Wagner remains the most intimate of opera composers and sees and portrays the complexity of human relationships.

JD: Many people are afraid of Wagner. They think he is very philosophical and profound and also rather scary — perhaps because of his tragic anti–Semitism.

JE: Yes, and for a whole generation of people Wagner was spoiled because of Hitler's horrible use of him.

JD: Exactly. Wagner died in 1883 and Hitler took over in Germany fifty years later. He was a thug who wanted to give his band of thugs some intellectual pretense. If Wagner had been alive during the Hitler period, he would probably have ended in a concentration camp since he would never have taken orders from a dictator or agreed with his lunacy.

JE: Those horrible associations have died off with the passage of time, and Wagner's wonderful *Ring* is being staged all over the world now with greater and greater frequency. This huge tetralogy is too wonderful to be ignored and every opera company in the world wants to stage it.

JD: What kind of Ring production do you like?

JE: I like the naturalistic ones best — like the productions at the Metropolitan and the Seattle Opera.

JD: I agree with you. I am so tired of the Eurotrash productions which totally ignore Wagner's stage directions. Many European directors seem to think that realism in the Ring means kitsch — but it does not have to. Realism does not have to reflect Walt Disney's view of nature.

JE: I too like a realistic or naturalistic production which is visually interesting, emphasizes the world of nature, which is so clearly the basis of the *Ring*'s world view. I am quite passionate about Wagner and feel very lucky to be a part of this incredible series of four operas. I think the most wonderful music in the whole cycle occurs in the five minutes after the Immolation. That music always brings tears to my eyes when I hear it backstage after the Immolation Scene. Some people think I sing too much Wagner, yet I really think he was one of the greatest geniuses of all art and of all time. I know some *Ring* groupies who will go anywhere in the world to see a *Ring* cycle, and I can understand that since Wagner's *Ring* generates that kind of excitement and adulation. I feel very fortunate to be able to recreate this great art, and what Wagner was as a person is totally irrelevant to his art.

JD: I agree completely.

VI. CONCLUSION

14. The Trouble with Wagner
John Louis DiGaetani

Wagnerians as a group often have an excessively worshipful approach to their favorite composer. I even recall some members of the Wagner Society of New York who insisted on referring to their favorite composer as the "Meister." Such an approach implies that Wagner remains the only great opera composer who could do nothing wrong and whose operas (or, as these fanatics would say, "music dramas") are incapable of any imperfections, but are instead absolutely perfect works of art. Such a rigid and religious approach — to these people Bayreuth equals the Vatican — strikes most other operagoers as laughable Wagnerolotry.

Most professional musicologists know very well the central flaw in Wagnerian opera: it is in fact a flaw obvious to all but the most irrevocably converted Wagnerians. Most knowledgeable opera experts have concluded that the flaw is clearly there, and perhaps it is time that even Wagnerians are forced to face the facts and admit the truth about this central flaw in the "Meister's" operas.

The flaw is, of course, that Wagner's operas tend to be too short. Wagner just did not know when he needed to continue with something marvelous he had stumbled upon; instead, he had the unfortunate habit of cutting off too quickly characters, musical ideas, and even whole operas.

Certainly the *Ring* cycle is full of examples of Wagner's unfortunate desire for concision at the expense of sufficient musical and dramatic development. In *Das Rheingold*— a mere one-act work after all — several of the characters clearly need much more development. Fasolt and Fafner, the two giants who possess the ring in the final scene, are cleverly delineated as separate characters, rather than as Tweedle-dum and Tweedle-dee. Fafner remains the more brutal brother, and is in fact the one who kills his own brother Fasolt at the end of the opera in order to own the ring. But not enough development appears in *Rheingold* to provide more information about the root of their rivalry and what causes Fafner to be the more violent of the two.

At the opposite extreme is Sieglinde, the great victim of *Die Walküre*. Her victimization is apparent in her first-act monologue, when she describes her horrible marriage to Hunding, which leads to her wonderful love music with her brother Siegmund. Certainly this love music is too short and needs to continue for at least another half-hour. The Fricka-Wotan relationship also needs more expansion. When was this marriage ever happy? How did it become so bitter? What *modus operandi* have these two characters developed to maintain their doomed and loveless relationship? Why didn't Wagner do more to answer these questions and to give these characters even greater reality?

Part of the reason was, unfortunately, his haste to get to *Siegfried*, the most comic of the four *Ring* operas, and certainly it would have been even funnier except for its unfortunate brevity. The wonderfully intense conflict between Alberich and Wotan in the second act clearly needs more dialogue. The depth of these characters' hatred of each other demands more development, as does their attraction to each other. Such an intense love-hate relationship necessitates greater action on stage between the two characters. And the wonderful, glorious love music between Siegfried and Brünnhilde at the end of the opera suffers from excessive brevity. Another twenty minutes of such sublime music is clearly needed; but no, yet again, Wagner cuts this short in his eagerness to finish the cycle.

Which explains why *Die Götterdämmerung* suffers most from Wagner's neurotic attraction to conciseness. The fascinating relationship between Gunther and Gutrune (another perhaps incestuous pair) cries out for greater dramatic action and more music. How wonderful if these two characters had more time on stage, and perhaps an extended love duet. The fascinating Hagen, their half-brother, and his dependence on his manipulative father Alberich, need more details. Of course these characters do have a wonderful scene together (Act II, scene 1), but this single scene teases rather than satisfies the viewer.

The Rhinemaidens at the end of the opera need more music to celebrate their final retrieval of their wonderful gold. That glorious finale at the end of the third act! I ask you: is it long enough? Of course not. But Wagner's neurotic haste also dooms the final *Ring* opera to be too short. Perhaps Wagner was a victim of his patron's eagerness to see all four of the operas on stage. King Ludwig's intense curiosity and Wagner's apparently (and unfortunately) natural desire to please his wealthy and powerful patron both share the blame for the *Ring's* alarming brevity.

So ignore the Wagnerians, I say, and let us all honestly face the sad truth about the central flaw in Wagnerian opera, particularly in the excessively brief *Ring* cycle. If only Wagner had had a bit more patience and stuck with his hasty inspirations a bit *longer*.

15. The *Ring* on Disc and on Video
Geoffrey Riggs

Audio Recordings

When it comes to the *Ring* discography, a broad divide has developed that, like many such divides, is derived partly from fact and partly from fiction. Chiefly, this divide centers around the centrality of the pioneering Georg Solti recording for Decca/London in the ears and hearts of many listeners versus the growing esteem for an earlier conductor's recordings, those of Wilhelm Furtwängler. For many, the differences between the two seem reflected in contrasting sets elsewhere in the catalogue, mostly later ones from later conductors who, to one degree or another, reflect similar stylistic contrasts. In the process, contrasts between these two have sometimes been exaggerated by critics to a point where similarities between them get overlooked.

Both Furtwängler and Solti are capable of projecting a rich sense of engagement in episode after episode. They seem able to communicate in a very personal way with an orchestra, making it easy for the listener to grasp the high stakes involved in Wagner's huge drama. In sharing this gift, they remain more similar to each other than strong adherents of either would generally admit.

This communicative strength is hardly a negligible achievement, since, in Wagner's *Ring*, the conductor ends up bulking larger than any other element in setting an individual stamp upon a recording. Here, the concept behind any performance necessarily entails interpretive choices on a grand scale. Ultimately, one perspective above all is needed to synthesize the sprawling elements in Wagner's masterpiece. That one perspective in a recording, where it is the ear alone that must convey the drama to the "spectator," can only be the conductor's.

With all the similarities between Furtwängler and Solti in their equal effectiveness as communicators, differences remain, and those differences reflect discrete performing traditions extending back about a century before either of these two sets of recordings were made.

A lot of ink — and energy — has been expended on the conducting style Wagner evidently preferred. Extrapolation has now become the order of the day, much of it highly speculative. Here's at least what we know. Wagner used a minimum of gestures in his actual conducting, which was, in his day, almost as famed as his composing. With this minimalist style, he would communicate (through the use of an evocative gaze, a subtle shift of the hands, and so on) constantly changing moods, dynamics, tempi. But again, none of this would be done demonstratively.

Wagner's physical gestures were marked more by a deliberately descriptive shaping of phrasing and dynamics, imparting the shape of a melody or a theme, than by the more conventional, precise indication of beats and musical measures.

The result would be an impression on the part of the listener of great fluidity, a mercurial emotional landscape that, at the same time, would be marked by quite smooth, seamless transitions that would rarely jar musically, though they could startle dramatically. One remark of Wagner's, concerning his own conceptions underlying the structure for his music dramas, links his claim of mastery in the art of transition (as a composer) with his concern that all be presented as "unending melody."

Granted, much of the above certainly sounds like a paradox. After all, if you are going to have constant shifts in moods, dynamics, etc., how are you — ever — to avoid jolts of the most obvious kind? Herein lies most of the controversy as to the "true" Wagnerian style. (A pesky rumor was recently floated that an old wax cylinder existed featuring Wagner actually conducting a scene from *Tristan und Isolde*, but it proved to be a hoax. In fact, no recording exists at all of Wagner performing.)

Wagner's own favorite conducting disciple was Anton Seidl, who was first the assistant conductor at Bayreuth and who then presided over a Golden Age of Wagner performance at the Metropolitan Opera. Unfortunately, this was in the 1880s and '90s, and no recordings exist of Seidl, who died in 1898. The definitive study of this period is Joseph Horowitz's *Wagner Nights*, 1994.

Seidl's conducting was marked by a simplicity of gesture similar to Wagner's, but he — apparently (fortunately, some of the New York critics of that time were alert, vivid and detailed in their descriptions) — achieved just as startlingly dramatic an effect as Wagner had, despite the apparent simplicity. In addition, the translucency that Seidl achieved in the orchestral line enabled singers to be clearly heard and their words to be readily understood.

In fact, in Heinrich Porges's contemporary account (*Wagner Rehearsing the Ring*) of the rehearsals for the first Bayreuth Festival — the *Ring* cycle in 1876 — Wagner always emphasizes how important a clear understanding of the words is for the audience, and elsewhere he is described putting up an inscription in the wings for his singers: "Take special care with the little notes, the big ones will take care of themselves." This inscription has been preserved and can be viewed by visitors to Bayreuth to this day.

In Seidl's performances, there was evidently a constant give and take between the orchestra and the singers to accommodate the singers in their constant adjustments for Wagner's shifts in emotional temperature, and this style was marked by a vividness and frankness that contributed in no small way to the popularizing of the Wagner canon as a miraculous voyage into the depths of the human psyche, for the performer and the listener alike.

The seeds of this mercurial approach may be in Wagner's own remarks, decades earlier, when he wrote that performing *Tannhäuser* properly entailed such extensive rehearsals that singer and conductor would eventually need no direct communication at all when effecting a critical transition. In fact, Wagner strongly implies that even subtle variations from night to night (unrehearsed, yet!) are just fine, so long as it is the *singer* who is calling the shots!

Much of this was also reflected in the conducting of Felix Mottl, apparently Wagner's second-favorite disciple, who won his approval during intensive rehearsals as assistant conductor at Bayreuth.

While no recordings exist of either Seidl or Seidl's chief conducting protégé (no less than Victor Herbert) performing Wagner, we do have a dimly recorded cylinder of Mottl conducting Wagner's "Kaisermarsch" (a pretty negligible piece). With the atrocious sound quality and so-so musical material, it isn't possible to tell much about Mottl here, but what does come through is an overarching sense of line and a surging presentational style of phrasing.

On a personal note, this listener learned the *Ring* cycle with (A) Solti's *Rheingold*, (B) a mix-and-match *Walküre* (Walter/Seidler-Winkler/Solti [Flagstad/Edelmann's Act III]), (C) Bodanzky's *Siegfried* (live from the Metropolitan with a somewhat cut Act III, but featuring Lauritz Melchior), and (D) Fjeldstad's *Götterdämmerung* (indifferent conducting but a memento of Flagstad's last Brünnhilde). Very shortly after that, it was on to the rest of the Solti *Ring* and, finally, to the two complete, "live" Furtwängler *Ring* cycles.

While *studio* recordings of Furtwängler's conducting heard up to then had shown great feeling, they had not suggested the drive heard in Solti. Consequently, drive had seemed inseparable from the energetically precise indicaton of beat and measure heard in Solti. It had not seemed possible that a "through-line" of energy and direction in Wagner could be generated any other way. But the two Furtwängler *Ring* cycles were recorded during live performances, and consequently they proved amazing.

First drawn to the *Ring* through hearing a grand vocal line from Gustav Neidlinger, Lotte Lehmann, Lauritz Melchior, Kirsten Flagstad, and the like, this listener had pegged Wagner's gigantic tetralogy as a sequence of stunning moments, highly dramatic but made up of apparently discrete units. Furtwängler's conducting in parts of his studio *Walküre*, made in 1954 with Moedl, Frantz, Rysanek and Suthaus, seemed to lack shape occasionally, and even Act I of his famed studio *Tristan und Isolde* with Flagstad and Suthaus did not seem to match the rest of that recording.

But both of his complete *Ring* cycles being live recordings makes all the difference. There is a sense of line that carries the listener through, without the apparent dependency on "exclamation marks" typical of the Solti school. Yes, there is less underlining and highlighting with Furtwängler than with Solti. For some, that may be a loss, but for others it is a net gain. Hard to imagine that one great moment can flow seamlessly into the next, that no matter how "exclamatory" individual moments of transition might be, there is always a theme, a melody of some kind, being "sung" by the orchestra. In addition, no matter how clearly an "unending melody" might be presented, it never seems to interfere with the vocal line, to compete with it. The words of the singers are usually reasonably clear, albeit somewhat compromised by merely-adequate-but-not-splendid sonics. At the same time, the emotional temperature seems duly volatile and mercurial in Furtwängler without disturbing the flow of the musical line. The emotional message is always compelling and vital, but it forms part of a greater — lyrical — whole, where no element appears to compete with any other.

It is this sense of downright competition that one hears when returning to Solti. Listening to live Furtwängler radically alters one's perspective on the younger maestro. One can still respect Solti sufficiently to appreciate his virtuosic strength with a clearly top-flight orchestra (the Vienna Philharmonic). But after hearing the two Furtwängler cycles, one can end up wondering just where, in Solti, the melody has gone! Granted, that's a slight exaggeration. After all, the melody has always been there. But, in a Dionysian effort to galvanize the hearer, Solti seems to be abandoning melody's claims in favor of other concerns bound up with orchestral brilliance and thunderous climaxes.

Only after realizing how radically a live Furtwängler document can alter one's perspective on the Solti style, and that of others of his school, does the aptness of some of the distinctions within the history of Wagnerian conducting assume proper importance. One has stumbled upon distinguishing characteristics that in fact reflect discrete schools of conducting.

If a Furtwängler epitomizes what Wagner and Seidl did in performance, then a turbocharged and meticulous Toscanini would have to be the most conspicuous and celebrated exemplar of a starkly contrasted school. Apparently, Solti started out as an assistant to Toscanini.

Toscanini's precise indications of beat and measure — rather than the shape of a phrase or a melody — are legendary; and these are characteristics that Solti adopted.

On the other hand, Furtwängler's physical style of conducting — sure enough — emphasized the general shape of phrasing and dynamics, much as Wagner's and Seidl's had. The beat and the measure were apparently secondary to him. And there are videos (thank goodness) of both Toscanini and Furtwängler clearly confirming these differences.

Last but certainly not least, Furtwängler was apparently a protégé of Felix Mottl.

This is not intended as a debunking of the Toscanini "precision" school. In fact, in the interests of brevity, I have somewhat oversimplified the differences in the two schools. Furthermore, there are a number of conductors who bridge the gap between the Furtwängler and Solti styles. So all is not black-and-white here. Some even regard Solti as not entirely of the Toscanini school either, although the similarities arguably remain more important than the differences.

And we should not give the back of our hand to the Toscanini school in any event; it remains as authentic and compelling a style for the wonders of Italian opera as the Furtwängler school is for the wonders of Wagner.

One can even understand how some might object that Solti, with his dramatic heightening of every moment, indeed reflects the mercurial degree to which singers under Seidl would seem to change emotional direction on a dime. After all, the burgeoning of interest in Wagner during the Seidl years was due as much to a kind of frenzy in the sung emotions as to the richness and flow of the music itself. What else could this be but a celebration of a Dionysian element, many may ask?

All of those arguments may be justified, but what distinguishes Furtwängler recorded in live performance is his capacity for combining undeniable variations in the emotional temperature with that fabulous sense of line of his, so reminiscent of the tantalizing descriptions we have of Wagner's great fluidity and smooth, seamless transitions.

And it remains more than merely suggestive for this listener that a sense of these distinct differences between Furtwängler and Solti was borne in forcefully before one was consciously aware of the historic facts behind the Furtwängler and Solti styles. The facts merely seem to confirm initial impressions.

The two Furtwängler readings are both from Italy, the earlier being a broadcast of a fully staged La Scala revival from 1950 with a few cuts and featuring Kirsten Flagstad as an untiring Brünnhilde, Set Svanholm and Max Lorenz as the two Siegfrieds, and Ferdinand Frantz as Wotan, with Josef Herrmann taking over as the Wanderer. Flagstad is the main attraction among the singers, although Frantz is certainly memorable as Wotan the thunderer. He is particularly exciting summoning Loge at the conclusion of *Die Walküre*, if less effective in the more inward moments. Herrmann does not have the same strong presence. His Gunther is preferable. Unfortunately, Svanholm's Siegfried, after a creditable Acts I and II, tires badly in the last act of *Siegfried* (some accounts claim food poisoning), while Max Lorenz is clearly past his prime, making heavy weather of his music throughout *Götterdämmerung*.

Ludwig Weber's keen Fasolt is indeed welcome, but surprisingly, in taking on all four principal bass roles, Fasolt, Hunding, Fafner (in *Siegfried*) and Hagen, he tires somewhat as the cycle progresses, showing distinct fatigue in *Götterdämmerung*. Apparently he was a distinguished Hagen; it is regrettable this reading does not show him at his best. Some of the other principals in the cast are Alois Pernerstorfer as Alberich, Peter Markwort as Mime, Joachim Sattier as Loge; Elisabeth Hongen as Fricka, the *Siegfried* Erda and the *Götterdämmerung* Waltraute; Albert Emmerich as Fafner (in *Rheingold*); Margret Weth-Falke as the *Rheingold* Erda and the First Norn; and Gunther Treptow and Hilde Konetzni as an uneven but sometimes exciting Siegmund and Sieglinde pair, with Konetzni also taking over as Gutrune and the Third Norn. Overall, this is a variable lineup, and the cuts can grate after a while. But Furtwängler is incandescent throughout, despite a relatively indifferent La Scala orchestra, and it is a rare treat to have a fully staged occasion like this one with Furtwängler at his most energized. This has been available on a number of specialty labels, including Music & Arts which probably boasts the best transfer to date.

Although Furtwängler's second *Ring* cycle, from RAI studios, 1953, cannot boast the same energy as a fully staged performance, nor the kind of vocal peaks offered by the likes of a Flagstad Brünnhilde, the overall cast is in fact generally preferable, with fewer lapses in quality. In addition, the restoration of all the cut passages is also welcome. This has been made available on EMI, and the general sound quality is preferable to the Scala broadcast. Again, the orchestral playing is strictly average. Perhaps some prospective listeners may look askance at Martha Mödl's Brünnhilde, especially after Kirsten Flagstad's, but in fact the voice is in good shape for the most part, and there are moments when Mödl conveys a poignancy of feeling second to none. An inspired artist. Ludwig Suthaus's Siegfried is not as attractive as Svanholm's, but since Radio Italiana (RAI) chose to broadcast the cycle one act a day, Suthaus does not encounter the fatigue problems Svanholm does, and he is in better command of the music than Lorenz. Frantz repeats his stalwart Wotan, and here we have his Wanderer as well.

With this cast filled out by the likes of Gustav Neidlinger for the *Rheingold* Alberich (Pernerstorfer is back for *Siegfried* and *Götterdämmerung*); Julius Patzak as the most musical and brooding Mime on discs; the young Wolfgang Windgassen as Loge and Siegmund; the imposing Margarete Klose as the *Siegfried* Erda, Waltraute and the First Norn; Gottlob Frick as the *Rheingold* Fafner; the radiant Sena Jurinac as Woglinde, the Third Norn and Gutrune; Elisabeth Grümmer as Freia; and even a star of the stature of Rita Streich as the Forest Bird, this whole performance is generally more accomplished and assured than the Scala reading.

That is not to say that there aren't some inequalities here all the same. Both Frickas lack stature to a degree, although Ira Malaniuk in *Rheingold* is at least respectable. Josef Greindl gained some fame at Bayreuth for his assumption of the principal bass roles, but his Fasolt, his *Siegfried* Fafner and his Hagen can sound pretty wobbly here, even though there's no denying the sheer power of his tones; and Ruth Siewert's *Rheingold* Erda hardly matches Klose's Erda in *Siegfried*. Konetzni repeats her Sieglinde in somewhat less fresh a voice than before.

Still, one is grateful to hear Furtwängler performing the uncut score with a more or less respectable cast and in reasonably acceptable sound.

The Solti reading on Decca/London has assumed legendary status, and it is doubtful that Wagner's orchestration has ever sounded more exciting. Solti and the recording's producer, John Culshaw, are to be commended for transferring to disc some of Wagner's precise directions with such meticulous care. One can learn almost every intricacy of the score purely by listening to this recording. There are some casting inequalities, though. With all the inspired insight and tenderness of Hans Hotter's Wotan in *Walküre* and *Siegfried*, his voice, particularly in *Walküre*, is in dire straits. The wobble and the occasionally off-pitch tones can be a trial. In a way, he complements Furtwängler's Ferdinand Frantz. Where Frantz can sound quite exciting when pulling out all the stops, Hotter can convey worlds of sorrow and an intimate history in a mere half-dozen hushed tones. He is especially gifted at this, and for many, that outweighs the vocal flaws. Ultimately, though, this Wotan is an acquired taste. George London's *Rheingold* Wotan can strike one as relatively crude, although there are not the same kinds of vocal problems here that we have in Hotter.

For most listeners, Birgit Nilsson's Brünnhilde is one of the most attractive things in this set. Here we have effortless, fearless top tones, and an abundance of energy throughout that readily matches much that's in the character. She may not have the sumptuous enveloping qualities of a Flagstad, nor the personal vulnerability of a Mödl. But there is rarely any question that here is the possessor of a strong resilient instrument, astonishing where Flagstad's is generous. Windgassen has now graduated to Siegfried and, in the recording studio, his voice usually sounds rested and well-managed. Its innate quality, though, is not the rich and heroic one ideally associated with the role. It is somewhat spindly, even reedy on occasion, and one sometimes has to listen through the instrument to appreciate the aplomb in Windgassen's singing. Apparently, he was brought in after recording sessions with Ernst Kozub revealed indifferent knowledge of the score, however commanding the instrument.

One can be grateful that here we get to hear Neidlinger's Alberich throughout the cycle, a Titanic characterization, chilling, bitter, filled with hate, but also with the capacity to project a true feeling of lament. Some have written of Alberich here as a fallen angel, and one can readily understand why. There is both nobility and squalor inherent in Neidlinger's tones, a masterly paradox that becomes clear upon listening. Unfortunately, his Nibelung sibling, Gerhard Stolze as the *Siegfried* Mime, seems too dependent on "shtick" to convey a rounded character. Evidently his interpretation was more compelling in the theater. Paul Kuen's musical manners as the younger Mime work better, although his voice is not in its first flush. Other assets in Solti's cast are a luxury pair of Frickas in Kirsten Flagstad and Christa Ludwig (who also sings the *Götterdämmerung* Waltraute, sharing it with Brigitte Fassbaender in *Die Walküre*), the terrifying Gottlob Frick repeating his superb Hunding and treating us to possibly one of the most lowering Hagens ever (Kurt Böhme is Fafner throughout and Fasolt is Walter Kreppel), the elegant Set Svanholm as Loge, James King and Regine Crespin as Siegmund and Sieglinde, and Dietrich Fischer-Dieskau and Claire Watson as Gunther and Gutrune. What remains special about this set is the naturalness with which everyone settles into their parts. It's been remarked that, with the vividness of this recording, it's easy to start thinking of Svanholm as Loge, not Svanholm, of Neidlinger as Alberich, not Neidlinger, of Ludwig as Waltraute, not Ludwig, and so on. That is a tribute to Culshaw's determination as a record producer in fashioning such a vivid soundscape for this set.

Essentially, the two Furtwängler sets and the Solti set form the nucleus of the *Ring* discography. Some others are well worthwhile, but it could be argued that many of those are best appreciated in relation to these three.

Naxos has put together a mix-and-match from the fabled Metropolitan broadcasts of the 1930s and early 1940s. There are cuts here, and the sound is only fair. Also, the artistic point of view shifts from the crisp veteran's baton of Artur Bodanzky to the young Erich Leinsdorf (heard in *Die Walküre*). Again, as in the Solti set, we have in *Die Walküre* a classic Wotan past his prime: Friedrich Schorr. But he is much finer, grand even, and almost five years younger, in *Rheingold* and *Siegfried*. Here, it is doubtful if Wotan's music has ever sounded so suave. Schorr projects a Wotan who is ever the patrician, incorporating tenderness where needed, impeccable musical manners, a fine sense of poetry — all within the framework of the lofty persona he has established. He conveys power and authority through austere reserve and great dignity rather than bluster. And the vocal beauty heard in his confrontation scene with Mime sets a standard rarely matched in others. As a bonus, we even get to hear him six years younger as Gunther. The three great Brünnhildes of those years, Helen Traubel, Kirsten Flagstad and Marjorie Lawrence, heard in that order, showcase the abundance of Wagnerian talent at that time. For good measure, we even have two more Brünnhildes heard in other roles: Dorothee Manski sings Freia, Gutrune and the Third Norn, and Astrid Varnay makes her Metropolitan Opera debut as Sieglinde. Siegfried is the indomitable Lauritz

Melchior throughout, in addition to doubling as Siegmund. His Siegfried is unique in that, even though he sometimes plays fast and loose with the notes (though not as recklessly as some have said), he has the inestimable virtue of making this taxing music sound downright easy! He has set a standard no one has yet surpassed. René Maison's Loge, Eduard Habich's Alberich, Karin Branzell and Kerstin Thorborg as Fricka (Thorborg also sings the *Siegfried* Erda), Alexander Kipnis's Hunding, Ludwig Hofmann's Hagen and Editha Fleischer's *Götterdämmerung* Woglinde all enhance a gala cast; and we hear Karl Laufkötter's Mime, Norman Cordon and Emanuel List's Fasolt and Fafner, Doris Doe's *Rheingold* Erda, Flosshilde, the *Walküre* Waltraute and the First Norn, and Kathryn Meisle's *Götterdämmerung* Waltraute.

Bodanzky's conducting has a fluid quality to it, which, to an extent, mirrors Furtwängler more than Solti. But Bodanzky's tempi are extremely quick in places. That plus the isolated spurts of energy he gives to certain passages makes a comparison with Solti equally apt. Bodanzky gives a lean taut reading, though not devoid of lyrical flow. His reading owes something to both conducting schools. Leinsdorf seems much more like Solti in the enthusiasm that drives him to highlight special moments and in somewhat more strict phrasing and accents.

Rudolf Moralt's conducting in a "live" Vienna cycle, from 1948–49, does not have much individuality. This document, available on Gebhardt and Myto, is worthwhile primarily for its *Siegfried*, Act III. We have a vocally stupendous Wotan in Ferdinand Frantz, whose untiring vocal line, though without the tenderness of a Schorr or a Hotter, is as rare as it is welcome, and he is heard here in his absolute prime. Gunther Treptow's Siegfried (he is also heard here as Siegmund, sounding better than at La Scala) boasts strong, clear tones that stand him in good stead for arduous music where, to say the least, the competition is hardly plentiful. Gertrude Grob-Prandl's *Siegfried* Brünnhilde is warm and ringing throughout. When she and Treptow join together for the *Siegfried* duet after Frantz's solid contribution in the first scene, we have experienced something rare in the discography: an uncut third act in the original German with all three principals in strong, fresh voice. Lest we forget, this is arguably the most difficult stretch, vocally, for all the protagonists. The balance of the cycle is variable, with a shallow-toned, quavery Helena Braun as Brünnhilde in *Walküre* (Grob-Prandl takes over in *Siegfried* and *Götterdämmerung*) and a blunt Alberich from Adolf Vogel. But it's worthwhile catching a vocally hale Ludwig Weber, here coming up to expectations as a fine Hagen.

Fritz Stiedry, too, is comparable to Moralt in that he keeps things going efficiently enough, without interposing himself that much, sometimes an asset. His reading can be heard in a New York cycle of a somewhat later vintage (1951) than the starry Naxos cycle. It has been released by Gebhardt.

Held over from the Bodanzky (Leinsdorf) cycle is Karin Branzell, now performing Erda, Astrid Varnay in the same role of Sieglinde, Kirsten Flagstad, although this time she is heard in *Walküre* instead of *Siegfried*, and Helen Traubel, this time in *Siegfried* and *Götterdämmerung*. Svanholm is both Loge and Siegfried, and Ferdinand Frantz is Wotan, but with Hans Hotter doing *Das Rheingold*. Other notables in the cast are the young Jerome Hines as Fasolt, Margaret Harshaw and Blanche Thebom sharing Fricka (Harshaw also takes on the *Götterdämmerung* Waltraute and the Third Norn), Jarmila Novotna as Freia, Erna Berger as Woglinde and the Forest Bird, the young Lucine Amara as Wellgunde, Regina Resnik as Helmwige and Gutrune and Herbert Janssen as Gunther. Also in the cast are Lawrence Davidson and Gerhard Pechner as Alberich (Davidson does *Das Rheingold*), Leslie Chabay and Peter Klein as Mime, and Deszö Ernster as Fafner and Hagen, with Gunther Treptow reprising his Siegmund.

Unlike the Naxos assemblage, these 1951 performances were actually presented as a cycle at the time. This, plus Stiedry's conducting throughout, gives the whole a much more unified feeling than the Naxos sequence. Especially intriguing for the New York audience was the presence of both Kirsten Flagstad and Helen Traubel in the same series.

Josef Keilberth, Clemens Krauss, Hans Knappertsbusch, Rudolf Kempe, Karl Böhm, Pierre Boulez, and Daniel Barenboim have led a number of Bayreuth sets over the ensuing 50 years, from the time of the Neu Bayreuth of the 1950s to the early 1990s. These cycles have been made available on a variety of labels, sometimes limited editions, sometimes commercial. Archipel, Melodram, Foyer, Gala, and Music & Arts have been some of the more venturesome labels, to whom we owe a distinct debt of gratitude. Philips has mass-produced both Böhm and Boulez, and Teldec has released a Barenboim.

Personally, Keilberth strikes this listener as the least distinctive of the seven. We are still fortunate to have some of his performances, since they occasionally catch one or two of the Bayreuth luminaries in exceptionally fresh vocal form. But although conscientious, Keilberth does not have the special gift of imparting a sweep and a clear identity to the whole.

Clemens Krauss somewhat parallels the combination of attributes heard in Bodanzky, although without such brisk tempi. He is also stronger at letting individual textures and colors dominate (although this contrast with Bodanzky could be a function of the so-so sonics in the Bodanzky set). Krauss was a disciple of Richard Strauss (as a conductor), who in turn studied with Hans von Bülow, the first conductor of *Tristan und Isolde*, among other things. Surprisingly, both the Strauss and Krauss styles do not have the same free and improvisatory quality one would expect of a tradition springing from one of Wagner's closest associates. There is, instead, something startlingly unindulgent and no-nonsense about it, alongside the undoubted mastery of lyric flow. Indeed, it's only with the Bayreuth school (Richter, Seidl, Levi, Mottl, and so on) that we come across vivid descriptions of the spontaneous, fluid style reflected in Furtwängler. Perhaps Von Bülow's style was in fact somewhat more "pulled in" than the relaxed style celebrated in a Seidl. After all, von Bülow did come from an earlier generation. Krauss brings a welcome discipline and energy to his conducting, in addition to its distinctive lyricism.

Hans Knappertsbusch is particularly inspired, even though there are some startling ensemble lapses in one or two of his extant sets. Still, when at his best, he equals Furtwängler's combination of flow and drive. The melody is always paramount, and his fluid style remains utterly natural, almost conversational, much of the time. Yes, his tempi can sometimes be slow, but he usually maintains forward momentum for all that. And, when well prepared, his orchestral forces are preferable to Furtwängler's. (The orchestral musicians at Bayreuth are considerably more adept than their Italian counterparts.) In many ways, for a set that combines fine sound and (usually) fine orchestral playing with an approach akin to Furtwängler's, plus the tingle of a live performance, a Knappertsbush *Ring* at Bayreuth is hard to beat. Moreover, Knappertsbusch learned his craft under Hans Richter, who conducted the first *Ring* cycle at Bayreuth in 1876, under the composer's close supervision. And, from contemporary descriptions of Richter, plus Knappertsbusch's own recordings, one gains a picture of a style that has much in common with the Seidl/Mottl tradition. If there is any set that may vie for its centrality with the Furtwängler/Solti sets, it might be one of the Knappertsbusch readings.

A naturalness of flow is what Rudolf Kempe also has, although with somewhat tighter tempi. Although not as individual as his immediate predecessors, it is misleading to peg him as nondescript. In fact, the naturalness and seeming inevitability of much that he does establishes its own special thumbprint. Nothing seems out of place or unduly highlighted, yet details still emerge clearly. Here is a maestro with an instinctive feel for the shape of the Wagnerian phrase.

Karl Böhm is extremely taut in his approach, which is sometimes an asset, sometimes not. The effect sometimes is to "dry out" the score (Bodanzky was also accused of this). While as disciplined as Krauss, and an inheritor of the same von Bülow/Strauss tradition, he does not have Krauss's lyricism. Clearly an accomplished musician, he simply does not have as much warmth (for once, this overused word fits perfectly) as a Krauss, or a Bodanzky, or a Knappertsbusch. Still, this cycle crackles with excitement throughout, and James King, in particular, in repeating his Siegmund, clearly benefits, as compared to his studio effort under Solti.

Pierre Boulez moves in the same direction as Böhm, only further. The clarity of detail and relative absence of portamento, of rounded attacks, is startling. This treatment, though, is remarkable for being extremely singer-friendly. (In fact, one of the problems in this set is just how much the singers here need coddling, despite an abundance of imagination among several of them.) Boulez's interpretive stance hands singers their cues with the greatest clarity; one has the feeling of something that has been swept clean. Some have even regarded the effect as slightly antiseptic. It might be, save that the energy throughout retains a human warmth.

With Daniel Barenboim, we return to a much more fluid style, not heard at Bayreuth for nearly three decades. Here is the mercurial approach of the authentic Wagnerian. Barenboim's is, in fact, an astonishing achievement, boasting some of the finest conducting in the discography. Barenboim knows how to build a scene better than anyone of his generation. He comes close to Knappertsbusch in the genius shown in rendering the steady ratcheting up of tension. And the sonics are also superb.

From Keilberth to Barenboim, about two generations of singers come and go at Bayreuth, affording a fascinating panorama of standards upheld, compromised, then partially restored.

The sheer number of noted Wagnerians across these decades can be pretty daunting. In roughly chronological order, sopranos include Inge Borkh, Astrid Varnay, Rita Streich, Martha Mödl, Regina Resnik (before becoming a contralto), Gré Brouwenstijn, Hilde Scheppan, Ilse Hollweg, Elisabeth Grümmer, Birgit Nilsson, Leonie Rysanek, Ingrid Bjoner, Aase Nordmo-Løvberg, Anja Silja, Erika Köth, Rachel Yakar, Hannelore Bode, Gwyneth Jones, Jeannine Altmeyer, Eva Johansson, Hilde Leidland, Nadine Secunde, Anne Evans and Eva-Maria Bundschuh. Contraltos include Ira Malaniuk, Maria von Ilosvay, Georgine von Milinkovic, Jean Madeira, Rita Gorr, Ursula Boese, Grace Hoffman, Hertha Töpper, Marga Höffgen, Ruth Hesse, Annelies Burmeister, Helga Dernesch (before switching to soprano), Eva Randová, Doris Soffel, Hanna Schwarz, Yvonne Minton, Gabriele Schnaut (before switching to soprano), Gwendolyn Killebrew, Ortrun Wenkel, Linda Finnie, Brigitta Svendén and Waltraud Meier. Tenors include Wolfgang Windgassen, Paul Kuen, Gunther Treptow, Bernd Aldenhoff, Max Lorenz, Gerhard Stolze, Erich Witte, Ramón Vinay, Josef Traxel, Ludwig Suthaus, Sándor Kónya, Fritz Uhl, Jon Vickers, Herold Kraus, Hans Hopf, Erwin Wohlfahrt, James King, Peter Hofmann, René Kollo, Heinz Zednik, Jess Thomas, Siegfried Jerusalem, Helmut Pampuch, Manfred Jung, Graham Clark and Poul Elming. Baritones include Gustav Neidlinger, Otokar Kraus, Zoltán Kelemen, Hermann Becht, Franz Mazura, Günter von Kannen and Bodo Brinkmann. Bass-baritones include Hermann Uhde, Hans Hotter, Theo Adam, Otto Wiener, Thomas Stewart, Jerome Hines (though a bass, heard in a brief stint as a remarkably mellifluous *Walküre* Wotan), Donald McIntyre and John Tomlinson. Basses include Ludwig Weber, Josef Greindl, Kurt Böhme, Arnold van Mill, Gottlob Frick, Martti Talvela, Gerd Nienstedt, Matti Salminen, Bengt Rundgren, Karl Ridderbusch, Fritz Hübner, Matthias Hölle and Philip Kang.

It is not possible to do justice to everyone here, but there are a few whose achievements were honored at the time and where it is possible to single out specific extant performances where they prove especially distinguished.

While Astrid Varnay's Brünnhilde displays a performer of uncommon imagination and an alert musician, her tones do not have the sympathetic qualities of a Flagstad or a Traubel. Moreover, there can be recurrent unsteadiness in her singing and a tendency to hit below the note. Still, one cycle where her instrument, while not particularly warm, sounds in good shape and is adroitly handled is the 1953 *Ring* performances under Clemens Krauss. Here, the line is suaver than in a 1952 performance with Keilberth, for instance, showing that there had been deliberate and diligent work done on her singing that year. The broad phrasing also signals extensive work on her breath control. Fortunately, her habitual attentiveness to words is not at all compromised by this new concentration on vocal discipline. She conveys a strongly individual character throughout, establishing a keen sense of development from Brünnhilde the warrior to Brünnhilde the woman in love to Brünnhilde the wronged woman bent on revenge. Her colleagues include Hans Hotter as Wotan, Wolfgang Windgassen as Siegfried, and Gustav Neidlinger as Alberich.

Martha Mödl did not bring such scrupulous musicianship to the role, nor are her top tones usually as responsive as Varnay's. But when they are, they can actually sound more generous than Varnay's. This is primarily due to the warmer and more giving qualities in the instrument itself. Her legato is also superior to Varnay's. These positive qualities are most in evidence in her rich middle and upper-middle tones. When the occasionally uncomfortable lunges to the top are relatively rare, Mödl can give real pleasure. Essentially, Mödl had been a mezzo with shining but unreliable notes on top. Switching to dramatic soprano proved costly in the long run. But she can be glorious when she is really on. Here is a warm, luscious instrument, capable of an infinite range of color, conveying a rich humanity in all she does. While in reasonably good control in Furtwängler's second *Ring* from 1953, she can be heard in even better shape earlier that year in Bayreuth under Josef Keilberth. Astonishingly, in the *Siegfried*, where the high tessitura ought to cause her the most problems, she delivers one of her finest performances on disc. Yes, some of the passagework is somewhat blurry, there are no trills, and so on. But the flow of rich, steady tone, steeped in the character and conveying an abundance of conflicting feelings, places these forty or so minutes up alongside the most inspiring interpretations we have from anyone at Bayreuth. It could be that the sheer brevity of Brünnhilde's role here accounts for the freedom and relaxation in Mödl's singing. There was no fatigue factor to mar alert concentration on the music and on what it is saying. Certainly, the results are magical. She is heard opposite the Siegfried of Wolfgang Windgassen, with Hans Hotter as Wotan and Gustav Neidlinger as Alberich.

Birgit Nilsson is best heard in the Böhm recording on Philips, a generally finer reading than the one for Solti. While we do not hear the abundance of feeling heard in Mödl, Nilsson shows more variety of expression here than in the recording studio. The influence of a superb director, Wieland Wagner, is also evident. Nilsson may not have the knack of highlighting specific words in the same way Varnay can, but there is the compensation of clearer, more direct tones than we hear in Nilsson's more erratic contemporary. (Surprisingly, considering the relative shortness of the period when their careers overlapped as dramatic sopranos, Varnay and Nilsson were exact contemporaries, both born in 1918.) In this Böhm performance, Theo Adam presents a disconcertingly gutteral Wotan, Wolfgang Windgassen is Siegfried and Gustav Neidlinger sings Alberich.

Gwyneth Jones's Brünnhilde has proved more controversial. In a reading under Pierre Boulez from 1979–80, Jones shows some of the imagination of a Varnay or a Mödl, but also some of the flaws. An effortful top like Mödl and an occasionally unsteady tone like Varnay mar a number of her scenes. But the intrinsic instrument is rich and powerful, rich in its abundance of expression and powerful against her admittedly less than stellar colleagues.

There are even moments when the coloring of the voice is actually beautiful in a generous way that can elude Varnay. An erratic vocalist, Jones is one rare performer who combines sumptuous tone with great imagination. It is regrettable that her many gifts are rarely under impeccable control. This is a Brünnhilde who aims for emotional impact above all. This serves to contrast her, effectively so, with some of her colleagues who seem more attuned (deliberately so) to the sparer emotional world of Pierre Boulez. His principals include Donald McIntyre, Hermann Becht and Manfred Jung as Wotan, Alberich and Siegfried. None of these sport voices anywhere near the caliber of Jones's, particularly Jung, whose Siegfried is particularly weak. But they are all effective actors (see Video Recordings, below).

The last Brünnhilde in this series is Anne Evans. A ready musician, she is distinguished more by adroit navigation of Brünnhilde's music than by any individuality. She is hardly uncommitted, but she is to be commended more for handling the vocal range of her two-octave-plus music with sure resonance throughout. At the same time, there is an occasional tendency to flatness, and the timbral variety of some of her predecessors is lacking. Hers is not as heroic an instrument as some we have heard, but it is not as spindly as some we encounter on video. She is surrounded by uncommonly consistent principals for that period. Günter von Kannen is hardly the world's greatest Alberich, but he is hardly a disgrace. John Tomlinson's Wotan is somewhat stronger, as Wotan should be, and Siegfried Jerusalem offers a highly resilient Siegfried (see below).

When it comes to Siegfried, Wolfgang Windgassen dominated this heldentenor role for almost 20 years. He did so by dint of clever handling of an essentially spinto or *jugendlich* instrument, not through brute vocal strength. Although the Solti cycle discloses an instrument that is occasionally reedy, the instrument has more juice to the tone during much of the 1950s. His younger self can be heard in the two 1953 cycles among others. But neither Keilberth nor Krauss find him as assured with the part as he was later on. Arguably, the best balance between matured experience with the role and still juicy tone is found in the 1956 Knappertsbusch cycle (the first of three Knappertsbusch *Rings*). Here, he is heard opposite the Brünnhilde of Astrid Varnay; Hans Hotter sings Wotan, and Gustav Neidlinger is the incomparable Alberich.

The other Bayreuth Siegfried to hold on to the role for a considerable time is the aptly named Siegfried Jerusalem. With a more attractive instrument than Windgassen, Jerusalem too does not own a traditional heldentenor voice. As with Windgassen, it is solid musicianship that carries him through. Jerusalem's contribution to the Barenboim production is amazingly sure and strong. He is capable of sustaining a lyrical quality while giving crucial heroic passages the sweep they need. Much of this may be due to Barenboim's sympathetic direction, whose inspired phrasing matches Jerusalem's and establishes a rapport rare in the discography. In the *Siegfried*, Jerusalem's one weakness is a tendency to sound throaty on occasion and to lapse into an overly emphatic attack here and there. But he stays the course and produces a melting performance for most of the final duet. The *Siegfried* is from 1992, but *Götterdämmerung* comes from 1991, and Jerusalem's is easily one of the finest *Götterdämmerung* Siegfrieds on disc in the last 25 years. Here, he fulfills his potential, delivering his finest performance of all, totally within the character, utterly musical from beginning to end, achieving the almost impossible task of rousing our sympathy for the essentially reactive character that Siegfried has now become.

During the first decade at Neu Bayreuth, Hermann Uhde and Hans Hotter shared the roles of Wotan. While contemporary accounts from those who attended usually single out Hotter as the more considerable interpreter, later generations not acquainted with the impact of these two on stage may find Uhde preferable. Certainly, as an aural experience, Uhde offers by far the steadier tone and the cleaner line. Furthermore, he is hardly an indifferent vocal actor, imparting great sorrow where needed and surpassing majesty to the climactic passages. He is heard in the Kempe recording in fine voice, where he emerges as one of the most effective Wotans of the whole Bayreuth series. Jerome Hines takes over from him for *Walküre* only, where his *bel canto* approach almost matches Uhde's. Others in the cast include Otokar Kraus as Alberich, Astrid Varnay and Birgit Nilsson as Brünnhilde (Varnay appears only in the *Walküre*), and Hans Hopf as Siegfried.

When it comes to Hans Hotter, listening to him is so different from seeing him that the listener may prefer to go with a choice where the health of his instrument is the prime consideration. He was always a telling vocal actor in any case, so one already has a thoroughly internalized reading from the moment Neu Bayreuth first opens its doors. Fortunately, we do have a relatively fresh-sounding Wotan from him in 1952 under Keilberth, although Uhde is heard in that *Rheingold*. Others in the cast are Astrid Varnay for Brünnhilde, Bernd Aldenhoff and Max Lorenz, two problematic Siegfrieds, and Gustav Neidlinger offering his always superb Alberich. If one wants to hear Hotter's Wotan throughout, one can choose the strong Clemens Krauss reading referenced above, where Hotter is still effective, even though his tones are not quite as easy as the year before. The most wonderful moments are those where Wotan's inner suffering is revealed. There is less strain here, and the spirit of a poet shines through. Hotter trusts Wagner's words implicitly, and the results, given the healthier instrument heard during these years, are infinitely preferable to the meal he can sometimes make of things under Solti.

The next generation sees basses taking over the part more. Donald McIntyre and John Tomlinson certainly sound like basses at any rate, and the upper register can be a bit of a stretch for both. McIntyre is heard with Boulez (see above), and, despite his great intelligence and commitment, we cannot count this one of his more successful appearances. The strain is pretty evident throughout. (For McIntyre at his best, sample one of his few rare outings in the bass repertoire: a studio Gurnemanz in *Parsifal* under Sir Reginald Goodall, made a number of years after this Wotan, shows that, thankfully, his instrument had not sustained irrevocable damage.)

John Tomlinson, too, is more bass than bass-baritone, but he is more assured at fielding the tricky heights in this role than McIntyre. There is still occasional strain on top, but clever phrasing helps integrate these dubious moments reasonably well. And that *sine qua non* of the better Wotans, an enlarging tenderness, is sometimes his as well; not to the same degree as an Uhde, a Hotter or a Schorr; but it's there nevertheless, and one is grateful to close this retrospective of Bayreuth highlights with a performance of such musicality and imagination. He can be heard on the Barenboim set.

The impact of the Solti set seemed to serve as a challenge to Herbert von Karajan. While preparing his Salzburg production, he committed his reading of the cycle to disc for DG, between 1966 and 1970. Despite the relative lack of a compelling emotional message in the Karajan recording, he at least strikes us as more "tuned in" to the flow of the musical line than is Solti. That doesn't necessarily mean he's better, since sheer dramatic excitement counts for much in the Solti, and with Karajan lacking some of that, his reading is still flawed. But if we go back to what has oriented this survey from the outset, Karajan tends to show more earmarks of the Seidl school than we hear in Solti.

An interpretation that is long on lyrical and poetic beauty, short on galvanic energy, pays off best in *Die Walküre*, where the relatively intimate quality of the drama and the sorrowful accents of the music yield huge dividends when approached in this way. Some observers regard Karajan's as the "chamber-music" *Ring*, and if there's any opera of Wagner's tetralogy that could be termed a domestic drama, it is *Die Walküre*. That, plus the happy accident that everyone in this *Walküre* is heard in fresh voice, makes this probably the finest installment in the Karajan cycle.

What remains attractive in Karajan's *Ring* here is a surprising emphasis on a compact, musical, vocal line, even though the voices as such are not uniformly rich and powerful. Equally surprising is the sympathetic way Zoltán Kelemen presents Alberich. Nobility is the dominant impression. That, along with two Wotans—Dietrich Fischer-Dieskau in *Rheingold* and Thomas Stewart in *Walküre*—who tend toward the gruff and the emphatic, throws one's usual sympathies off balance. This is less so in *Walküre*, where Alberich is not heard from and where Stewart tones down some of the emphasis, but it is startling hearing the theft in *Rheingold*, Scene 4 enacted in noble tones by Kelemen and predatory accents by Fischer-Dieskau. The magnitude of Wotan now turning thief is brought home forcefully, especially with Alberich sung so sympathetically.

Jess Thomas can also sustain fine sympathy in certain of his recordings, but, as with Windgassen and Jerusalem, his young Siegfried is more a *jugendlich* than a heldentenor. And unlike Windgassen and Jerusalem, the strain shows more. Hearing him in person made one less aware of a growing unsteadiness in the tone at that time. But DG's mikes mercilessly expose the results of his taking on Siegfried and Tristan. Attractive phrases alternate with uncomfortable moments where a tremolo is very evident. He continued with this demanding repertoire for quite a while after this recording was made, and he continued being effective in the house. The innate attractiveness of his vocal timbre and his musical phrasing stood him in good stead. An excellent presence on stage and a likable stage persona also counted for much, but the listener, if not the spectator, ends up missing the needed security in this music. Helge Brilioth does much better in the *Götterdämmerung*. He may not have the insight or the variety of some others, but the sturdy vocalism is welcome. He may not project much character, but the natural conversational style he and Karajan adopt works well in context. The result is shapely and musical throughout.

Régine Crespin and Helga Dernesch share Brünnhilde, Dernesch taking over for *Siegfried* and *Götterdämmerung*. Crespin and Dernesch both give much more vulnerable readings of this role than is the norm, and the warm loveliness of Dernesch's instrument at that time seemed a welcome contrast to the haughtier tones of Nilsson. There wasn't just one way to deliver this role after all. Dernesch, like Mödl before her, had started as a mezzo (see roster of Bayreuth contraltos above), but her top here is actually considerably easier than Mödl's ever was, notwithstanding her having eventually to give up the soprano repertory altogether by the 1980s. Crespin as well eventually switched to mezzo. But she started out as a soprano, and her voice is still fresh and vibrant in this *Walküre*.

In fact, it's salutary to recall here Karajan's entire *Walküre* cast, since it may be the most consistently vocalized reading on disc. Others may have grander peaks, but the consistent musicality here stamps this offering as at least preferable, by and large, to the Solti *Walküre*. In order of appearance, Siegmund and Sieglinde are Jon Vickers and Gundula Janowitz, and Hunding is Martti Talvela. Alongside Crespin's Brünnhilde, a mellowed Thomas Stewart sings Wotan, and Fricka is Josephine Veasey.

A curiosity, somewhat off the beaten track, is an account conducted by Hans Swarowsky, made in 1968. Aspects of this recording are fairly slipshod, but there are some attractive voices, even though their performances are occasionally sketchy at best. Most striking, the tenor singing Siegfried has a genuinely attractive timbre, and one has to wonder why he is not better known: Gerald McKee. Yes, many details of his reading are certainly improvisatory, to say the least, but this is a real talent, and, if not the most profound of interpretations, there are many far worse, vocally. Nadezda Kniplova sings Brünnhilde, Rolf Polke Wotan, and Rolf Kühne Alberich.

Sir Reginald Goodall's set is not off the beaten track, particularly when it comes to Goodall's own place in the hierarchy. Furthermore, there's some handsome singing through-out this set that rewards close listening. This one, though, can never be slotted as a reference, fine as it is, since it is sung in English translation. That aside, Goodall's contribution is thor-oughly within the Seidl/Mottl tradition. He may not always sustain the tension of a Furtwän-gler, a Knappertsbusch or a Barenboim at their best, but his control of the musical flow is actually superior to Barenboim's, for instance, and his mastery of transition and the "endless melody" is awe-inspiring. Tempi are another matter. Even slower than Knappertsbusch, cer-tain of the scenes can lose some impact. Yet, while the last act of *Siegfried* is sometimes as slow as any sequence in this set, it functions triumphantly as the climactic sequence of the whole performance. Here, tension and melody and flow come together marvelously. And Alberto Remedios as Siegfried and Rita Hunter as Brünnhilde truly *sing* that closing duet. They don't scream it, approximate it, or bark it. Better yet, they sing it with true attentive-ness to the meaning of what they're singing. While we may regret the English translation, it is quite likely that their alertness to meaning was significantly helped by singing this in their native language.

The Goodall entry is a triumph of ensemble, and the absorption of these artists in their roles and the way they relate to each other demonstrate the care with which Goodall prepared his principals. Norman Bailey may not be the most attractive-voiced Wotan on disc, but he's at least musical and direct, and Derek Hammond-Stroud's Alberich is especially effective in those scenes where he must stand up to the god. A worthy recording and a worthy memento of a conductor whose grasp of this cycle places him among the top interpreters.

Marek Janowski's reading for Eurodisc in 1980–83 is at an opposite pole, though not necessarily bad for all that. Details are sometimes deftly applied and there is a welcome sense of commitment evident at crucial moments, such as the opening measures of *Siegfried*, Act 3, where Janowski's mastery of detail strongly pays off. What he lacks is consistent mastery of mood, certain moments becoming segmented off from the whole. Unfortunately, Janowski's Wotan, Theo Adam, is consistently guttural and over-emphatic throughout. Kollo's Siegfried at least has the advantage of an attractive instrument, but there are some signs of wear, and he occasionally resorts to over-emphasis as well. At the same time, there are moments where Kollo conveys a solid understanding of his role, sustaining our sympathy at certain critical moments in *Siegfried* most especially. On the other hand, Jeannine Altmeyer's Brünnhilde, however sloppy she sometimes is, does have the advantage of a consistently warm sound used with some heart. She is not a world-beater, but in this company her shining tones are a wel-come relief from other afflictions. Fortunately, Siegmund Nimsgern's Alberich is not one of those afflictions. Here is a strong presence, guided with sure musical control and exerting the charisma needed in his confrontations with Wotan (not hard to make an impact, given Adam's travails). Other individual performers are welcome here as well, even though, taken together, they do not add up to as compelling a reading as one might expect. It is nice to welcome Matti Salminen's pulverizing Hagen and Fafner in this recording, along with Yvonne Minton's attractive Fricka, Lucia Popp's Woglinde, Hanna Schwarz's Flosshilde and the Siegmund and Sieglinde of Siegfried Jerusalem and Jessye Norman.

James Levine's reading for DG is marked by a meticulously prepared Metropolitan orches-tra and a tendency to excel at individual moments rather than a larger sweep. But those indi-vidual moments can be quite compelling. His tempi are on the slow side, though not as slow as Goodall's, for instance. What he seems to lack is the thread that links the more slowly played sections together. Goodall, for all his occasional lack of energy, rarely leaves one under the impression that the music has no clear trajectory.

Levine's soloists are generally distinguished, sometimes more than that. Ekkehard Wlaschiha is *the* great Alberich who follows in the footsteps of his great predecessor, Gustav Neidlinger. He inherits from him the capacity to be spine-tinglingly mean yet musical at the same time. With a staggering range that conquers the heights and depths of this music with ease, he is also a born actor's actor, making every moment alive and painfully honest. Everything here counts, and all is integrated superbly into a gripping portrayal of one with limited vision, but with longings that are no less painful for being inchoate and tantalizing. Wlashiha's Alberich is a creature only half-formed inside, frighteningly and brilliantly so. Christa Ludwig's Fricka is also about the pain of rejection. We have already encountered her Fricka in the Solti *Walküre* twenty years earlier. Remarkably, she is still going strong here, and, wonder of wonders, the portrayal has even developed beyond where it was in the 1960s, not just dramatically but vocally. There is a keener sense of personal injury now, yielding more fiery climaxes and an even more dejected sense of quietude when (momentarily) defeated. This is carried into her *Rheingold* Fricka, and we are grateful to hear this unique artist develop the entire role so inevitably from a still loving but uneasy beloved to a bitter, hurt mistress of a loveless home. By now, Jessye Norman's vocal reserves seem infinite, and the grandeur she gives to Sieglinde may be unique. But is it desirable? In the last act, it's hard to conceive that the more slender-voiced Brünnhilde of Hildegard Behrens can offer succour to a heroic Sieglinde like this! But perhaps it's unfair to demur at a Sieglinde for the Brünnhilde who sings at her side. After all, Wagner originally wanted for Sieglinde Marianne Brandt, an artist who, like Norman, alternated soprano and mezzo and had an enormous range. Norman fully answers that description, and it's revelatory to hear the most taxing passages in this role done with such ease. This set also boasts Golden-Age quality basses, with Kurt Moll singing Fasolt, Hunding, and the *Siegfried* Fafner, and Matti Salminen repeating his superb Hagen. In fact, this Hagen has now developed into a towering portrayal, on a par with Wlaschiha's Alberich and Ludwig's Fricka. In *Siegfried* and *Götterdämmerung*, four fine artists appear for the first time in this cycle: Kathleen Battle as a sparkling Forest Bird, Cheryl Studer as an involved and involving Gutrune, Hanna Schwarz as a vivid and always musical Waltraute and Helga Dernesch as one of the grandest First Norns on disc.

And the top three principals? Equivocal. Granted, one doubts that sheer vocal fitness has ever been matched to Wotan's music more aptly than in James Morris's performance. He is also able to obey all of Wagner's demanding phrase markings without exception. There is, though, an occasional lack of variety to his singing. Everything is intoned authoritatively, even menacingly sometimes. The effect can be a trifle wearing. Nevertheless, it's still a relief after hearing so many Wotans strangling on the music. If there's any demur vocally, it's a tendency to throatiness in the lowest notes. Behrens' Brünnhilde may seem spindly alongside Norman's Sieglinde and Morris's imposing Wotan, but she brings considerable heart to her portrayal and much variety of shading. The spindliness is felt most in passages with a lower tessitura. Here, choppiness of line and distinct unsteadiness take over. Reiner Goldberg's Siegfried shows signs of a once-handsome instrument, but failure to capitalize on its expressive potential and a few downright unattractive sounds strongly suggest a fading ability to control it.

Bernard Haitink establishes more of a through-line to the score than we hear from Levine. Not as incandescent as Barenboim at his best, there is still something very steady and reassuring to this reading. Nothing seems out of place; all is in proportion. A rare gift.

This set reverses the Karajan pattern of a noble Alberich and a gruff Wotan with a vengeance: we repeat James Morris's imposing Wotan just heard under Levine, and Alberich is sung by a former Wotan, but a distinctly guttural one, Theo Adam. We hear Goldberg again, but this time as Siegmund, and Cheryl Studer is an appealing Sieglinde. Matti Salminen has switched roles as well, this time singing a superb Hunding. Marjana Lipovsek and Waltraud Meier are a formidable pair of Frickas (Lipovsek comes back as the *Götterdämmerung* Waltraute), and we have a shimmering Forest Bird from Kiri Te Kanawa. The rare presence of a *bel canto* and Mozart specialist for Gunther, Thomas Hampson, gives the role an uncommon elegance, affording a rich contrast with the plainer vocal style of John Tomlinson's Hagen.

Unfortunately, Eva Marton's Brünnhilde is afflicted with a wobble and pitch problems. Even beyond this, the vocal palette is essentially loud and louder, making it hard to discern any real interpretation. Possibly this is the sad result of a lost opportunity, since Marton made a positive impression in the hall earlier in her career; and perhaps she could have contributed a vocally stronger Brünnhilde earlier, if not a more fully thought-out one. Oddly, though Jerusalem's Siegfried shows clearly better musicianship than his partner's, he does not deliver the role in the same winning way of his Bayreuth reading. What makes this especially odd is that his unsatisfactory older Siegfried here, which was arguably the finest achievement of the Barenboim cycle, comes from 1991, the same year as the Barenboim performance.

Some more recent sets feature various unknowns, singers who have yet to make their mark internationally. From Karlsruhe, 1993–95, Günter Neuhold conducts a performance featuring Carla Pohl as Brünnhilde, John Wegner as Wotan, Wolfgang Neumann and Edward Cook sharing Siegfried, and Oleg Bryjak as Alberich. It is a delight to single out Mette Ejsing's deeply stirring Erda in *Rheingold*.

Even more recent, made around the turn of this century, is Gustav Kuhn's account on Arte Nova. Here, Elena Cornotti, Elisabeth-Maria Wachutka and Eva Silberbauer are the three Brünnhildes; the Wotans are Albert Dohmen, Duccio dal Monte and Juha Uusitalo; and Alberich is Andrea Martin. This set is most notable for the Siegfried of Alan Woodrow. He is not the most scrupulous of singers, but his voice shows tremendous promise, combining as it does lyricism and dramatic strength. One to watch closely.

Video Recordings

The *Ring* on Video has not had nearly as long a history as it has in audio recordings, but one or two of the offerings have made quite an impact, starting with the Boulez production from Bayreuth already discussed. Not only Boulez but this performance's producer, Patrice Chéreau, stripped the work of much of its traditional Romantic rhetoric. Chéreau presented it as an allegory of the capitalist world, partly taking his cue from George Bernard Shaw's study of the *Ring* cycle, *The Perfect Wagnerite*. This meant a gritty presentation with the characters nowhere near as noble as usually seen. Wotan especially becomes more the ruthless captain of industry than anything else.

Presented this way, the spotty singing works somewhat better than as purely an aural experience on one's sound system. *Walküre* becomes very powerful in this reading, because both Siegmund and Sieglinde are especially vulnerable to all the cruel intrigue around them. They are never more victims than in this staging, and both Peter Hofmann and the winning Jeannine Altmeyer become extremely sympathetic figures. *Walküre* is the high spot of this video.

Perhaps intended as a strong corrective to this was the Metropolitan Opera production, introduced in the late 1980s, where Otto Schenk, its producer, presented a performance far closer to Wagner's original staging than any other production of that time or now. (The Metropolitan still gives it to this day.) The video comes from 1989–90. We see here an entirely traditional staging, and some of the outdoor scenes are actually quite enticing. Characterization, though, is more spotty than in the Boulez. Certain interpreters, Wlaschiha as Alberich, Ludwig as Fricka and Salminen as Hagen, are as strong dramatically as they are vocally, very much like their performances on the Levine CD. But, even when one of the principals might be utterly in his part, the rapport between that artist and someone else on stage can fall into the routine. One rarely forgets one is watching singers singing, not the case with the Boulez.

Of course, the overpowering presence of James Morris as Wotan becomes enormously effective on video. Perhaps not the most insightful of Wotans, he is never less than credible as this implacable figure, initially blind to his own frailties. I find that his best work is in *Rheingold*, where the conflict between "Lord of the Manor" (so to speak) and his own careless greed is most in evidence. Complexity of inner torment (which overtakes him later on) may not draw on Morris's greatest strengths. The chief difference between this video and the Levine CD is in its Siegfried. Instead of Goldberg, we have Siegfried Jerusalem. Again, curiously enough, Jerusalem fails to live up to his superb command of the role under Barenboim. There is considerable effort, and he sounds sorely fatigued in spots. And, again, as with his disappointing showing under Haitink, this was made around the same time as the Barenboim; frustrating.

From Munich, around the same time, we have a more avant-garde production under Wolfgang Sawallisch. The producer is Nikolaus Lehnhoff. Location, both of place and time, is hard to pin down here. Futuristic images alternate with Art Deco to produce a weird assortment of contrasts that sometimes collide with each other in an odd way. But the characterization and the interaction of the principals are worked out brilliantly.

First and foremost is the *Walküre* confrontation between Wotan and Fricka. Robert Hale and Marjana Lipovsek depict a couple who know exactly how to get under each other's skin. And deeply resentful as Lipovsek's Fricka is, there is the slight hint that Fricka, at least, enjoys doing that. Wit and hair-raising bitterness combine here in a theatrical *tour de force*. All the principals here are similarly attuned to their parts; in no particular order: Hildegard Behrens presents an even more multi-faceted Brünnhilde than with Otto Schenk, and her vocalism is somewhat cleaner as well. Ekkehard Wlaschiha's Alberich is simply tremendous from beginning to end. Unfortunately, René Kollo's Siegfried is caught far too late. He is frequently flat and unsteady, with badly pressured tone throughout. Here is a true artist who thoroughly understands his role, a careful musician. It's a shame his vocal travails should cast such a pall over a finely judged interpretation — and over a generally brilliant production as well. This performance is also available on CD, from EMI.

Finally, it's useful to view a video of the Barenboim performance. This production was by Harry Kupfer, and here too the production has gone in for certain distinctly futuristic effects. In addition, there is something hard and cold about the decor. But the characterizations are sometimes deeply touching, and this presentation has the triple virtue of having consistently respectable, if not uniformly sumptuous, singing throughout (unlike the previous videos from Bayreuth and Munich), thoroughly worked-out characterizations (unlike the Levine video) and superb conducting.

Probably the most emotional moment, albeit utterly unsanctioned by the original, is a chance meeting between Wotan and Brünnhilde during the most wrenching themes of the Funeral Music in the final act of the whole cycle. Gazing sorrowfully at the slain Siegfried, they quietly comfort each other. This image has dominated my recall of the entire production ever since I saw it. Unforgettable. What with Jerusalem being at his finest in *Götterdämmerung*; with this moment for Wotan and Brünnhilde in the final act; with Evans, who can be uneven, also smartening up somewhat in this installment; and with Barenboim at his most inspired, this cycle ends on an exalted plane unmatched by any other video presentation. There are bumps along the way, but the cumulative effect of this performance, despite the eccentricities of decor, make the bumps entirely worthwhile. This is a *Ring* cycle to see and see again.

Bibliography

The following list of sources represent those that I have found most valuable, as background information and as actual renditions of the Ring.

Audio and Video Resources

EMI Records. *Ring des Nibelungen, Vol. 60* (Compact Disc). International Masters. 1999.
Jenkins, Speight. *Enjoying Wagner's Ring* (4 Audio Cassettes). HighBridge, June 1996.
The Ring Disc: An Interactive Guide to Wagner's Ring Cycle. (CD) Complete Solti recording, piano-vocal score, German/English libretto, analysis of leitmotifs, commentary, essays, production photos, search functions. (Pentium processor PC and Windows 95 or Windows NT. New pressing states, "Macintosh users: Ring Disc runs fine on G3 Mac with Virtual PC & 64 MB RAM.")

Books, Librettos, and Music

Aberbach, Alan David. *Ideas of Richard Wagner: An Examination and Analysis of His Major Aesthetic, Political, Economic, Social, and Religious Thoughts* (revised). Lanham, Md.: University Press of America, 1987.

Bassett, Peter. *The Nibelung's Ring: A Guide to Wagner's* Der Ring des Nibelungen. Australia: Wakefield, 2004.

Besack, Michael. *The Esoteric Wagnerå: An Introduction to* Der Ring Des Nibelungen*: Esoteric Journeys through Poetry and Song.* Oakland: Regent, 2004.

Björnsson, Árni. *Wagner and the Walsungs: Icelandic Sources of Der Ring des Nibelungen.* Trans. Anna Yates and Anthony Faulkes. London: Viking Society for Northern Research, 2003.

Bolen, Jean Shinoda. *Ring of Power: The Abandoned Child, the Authoritarian Father, and the Disempowered Feminine.* San Francisco: HarperSanFrancisco, 1993.

_____. *Ring of Power: Symbols and Themes, Love vs. Power in Wagner's Ring Cycle and in Us.* York Beach, Me.: Nicolas-Hays, 1999.

Brink, Louise. *Women Characters in Richard Wagner: A Study in the Ring of the Nibelung.* New York: St. Martin's, 1974.

Buller, Jeffrey L. *Classically Romantic: Classical Form and Meaning in Wagner's Ring.* Philadelphia: Xlibris, 2001.

Caggiano, Philip, ed. *Ring: Four Plays for Children.* New York: William Morrow, 1982.

Cicora, Mary A. *Mythology as Metaphor: Romantic Irony, Critical Theory, and Wagner's Ring.* Westport: Greenwood, 1998.

_____. *Wagner's Ring and German Drama: Comparative Studies in Mythology and History in Drama.* Westport: Greenwood, 1999.

Cooke, Deryck. *I Saw the World End: A Study of Wagner's Ring.* London/New York: Oxford University Press, 1992.

Cord, William O. *An Introduction to Richard Wagner's Der Ring des Nibelungen: A Handbook* (revised second edition). Athens: Ohio University Press, 1995.

_____. *Teutonic Mythology of Richard Wagner's "The Ring of the Nibelung" Vol. 1: Nine Properties.* Lewiston, N.Y.: Edwin Mellen, 1989.

_____. *Teutonic Mythology of Richard Wagner's "The Ring of the Nibelung." Vol. 2: The Family of Gods.* Lewiston, N.Y.: Edwin Mellen, 1990.

_____. *Teutonic Mythology of Richard Wagner's "The Ring of the Nibelung." Vol. 3: The Natural and Supernatural Worlds.* Lewiston, N.Y.: Edwin Mellen, 1990.

_____. *201 Questions (and Answers) on* Der Ring des Nibelungen (2nd Ed., revised). San Francisco: The Wagner Society of Northern California, 1998.

Corse, Sandra. *Wagner and the New Consciousness: Language and Love in the Ring.* Rutherford: Fairleigh Dickinson University Press, 1990.

Culshaw, John. *Reflections on Wagner's Ring.* New York: Viking, 1976.

_____. *Ring Resounding* (First Limelight edition). New York: Amadeus, 1987.

Darcy, Warren. *Wagner's Das Rheingold* (reprint). New York: Oxford University Press, 1996.

Day, David and Lee, Alan (illus.). *Tolkien's Ring.* New York: Barnes & Noble, 1999.

De Rico, Ul and Solti, Georg. *The Ring of the Nibelung.* New York: Thames & Hudson, 1980.

Deathridge, John, and Dahlhaus, Carl. *The New Grove Wagner.* New York: Norton, 1984.

DiGaetani, John Louis (ed.). *Penetrating Wagner's Ring: An Anthology* (reprint). New York: Da Capo, 1991

_____. *Wagner and Suicide.* Jefferson, N.C.: McFarland, 2003.

Donington, Robert. *Wagner's 'Ring' and Its Symbols: The Music and the Myth* (third edition). London: Faber and Faber, 1974.

Ewans, Michael. *Wagner and Aeschylus: The Ring and the Oresteia.* New York: Cambridge University Press, 1983.

Fay, Stephen. *The Ring.* Dover, N.H.: Longwood, 1985.

Fisher, Burton D. *Exploring Wagner's Ring.* Coral Gables: Opera Journeys, 2000.

_____. *Wagner's The Ring of the Nibelung.* Coral Gables: Opera Journeys, 2002.

Fricke, Richard. *Wagner in Rehearsal, 1875–1876* [from his diaries]. Trans. G. Fricke. Stuyvesant, N.Y.: Pendragon, 1996.

Highwater, Jamake. *Dark Legend.* Bridgewater, N.J.: Replica, 1999.

Hollander, Lee M., ed. and trans. *The Poetic Edda.* Austin: University of Texas Press, 1986.

Holman, J. K. K. *Wagner's Ring: A Listener's Companion and Concordance* (Foreword by Peter Allen). Portland, Ore.: Amadeus, 1996.

Horowitz, Joseph. *Wagner Nights: An American History (California Studies in 19th Century Music,* No 9). Berkeley: University of California Press, 1994.

Kitcher, Philip and Schacht, Richard. *Finding an Ending: Reflections on Wagner's Ring.* Oxford/NewYork: Oxford University Press, 2004.

Kobbé, Gustav. *How to Understand Wagner's Ring of the Nibelung.* New York: AMS, 1976.

Lee, M. Owen. *Athena Sings: Wagner and the Greeks.* Toronto: University of Toronto Press, 2003.

_____. *Wagner's Ring: Turning the Sky Round* (first Limelight Edition). New York: Amadeus, 1994.

Levin, David J. *Richard Wagner, Fritz Lang, and the Nibelungen: The Dramaturgy of Disavowal.* Princeton: Princeton University Press, 2000.

Littlejohn, David. *Ultimate Art: Essays Around and About Opera.* Berkeley: University of California Press, 1994.

Magee, Bryan. *Aspects of Wagner* (second edition). Oxford/New York: Oxford University Press, 1988.

_____. *The Philosophy of Schopenhauer* (with appendix: "Wagner and Schopenhauer"; revised, enlarged). Oxford/New York: Oxford University Press, 1997.

Magee, Elizabeth. *Richard Wagner and the Nibelungs.* Oxford/New York: Oxford University Press, 1991.

McMullen, Jim (illus.) and Robb, Stewart (trans.). *The Ring of the Nibelung* (Der Ring des Nibelungen). New York: Penguin, 1960.

Millington, Barry. *Wagner* (revised). Princeton: Princeton University Press, 1992.

_____. (Ed.) and Spencer, Stewart (ed. and trans.) *Wagner in Performance.* New Haven: Yale University Press, 1992.

Newman, Ernest. *Wagner Operas* (reprint). Princeton: Princeton University Press, 1991.

_____. *Wagner Operas, Vol. 1* (second edition; first Harper Colophon edition). London: HarperCollins, 1983.

_____. *Wagner Operas, Vol. 2* (first Harper Colophon edition). London: HarperCollins, 1983.

Nibelungenlied (unabridged), trans. D. G. Mowatt. Mineola: Dover, 2001.

Medieval Epics: Beowulf, the Niebelungenlied, the Song of Roland, and the Cid (Modern Library Series), trans. W. S. Merwin, Helen M. Mustard, and William Alfred. New York: Random House, 1998.

Ostwald, Peter F. and Zegans, Leonard S., eds. *Threat to the Cosmic Order: Psychological, Social and Health Implications of Richard Wagner's Ring of the Nibelung.* (first edition). Madison, Ct.: International Universities Press, 1997.

Porges, Heinrich and Jacobs, Robert L. (trans.) *Wagner Rehearsing the Ring: An Eye-Witness Account of the Stage Rehearsals of the First Bayreuth Festival.* Cambridge: Cambridge University Press, 1983.

Porter, Andrew (trans.) and Fraser, Eric (illus.). *The Ring of the Nibelung* (Der Ring des Nibelungen). Libretto: English and German (first edition; first American edition). New York: Norton, 1976.

_____. *Der Ring des Nibelungen* (Ring of the Nibelung). Libretto: German and English. New York: Norton, 1977.

_____ and John, Nicholas (ed.). *Das Rheingold* (The Rheingold). Libretto in German and English. New York: Riverrun, 1986.

_____ and _____. *Die Walküre* (The Valkyrie). Libretto in German and English. New York: Riverrun, 1990.

_____ and _____. *Siegfried.* Libretto in German and English. New York: Riverrun, 1984.

_____ and _____. *Götterdämmerung* (Twilight of the Gods). Libretto in German and English. New York: Riverrun, 1984.

Rackham, Arthur (illus.) and Armour, Margaret (trans.). *Der Ring des Nibelungen* (The Ring of the Nibelung). Librettos: English & German (2-volume Set). New York: Abaris, 1976.

_____ and Spero, James (illus.). *Rackham's Color Illustrations for Wagner's Ring*, Based on Work by Richard Wagner. Mineola: Dover, 1991.

Richardson, Herbert Warren. *New Studies in Richard Wagner's "The Ring of the Nibelung."* Lewiston, N.Y.: Edwin Mellen, 1992.

Russell, P. Craig and Mason, Patrick (trans.). *The Ring of the Nibelung Volume 1.* Portland, Ore.: Dark Horse Comics, 2002.

Sabor, Rudolph (trans.). *Richard Wagner, Der Ring des Nibelungen.* Librettos with Translations and Commentaries, Boxed 5-Volume Set. London: Phaidon, 1997.

_____. *Richard Wagner, Der Ring des Nibelungen.* A Companion Volume. London: Phaidon, 1997.

_____. *Das Rheingold.* Translation and Commentary (Libretto in German and English). London: Phaidon, 1997.

_____. *Die Walküre* (The Valkyrie). Translation and Commentary (Libretto in German and English). London: Phaidon, 1997.

_____. *Siegfried.* Translation and Commentary (Libretto in German and English). London: Phaidon, 1997.

_____. *Götterdämmerung* (Twilight of the Gods). Translation and Commentary (Libretto in German and English). London: Phaidon, 1997

Shaw, George Bernard. *Major Critical Essays: The Quintessence of Ibsenism, The Perfect Wagnerite, The Sanity of Art.* New York: Penguin, 1990.

_____. *The Perfect Wagnerite: A Commentary on the Niblung's Ring.* New York: Dover, 1967.

Spencer, Stewart. *Wagner Remembered.* New York: Faber & Faber, 2000.

_____ (trans.) and Millington, Barry, (ed.). *Wagner's Ring of the Nibelung* (second edition). New York: Thames & Hudson, 2000.

Sturluson, Snorri. *The Prose Edda.* Trans. J. Young. Berkeley: University of California Press, 1954.

Tanner, Michael. *Wagner* (reprint). Princeton: Princeton University Press, 2002.

Thomas, Roy and Kane, Gil. *Richard Wagner's the Ring of the Nibelung* (DC Comics' adaptation of the Ring into a "graphic novel"), 1-volume edition. California: Express, 1997.

Tietz, John. *Redemption or Annihilation?: Love Versus Power in Wagner's Ring.* New York: Peter Lang, 1999.

Westernhagen, Curt von and Whittall, Arnold and Mary (trans.). *Forging of the "Ring."* Cambridge: Cambridge University Press, 1976.

Wagner, Cosima. *Cosima Wagner's Diaries, An Abridgement* [1869–1882]. Ed. G. Skelton. New Haven: Yale University Press, 1997.

Wagner, Richard. *Actors & Singers.* Trans. William Ashton Ellis. Lincoln: University of Nebraska Press, 1995.

_____. *The Art-Work of the Future and Other Works.* Trans. W.A. Ellis. (reprint). Lincoln: University of Nebraska Press, 1993.

_____. *Götterdämmerung* (Twilight of the Gods). In full score (Sheet Music). Mineola: Dover, 1995.

_____. *Das Rheingold.* In full score (Sheet Music). Trans. Stanley Appelbaum. Mineola: Dover, 1991.

_____ and Humperdinck, Engelbert. *The Ride of the Valkyries and Other Highlights from The Ring.* In full score (Sheet Music). Mineola: Dover, 1996.

Wagner: Ring of the Nibelung. New York: Value, 1988.

_____. *Siegfried.* In full score (Sheet Music Dover Opera and Choral Scores). Mineola: Dover, 1995.

_____. *Siegfried.* Partitura (Piano/Vocal Score Sheet Music). Budapest: Konemann Music, 2000.

_____. *Die Walküre* (The Valkyrie). Complete Vocal and Orchestral Score (Sheet Music). Mineola: Dover, 1978.

Wagner, Wilhelm and Anson, W. S. (intro.). *Great Norse, Celtic and Teutonic Legends* (Unabridged Edition). Mineola: Dover, 2004.

White, David A. *Turning Wheel: A Study of Contracts and Oaths in Wagner's Ring.* Selinsgrove, Pa.: Susquehanna, 1988.

Williams, Simon. *Richard Wagner and Festival Theatre.* Westport: Greenwood, 1994.

Winkler, Franz E. and Dejong, Elizabeth (illus.). *For Freedom Destined: The Mythology of Wagner's Ring Operas and Parsifal.* Great Barrington: The Orion Society, 1981.

Winterbourne, Anthony. *Speaking to Our Condition: Moral Frameworks in Wagner's Ring of the Nibelung.* Rutherford: Fairleigh Dickinson University Press, 2000.

About the Contributors

STEVEN R. CERF is a professor of German at Bowdoin College in Brunswick, Maine. He received his Ph.D. from Yale University in Germanic languages and literatures. His areas of specialization are Thomas Mann, opera as literature, and the Holocaust.

JOHN LOUIS DIGAETANI is a professor of English at Hofstra University. He received a B.A. from the University of Illinois, his M.A. from Northern Illinois University, and his Ph.D. from the University of Wisconsin. His books include *Richard Wagner and the Modern British Novel*; *Penetrating Wagner's* Ring: *An Anthology*; *Wagner and Suicide*; *Carlo Gozzi: A Life in the 18th Century Venetian Theater, an Afterlife in Opera*; *Puccini the Thinker*; *A Search for a Postmodern Theater*; and *An Invitation to the Opera*.

NEIL K. FRIEDMAN received a B.A. from Lawrence University and a Ph.D. in political science from Stanford University. He teaches in the Business and Liberal Arts Program at Queens College, City University of New York, and is an active member of the Wagner Society of New York.

BARBARA JOSEPHINE GUENTHER has degrees in music and in English literature from Nazareth College, the University of Michigan, and the University of Wisconsin. She teaches courses in writing and in Romanticism at the School of the Art Institute of Chicago. She is active as a singer in a number of choral groups, including Northwestern University's Symphonic Chorus and the Apollo Chorus in Chicago.

BRIGITTE HELDT is a professor of music at the University of Regensburg in Germany. She received her Ph.D. in musicology and pedagogy from Ludwig-Maximilians University in Munich. She has written a book entitled *Richard Wagner and Tristan und Isolde*, and her scholarly interests include music of the nineteenth century and musical pedagogy.

JAMES K. HOLMAN is the author of *Wagner's* Ring: *A Listener's Companion and Concordance*. He is chairman of the Wagner Society of Washington, D.C. He is a former trustee of the Washington National Opera, and is on the board of the American Friends of the English National Opera. He writes and lectures on Wagner, and resides in Washington, D.C.

GREGORY KERSHNER is a professor of German at Hofstra University. His Ph.D. in German is from the University of California at Davis, and he has a master's degree in international affairs from Columbia University. His specialty is German literature of the nineteenth and twentieth centuries, and he has taught and lectured on these topics in the New York City area.

249

JOANN P. KRIEG is a professor of English at Hofstra University, where she teaches American literature and American studies. A specialist in the life and work of Walt Whitman, she has edited a volume of essays on the poet and is the author of *A Whitman Chronology* and *Whitman and the Irish*.

ERICK NEHER has a B.A. from Harvard College and an M.S. in performance studies from New York University. He was an associate editor at *Opera Monthly* magazine and has written for other publications and lectured extensively for the Wagner Society of New York. He lives in New York City and is executive marketing director of the Hearst Group.

GEOFFREY S. RIGGS has been a guest lecturer at Juilliard, the Richard Tauber Institute, and the Wagner Society of New York. He has written *The Assoluta Voice in Opera, 1797–1847* and articles and reviews for *Opera Journal, Listener Magazine, Wagner Notes, Review of Reviews, Stagebill,* and other publications. He lives in New York and shares Webmaster duties for Operacast.com with his wife Elizabeth.

STEWART SPENCER studied German and French at Oxford University and taught medieval German literature at London University. Now a freelance translator, he is the author of *Wagner Remembered* and the co-author, with Barry Millington, of *Selected Letters of Richard Wagner, Wagner in Performance,* and *Wagner's* Ring *of the Nibelung.* He has translated books on Wagner, Liszt, Mozart, and Bach.

NICHOLAS VAZSONYI is a professor of German and director of the German Studies Program at the University of South Carolina. He has published extensively on German literature and culture from the eighteenth to the twentieth centuries. His books include *Lukacs Reads Goethe: From Stalinism to Aestheticism*; *Searching for Common Ground: Diskurse zur Deutschen Identität 1750–1871*; and *Wagner's Meistersinger: Performance, History, Representation.*

Index